LETTING BE

LETTING BE

FRED DALLMAYR'S COSMOPOLITICAL VISION

edited by

STEPHEN F. SCHNECK

University of Notre Dame Press

Notre Dame, Indiana

Manufactured in the United States of America

Library of Congress Cataloging-in-Publication Data

Letting be : Fred Dallmayr's cosmopolitical vision / edited by Stephen F. Schneck.
    p.   cm.
Includes bibliographical references and index.
ISBN-13: 978-0-268-04124-3 (pbk. : alk. paper)
ISBN-10: 0-268-04124-5 (pbk. : alk. paper)
1. Political science—Philosophy. 2. Dallmayr, Fred R. (Fred Reinhard), 1928–
3. Cosmopolitanism. 4. Internationalism. I. Schneck, Stephen Frederick, 1953–
JA71.L447   2006
320.092—dc22
2006018618

Contents

Preface ix

Introduction: Dallmayr's "Letting Be" 1
Stephen F. Schneck

PART I.
POLITICAL THEORY AND MODERN PHILOSOPHY

ONE
Seeing the Sovereign: 33
Theatricality and Representation in Hobbes
Tracy B. Strong

TWO
The Next Enlightenment: Aesthetic Reason in 55
Modern Art and Mass Culture
Morton Schoolman

THREE
Multicultural Cosmopolitanism: Remarks on 88
the Idea of Universal History
Thomas McCarthy

FOUR
The Other Politics: Anthropocentrism, Power, Nihilation 114
Krzysztof Ziarek

PART II.
MULTICULTURALISM AND COMPARATIVE POLITICAL THEORY

FIVE
Encounters with Modernity and Tradition   141
Ronald J. Terchek

SIX
Between Athens and Jerusalem (or Mecca): A Journey   167
with Dallmayr, Strauss, Ibn Rushd, and Jabiri
Michaelle Browers

SEVEN
Letting Being Be: Cross-Cultural Encounters in   183
a University Setting
Neve Gordon

EIGHT
Mestizo Democracy: Lateral Universality Begins at Home   205
John Francis Burke

NINE
Transversality and Comparative Political Theory: 230
A Tribute to Fred Dallmayr's Work
Hwa Yol Jung

PART III.
GLOBALISM AND COSMOPOLITICS

TEN
New Ways of Being Selves in the World: 253
Fred Dallmayr's Search for a Political Theory of Compassion
Franke Wilmer

ELEVEN
Cosmopolitanism and Its Problems   272
Chantal Mouffe

TWELVE
Civility and Dialogue in the Cosmopolitan Consensus   286
on Rights
David Ingram

THIRTEEN
A Thought Experiment on Cross-Cultural Dialogue   310
and Peacemaking
Calvin O. Schrag

Response   320
Fred Dallmayr

Dallmayr Bibliography   346

Contributors   360

Index   365

Preface

Gathered in this volume are essays from fourteen scholars representing different disciplines and fields of study—from comparative literature, philosophy, and political theory—who have written in honor of Fred Dallmayr on the occasion of his seventy-fifth birthday. The authors have adopted differing vantage points within the complexity of Dallmayr's writings for considering his thought, and the volume is arranged to reflect this range of perspectives.

The editor's introduction, which is intended as a general introduction to Dallmayr's thought, traces a path in his writings from the 1960s to the present. Following the introduction the first section of the volume, titled "Political Theory and Modernity," offers essays from Tracy Strong, Thomas McCarthy, Krzysztof Ziarek, and Morton Schoolman. These essays take their intellectual bearings from Dallmayr's well-known, critical assessment of modernity, modern Western political theory, and modern philosophy. The second section of the volume, "Multiculturalism and Comparative Political Theory," has essays from Ronald Terchek, Michaelle Browers, Neve Gordon, John Francis Burke, and Hwa Yol Jung. The essays in this section address Dallmayr's interest in comparative political theory and weigh the theoretical implications of non-Western political thinking and of dialogues among civilizations. Finally, the third section of the volume, "Globalism and Cosmopolitics," has essays from Francke Wilmer, Chantal Mouffe, David Ingram, and Calvin Schrag, all of which speak to the possibilities of global, shared, multipolar, or—in Dallmayr's words—a "cosmopolitical" framework for civilization.

Fred writes in his response at the end of volume that the occasion of his seventy-fifth birthday is not so much about accomplishment, but rather an opportunity. One might quibble about his modest dismissal of accomplishment. A glance at the rich and lengthy list of books and publications in the Dallmayr bibliography surely demands that such extraordinary scholarship be celebrated and feted. But, indeed, this is a moment of rare opportunity. For us, Fred—for your friends, colleagues, and students—this is an opportunity to express our gratitude for your scholarship, discourse, and friendship. We are grateful for the ways, mundane and profound, that your "letting be" has provoked, shaped, and inspired us.

Stephen F. Schneck

Introduction: Dallmayr's "Letting Be"

Stephen F. Schneck

"From all mountains I look out for fatherlands and motherlands; but home I found nowhere," Zarathustra states. "Strange and a mockery to me are the men of today to whom my heart recently drew me; and I am driven out of fatherlands and motherlands. Thus I now love only my *children's land*, yet undiscovered, in the farthest sea: for this I bid my sails search and search."

Friedrich Nietzsche

This volume of essays is presented as a festschrift to honor Fred Dallmayr on the occasion of his seventy-fifth birthday. Gathered here, the authors celebrate Fred's life, his lifetime of scholarship, and the rich contribution of his thought and writings to political theory, to comparative political theory, to political science, and to philosophy. The range and scope of the scholarship represented by these assembled authors reflects Dallmayr's own astonishing breadth of scholarship. In an intellectual career that spans nearly fifty years, he has written eighteen books, edited more than a dozen others, and has contributed many journal articles and book chapters.[1]

This scholarly output presents an imposing challenge to those who would introduce and explain his work. How does one introduce a thinker who has engaged the broad spectrum of ideas of Jürgen Habermas and Martin Heidegger, Michel Foucault and Charles Taylor, Jacques Derrida and Abdolkarim Soroush—not to mention phenomenology, philosophy of language, critical theory, hermeneutics, deconstruction, and a rich collection of non-Western thinkers, both classical and contemporary? Moreover, the last decade has seen Dallmayr's works expanding into the developing field of comparative political thought. His most recent books, *Beyond Orientalism* (1996), *Alternative Visions* (1998), *Achieving Our World* (2001), *Dialogue among Civilizations* (2002), *Peace Talks—Who Will Listen?* (2004), and *Small Wonder* (2005), weave discursively across the old historical and geographical borders of thought, crossing North and South, East and West, ancient and modern. These works place non-Western political thinkers—Gandhi, Confucius, Ibn Rushd, and many others—into multilayered interplays of consideration about justice, peace, democracy, law, rights, globalization, and politics itself along with the canonical thinkers and approaches of Western political philosophy. How, indeed, can one fully comprehend and introduce the complexity of Fred Dallmayr's thought?

And, yet . . . . The quotation from Nietzsche that serves as this introduction's epigraph, although cited by Dallmayr in an early work in support of what might then have been called "practical ontology," equally speaks to the "cosmopolitical" efforts at the center of his more recent thinking. For, despite the daunting range and the complexity of his many themes, topics, and inspirations, an utter integrity, a common framework of concerns, and a unifying, scholarly approach thread his many works into a compelling political theory.

That theory, of course, should in no way be considered a system. From the beginning Dallmayr has been critical of programmatic ideas and the ideologies, the micro- and macro-certainties, and the closures of thought that systematic theories engender. Quite differently, the turns of theoretical effort that run through his many books are—perhaps like the light steps so praised by Nietzsche's Zarathustra—open, discursive, wondering, rigorous, and adventurous. Thinking, Dallmayr repeatedly tells us, revolves between the one and the many, between identity and difference, between *Heimat* and what is *unheimlich*, between the deep familiarities of *Lebenswelt* and the luminous but provocative otherness of what the poet Eichendorff called *schöne Fremde*—beautiful strangeness. Moreover, Dallmayr's goal is never a resolution or end to openness, wonder, discourse, rigor, and adventure, but rather an enrichment of the same in ever-widening circles of engagement and reflection. Much more than a matter of epistemology, the implications of his vision point toward imperatives for subjectivity and sociality, ethics and ontology, politics and civilization.

A hermeneutical quality was ever evident in this. The discursive, open-minded interplay between identity and difference coupled with the ongoing enlargement and enrichment of identity through difference, processes which define the hermeneutic circle, are also hallmarks of Dallmayr's thought. But, it would be a mistake to see Dallmayr's hermeneutical "letting be" only in terms of its openness to and delight in the interplay of difference. It would be equally mistaken to understand his sense of the corresponding hermeneutical enlargement and enrichment of identity as seamless or enclosing. His is a hermeneutics of a different kind, which he explains by distinguishing his thought from the much-admired hermeneutics of Hans-Georg Gadamer:

> In *Truth and Method* Gadamer at one point expresses the central maxim of philosophical hermeneutics: "To recognize oneself (or one's own) in the other and find a home abroad—this is the basic movement of spirit whose being consists in this return to itself from otherness." But clearly this maxim engenders, and needs to be complemented by, another maxim: namely, the challenge to recognize otherness or the alien in oneself (or one's own).[2]

Dallmayr's "letting be," much akin to his reading of Martin Heidegger's "letting Being be," should be construed neither as a conservative acceptance of self-identity nor as a nonengaged indifference to difference. Instead, endeavoring to privilege neither identity nor difference, the hermeneutic circle for Dallmayr must also be one of thoroughgoing critique and praxis.[3] And, indeed, what joins together Dallmayr's many essays and explorations, what inheres within his "cosmopolitan" understanding of the contemporary world, and what lends his analyses their imperative is this same "letting be."

CRITICAL PHENOMENOLOGY, LANGUAGE, PRACTICAL ONTOLOGY

In the late 1960s, Fred Dallmayr began to turn in his intellectual work from the field of comparative politics toward political theory.[4] He had completed a doctorate in law in his native Bavaria, then came to the United States in the late 1950s and earned a doctorate in political science at Duke University.[5] The fruit of his turn included pieces on Thomas Hobbes, existentialism, ethics, and Leo Strauss, but perhaps the momentum of his research in those years concerned critical theory, phenomenology, and the idea of the social sciences.

The methodology debates that rocked the English-speaking circles of the social sciences in the late 1960s and early 1970s—perhaps partly in response to Thomas Kuhn's *The Structure of Scientific Revolutions,* published in 1966—invited theorists to reconsider a perennial question: how knowledge of others is possible. In the United States the reconsideration centered around several theoretical landmarks, some of which were canonical elements from the classics of social science, including Max Weber's *Verstehen* and Wilhelm Dilthey's distinction between the historical and the natural sciences. Others were then more recent, such as Peter Winch's use of E. E. Evans-Pritchard's Azande research to argue for radical limits to human science or Alfred Schütz's attack on behavioralism for its unacknowledged reliance on the notion of the lifeworld. To some extent these same methodological debates and explorations of the philosophy of the human sciences also were background for the development of key features of Dallmayr's thinking.

The ideas of Jürgen Habermas also came to be part of these explorations. Dallmayr was among the handful of scholars at the center of introducing the thinking of Habermas to an American academic audience.[6] Habermas was, of course, already a prominent partisan in the somewhat earlier wave of the *Methodenstreit* that had swept through German academia in the late 1950s and early 1960s. Against those in the methodology debates who—following Winch or Schütz or similar thinkers—were arguing for sweeping limits to the possibility of enlightened human sciences, Habermas had insisted on the possibility of such science through the use of rigorous theoretical and practical critique. Habermas's famous debate with Gadamer regarding hermeneutics during this period seems in many ways to have framed the discussion for Dallmayr's different consideration of these questions and issues then emerging. With the Habermas scholar Thomas McCarthy, Dallmayr organized in 1977 an edited volume of materials in social theory and the philosophy of the social sciences that addressed varying approaches for how knowledge of others is possible and could be "scientific." Not only Habermas's critical theory, but also hermeneutics, *Verstehen* theories, phenomenology, ethnomethodology, and lifeworld are part of that volume's collection.[7]

Dallmayr's own thinking regarding these themes plainly embraced the openness, the tolerance, the intellectual and ethical humility, the decentered subjectivity, and the consciousness-constitutive roles that world, history, and sociality played in approaches such as phenomenology and hermeneutics. Yet, at the same time, Dallmayr passionately endorsed aspects of critical theories such as Habermas's for their promise to unearth, raise to consciousness, and critique these same deep, often hidden, and repressive constitutive structures. Dallmayr's direction, accordingly, was to pursue an approach for the human sciences, politics, and ethics that joined openness with critique, understanding with emancipation.

His subsequent book, *Beyond Dogma and Despair* (1981), illustrates his efforts.[8] Subtitled *Toward a Critical Phenomenology of Politics,* the book's various considerations of authors and approaches are deployed toward balancing critical theory and phenomenology, while also challenging elements of both approaches that might undercut or preclude such balancing. Dallmayr, for example, criticizes what might be called the "Cartesian" or "Enlightenment" exaggerations in some critical theories of the emancipatory qualities of reason. Conversely, Dallmayr, drawing much from the analysis of the critical theorist Karl-Otto Apel, questions the thinking of those like Winch, for whom the human sciences offer no hope of either emancipation or critique. Between these extremes, Dallmayr explores the possibility of an approach that facilitates what he believes is theoretically and practically viable from the concerns of both sides: critical phenomenology. In an introductory passage, Dallmayr explains that he wants to draw on both critical theories and phenomenology with an aim "to combine their strengths or merits while avoiding their shortcomings." Regarding phenomenology he hopes to avoid an approach that "leans in the direction of a purely descriptive exercise" or "that is both normatively and politically 'neutral.'" The remedy for such leaning, he indicates, is for phenomenology somehow "to marshal the resources of critical reflection and judgment" found, for example, in critical theories.[9] And yet he goes on to make it clear:

> [C]ritical reflection cannot or should not be viewed as self-sufficient, for that would conjure up the peril of "critical criticism" or of narrowly rationalistic "apriorism." To gain its bearings and to avoid self-enclosure, critical thought must hearken back to the lessons of "phenomena" and of concrete experience, remaining alert to pre-reflective underpinnings of reflection, or of the linkage of thought and non-thought. In this manner, critical judgment and the study of phenomena are related in a precarious

balance, neither side being able to claim primacy or to provide a secure primordial starting point.[10]

In key chapters of *Beyond Dogma and Despair,* Dallmayr offers perspectives on the possibility of this "critical phenomenology" that speak to both the limits of understanding and historicism on one hand, and the limits to reason and critical epistemology on the other. Enzo Paci's critical phenomenology, Paul Ricoeur's depth hermeneutics, and especially Maurice Merleu-Ponty's phenomenological, open-ended dialectic are given special attention. And, as always for Dallmayr, the ethical and political implications of these revolutions between critique and openness, emancipation and understanding, are never far from his considerations.

Within a short period, however, a slight shift in Dallmayr's terms and his approach to these issues is evident. The shift is subtle; he speaks of a theoretical perspective that "might be labeled *critical post-phenomenology;* but it might also (and perhaps better) be described as *practical ontology*—provided *ontology* is not confused with an ontic objectivism and the term *practical* is not narrowly or exclusively identified with subjective intentional activity."[11] The poststructuralist thinking of Jacques Derrida and of Michel Foucault, references to which were becoming prominent in Dallmayr's writings during this time, may in some way have raised certain concerns for phenomenology's purported proclivity for complaisance and even naive positivism. Yet the understandings of intersubjectivity and decentered subjectivity that characterize many phenomenological considerations of human agency remain a centerpiece of Dallmayr's *Twilight of Subjectivity,* which he wrote during this period. There, in his consideration of Alfred Schütz's thought, for example, Dallmayr lauds Schütz's natural attitude phenomenology, the intersubjectivity of Schütz's conception of the lifeworld, and especially Schütz's move away from the capitalized subject of Edmund Husserl's more transcendental approach, but he worries that such phenomenology does this only "at a price," including the loss of "normative standards applicable both to the validation of cognitive claims and to the justification of social practices."[12]

Twilight of Subjectivity, however, also evinces an obverse worry about critical theory and its "rationalist proclivity." That proclivity, Dallmayr explains, is all too often wedded to teleological or utopian hopes for rational subjectivity. In the work's appendix, especially, Dallmayr takes to task any critical theory that looks to find in the processes of critique a teleological emancipation from what one unfortunate critical theorist called "the slime of history." "The conception of critique as the termination of natural or historical conditions appears both untenable and obnoxious: stripped of its prereflective beginnings reason turns either into idle curiosity or an instrument of domination. On the level of praxis, emancipation construed in this manner vitiates the formation of character; for where should human responsibility and care be *practiced* if not in concrete communities?"[13]

Dallmayr's presents practical ontology, with its decentered (but not abandoned) subjectivity, as oscillating between the more extreme directions of phenomenology and critical theory. He quotes from Merleau-Ponty's *The Visible and the Invisible,* for example, maintaining that "[w]e do not have to choose between a philosophy that installs itself in the world itself or in the other and a philosophy that installs itself 'in us.'" We need not choose, Dallmayr glosses, "between an internal and external perspective" wherein choosing either perspective would leave world and person, object and subject, other and self isolated and opposed. Indeed, we *ought* not choose between such alternatives because, continuing with Merleau-Ponty "these alternatives are not imperative, since perhaps the self and the non-self are like the obverse and the reverse and since perhaps our own experience *is* this turning round that installs us far from 'ourselves,' in the other, in the things."[14]

Dallmayr was invited to present in the spring of 1981 that year's address as part of the Loyola Lecture Series in Political Analysis at Loyola University in Chicago, which subsequently became the basis of his book *Language and Politics* (1984).[15] Practical ontology, while not explicitly addressed in the work, is nevertheless what patently is at stake in the context of language's obvious ontological and pragmatic dimensions. The preface, indeed, invokes the twinned Aristotelian definitions of humankind: *zoon politikon* and *zoon logon ekhon*—the latter of which Dallmayr interprets in the fashion of Heidegger (for whom, famously, "language is the house of Being") as a being endowed with language.[16] Language and politics are not only inseparable, but their multilayered connections have the character of practical ontology. Dallmayr's wide-ranging consideration in the work surveys ordinary language philosophy, constructivists, hermeneutics, semiotics, deconstruction, the Vienna Circle, ideal speech situations, structuralism, and more. Chomsky, Husserl, Searle, Wittgenstein, Saussure, Gusdorf, Derrida, Apel, Quine, Arendt,

Ryle, Lévi-Strauss, Frege, and many other theorists are weighed. Nevertheless the edges and conditions of practical ontology within the context of the consideration of language and discourse are at the center of Dallmayr's analyses.

Richard Rorty's and Michael Oakeshott's theories are illuminated as one such edge: radical "polyphony." Rorty's *Philosophy and the Mirror of Nature*, at the time only recently published, had invigorated theorists' renewed interest in language.[17] Michael Oakeshott's writings had greatly influenced academic political theory through criticism and interpretations from such scholars as Sheldon Wolin and Benjamin Barber, among others.[18] The conception of language in the thinking of Rorty and Oakeshott, according to Dallmayr's analysis, was utterly open (utterly polyphonic) in that meaning was merely an ad hoc determination of pragmatic utility by any speaker. As such, a certain attractiveness is evident from a political perspective suggesting, as it does, the possibility of untrammeled tolerance and liberality. Conversations would "exhibit no privileged speakers, no 'lead instruments,' no first and second strings." No one "would have the final word—mainly because there is no such final word." So utterly pragmatic as to deny the ontological dimension of language, though, Dallmayr argues that were Rorty and Oakeshott right, then language would be doomed to drift into "empty rhetoric," "idle chatter," and "disconnected soliloquies," much like the Babel metaphor that Oakeshott himself put to use in several essays.[19]

A second edge to practical ontology explored by Dallmayr in *Language and Politics* is evident in his consideration of Paul Ricouer's transcendental hermeneutics and Jürgen Habermas's then recent theory of universal pragmatics. "Transcendental" and "universal" might be construed as signaling a worrisome "uni-phonic" insistence or even closure in these theories. Dallmayr, interestingly, does not entirely agree. Although he endorses Karl-Otto Apel's criticism of the "rationalistic reconstruction" process that was so central for Habermas's universal pragmatics, he nevertheless also accepts the transcendental or universal aspirations of approaches such as Ricouer's hermeneutics and Habermas's universal pragmatics.[20] Hermeneutics, moreover, receives Dallmayr's warmest attention. Drawing much inspiration from Heidegger, Dallmayr stresses the "clarifying" operation of the hermeneutic circle in its spiraling between preunderstanding and interpretive clarification. He follows Ricouer's hope for a "highest task for hermeneutics," which he calls "critical exegesis or the 'critical function' of hermeneutics."[21]

Finally, a third edge to Dallmayr's own approach is evident in the book's consideration of poststructuralist theories of language. Such theories begin with profound suspicions of universal or transcendental aspirations, such as Ricouer's. Critical exegesis as deployed, for example, in Foucault's genealogy or Derrida's deconstruction aims not at clarification, but at problematizing confidence in clarity itself. Most importantly, hermeneutics' hoped for enrichment or enlargement of identity (or even *Bildung*) through the assumed universal possibilities of language would be denied if, as poststructuralists maintain, "words are weapons" or discourse is but a deployment of relations of power. Referencing the analysis of Hayden White, who calls these radically poststructuralist theories "absurdist," Dallmayr balks at the extremes of such thinking. Agreeing with White, he notes that these "absurdist critics tend to cultivate an abnormal if not pathological brand of exegesis."[22]

CRITICAL ENCOUNTERS

Language remains a recurring focus of Dallmayr's thinking, central for understanding his conception of "letting be" and the cosmopolitical. After *Language and Politics,* however, he returns in the 1980s more forcefully to the issues of critique, subjectivity, and modernity. Dallmayr's *Polis and Praxis* (1984), *Critical Encounters* (1987), and *Margins of Political Discourse* (1989) in many ways are organized as a three-sided comparison of poststructuralist approaches, critical theory approaches, and hermeneutics/lifeworld approaches.[23] Heidegger's thinking is increasingly brought to the foreground in these studies as Dallmayr begins more directly to articulate his emerging idea of practical ontology.

The praxis or practical aspect of his practical ontology receives weighty attention. Most important for Dallmayr is that such praxis be carefully distinguished from the emphasis on an individual, rationalistic, acting subject, which has been the prominent theoretical understanding of practice in the Western tradition, especially in the modern era. He takes up Heidegger's thought as his principal lens through which to study the issue. Yet his is not that generic interpretation of Heidegger that commonly overweighs the importance of *Being and Time.* In *Polis and Praxis,* offering a perceptive analysis of Heidegger's works, Dallmayr suggests three rough stages in the trajectory of Heidegger's thinking over his lifetime: a "decisionist" (or vaguely existentialist) early stage culminating perhaps in 1930; a middle period in which subjectivity is decentered in the history of Being; and a third stage beginning about the time of the *Letter on Humanism* (or perhaps, as Dallmayr also suggests, with Heidegger's 1936 lectures on Schelling and freedom), wherein even *Dasein* is understood within "letting Being be" or, phrased differently, within "the destiny of Being."[24]

Heidegger's post-1930 thinking, within which such terms as "act," "will," and "cause" are more ontologically understood, seems in many ways consistent with the practical ontology that is the hallmark of Dallmayr's own thinking at this time. Dallmayr notes that Hannah Arendt, too (especially the Arendt of *The Human Condition*), found inspiration in Heidegger's post-1930 writings. In an early chapter of *Polis and Praxis,* the ideas of Arendt and Heidegger are compared with the thought of Michel Foucault, and the three thinkers are to some degree positioned against Habermas's arguments. Organized in this way, they are presented with sympathy and with an emphasis on their similarities. Central in Dallmayr's presentation is the "agonistic" dimension that he discerns in each of the three thinker's approach. He writes in the book's introduction:

> Together with Arendt and Foucault, I view politics basically as an "agonal" undertaking—that is, as a tensional, serious-playful contest revolving around the quality or excellence and ultimately the very "point" of political life. Using slightly different vocabulary, politics can also be described as the cultivation of a particular interhuman "practice": namely, the practice of "friendship"—a term denoting not so much personal intimacy as a public relationship steeped in mutual respect and a willingness to let one another "be."[25]

Dallmayr uses his consideration of the agonistic in Foucault, Arendt, and Heidegger, moreover, to telegraph his growing concern with the direction of Habermas's critical theory and its then formulation around the idea of communicative action. In this, he follows threads from earlier remarks by Habermas regarding Arendt and Heidegger and brilliantly anticipates and ripostes Habermas's subsequent criticism of Foucault and other poststructuralists as "neoconservatives" and "positivistic."[26] Dallmayr insists against Habermas that these thinkers offer prospects for compelling critique and, far from being tacitly conservative, point toward the possibility of enriching the human condition (the *polis* of Dallmayr's book's title) in the sense of a unique pluralism "based on mutual respect." And that respect, he quotes from Arendt, would be "'not unlike the Aristotelian *philia politike'*" in that it would not be one of "merger and identity."[27]

In his subsequent book, *Critical Encounters*, Dallmayr sharpens the focus of his differences with Habermas. Arguably, Theodor Adorno at this juncture replaces Habermas as Dallmayr's principal partner in conversation with critical theory. But, advising his readers that he intends to more clearly profile his own thinking and to accentuate the differences he has with other thinkers, Dallmayr here takes pains also to more sharply distinguish his own practical ontology from the more Kantian aspects of Hannah Arendt's agonal *polis;* from the less rigorous or less critical aspects of phenomenologies and hermeneutics; from the positivist aspects of neopragmatisms that may too quickly settle (or even close) around what "sells"; and from the "anti-humanist" (or better the "anti-cosmopolitan") extravagances of poststructuralists. No other book among his many titles is as revealing of Dallmayr's theoretical efforts.

An intriguing consideration of *Bildung* in *Critical Encounters* offers perspective and leverage for many of these comparisons. Commonly translated as "education," the German word also evokes classical humanistic aspirations for personal formation toward maturity and for the enriching of ethnos and ethos, as well as a sense of caring for civilization and its continuation. At many levels and in complex ways (theoretical, pragmatic, aesthetic, and ethical) a particular understanding of *Bildung* lies near the heart of Dallmayr's thinking.[28] Dallmayr raises the matter in *Critical Encounters* within his assessment of the famous 1981 Derrida–Gadamer encounter in Paris, and in conjunction with an argument that Gadamer's hermeneutical approach remedies two worrisome tendencies in Derrida's poststructuralism and deconstruction.

One such tendency derives from what Dallmayr suggests is deconstruction's stress on "rupture and radical otherness" by which it "seeks to uproot and dislodge the inquirer's comfortable self-identity."[29] Carried to extremes, such measures would likely militate against rich participation with others in common ethical, cultural, political, or civilizational endeavors. Given its suspicion of common endeavors and its insistence on the incommensurability of ever-transient self-identity, moreover, deconstruction may also incline, as a second tendency, toward solipsism and escapist disengagement from the world and others. Gadamer's hermeneutics, Dallmayr contends, offers an approach that is more engaged and participatory, holding open the aspirations of *Bildung*.

> His [Gadamer's] Paris comments presented "the capacity of understanding" as a "basic human endowment which sustains social life," while the possibility of consensus was described as prerequisite of "all human solidarity and the viability of society." Seen from this perspective, social and political interaction clearly requires ethical engagement or the reciprocal display of "good will"—though an engagement which in its more intense or accomplished modes, makes room for non-intentional playfulness. This combination or sequence seems to me to be the gist of "*Bildung*" or of public education and culture. Again, Gadamer deserves praise for having rescued this notion from its contemporary oblivion or effacement. "Viewed as elevation to a universal or common vista," he writes in *Truth and Method*, "*Bildung* constitutes a general human task." The task requires sacrifice of (mere) particularity for the sake of something common or universal—where sacrifice of particularity means, in negative terms, the curbing of desire and hence freedom from the object of desire and freedom for its objectivity.[30]

Dallmayr values deconstruction for its insouciant unmasking or unearthing of hidden structures, repressions, hegemonies, and similar closures of discursive interactions. He edges away, however, when with its "emphasis on discontinuity and fragmentation" it "shades over into a celebration of indifference, non-engagement, and indecision."[31]

The discursive, engaged, and yet open *Bildung* for which Dallmayr hoped, however, must be considered carefully. While the concept reveals in Dallmayr's thought fascinating affinities and potential pathways from which to survey the political theory literatures of civic virtue, religion, civil society, local community, and so forth, he does not fully elaborate the notion as it relates to either his practical ontology or cosmopolitan ideas. Furthermore, Dallmayr certainly does not embrace fully the universal or metaphysical dimensions of the concept as it has been traditionally presented, or even the slightly more limited versions suggested by the hermeneutics of not only Gadamer but also Ricouer. A revealing illustration of Dallmayr's unique take is evident in his review of the arguments of Alasdair MacIntyre. MacIntyre's *After Virtue*, at first glance, would seem in many ways to be in some harmony with Dallmayr's concerns regards Derrida's deconstruction. After all, MacIntyre stresses the importance of continuity, ethical and intellectual formation, and the virtues of fully participating in common moral and civilizational efforts.[32] Yet, Dallmayr's difficulties with MacIntyre's thesis are legion, beginning with an utterly sweeping indictment of the metaphysical teleology on which MacIntyre's thesis rests. "Virtue," Dallmayr writes, "cannot be grounded on 'heteronomy' nor ethics be construed as an external fiat imposed on man."[33] *Bildung*, as it were, ought not (cannot) be a process of formation from above nor a squeezing of humankind into some predetermined order—historical or teleological.

Dallmayr's 1989 *Margins of Political Discourse* continues the elaboration and exploration of these themes. The paired concerns against order and disorder so palpable in his considerations of MacIntyre, Gadamer, and Ricouer vis-à-vis poststructuralism resurface in chapters on "Eric Voegelin's Search for Order" and most keenly in Dallmayr's analysis of so-called "postmodernism" in the book's central chapter "Postmodernism and Political Order." Somewhat in parallel with his critique of MacIntyre in *Critical Encounters*, Dallmayr finds theoretical harmonies between Voegelin's approach and some hermeneutical theories, including Paul Ricouer's. Further, he finds Voegelin's interpretations of ancient thinkers, particularly Plato, to be sensitive and revealing. Nevertheless, Dallmayr expresses much hesitation with Voegelin's ultimate contention that a privileged moral order in consciousness and in history depends on a dualistic (albeit unresolved) metaphysical order that corresponds with Christian Revelation. Indeed, with less hesitation than was evident in *Critical Encounters*, in *Margins of Political Discourse* Dallmayr expresses appreciation for difference and disruption. Favorably citing Bernhard Waldenfels, for example, he maintains that in the present condition "[w]hat is needed here is a preservation of differences, a tolerance of ambiguities, and at the same time a resistance to forced unity."[34] Indeed, almost in response to Voegelin's consuming search for order, Dallmayr insists on the need for maintaining an appreciation for what is not order. But his sense of this need is modulated in an interesting way: "We must distinguish between 'disordered' or disorderly in the sense of a rule violation governed by the binary matrix of an order, and a rule-less or unruled dimension on the other side of order which we may call the 'unordered.'"[35] The need for differences and toleration of ambiguities, for Dallmayr, would invoke not a celebration of the "disordered" but instead a reverence for the "unordered."

This distinction is also in evidence in Dallmayr's sympathetic, but measured, assessment of Ernesto Laclau and Chantal Mouffe's *Hegemony and Socialist Strategy*.[36] Laclau and Mouffe argue for poststructuralism as the basis for a positive political theory, but also eschew the anarchism that so many other scholars have surveyed from that approach. As the book's title suggests, the endeavor weighs linkages between poststructuralist thinking and socialism, and includes in its pages many reconsiderations of traditional socialist thinkers in light of poststructuralism. Dallmayr's hesitations, however, center around what he considers to be formulations of Laclau and Mouffe that take their bearings from disorder rather than the unordered:

> Small wonder that on such premises antagonisms begin to shade over into total conflict—as happens in a passage which finds the "formula of antagonism" in a "relation of total equivalence where the differential positivity of all . . . terms is dissolved." Flirtation with nothingness is also evident in the statement that experience of negativity is "not an access to a diverse ontological order, to something beyond differences, simply because . . . there is no beyond."[37]

Margins of Political Discourse, however, also signals an emerging element in Dallmayr's thought. The idea of "cosmopolis" had been a minor theme in Dallmayr's writings at least since 1984. The pluralism, respect, friendship, and "letting be," for example, that Dallmayr explored at the heart of *Polis and Praxis* also coincided with one of his first uses of the term "cosmopolis," which he there associated with a global arrangement of "closeness and distance" that "can curb the arrogance of State-centered force."[38] In *Margins*, though, cosmopolis moves to the forefront. For the ancient Stoics the term had designated a universalized *polis*, not of this world but of spirit, in which all of humankind were equally citizens, equally subject to the transcendental law of the "cosmic city," and which properly served as criterion and inspiration for earthly politics, law, and government. Dallmayr's use of the term "cosmopolis" pointedly refers not to a separate, perfect realm. For him, it points instead toward immanent practices and efforts to rethink the political in the contemporary world that would cross over the usual margins of Western thought. A chapter on Mohandas Gandhi, for example, hints at the broader directions Dallmayr's thought would subsequently move. But a fulsome elaboration of his understanding of cosmopolis would not appear for a few years.

Indeed, the publishing of Hugo Ott's *Martin Heidegger* and, more significantly, the publication and translation of Victor Farias's *Heidegger and Nazism* in the late 1980s, impressed on Dallmayr a more immediate task.[39]

DALLMAYR AND HEIDEGGER

Heidegger's writings have long been inspiring and provocative for Dallmayr's own thinking and rethinking. In Dallmayr's early books, such as *Twilight of Subjectivity*, Heidegger's thought was instrumental in the analysis of the pathologies of Enlightenment individualism, rationalism, and subjectivity. More importantly, Dallmayr's key theoretical argument from those years, the argument for decentered subjectivity, owes much to his theoretical mining of Heidegger's post-1930 writings.

Heidegger's thinking was also of central importance for Dallmayr as he gradually refined, over the course of several decades, his own distinctive ontological attitude: namely, "letting be." It might well be argued that a contrail of sorts can be discerned in the wake of Dallmayr's writing on this point, evident from his engagement and reengagement with Heidegger's works through the decades. Earlier books and essays, where the attitude or approach was best described as "critical phenomenology," used Heidegger's thinking to balance a more phenomenological perspective against the overly epistemological and even rationalistic excess of various critical theories. Likewise, Heidegger's thinking was presented as if to remind critical theorists and lifeworld advocates that critique and understanding, if Heidegger is right, are characteristic features of "letting Being be." As Dallmayr reoriented the focus of his thought toward "practical ontology," however, Heidegger's ideas move to a more foundational place. Spurred perhaps by thinkers like Derrida, Dallmayr's presentation of Heidegger's importance at this point is no longer so much about epistemology, such as understanding others or even clarifying the constitution of consciousness. Rather, it is for rethinking the possibilities and responsibilities of praxis (especially understood politically, ethically, and civilizationally) without reliance on either classical or Enlightenment models of subjectivity and agency.

In *Between Freiburg and Frankfurt* (1991) and *The Other Heidegger* (1993), Dallmayr takes this another step and in so doing nudges his developing understanding of "letting be" toward what at this time he calls "critical ontology." Where previously the stress was either on using Heidegger's thought to balance critical theory or on finding in Heidegger's understanding of Being a common ground for critique, practice, and understanding, the stress now swings toward the inherently critical character of fundamental ontology itself.

In the introduction to *Between Freiburg and Frankfurt* the argument is put squarely. Heidegger from the first, we are told, "did not champion a substantive or objectifiable ontology but rather a mode of radical questioning unsettling received answers; to this extent, his 'fundamental ontology' involved simultaneously a program of critical "deconstruction" [*Destruktion*] aimed at traditional philosophical doctrines and worldviews." Heidegger's, in other words, is defined as a "critique-engendering ontology."[40] In one sense, of course, nearly all Heideggerian scholars would agree with Dallmayr's new terminology. The fundamental ontology at the center of Heidegger's thinking, even before 1930, is presented in the context of Being making a "caring" issue of itself. Dallmayr agrees, noting that "Being for Heidegger was never a doctrine or positive proposition but rather a question or problem," and indeed that for Heidegger "a central view of 'being'" was its "'openness' toward otherness or unfamiliar horizons."[41] Where Dallmayr breaks new ground, however, is in his claiming that "Heidegger's work can be seen as [a] primary exemplar of a perspective combining ontological reflection with post-Kantian (not subject-centered) critique."[42]

Still, certain theoretical hesitations concerning Heidegger are highlighted as they bear on Dallmayr's hoped-for critical ontology. The writings of the critical theorist Theodor Adorno, with special reference to Adorno's *Negative Dialectics*, are deftly employed in this regard. Most important among Dallmayr's theoretical hesitations is Heidegger's own apparent hesitancy to unleash or deploy the critical dimension of his fundamental ontology. Following Hermann Mörchen's observations on this, Dallmayr argues that "the 'weakest' point in Heidegger's work—in light of his own 'understanding of being'—is the fact that his neglect of the 'concrete tasks' of social and political life, his 'untimely' attitude à la Nietzsche, *may* be construed as an 'escape from a concrete immersion into temporality.'"[43] In this, Dallmayr shares a concern raised by many critical theorists who perceive in Heidegger's thought an unfortunately gentle treatment of *what is*, of reality's status quo, as if the world were already redeemed and reconciled. Nodding in this direction, Dallmayr recommends Adorno: "One of Adorno's most relentless objections—which supporters of Heidegger should carefully heed—is the charge of an 'affirmative' stance blindly endorsing existing conditions or the 'powers that be.' Perhaps, in cultivating his social distance, Heidegger did not always sufficiently guard against the peril or lure of this stance."[44]

Between Freiburg and Frankfurt was published almost simultaneously with the appearance of Hugo Ott's *Martin Heidegger* and Victor Farias's *Heidegger and Nazism*, but it preceded the notoriety of *l'affaire* Heidegger in the early 1990s, which was ignited in Western intellectual circles by the works and subsequent indictments on the part of such authors as Richard Wolin.[45] Together the arguments of these various books compile a case detailing Heidegger's purposeful endorsement of and participation in National Socialism. Moreover, persuasive theoretical arguments are advanced by some for affinities between themes in Heidegger's own writings (especially, but not solely before 1933) and aspects of his involvement with National Socialism.

In the charged and sometimes polemic atmosphere of those years, Dallmayr wrote one of his best-known books, *The Other Heidegger*. The work is neither an apologia nor an effort to look away from, deflect, or soft-pedal any indictment of Heidegger's participation with the Nazi Party. Instead, as Dallmayr puts it in the preface, his 'concern is to lay out for political theory a broader portrayal of Heidegger's thought, "a more complex picture, akin to a multilayered tapestry—a tapestry in which his fascist involvement is *one* (easily the most deplorable) strand, but not the only and not even the dominant one."[46] Within this broader portrayal, Dallmayr's thinking nevertheless is guided by several landmarks in Heidegger's writings: the then recently published *Beiträge zur Philosophie* (along with his 1936 Schelling essay on freedom), the *Zollikon Seminars,* the *Letter on Humanism,* and several of Heidegger's interpretations of Hölderlin's hymns. Spanning the period from immediately after Heidegger's infamous rector's address to 1945, these writings, Dallmayr suggests, "adumbrate a broadly ontological perspective of 'letting-be' in which different elements or modalities of being are related without mutual intrusion," "granting each other space in the interstices of presence and absence, arrival and departure."[47]

Dallmayr's own "letting be" is lent fresh perspective, accordingly. In his brief review of the *Beiträge*, for example, a work that Heidegger himself described as a groundwork for a new beginning in his thought, Dallmayr points to terms that he believes are insightful for comprehending where Heidegger was heading: "awe," "reserve," "reticence," "premonition," and "renunciation." Dallmayr's reading of these terms finds them at odds with fascism's valorization of "will" and at odds with the closures of thinking that define all ideologies. Awe is associated with wonder. "Reserve," Dallmayr relates, "is said to form the midpoint between awe and reticence, which is not so much shyness or bashfulness as the willingness to 'let being be' in whatever mode it may happen or occur (particularly in the mode of absence or withdrawal)." He goes on to say:

> Premonition, or surmise, opens the view to the dimensions of disclosure and concealment, and specifically to the sense of being's withdrawal or its happening in the mode of refusal, or self-refusal (*Verweigerung*). Once being is seen to happen as or through refusal, a refusal heralding not vacuum but an absent mode of presencing, then human acceptance of this refusal can only take the form of renunciation (which signals not rejection or indifference but a radical type of engagement).[48]

Dallmayr's parenthetical insertion that describes such "letting be" as "a radical type of engagement" should be provocative. Heidegger himself admitted in the *Beiträge* of worries that his thinking would be construed as "cowardly weakness." Indeed, why does not such "letting be" more likely devolve into mere disengagement or, worse, a quiet sinking into the unrippled pond of familiar identity? Dallmayr's responses to such questions are many, but none are perhaps as compelling as those that surround his take on Heidegger's 1942 lectures on Hölderlin's poem *Der Ister.*

Der Ister is an archaic name for the Danube, the storied river that connects Occident and Orient, poetically connects modern Europe with its Hellenic roots, and that has its source in Heidegger's Swabian homeland. Hölderlin's poem speaks of these linkages and crossings in terms evocative of Odysseus's fated wanderings from East to West and back, while also conveying gratitude for the river's opening of the heartland of Europe for building and dwelling. Dallmayr, following Heidegger, embraces the conjoining of the crossings, the ever-shifting and wandering character of the river, and the hope for homecoming. For him "the stream means a journey or wandering that incipiently heralds an impending homecoming or the possibility of 'being at home' (*Heimischsein*)." Such "[h]omecoming," such "letting be," Dallmayr translates from Heidegger, must ever be "a transit through other otherness."[49] Crossing borders between East and West, antiquity and modernity, by Dallmayr's account, "letting be" is neither complacent nor uncritical, but instead a rigorous but light-stepping sojourn between dwellings and distant lands, with homecoming not a promise but a hope.

Cosmopolitics

In the mid 1990s, following the publication of *The Other Heidegger,* Dallmayr began more purposively to address his thinking to the themes and issues of comparative political theory, elements of which had always had much interest for him and which had been explored in key essays of previous works. Although his engagement with such themes would come, gradually, to encompass his intellectual efforts, it would be incorrect to interpret comparative political theory as an abrupt theoretical turn in Dallmayr's thought. The continued working through of his idea of "letting be," which began with his critical phenomenology in the 1970s and was always near the center of his efforts, remains central to his writings and analyses of the last decade. Indeed, his fervent interest in non-Western thinkers, and his auspicious considerations of these thinkers and ideas against the background of Western philosophy and political theory, can well be understood in itself as the "homecoming through otherness" of "letting be."

Yet still, changes of emphasis and a difference of ambience in the new works cannot be overlooked. Gadamer's thought and philosophical hermeneutics in general begin to be given more prominence and more authority in Dallmayr's writings. Emphases on the agonal character of "letting be" are muted and more hope is entertained for progress in easing bitterness and mediating conflict. A slightly greater lean toward embracing difference may also be discerned. By no means do such shifts of emphasis convey an endorsement of the hermeneutics of consensus let alone one of universal understanding, but titles that speak of "global village," "peace," and "achieving our world," even if understood in the context of the critical dimension of "letting be," hint at implications that deserve to be carefully weighed.

The breakthrough book for this refocusing of Dallmayr's thought was *Beyond Orientalism* (1986), which appeared a few years after *The Other Heidegger.*[50] The title, of course, is in reference to Edward Said's well-known *Orientalism* (1979), which argued that Western cultural and social scientific studies of the Middle East effected a regime of knowledge that hegemonically reified the cultures of the region (even for Middle Easterners' own self-understanding). Endeavoring to explore "beyond" Said's careful analysis of orientalism, Dallmayr assesses alternatives to the approaches of traditional cultural and social scientific studies. In particular, something like "letting be" hints at the possibility of radical appreciation of cultural difference, nonhegemonic understanding, while also—in part because of its appreciation of difference—demanding a thoroughgoing critical attitude. Called here a "hermeneutics of difference," Dallmayr elaborates the concept by revisiting the Gadamer/Derrida comparison that had been so theoretically formative for his earlier *Critical Encounters.*

Put simply, such a hermeneutics of difference would eschew the identity-closing "fusion of horizons" associated with hermeneutical theories that beg overcoming of difference. Like Derrida's deconstruction, difference not only is tolerated, but endorsed and preserved. Yet, unlike many interpretations of Derrida's deconstruction, conflict among difference is muted and localized understandings across the margins and edges of difference are possible and additive.[51] *Beyond Orientalism* presents several case examples that Dallmayr believes illustrate how something akin to this hermeneutics of difference might work, including an exegesis of the work of the philosopher and Indologist Wilhelm Halbfass and a consideration of affinities between Heidegger's later philosophy and Indian mysticism. Nevertheless, even though *Beyond Orientalism*'s hermeneutics of difference remains utterly consonant with the direction of his previous studies, the book also reconnects with translocalized hopes for harmony and peace (while respecting difference) that were broached in Dallmayr's earlier, tentative steps toward what he called "cosmopolis." Accordingly, the last portions of the book survey an idea of a multicultural world that would be democratic and, ostensibly, nonhegemonic.

Such translocalized hopes, arguably, were inspiration for *Alternative Visions* (1998), which continues and accelerates Dallmayr's interest in looking beyond Western thought for a richer and more persuasive response to the intellectual hegemony that he associates with Enlightenment rationalism and subjectivity.[52] Indeed, Western intellectuals with whom Dallmayr is otherwise quite sympathetic, such as Theodor Adorno and Edward Said, are chided for what might be termed their "conservative" and passive reluctance to move beyond merely abstract critique and European/American modes of analysis. As heirs to the Enlightenment West's suspicions of faith and tradition, such thinkers are profoundly handicapped in their ability to recover or value the salient lifeworlds of the non-Western world or even the nonsecular elements of traditional lifeworlds in Western societies themselves. The upshot, Dallmayr contends, is a worldview that abandons all that is not explicable (within the contours of Enlightenment rationality and subjectivity) as unresolvable "non-identity." In the introduction, he cites Michel Foucault with approval regarding the present need to "resist the blackmail of the Enlightenment" wherein one is forced to choose between identity defined by Enlightenment rationalism and the non-identity of mere "irrationalism."[53]

Drawing from a reading of Gadamer's hermeneutics that recommends proceeding "from the vantage of situated modes of self-understanding," Dallmayr's argument here more strongly emphasizes local difference than had *Beyond Orientalism*.[54] The critic of the Enlightenment, Johann Gottfried Herder, provides Dallmayr a perspective on the process of such a hermeneutics in which the circle would not move in abstraction or generalization from local difference toward transcendental understanding, but instead by circling down ever-more richly into particular difference with the hope of ontological discovery. Such an approach, Dallmayr anticipates, would yield the possibility of movement toward the subtitled "global village," while not "damaging the integrity of local lifeworlds" via assimilation from above.[55] Avoiding the counter-Enlightenment (and therefore, Enlightenment-inspired) trope of romanticizing so-called authentic traditions or escaping from the allegedly gray disenchantment that many critics associate with the momentum of modern Western rationalism, *Alternative Visions* instead advocates a broadening discourse among a world of lifeworlds in which the Western is simply not privileged and all lifeworlds are affirmed, not assimilated, but still share an equal respect in a cosmopolitical, global village.

The rub, naturally, is how this might be done. In *Achieving Our World* (2001), Dallmayr offers a provocative litany of suggestions. As he relates in the preface, "this book seeks to explore or uncover viable interconnections or linkages between elements of our world, linkages that might be conducive to some kind of mutuality, reciprocal recognition, and peace."[56] His thinking here, moreover, crystallizes around specific, pragmatic proposals: democratic practices (not only within and among the institutions of nation-states, but also beyond the limits of the modern nation-state); cosmopolitan law, rights, and institutions; a cosmopolitan *Bildung* or civic culture; and so forth. Surveying such ideas, Dallmayr refers to a broad spectrum of thinkers and writings, including David Held, Anthony Giddens, Elise Boulding, Stephen Toulmin, Richard Falk—even Immanuel Kant's *Zum ewigen Frieden.* How such cosmopolitan projects would emerge, how they would find efficacy outside the contemporary age's relations of power, and how they would not compromise local lifeworlds and identities are questions for which Dallmayr's answers are tentative. But, straightforwardly, the direction of his interest is toward global, multicultural, cross-cultural arrangements, for which the proper metaphor perhaps lies somewhere between mosaic and orchestra.

Friendship, the compelling and frequently explicit theme in *Achieving Our World,* might well be more than metaphorical for Dallmayr's own understanding of the cosmopolitical. A surprising move against the thinking of Derrida on the topic of friendship (in conjunction with friendlier interchanges with Thomas McCarthy and Calvin Schrag) reveals much. Derrida's account of friendship, showcased in his book *Politics of Friendship,* reflects the basic tenor of well-known deconstructive arguments and stresses the self's uncompromising incommensurability with the other, such that friendship appears as radicalized, nonintrusive, and nonreciprocal respect for the ever distant other.[57] In response, Dallmayr evidences instead sympathy for Aristotle's *philia.* "If people are friends," he quotes from the philosopher, "they have no need of justice, but if they are just they need friendship in addition; and the justice that is most just seems to belong to friendship."[58] Lamenting that already such "ancient notions like 'concord' (*homonoia*) or 'communion' (*consensio*) have been increasingly problematized if not entirely eclipsed" in the emergence of Western civilization's conception of self and other, Dallmayr worries that Derrida's thinking absolutizes the problem.[59] Derrida's "friendship as noncommunity," he writes, with "[i]ts goal 'not to give in to proximity or identification, to the fusion of you and me,' but rather 'to place, maintain or keep an infinite distance within *good friendship,*'" would dismiss any hope for the concord so needed for genuine praxis and shared social practices.[60] Dallmayr continues: "The costs or negative side effects of this dismissal—thematized under such labels as 'anomie,' 'world-alienation,' and *'trahison de tous par tous'*—are not entirely ignored, and occasionally even deplored, but without any effect on the general orientation."[61]

Friendship (indeed "self-transgressive friendship"), as well as considerations of self, other, and their relationship are also threads that run through Dallmayr's subsequent book, *Dialogue among Civilizations* (2002). The title echoes the former Iranian president Mohammad Khatami's 1998 United Nations resolution, which was itself something of a response to Samuel Huntington's perceived "clash of civilizatons."[62] Dallmayr opens his book with a few lines from Hölderlin's poem "Remembrance":

> But good is it
> To have dialogue [*Gespräch*] and to talk
> About the heart's thought, and to listen much
> About the days of love,
> And about deeds that have happened.

He reiterates Heidegger's gloss of these lines, noting that "dialogue, for the poet, involves not only speech and counter-speech, statements and rejoinders, but also a kind of world-disclosure: namely, the opening-up of a space or shared matrix holding the speakers silently together."[63]

That "space" represents Dallmayr's hope. Not enmity, conflict, and the "clash" cited by so many as the way to a new world arrangement; Dallmayr instead proposes "space" for mutual world-disclosure through dialogue and discursive openness. Such a process, wherein all speakers and listeners are mutually enriched and matured in a "shared matrix" of world-disclosure, ought be recognized, he thinks, as the hoped-for "civilizing process for our global age."[64] The hermeneutical quality of such a "civilizing process" is unmistakable and, indeed, familiar names such as Ricouer and, even more, Gadamer are recommended in the book. But, this "civilizing process" is more than just a way of knowing or even of *Bildung*. Civilization has its etymological roots in the Roman *civitas*, as in a book Dallmayr describes as "magisterial"—Augustine's *Civitas Dei*, or *City of God*. Accordingly, he speaks of the "civilizing process" in such terms:

Whatever its other dimensions, the emerging global community will also be a "city"—though not on the model of the nation-state— governed by fair rules of conduct and attentive to the demands of good (responsible/accountable) government. Above all global civil life will have to nurture the virtues of practical-political citizenship; that is, commitment to social justice and the rule of law, and a willingness to shoulder the sobering demands of civic "prudence" (*phronesis*). In addition, however, attention needs to be accorded to civilization's corollaries or supplements, speaking to us in their distinctive registers. In sum, civilizational dialogue will have to be a multi-lingual discourse carried on in multiple tonalities, including the tonalities of politics, religion, philosophy, and ecology.[65]

The Roman *civitas,* of course, is what the Greeks called *polis*—and for the classically educated Dallmayr, the linkage is surely automatic. And, in this, an intriguing convergence of his ideas presents itself. The "civilizing process," which is at once thoroughly associated in *Dialogue among Civilizations* with dynamics of discourse and with the "letting be" that had long been center stage in Dallmayr's theory, is a process integral with his increasingly prominent hopes for *cosmopolis.*

Toward the end of the volume, in an essay entitled "What is Self Rule? Lessons from Gandhi," many of the elements of this convergence become apparent. The essay begins with reflection on Gandhi's famous *Hind Swaraj,* focusing on the Hindi word *"swaraj"* or self-rule. Following Gandhi, Dallmayr stresses the multiple imperatives of *swaraj:* freedom, independence, self-restraint, maturity, self-reliance, and being true to oneself. In Gandhi's usage, the term becomes freighted politically, psychologically, religiously, and philosophically with implications for home rule, democracy, Indian identity, law, pluralism, but especially with the idea and practice of passive resistance toward liberation. Dallmayr reminds us of the multiple scales on which to weigh these aspects, which even for Gandhi went far beyond independence from England—establishing a multicultural democracy, encouraging religious toleration, turning inward to lay down a new constitutional order, or looking outward for a world arrangement of pluralist but mutually supportive self-determination. Thus, conveying tonalities that include home with self-reflection, while equally invoking the measure of ongoing self-transformation for authenticity, *swaraj* resonates with the critical and practical dimensions of Dallmayr's understanding of "letting be."

Moreover, a crucial aspect of his hoped-for cosmopolitical progress is also lent fresh perspective. Conceived not as a progressive imposition of an abstract or universalized identity, the "shared matrix" and its "civilizing process," instead, must be akin to the practice of *swaraj,* in the sense of enhancing different authenticities but demanding "self-rule." Quoting Charles Taylor at length, Dallmayr agrees that such "authenticity points us towards a more self-responsible form of life" that, as Taylor says, "opens up an age of responsibilization."[66] With Taylor and Gandhi, Dallmayr insists that the hoped-for "civilizing process" is not a dream. Through practical efforts, hearts and minds can be changed, and ground can be gained—at least for a while.

Peace

One of Dallmayr's most recent books (noting, however, that two more are in process), *Peace Talks—Who Will Listen?* (2004), builds on the Gandhi-inspired hope for not dreaming, but "doing" *swaraj* and for substantive progress through practical efforts to change hearts and minds.[67] Written against the backdrop of the United States' war in Iraq, his book is an eloquent and compelling plea for peace—and, from so many vantage points, his thoughts here frame anew the "letting be" that has been so near the heart of his thinking throughout his intellectual life. It is a book, of course, of political theory and politics; but, equally, *Peace Talks* is a book of philosophy, prayer, and poetry. It praises what Norberto Bobbio (much like Jane de Chantal and Gandhi) recommends as "little virtues," such as meekness, gentleness, littleness, simplicity, and perhaps even extending to what Erasmus called "folly." And, at its heart, Dallmayr's *Peace Talks* endorses a measured vision of nonviolence. Citing Lech Walesa, Martin Luther King, Gandhi, Vaclav Havel, and Nelson Mandela, he calls on the world's intellectuals, instead "of joining the champions of *realpolitik,*" "to join the great humanitarian benefactors of the last century and to champion, whenever and wherever feasible, the course of nonviolence and *satyagraha.*"[68]

Peace "talks," he says, referring to the opening line of Erasmus's *The Complaint of Peace.* But, more powerfully, it calls. Speaking again of a "civilizing process," he reframes the term: "The difficult task is that of 'civilizing humanity': that is, of channeling inclinations and desires in the direction of justice, goodwill, and friendliness. To this extent, peacemaking is never finished. The plaintiff voice of Peace remains forever 'calling': calling us to a promised dwelling place."[69]

Those of us who know Fred Dallmayr perhaps have some inkling of what he means by "a promised dwelling place." At once, the word "dwelling" reminds us of Fred's breathtaking reading of Heidegger's "dwelling poetically" and of the *Bildung* of Heidegger's "Building Dwelling Thinking." It reminds us of Dallmayr's thoughtful readings of Hölderlin's "*Der Ister*," of Hannah Arendt's *vita activa*, of Aristotle's *philia*, of Gandhi's *swaraj*, of Zarathustra's "children's land," and of Heraclitus's invitation to join him at his stove because "Here, too, gods dwell." We know, too, that the "promised dwelling place" of which he speaks must also somehow be a city (*civitas, polis*)—a city of little virtues, friendliness, nonviolence, noisy with discourse, yet listening for peace, and "letting be."

NOTES

1. See the Dallmayr bibliography in this volume.

2. Fred Dallmayr, *Critical Encounters: Between Philosophy and Politics* (Notre Dame, Ind.: University of Notre Dame Press, 1987), p. 157. The quotation is from Hans-Georg Gadamer, *Truth and Method* (New York: Seabury Press, 1975), p. 15.

3. Cf. Fred Dallmayr, *The Other Heidegger* (Ithaca: Cornell University Press, 1993), pp. 64, 98; Fred Dallmayr, *Between Freiburg and Frankfurt: Toward a Critical Ontology* (Amherst: University of Massachusetts Press, 1991), pp. 66–67; and *Critical Encounters*, pp. 66–72.

4. Dallmayr's first book, for example, dealt with the implications of governments' use of emergency powers for freedom and civil liberties. Fred Dallmayr and Robert S. Rankin, *Freedom and Emergency Power* (New York: Appleton-Century-Crofts, 1964).

5. Biographical information can be found in Stephen White's *Lifeworld and Politics: Essays in Honor of Fred Dallmayr* (Notre Dame, Ind.: University of Notre Dame Press, 1989). See especially White's introduction. Cf. Dallmayr's autobiographical remarks related to the formation of his theory in *The Other Heidegger*, pp. 1–8. An interesting earlier take on Dallmayr's political theory is David M. Rasmussen's "Fred Dallmayr: The Odyssey of Reconciling Reason," *Human Studies* 21 (1998).

6. For example, see Dallmayr's edited volume, *Materialenband zu Habermas' Erkenntnis und Interesse* (Frankfurt: Suhrkamp Verlag, 1974).

7. Fred Dallmayr and Thomas McCarthy, *Understanding and Social Inquiry* (Notre Dame, Ind.: University of Notre Dame Press, 1977). See also McCarthy's essay in this festschrift.

8. Fred Dallmayr, *Beyond Dogma and Despair: Toward a Critical Phenomenology of Politics* (Notre Dame, Ind.: University of Notre Dame Press, 1981).

9. Ibid., pp. 3–4.

10. Ibid., p. 4.

11. Fred Dallmayr, *Twilight of Subjectivity: Contributions to a Post-Individualist Theory of Politics* (Amherst: University of Massachusetts Press, 1981), p. 5.

12. Ibid., p. 53.

13. Ibid., p. 287.

14. Maurice Merleau-Ponty, quoted in ibid., p. 36. The quotation from Merleau-Ponty is from *The Visible and the Invisible,* trans. Alphonso Lingis (Evanston, Ill.: Northwestern University Press, 1968), pp. 159–60.

15. Fred Dallmayr, *Language and Politics: Why Does Language Matter to Political Philosophy?* (Notre Dame, Ind.: University of Notre Dame Press, 1984).

16. Ibid., p. ix. The traditional interpretation of *zoon logon ekhon* is "rational creature." Dallmayr and Heidegger understand *logos* to mean "word" as well as "rational thought."

17. Richard Rorty, *Philosophy and the Mirror of Nature* (Princeton: Princeton University Press, 1979). See also Rorty's *The Linguistic Turn: Recent Essays in Philosophical Method* (Chicago: University of Chicago Press, 1976).

18. See, e.g., Michael Oakeshott's *Rationalism in Politics, and other Essays* (New York: Basic Books, 1962), and *On Human Conduct* (Oxford: Clarendon Press, 1975).

19. Dallmayr, *Language and Politics,* pp. 176–77.

20. Cf. ibid., pp. 139, 115–17.

21. Ibid., pp. 143–44.

22. Ibid., p. 169. Cf. Hayden White, *Tropics of Discourse: Essays in Cultural Criticism* (Baltimore: Johns Hopkins University Press, 1978), p. 278. To be sure, Dallmayr objects to the flamboyant tone of White's assessment, but he agrees with the general analysis.

23. Fred Dallmayr, *Polis and Praxis* (Cambridge: MIT Press, 1984); *Critical Encounters;* Fred Dallmayr, *Margins of Political Discourse* (Albany: SUNY Press, 1989).

24. Dallmayr, *Polis and Praxis,* p. 109.

25. Ibid., p. 9 With the emphasis on "be," he references Heidegger's "letting Being be."

26. Habermas's *Philosophische Diskurs der Moderne* (Frankfurt: Suhrkamp Verlag), where these criticisms were leveled, was not published until 1985.

27. Dallmayr, *Polis and Praxis,* p. 101.

28. I remember attending a Dallmayr seminar on Heidegger at the University of Notre Dame in the winter of 1981, where at one point, in conjunction with his exegesis of Heidegger's "Building Dwelling Thinking," he expanded at length on *Bildung* and its central place in Heidegger's post-1930 and particularly his post-1945 thought.

Dallmayr's own sensibilities in this regard seemed very much in keeping with his account of Heidegger's understanding of *Bildung.*

29. Dallmayr, *Critical Encounters,* p. 157.

30. Ibid., pp. 156–57. The quotation is from Gadamer's *Truth and Method,* p. 13.

31. Dallmayr, *Critical Encounters,* p. 155.

32. Alasdair MacIntyre, *After Virtue: A Study in Moral Theory* (Notre Dame, Ind.: University of Notre Dame Press, 1984).

33. Dallmayr, *Critical Encounters,* p. 206.

34. Dallmayr, *Margins of Political Discourse,* p. 107.

35. Ibid., p. 104. The quotation is from Bernard Waldenfels, *Ordnung in Zwielicht* (Frankfurt: Suhrkamp Verlag, 1987), pp. 10–11.

36. Ernesto Laclau and Chantal Mouffe, *Hegemony and Socialist Strategy: Towards a Radical Democratic Politics,* trans. Winston Moore and Paul Cammack (London: Verso, 1985). See also Mouffe's essay in this festschrift.

37. Dallmayr, *Margins of Political Discourse,* p. 133. The quotations are from Laclau and Mouffe, *Hegemony and Socialist Strategy,* pp. 125–26, 128–29.

38. Dallmayr, *Polis and Praxis,* p. 9.

39. Cf. Hugo Ott, *Martin Heidegger: Unterwegs zu seiner Biographie* (Frankfurt: Campus Verlag, 1988); and Victor Farias, *Heidegger et le nazisme* (Paris: Verdier, 1987).

40. Dallmayr, *Between Freiburg and Frankfurt,* p. 3.

41. Ibid., pp. 56, 54.

42. Ibid., p. 31.

43. Ibid., p. 64. The emphasis is in Hermann Mörchen's *Adorno und Heidegger: Untersuchung einer philosophischen Kommunikationsverweigerung* (Stuttgart: Klett-Cotta, 1981) pp. 242–44.

44. Dallmayr, *Between Freiburg and Frankfurt,* p. 67.

45. See Richard Wolin, ed., *The Heidegger Controversy: A Critical Reader* (New York: Columbia University Press, 1991).

46. Dallmayr, *The Other Heidegger,* p. ix.

47. Ibid., p. 10.

48. Ibid., p. 98.

49. Ibid., p. 161. The Heidegger quotation is from *Hölderlins Hymne "Der Ister,"* in *Gesamtausgabe,* vol. 53, ed. Walter Biemel (Frankfurt: Klostermann Verlag, 1984), p. 60.

50. Dallmayr, *Beyond Orientalism: Essays on Cross-Cultural Encounter* (Albany: SUNY Press, 1996). For reasons of rhetoric and space I am not reviewing Dallmayr's intriguing work on Hegel: *G. W. F. Hegel: Modernity and Politics,* rev. ed. (Lanham, Md.: Rowman and Littlefield, 2002).

51. Dallymayr's *Beyond Orientalism,* the chapter "Gadamer, Derrida, and the Hermeneutics of Difference."

52. Dallmayr, *Alternative Visions: Paths in the Global Village* (Lanham, Md.: Rowman and Littlefield, 1998).

53. Ibid., p. 2.

54. Ibid., p. 7.

55. Ibid., p. 132.

56. Fred Dallmayr, *Achieving Our World: Toward a Global and Plural Democracy* (Lanham, Md.: Rowman and Littlefield, 2001), p. ix.

57. Jacques Derrida, *Politics of Friendship,* trans. George Collins (London: Verso, 1997). Cf. Derrida, "The Politics of Friendship," *Journal of Philosophy* 85 (1988). See also the essays by Schrag and McCarthy in this festschrift.

58. Dallmayr, *Achieving Our World*, p. 159. The Aristotle quotation is from *Nicomachean Ethics* 1155a25 (bk. 8, 9.35), trans. Terence Irwin (Indianapolis: Hackett, 1985).

59. Dallmayr, *Achieving Our World*, p. 147.

60. Dallmayr, Ibid., p. 164. The quotations are from Derrida's *Politics of Friendship*, pp. 64–65.

61. Dallmayr, *Achieving Our World*, p. 165.

62. UN General Assembly Resolution 53/22 (November 4, 1998). Cf. Samuel Huntington, *The Clash of Civilizations and the Remaking of World Order* (New York: Simon and Schuster, 1996).

63. Fred Dallmayr, *Dialogue among Civilizations: Some Exemplary Voices* (New York: Palgrave Macmillan, 2002), p. 13. See Friedrich Hölderlin, *Sämtliche Werke,* vol. 2, *Gedichte nach 1800*, ed. Friedrich Beißner (Stuttgart: Große Stuttgarter Ausgabe, 1946), p. 133. Cf. Heidegger, *Gesamtausgabe*, vol. 4, *Erläuterungen zu Hölderlins Dichtung,* ed. Friedrich-Wilhelm von Hermann (Frankfurt: Klostermann, 1981), pp. 123–24.

64. Dallmayr, *Dialogue among Civilizations*, p. 26.

65. Ibid., p. 30.

66. Ibid., p. 228. The quotations are from Charles Taylor, *The Ethics of Authenticity* (Cambridge: Harvard University Press, 1992), pp. 68, 74.

67. Fred Dallmayr, *Peace Talks—Who Will Listen?* (Notre Dame, Ind.: University of Notre Dame Press, 2004). His most recent book, *Small Wonder: Global Power and Its Discontents* (Lanham, Md.: Rowman and Littlefield, 2005) appeared too recently to include in this review.

68. Ibid., pp. 130–31.

69. Ibid., p. 21.

PART I.

POLITICAL THEORY

AND MODERN PHILOSOPHY

Seeing the Sovereign: Theatricality and Representation in Hobbes

Tracy B. Strong

One of Fred Dallmayr's earliest essays—one published in two different versions—concerns the affinities between Hobbes and existentialism.[1] It is already wonderfully characteristic of what we would come to think of as Fred's voice: there is little, but polite, truck with standard interpretations; there are surprising juxtapositions about which one would not have otherwise thought; there is, as always, the focus on how the writer being considered reaches us on the "level of basic human experience."[2]

Toward the end of that article, after exploring points of intersection between Hobbes, Sartre, Camus, and Merleau-Ponty, Dallmayr notes that Hobbes does not seem to pursue his own thought to its end: "The stipulation of a common power whose decisions ultimately derive from human will clearly introduces an element of contingency into the operation of the commonwealth."[3] Fred thereby notes that there are implications in Hobbes's argument about the sovereign that Hobbes does not draw out, and he pretty much concludes the article on that note. I propose here to continue Fred's thought, if possible, in an attempt to draw out some of those implications.

The Hobbesian sovereign is a tempting creature: tempting because we want to think of him/it both as omnipotent and as a creature—because it is we who have made him, and not he himself.[4] He offers the reader the image of a being who is our own and yet somehow more than we are. The famous frontispiece of *Leviathan* is noteworthy in this respect. It shows an immense but very human giant towering above the horizon. In front of the giant is laid out a well-ordered city; around it are signs of human husbandry and agriculture. The giant is such that no one living in the city or working on the land could possibly *not* see him; he is unavoidable. One imagines going out in the morning to take in the milk: the sovereign cannot be missed and is just where he was when you went to bed.

His body is made up of many discrete individuals who differ among themselves in their dress (and thus their status). Each of them faces the giant. We know that Hobbes took an active part in the composition of this frontispiece. We know also that an earlier version of the drawing showed the individuals making up the giant's body facing outward, toward the reader. It is not unreasonable to suppose that Hobbes wished them to face the other way so that they may be seen from behind, just as one sees the fellow members of an audience when at the theater.[5] The sovereign is first and foremost a being present to our sight.

There are two aspects to this presence. First, the sovereign is an object of sight; second, the sight of the sovereign is *in* sight, much as he would be if on a stage in the theater. The important thing about the object of sight in the theater is that what I see does not see me; the relation is intransitive and not reciprocal. But, then, what kind of person is it that is seen by me but does not see me? The short answer is that for Hobbes it is the sovereign; and, to explore Hobbes's understanding of sovereignty, one must understand the importance of the fact that the sovereign is centrally the object of sight for Hobbes. This in turn requires an explanation of what Hobbes means by calling the sovereign a "person," a concept of considerable complexity.

After asserting in his response to Bishop Bramhall that the "civil laws are nothing else but the commands of him that hath the sovereign power, concerning the future actions of his subjects," Hobbes continues: "What verbal command of a king can arrive at the ears of all his subjects, which it must do ere it be a law, without the seal of the person of the commonwealth, which is here the Great Seal of England?"[6]

This tells us that the term "persons" is first and foremost for Hobbes a term for the locus of and the possibility of power. This is true whether the person is "natural" (considered simply as a human being) or "civil" (considered in his or her political capacity, here emblematized in and by the Great Seal). In *Leviathan*, we thus read:

> The greatest of human powers, is that which is compounded of the powers of most men, united by consent, in one person, natural, or civil, that has the use of all their powers depending on his will; such as is the power

of a common-wealth: or depending on the wills of each particular; such as is the power of a faction or of divers factions leagued. Therefore to have servants, is power; to have friends, is power: for they are strengths united.[7]

Persons are or can be made of human beings. In this analysis, it is the existence of persons that makes power possible, at least for human beings. Persons permit, in a manner I shall examine, the intensification of power. Additionally and importantly, the idea of "person" applies not just to (ordinary, mortal) human beings. In chapter 15 of *Leviathan*, we find that "the detaining of debt, is an injury to themselves; but *robbery and violence, are injuries to the person of the commonwealth*." The italics are mine and underline Hobbes's conception of a commonwealth.

All this means that Hobbes's understanding of person needs still further explication. In his response to Bishop Bramhall, he discusses the idea in the context of the Trinity and the nature of God. Hobbes wants to hold that God is both corporeal and infinite. Bramhall had objected that this subverted the doctrine of the Trinity on the general grounds that nothing corporeal could be other than singular. Hobbes retorts that just as one can be at the same time three persons (he adduces a letter of Cicero's; see below), so also can God be Tri and Une. Leaving aside the dubious orthodoxy of Hobbes's claim, it is clear that what is at stake is the definition of person. Hobbes writes:

> And thus we have the exact meaning of the word person. The Greek tongue cannot render it; for prosopon is properly a face, and, metaphorically, a vizard of an actor upon the stage. How then did the Greek Fathers render the word person, as it is in the blessed Trinity? Not well. Instead of the word person they put hypostasis, which signifies substance; from whence it might be inferred, that the three persons in the Trinity are three Divine substances, that is, three Gods. The word prosopon they could not use, because face and vizard are neither of them honorable attributes of God, nor explicative of the meaning of the Greek church.[8]

A parallel argument had already been made in the famous chapter 16 of the English-language version of the *Leviathan*:

The word person is Latin: instead whereof the Greeks have prosopon, which signifies the face, as persona in Latin signifies the disguise, or outward appearance of a man, counterfeited on the stage; and sometimes more particularly that part of it, which disguiseth the face, as a mask or vizard: and from the stage, hath been translated to any representer of speech and action, as well in tribunals, as theatres. So that a person, is the same that an actor is, both on the stage and in common conversation; and to personate, is to act, or represent himself, or another; and he that acteth another, is said to bear his person, or act in his name; (in which sense Cicero useth it where he says, *Unus sustineo tres personas; mei, adversarii, et judicis,* I bear three persons; my own, my adversary's, and the judge's;) and is called in divers occasions, diversely; as a representer, or representative, a lieutenant, a vicar, an attorney, a deputy, a procurator, an actor, and the like.[9]

Hobbes's discussion here is notable on several counts. First, it argues that the idea of face and person are particularly and exclusively human and that they cannot be accurately applied to the early Greek Fathers' understanding of the being of the Christian God.[10] In fact, they cannot be applied to God at all, for God has no face in any human sense of the term. As such, Hobbes's discussion here reemphasizes the this-worldliness of his concerns, or more accurately his insistence that our understandings be of this world.

Second, by its emphasis on face, the above passage implies that seeing is a particularly human trait. Indeed, Hobbes goes so far as to deny that God actually sees. In *De Cive,* he writes that "when we attribute sight . . . to him [God], or knowledge, or understanding, which in us are nothing else but a tumult of the mind, raised from outward objects pressing the organs; we must not think that any such thing befalls the Deity; for it is a sign of power depending upon some other, which is not the most blessed thing."[11] And as the sovereign is a "mortal God,"[12] it follows that the sovereign also needs not sight (for if He were sighted it would follow that He might then miss something).

A third consideration comes from the question as to who or what Cicero might be in his bearing of three persons. In his response to Bramhall, Cicero is said to be a "substance intelligent, one man." Hence it is possible to be the same man and many persons.[13] Whatever a person is, it is something that sight can give us—a "Conception," as Hobbes says. A conception is defined by Hobbes in the *Elements of Law* as "imagery and representations of the qualities of things without us."[14] Conception is in turn a human quality, for we have no (actual, proper) conception of God.[15]

Persons are thus constructs, human, and the object of sight. This complex idea of person is absolutely central in Hobbes's political philosophy.[16] As laid out in the two passages above, it includes a number of facets. Importantly, a person is for Hobbes the same "that an actor is" on stage.[17] Hobbes gives some idea of what that entails when he writes, for instance, that "[t]he king of Persia, honored Mordecai, when he appointed he should be conducted through the streets in the king's garment, upon one of the king's horses, with a crown on his head, and a prince before him, proclaiming, thus shall it be done to him that the king will honor."[18] The king places Mordecai in the theatrical sight of the populace: what matters about persons is how they appear to one another or, more accurately, are seen by one another. A person is, then, centrally for Hobbes a performance or a representation.

What does it mean to say that theatricality is the model for persons? Three things seem important. First, it implies, at least, that being seen is central to being at all. Second, it also implies that how one appears to others is how one is. Last and most crucial, it requires that others acknowledge you as and in your performance. One will only know from seeing. Hobbes goes so far as to suggest that what we see we will know better than we know ourselves. For example, in a letter from 1634, he responds to a friend's query as follows:

> For your question, why a man remembers less his own face, which he sees often in a glass, than the face of a friend that he has not seen of a great time, my opinion in general is, that a man remembers best those faces whereof he has had the greatest impressions, and that the impressions are the greater for the oftener seeing them, and the longer staying upon the sight of them. Now you know men look upon their own faces but for short fits, but upon their friends' faces long time together, whilst they discourse or converse together; so that a man may receive a greater impression from his friend's face in a day, than from his own in a year; and according to this impression, the image will be fresher in his mind.[19]

In general, Hobbes uses the term "sight" to describe evidence that one has trouble denying. "First sight" is his common term for that which is evident.[20] The task comes in making an object in sight such that no one can be mistaken about it. Thus, for Hobbes, the task is to make sovereignty appear in such a manner that no one cannot but see it for what it is.

Here the matter becomes complex. We do not see ourselves as we are—that is, our sight of ourselves betrays us. Hobbes here makes an important assimilation of the idea of reading to that of understanding. As human beings are so confused as to what words actually mean, Hobbes writes in the *Elements of Law* that self-knowledge must proceed from looking into the self. As "it is," writes Hobbes, "impossible to rectify so many errors of any one man . . . without beginning anew from the very first grounds of all our knowledge . . . and, instead of books, reading over orderly one's own conceptions: in which meaning I take *nosce teipsum* for a precept worthy the reputation it hath gotten." This reputation is made more explicit in the introduction to *Leviathan:*

> [T]here is another saying not of late understood, by which they might learn truly to read one another, if they would take the pains; and that is, *nosce teipsum*, read thyself: which was not meant, as it is now used, to countenance, either the barbarous state of men in power, towards their inferiors; or to encourage men of low degree, to a saucy behavior towards their betters; but to teach us, that for the similitude of the thoughts and passions of one man, to the thoughts and passions of another, whosoever looketh into himself, and considereth what he doth, when he does think, opine, reason, hope, fear, &c. and upon what grounds; he shall thereby read and know, what are the thoughts and passions of all other men upon the like occasions.[21]

The translation of *nosce teipsum* as "read thyself" is quite dramatic.[22] Reading is the knowledge gained through sight.[23] A number of qualities stand out. What is read—self-knowledge—will be the same for everyone. It neither justifies domination nor rebellion. It will give us generally valid information. Why then are things so bad? Hobbes's answer is that self-knowledge is hard to come by. Humans want to resist it. In the appendix to the Latin edition of *Leviathan* he writes: "Natural law is eternal, divine and inscribed only in human hearts. But there are very few men who know how to examine their own heart and read what is written there. Thus it is from written laws [from laws that have authority behind them] that men know what they must do or avoid."[24]

The internal writing that is in each of our hearts is hard to read. Humans thus need external written laws, set down by one who can read the human heart, in order to know what it is in their hearts to do. From this it would follow that Hobbes seeks to make the Leviathan—the sovereign—an object of sight such that what all see there will in fact be what could have been read in their own hearts. The sovereign is, thus, our self constructed as an object of sight. When we see the Leviathan over the horizon, we are in fact seeing ourselves, in the way we would do so in a theater.

What does it mean to say that we see ourselves in a theater?[25] Theater is when "[p]eople act and play their own parts," Hobbes tells us in the "Answer to the Preface before Gondibert." The important word is "own." With this notion, the general equality of the speakers, the notion of a voice in each, one might be tempted to think that Hobbes is here reactivating the classical notion of the agora.[26] Yet this is wrong, or rather misleading: the classical notion of the agora conceived of it as physical space. In the classical Greek democracies, the agora was that which defined them as different from those whom Herodotus called the "barbaric peoples" of the East, whose states were founded on invisibility, thus on secrecy or deceit. However, this visibility is not simply an ethical requirement of transparency and truth. What Hobbes understood is that the idea of a person includes an aesthetic dimension: it must be made manifest and perceived in gestures and symbols, perhaps even in ceremonies. The requirement of visibility thus "puts up a front"; it exposes—and must risk itself—to public scrutiny, just as do performers on a stage. In other words, Hobbes's conception of sovereignty involves a transformation of the conception of political space.[27]

Such a change was historically necessary. In the seventeenth century, the legitimacy of the English state, with its origins in Norman Conquest, was denied by such groups as the Levelers and the Diggers on the grounds that conquest conferred no right to govern. History had settled nothing. "We may have been conquered," they said in effect, "but that means nothing, for one day we will conquer the conquerors." The English Revolution gave substance to the potential of this claim; it required a justification of governance on a basis other than that of conquest or inheritance—categories that had received their early modern formulation in Machiavelli. It fell to Hobbes to rouse thought from its historical slumber and found modern political philosophy by uniting contract with sovereignty.[28] To the warring partners of the civil war, Hobbes said in effect that it did not matter who won and who lost the historical war, at least not in the long run. The state that was established by the contractual elaboration of sovereignty was, Hobbes argued, what each, whether in victory or in defeat, actually wanted.[29]

Hobbes deployed two central arguments to demonstrate his claim that the sovereign was, in the end—or rather, at the beginning—us. The first is the claim that he (or someone like him) saw better than we did how it was with each of us. In the *Elements of Law*, Hobbes's intention is explicitly "to put men in mind of what they know already, or may know by their own experience."[30] In the preface to *De Cive*, he sets down as a "principle known to all men and denied by none" that every man "will distrust and dread in each other." He then goes on to ask what is one to make of those who would deny such a principle. As I noted above, for Hobbes the political problem comes from the fact that humans deny that which they know. One therefore needs dramatically to remind them of the reality of their experience: "It may seem strange, to some man that has not well weighed these things, that nature should thus dissociate, and render men apt to invade and destroy one another. And he may, therefore, not trusting to this inference made from the passions, desire perhaps to have the same confirmed by experience."[31] And he proceeds to tell a little story, asking who does not go armed when on travel, does not lock one's chests, and so forth. "Look at your own life—don't think about it," seems to be Hobbes's message. For Hobbes, human use will and can teach us the meaning; however, a sovereign must be constructed so as to embody it so that we can see it.

To enable such a construction, Hobbes's second crucial argument has to do with representation. The reason that one cannot complain against the sovereign is that the sovereign represents one's own will as one would understand it except for the fact that we deny ourselves knowledge of ourselves. The grounds for this argument were set again in chapter 16 of *Leviathan*, a chapter with no parallel in *De Cive* and one that Hobbes added to the English version of *Leviathan*. There he argues that representation is a species of ownership, whereby those who authorize the sovereign owns his actions. The sovereign is, so to speak a "me" that I have constructed, whose actions are mine as I am their sole owner. Artificial persons—such as a sovereign—have nothing of their own. (So for instance, William the Conqueror is said never to have owned anything as sovereign, the fields and forests "being reserved to him in his private capacity.") But because that which is owned are those of my actions that I would sooner give up in most circumstances (because it is hard for me to read my heart, because I do not like what is in my heart), I am— must be—bound to those actions in an irredeemable manner.

That which represents me is thus, for Hobbes, a me over which I can have no control, because control is contradictory to the terms of the representation. We should obey an authority, even and perhaps especially one that we have authorized. Yet this authority is ourselves as our own fathers or superegos: we have met the king and he is us.[32] Revolt becomes a form of violence to the self, perhaps of suicide.

| What does it mean to see oneself on stage, as it were, as the sovereign? In 1586, Elizabeth I gave a speech to Parliament members. "We Princes," she told them, "are set on stages, in the sight and view of all the world duly observed."[33] Her Majesty's not unrueful recognition of her own visibility is consequent to her understanding of herself as a person in public space. One senses that Elizabeth would have preferred not to be so set before her world, but also that she knew that she had no choice. Elizabeth's recognition of her visibility manifests a change that takes place loosely in the period between Machiavelli and Hobbes.

In Hobbes, visibility is key to the stability of the realm. Speaking of a good polity, he writes in the preface to *De Cive* that subjects "reverenced the supreme power, whether residing in one man or in a council, as a certain visible divinity." Elsewhere, the setting up of a "visible mark" is understood to be the first step man makes as he rises above beasts.[34] In *Leviathan*, finally, the defining quality of successful sovereignty is that he can be seen:

> The final cause, end, or design of men, (who naturally love liberty, and dominion over others,) in the introduction of that restraint upon themselves, (in which we see them live in commonwealths,) is the foresight of their own preservation and of a more contented life thereby; that is to say, of getting themselves out from that miserable condition of war, which is necessarily consequent (as hath been shown), to the natural passions of men, when there is no *visible power* to keep them in awe, and tie them by fear of punishment to the performance of their covenants,

and observation of those laws of nature set down in the fourteenth and fifteenth chapters.[35]

It is important to mark the change Hobbes is instituting, approaching the matter differently than Machiavelli. In Machiavelli, the central question concerning the power and legitimacy of the prince was famously answered in terms of love and fear. The Machiavellian prince was constantly in need of eliciting, either by seduction or terror, the passion and the approval of his subjects. *The Prince* is a kind of handbook for the political use of emotions. For example, it is important not to elicit emotions in the populace that cannot be controlled. If you conquer a city that loves liberty, you should put the populace to the sword because the love of liberty cannot be controlled. Likewise, the prince should not interfere with the women among his subjects because that gives rise to an emotion that will not be forgotten and that no technique can divert to his own interests and estate.

By the time we get to Hobbes, this is clearly no longer the case. We might even say that what had been technique in Machiavelli becomes ontology in Hobbes. What has happened? Here a recent article by Paul Dumouchel is of help.[36] He argues not just that representation is central to Hobbes's idea of sovereignty, but that the Hobbesian sovereign is defined in and by the fact that he represents. Representation is understood here in a double sense, both reflexively as he who wants to give expression to someone or something (as is the case in theater), and nonreflexively as having the job to be the delegate of someone else. In both cases, to represent is to be an actor.[37] Hobbes's originality at this juncture lies in his wishing to join both meanings. The sovereign must be seen, must hold himself on stage, must be a persona not in order to attract votes or approval—or to evoke fear—but because that is what makes him the sovereign. In fact, it is only by seeing him as this persona that the subjects can come to a common understanding. The public theatrical image of the sovereign brings about the political unity of the subjects. As Dumouchel writes, "this image does not represent anything other than the power of the multitude, a power it constitutes through the very act of representing it" (57).

Thus, even in the case that appears to be the most uncongenial to democratic public space (uncongenial because, according to Hobbes, the sovereign is established by a contract to which he is not party), the question of visibility in general and of visibility as a public staging remains basic. Hobbes places it at the heart of political thought. Theatricality is no longer understood merely as an instrument of power, it is its very essence, the essence of political visibility. This is certainly why, from the Enlightenment on, the rediscovery of democratic political space came as a reaction against this theatricality, to the point of trying to deny the existence of a staging power (even as this power continues to delineate the space of visibility).[38]

Subsequent thinkers learn from Hobbes (even when they denounce his program) how to push as far as possible his conception of the theatrical necessity in sovereign power. They understand, in other words, that theatricality is not an accident nor a simple tool, but the very being of power. Hobbes, we might say, is the first political thinker to see the power of the medium. And, in doing so, he initiates a process whereby the representation of power will eventually come to fulfillment in the power of representation. In doing so, however, Hobbes unwittingly sets the conditions for modern democracy.

Once again, the arguments of *Leviathan*'s chapter 16 are central. The construction of the visible sovereign is made possible by the distinction between authors and actors. The sovereign is for Hobbes an artificial—that is constructed—actor. The authors are those who construct him. In a famous passage, Hobbes writes:

> Of persons artificial, some have their words and actions owned by those whom they represent. And then the person is the actor; and he that owneth his words and actions, is the AUTHOR: in which case the actor acteth by authority. For that which in speaking of goods and possessions, is called an owner, and in Latin dominus, in Greek kyrios; speaking of actions, is called author. And as the right of possession, is called dominion; so the right of doing any action, is called AUTHORITY. So that by authority, is always understood a right of doing any act: and done by authority, done by commission, or licence from him whose right it is.

The theatricalizing of sovereignty permits an assembly of the populace (for Hobbes, all citizens) solemnly to partake in a dramatic genesis of sovereignty. It is thus as appearance and theater that sovereignty achieves the reality of its own being. As Fred Dallmayr pointed out in the 1960s, Hobbes did not fully grasp the implication of his move.

Necessary to the theatricalizing of sovereignty is the author. We are each of us author of the sovereign. The sovereign's acts are thus our own rational acts. They embody that hard to achieve self-knowledge (which is one of the reasons why resistance to the sovereign is an epistemologically meaningless act for Hobbes). Thus, Hobbes can quite consistently write that "if he that attempteth to depose his sovereign, be killed, or punished by him for such attempt, he is author of his own punishment, as being by the institution, author of all his sovereign shall do: and because it is injustice for a man to do any thing, for which he may be punished by his own authority, he is also upon that title, unjust."[39]

Let us see what happens in Hobbes's text:

> A multitude of men, are made one person, when they are by one man, or one person, represented; so that it be done with the consent of every one of that multitude in particular. For it is the unity of the representer, not the unity of the represented, that maketh the person one. And it is the representer that beareth the person, and but one person: and unity, cannot otherwise be understood in multitude.

As each person represents himself in the same way, each finds himself represented by the same representer, namely, the sovereign. In such a vision, the multitude is made one, that is, is given a common identity consequent to the fact that each has constructed the same representer. The unity attained both requires and retains the multiplicity of each author.[40] Hobbes continues:

> And because the multitude naturally is not one, but many; they cannot be understood for one; but many authors, of every thing their representative saith, or doth in their name; every man giving their common representer, authority from himself in particular; and owning all the actions the representer doth, in case they give him authority without stint: otherwise, when they limit him in what, and how far he shall represent them, none of them owneth more, than they gave him commission to act.

Hobbes says that whatever is authorized is, and is only to that extent, given over to the representer (sovereign). Any acts that the sovereign undertakes within this commission are in fact the acts of the authorizers and cannot be disclaimed. And Hobbes leaves it pretty much at that. The next book of *Leviathan* is an examination of logical consequences of authorizing the sovereign to exercise one's right of nature to defend oneself. It is worth noting in passing that in no ways is this vision one of a single proto-totalitarian figure. The very next paragraph holds:

> And if the representative consist of many men, the voice of the greater number, must be considered as the voice of them all. For if the lesser number pronounce (for example) in the affirmative, and the greater in the negative, there will be negatives more than enough to destroy the affirmatives; and thereby the excess of negatives, standing uncontradicted, are the only voice the representative hath.

This simply means that the sovereign can be composed of many individuals. In fact, the people are the sovereign, which can theatricalize itself on the political stage as one, many, or all. The sovereign is said to "bear [my] person."[41]

Hobbes here opens a doorway through which he is unwilling to pass. His image of the authorizing process is, I have argued, theatrical. It consists of establishing an actor on a stage who can be a first sight recognized for what he is: our legitimate sovereign. Yet it is at this point that Hobbes reverts to a passive understanding of the citizenry/audience. Hobbes will repeat again and again that we can do nothing about the sovereign's actions because they are ours. But what this fails to realize is that Hobbes has, in the process of authorizing the sovereign, tacitly empowered the author. In his article on Hobbes and the existentialists, Dallmayr writes that "[t]he stipulation of a common power whose decisions ultimately derive from human will clearly introduces an element of contingency into the operation of the commonwealth."[42]

Asking about the source and import of this contingency raises the question concerning the relation of the people to the actor they have authorized to be their sovereign. Such authorization is essential to modern politics. There is a tendency in much modern thought, however, to share with Hobbes the feeling that this relation is one of passivity.[43] Hobbes celebrated this passivity; many now decry it. But they share the same vision.

I think this is mistaken because it fails adequately to grasp the actual nature of the audience relationship. I repeat that such a relationship is necessary—the spatial agora of the Greeks cannot be recreated. Nevertheless, there are still resources in the audience relation that Hobbes either does not see or does not see fit to tap. Rousseau understood this when he suggested that for Hobbes the English were only free at the moment of authorizing, after which "ils retombent dans l'hobbisme le plus parfait," and he condemned Hobbes for it. At least, however, an instant of freedom was made possible. A more complex vision of the audience relationship can be found in the work of Rousseau and of Nietzsche. I can only point at their understandings here.[44]

The second book of the *Social Contract* is an exploration of the way in which "laws" are established, that is, sovereignty. "Laws" needs here to be placed within quotation marks in order to draw attention to the fact that Rousseau has an explicitly somewhat technical use of the term.

In the first version of the *Social Contract*, Rousseau had placed his discussion of law in the first book. As the book matured he came to see that it required a separate and preliminary discussion of the sovereign as that which makes law possible. Already in the early version, however, he had recognized the centrality and novelty of his concept. Having proclaimed in *Emile* that "this subject is completely new: the definition of the law is still to be made,"[45] he here boldly declares that what is called "law" is "properly only the conditions of civil association." The mood of this section is rhapsodic: it is "only to law that humans owe justice and liberty.... [Law] is the celestial voice which dictates to each citizen the precepts of public reason.... Without law an existing state (*l'état formé*) is only a body without soul, for it is not enough that each be subject to the general will; one has to know it to follow it."[46]

"Law" is thus that which makes it possible to live generally by one's will. Rousseau describes a law as follows:

> [W]hen an entire people gives a law for the entire people (*statue sur tout le peuple*) it considers only itself. And if a relationship is thus formed, it is from one point of view a relationship of the entire object with the entire object from another point of view, without any division of the whole. Thus the matter for which a law is given (*sur laquelle on statue*) is general in the same way that is the will which gives the law. It is this act that I call a law.[47]

For Rousseau, a law thus requires that a people be able to see itself as a people, to stand outside itself and, as itself, constitute itself. The object of a law is therefore always general in the sense that the general will is general. It considers "the citizens in a body" and sees all actions in a general or common manner, that is, as the same for you as they are for me. To act in such a manner is for Rousseau what is meant by "sovereignty."

Following the terms of this analogy, we might then think of the sovereign as being for Rousseau the perfect user of the language of community, of the common tongue. The sovereign is that which does not make a mistake, since it is, as it were, grammar in action. The sovereign exists then only in the present as it can in no way "bind itself for the future."[48] And for it to have existence in the present it must be by means of the doubleness that each individual can introduce into him or herself. Each contracts "as it were," says Rousseau, with him or herself. The most important thing to realize about this relationship of self seeing the self is that it cannot be guaranteed. The essence of commonality holds its right from the fact that it can claim no right, that is, it can claim no thing that is not itself.[49] As with Hobbes, at least on the surface, "the sovereign, by the mere fact of being, is always what it ought to be."[50] If what Rousseau calls the "sanctity" of the contract should be violated by any act that would be contrary to its being, then the contract would carry no obligation. Indeed, the notion of obligation is inappropriate here as sovereignty collapses the time dimension of political society into the present.[51]

The sovereign for Rousseau, therefore, is the citizens, that is, the individuals of a commonalty when they are acting as members of that community, as citizens. "Indeed," he says, "each individual can as a human being have a particular will that is contrary or dissimilar to the general will which he has as citizen."[52] The social contract—what Rousseau often telling calls the "fundamental compact"—substitutes a legal and conventional equality for physical inequality,[53] and it is precisely this conventional equality that is constitutive of and established by citizenship. There is no viable notion of citizenship without commonalty, thus without equality. The conventional equality exists as, and only as, that which has been acknowledged to be common between me and you.

But why is it that such sovereignty can neither be alienated (given over to someone else) nor even represented (given on loan, as it were)? How can something be really mine if I cannot give it away, or at least let it be borrowed? Rousseau's understanding was that since the sovereign is me, while one might say that it represents me, in no way do I give my self over to it or become passive in relation to it.[54]

The first thing to recall is that sovereignty does not exist over time or even in time. Whereas the establishment of sovereignty took place in a kind of absolute moment, after that the sovereign had *durée*. For Rousseau, rather, each moment of sovereignty is "absolute, independent of the preceding, and never does the sovereign act because he willed, but only because he wills."[55] This thought, given formulation in several places in Rousseau's drafts as he worked on the *Social Contract,* appears in final form as "yesterday's law carries no obligations today."[56] In a gesture to the pragmatics of politics, Rousseau goes on to indicate that "consent is presumed from silence." What should not be missed here, however, is that sovereignty and thus the being of political society is held to exist solely in the present tense. Not only can the future not be tied down, but it should not be named. Thus there is not, nor can there be, to speak precisely, "any kind of obligatory fundamental law for the body of the people, not even the social contract."

No "kind of fundamental law"! Rousseau really means it when he says that political society is made possible and continues in its existence because of the free human will. Against Hobbes, and insofar as the idea of obligation consists of a binding of the will to a future, Rousseau rejects the idea that political society rests on obligation. If I am obliged, I am available as a representation; I have represented myself to the future. The strictures that Rousseau places on the representation of sovereignty derive from the nontemporal quality of sovereignty. If something exists only in the present, then its only existence derives from the activity that it requires of those that engage it. Rousseau thus picked up on the aesthetic dimension present in Hobbes's discussion of sovereignty and worked through its implications. Sovereignty is like a work of art in the sense that it exists only in the present. It is thus in constant dialogue with those who are its audience and its continuing authors.

This process, initiated but not completely worked through by Hobbes, was developed radically in Rousseau and finally worked out in Nietzsche, an author not often associated with Hobbes (or Rousseau). In *The Birth of Tragedy,* Nietzsche advances an argument about the politico-cultural importance of Greek drama, giving an account of the kind of audience that Greeks were for tragic theater.

A public of spectators as we know it was unknown to the Greeks: in their theaters, the terraced structure of the concentric arcs of the place of spectatorship (*Zuschauerraumes*) made it possible for everyone actually to overlook the whole world of culture around him and imagine in sated contemplation that he was a chorist.[57]

The German word for "overlook" is *übersehen,* and it permits the double meaning of "survey" and "fail to see." The audience is in "sated contemplation," that is, there is nothing missing from what it is the audience of. During this time, the audience finds itself in the "place of spectatorship." It knows that everything occurring before it cannot be affected by its actions. (This is what Nietzsche means by a "dionysian" state—the erotic origins of Dionysus are key.) The spectator will not therefore, Nietzsche indicates, "run up on stage and free the god from its torments."

As characters, the actors on stage are in the presence of the audience but the audience is not in their presence. There is no way in which the audience can, as audience, compel the action on stage to acknowledge it. The audience, in the *Birth of Tragedy,* is in a dionysian state; so also is the chorus on stage, in view of the audience. Through the chorus, Nietzsche argues, the audience is swept up onto the stage to contemplate the action but not to affect it. (The chorus never does anything in Aeschylean tragedy.) Nietzsche writes: "The proceeding of the tragic chorus is the dramatic protophenomenon: to see oneself [as embodied in the chorus—TBS] transformed before one's very eyes [as spectator—TBS] and to begin to act as if one had actually entered into another character."[58] Here the audience is in relation to a politico-cultural exemplar of itself. It finds itself compelled to enter into a character that has to deal with a particular politico-cultural issue (such as the meaning of law, in *Antigone*). One is not then called only to a "higher self" by tragedy—one is called to take concern for a matter that affects the public. But only those who can respond to tragedy as a real audience will find themselves so called. Nietzsche's strictures against Socrates and Euripides are that they make this impossible. Indeed, the whole of the *Birth of Tragedy* may be seen as a test whether one is capable of such a relation to the performance. The notion of transformation is key: against Aristotle who had argued that the purpose of tragedy was self-recognition, Nietzsche is arguing that it is self-transformation.

What Nietzsche and implicitly Rousseau argued is that a true understanding of what it means to be an audience for the theater of politics involves something other than a passive relationship. There is such a relationship, but it is a particular type of passivity that also requires that the audience understand itself as participating in the play and the characters of which it is the author.

The qualities of theatricality induce an intransitive, nonreciprocal relationship between those involved. This is most obvious in "real" theater, but it inheres in all that in politics pertains to the realm of the ritual, the symbol, the ceremony. But it is not "passive." All speaking admits of a response if only one in another space: a speech from the throne, for instance, or a radio or television address. Speech of this kind is intransitive, but it is not thereby political or passive.

When Aristotle identified the possession of speech as characteristically human, he meant the quality that our words have such as to require a response to them from another human being. This means that I act with the expectation that my actions will elicit a response to them from you. The response can be positive or negative but my action is undertaken with the sense that you will not be able to remain indifferent. When, for instance, African Americans and whites demonstrated (note the theatricality of the term) and "sat in" at segregated lunch counters in the American South during the 1960s, they did so with the (correct) expectation that the segregationist owners could not remain indifferent to what was happening. The demonstrators sought to elicit a judgment from those owners about the sit-in, a judgment that they expected, over time, to reflectively acknowledge the correctness of their actions. And they were right.[59]

Thus, no matter how a particular individual (or a group by means of that individual) achieves a position of power, s/he is in a position of public visibility—in the public eye, as we say. Such a person is then required—in the sense of having no choice—to speak in front of others, to make decisions concerning the community, and to justify those decisions when called on. (Indeed, even silence becomes public and takes on the meaning of a judgment or choice for everyone to assess.)

The sovereign in Hobbes is thus in public sight—that is, s/he embodies an image of what may be expected, indeed, required, of him or her. This is what Hobbes failed to grasp fully and is the source of the contingency that Dallmayr found and approved in the existentialists. What is clear is that precisely the process by which we establish the sovereign requires of us that we require of it. The conditions of its establishment make passivity impossible.

It is as if the author not only abrogates for himself the (symmetrical) position of the sovereign, but also makes it more possible. The *auctor* becomes *auctoritas*. Thus, as spectators and citizens we forgo and retain the omnipotence that Hobbes found in the sovereign.

NOTES

1. Fred Dallmayr, "Hobbes and Existentialism: Some Affinities," *Journal of Politics* 31, no. 3 (August, 1969): 615–40.

2. Ibid., pp. 615–16.

3. Ibid., p. 639.

4. The Anglican reader will recognize a borrowing from the "General Confession" in the *Book of Common Prayer*.

5. For a discussion of the frontispiece, see my "How to Write Scripture: Words and Authority in Thomas Hobbes," *Critical Inquiry* 20, no. 1 (Autumn 1993) and the works cited therein. To be added to the works discussed there is Horst Bredekamp, *Thomas Hobbes: visuelle Strategien. Der Leviathan: Urbild des modernen Staates. Werkillustrationen und Portraits* (Berlin: Akademie Verlag, 1999). Bredekamp argues that the body of the Leviathan draws on the *corpus hermeticum* (pp. 61ff).

6. Thomas Hobbes, "Answer to Bishop Bramhall," in *English Works*, vol. 5 (Molesworth, 1831). Citations to Hobbes are from the Molesworth edition.

7. Thomas Hobbes, *Leviathan*, chap. 10.

8. Hobbes, "Answer to Bishop Bramhall."

9. Hobbes, *Leviathan*, chap. 16.

10. For a discussion of Hobbes's attitude toward religion, see my "How to Write Scripture," and "When Is a Text Not a Pretext: A Reply to Professor Silver," in the same issue.

11. Thomas Hobbes, *De Cive*, chap. 14; the parallel passage in *Leviathan* is chap. 34.

12. Hobbes, *Leviathan*, chap. 17. Is it worth reflecting here that the Christ was a mortal God?

13. A similar and more aesthetically radical version of this is given in David Hume, *A Treatise of Human Nature*, I, iv, 6, where Hume compares the mind to a theater and then remarks: "In this respect, I cannot compare the soul more properly to any thing than to a republic or commonwealth, in which the several members are united by the reciprocal ties of government and subordination, and give rise to other persons who propagate the same republic in the incessant changes of its parts. And as the same individual republic may not only change its members, but also its laws and constitutions; in like manner the same person may vary his character and disposition, as well as his impressions and ideas, without losing his identity."

14. Thomas Hobbes, *Elements of Law,* I, 1.

15. Hobbes, *De Cive,* chap. 14.

16. Hanna F. Pitkin was probably the first to give an extended analysis of why. See her *The Concept of Representation* (Berkeley: University of California Press, 1978).

17. Hobbes, *Leviathan,* chap. 16.

18. Ibid., chap. 10.

19. Thomas Hobbes, "Letter to a Friend in England," from Paris, October 21/31, 1634, in Thomas Hobbes, *The Correspondence,* ed. Noel Malcolm (Oxford: Clarendon Press, 1997), pp. 22–23.

20. See, e.g., Hobbes, *Leviathan,* chap. 26: "In which definition, there is nothing that is not at first sight evident. For every man seeth, . . ." Hobbes does also use the term for that which may appear to be evidence but can be shown not to be.

21. Hobbes, *Leviathan,* intro. For a full discussion of reading in Hobbes, see my "How to Write Scripture."

22. *Noscere* means to gain knowledge from an action. Here the action dominates.

23. This is a relatively new—post-fourteenth-century—development, however. See the fascinating discussion in Ivan Illych, *In the Vineyard of the Text* (Chicago: University of Chicago Press, 1995).

24. Thomas Hobbes, "Appendix to Latin *Leviathan,*" in *Leviathan,* ed. F. Tricaud (Paris: Sirey, 1990), p. 760.

25. This entire discussion is complexly related to what Francis Bacon wrote in *The New Organon,* I, xliv: "Lastly, there are Idols which have immigrated into men's minds from the various dogmas of philosophies, and also from wrong laws of demonstration. These I call Idols of the Theatre; because in my judgment all the received systems are but so many stage-plays, representing worlds of their own creation after an unreal and scenic fashion." For Hobbes, what we see in perceiving the Leviathan is not a "received system."

26. The following paragraph draws on Marcel Hénaff and Tracy B. Strong, eds., *Public Space and Democracy,* introduction to pt. 1 (Minneapolis: University of Minnesota Press, 2002). See also Paul Dumouchel's essay on Hobbes in the same volume.

27. It is not wrong, but it is potentially misleading, to argue as does Michael Walzer that Hobbes's achievement consists in replacing the metaphor of the family with that of the body. See his "On the Role of Symbolism in Political Thought," in *The Self and the Political Order,* ed. Tracy B. Strong (London: Blackwells, 1990).

28. See Hobbes, *Elements of Law,* II, 2, 15: 15. "Likewise a man is released of his subjection by conquest; for when it cometh to pass, that the power of a commonwealth is overthrown, and any particular man thereby, lying under the sword of his enemy yieldeth himself captive, he is thereby bound to serve him that taketh him, and consequently discharged of his obligation to the former. For no man can serve two masters." Dominion by conquest ("despotical") produces "servants" (*Leviathan,*

chap. 20). *De Cive* is about the "Philosophical Elements of a True Citizen Liberty." It is worth reflecting on the fact that the term "citizen" appears eighteen times in *De Cive* and only once in *Leviathan*. This is because *Leviathan* has a broader scope, seeking to show that "the rights and consequences of both paternal and despotical dominion, are the very same with those of a sovereign by institution" (*Leviathan*, chap. 20).

29. See the discussion in Michel Foucault, *Pour défendre la société* (Paris: Gallimard, 1997), pp. 21–100.

30. Hobbes, *Elements of Law*, I.1.2.

31. Hobbes, *Leviathan*, chap. 13.

32. Thus were one to follow Foucault and cry "off with his head," it would be our own that falls. This merely points at how complex the Foucault move is. For further reflection on one's own head falling, see Nathaniel Hawthorne, "The Custom House," in *The Scarlet Letter* (New York: Library of America, 1983), pp. 153–57.

33. Cited in Stephen Greenblatt, *Renaissance Self-Fashioning* (Chicago: University of Chicago Press, 1980), p. 167.

34. Hobbes, *Elements of Law*, I, 5.

35. Hobbes, *Leviathan*, chap. 17, my italics. Cf. chap. 29: "For the civil authority being more visible, and standing in the clearer light of natural reason, cannot choose but draw to it in all times a very considerable part of the people."

36. Paul Dumouchel, "Persona: Reason and Representation in Hobbes," in *Public Space and Democracy*, ed. Hénaff and Strong.

37. Compare here Pitkin, *The Concept of Representation*, chaps. 1 and 2.

38. Cf. Jonas Barish, *The Anti-Theatrical Prejudice* (Berkeley: University of California Press, 1981).

39. Hobbes, *Leviathan*, chap. 17.

40. This is one reason that Richard Flathman finds in Hobbes the resources of a liberalism adequate to modern times. See his *Thomas Hobbes: Skepticism, Individuality and Chastened Politics* (New York: Sage, 1993).

41. *Leviathan*, chap. 17.

42. Dallmayr, "Hobbes and Existentialism," p. 639.

43. Dallmayr notes (ibid., p. 638) the "relative tranquility" of the Hobbesian state. Something like this is, it seems to me, at the root of the arguments in Leo Strauss, *The Political Philosophy of Hobbes* (Chicago: University of Chicago Press, 1936), and of the ambivalence that Carl Schmitt finds in *Le Léviathan dans la doctrine de l'état de Thomas Hobbes* (Paris: Seuil, 2002), a book written originally in 1938 whose author does not cite but certainly knew the Strauss work. See also Etienne Balibar's introduction to the Schmitt volume.

44. The following paragraphs draw on my *Jean Jacques Rousseau: The Politics of the Ordinary* (New York: Sage, 1993), chap. 3.

45. *Emile*, 5 *Oeuvres Complètes* (hereinafter *OC*), vol. 4 (Paris: Gallimard, 1960–). Works are cited by internal division and page number in the Gallimard edition.

46. *Social Contract* (hereinafter *SC*) (1st version) I.7, *OC* III, p. 310.

47. *SC* II.6, *OC* III, p. 379.

48. *SC* II.1, *OC* III, p. 369.

49. See here Michel Foucault's parallel discussion of what a right that one had no right to claim would be. See James Bernauer and David Rasmussen, eds., *The Final Foucault* (Boston: MIT Press, 1988).

50. *SC* I.7, *OC* III, pp. 362–63.

51. Hence Rousseau has no need for what Rawls calls "the principle of fidelity"—the continuity over time of a rational choice for the chooser, which would underlie and ensure the morality of the institution of, for example, promising. See John Rawls, *A Theory of Justice* (Cambridge: Harvard University Press, 1971), p. 346.

52. *SC* II.2; *OC* III, p. 363.

53. *SC* I.9; *OC* III, p. 367.

54. A further exploration of this requires analyzing the centrality of music to Rousseau. See C. N. Dugan and Tracy B. Strong, "'A Language More Vital than Speech': Music, Politics and Representation in Rousseau," in *The Cambridge Companion to Rousseau,* ed. Patrick Riley (Cambridge: Cambridge University Press, 1999).

55. *Fragments politiques, OC* III, p. 485.

56. *SC* III.11; *OC* III, p. 424.

57. *Birth of Tragedy* (hereinafter *BT*) 8.III$_1$, pp. 55–56. Works are cited by internal division and from the Colli and Montinari edition, *Werke Gesammelte Ausgabe* (Berlin: Gruyter, 1966ff), by section and (subscript) volume number and page.

58. *BT* 8.III$_1$, p. 56.

59. For the idea of "reflective judgment" and its political difference from John Rawls's notion of "reflective equilibrium," see Stanley Cavell, *Conditions Handsome and Unhandsome* (Chicago: University of Chicago Press, 1990), pp. 104ff.

TWO

The Next Enlightenment:
Aesthetic Reason in Modern Art
and Mass Culture

Morton Schoolman

Political theorists of my generation and educated in the United States were fortunate to have been preceded by two generations of North American political theorists whose work secured a place for political theory in the American university system. Following World War II, political theory, and political theorists, led a somewhat precarious existence in American political science departments. Owing as much to the politics as to the theoretical disputes surrounding the versions of the European *Methodenstreit,* the *Werturteilsstreit,* and the *Positivismussstreit* that colonized American political science, political theory found itself under attack and struggling for academic space. Political theorists engaged in intellectual battles with positivist and empiricist political science throughout the 1960s and well into the 1970s, battles that continue in various forms to the present. Originally the stakes included not only the fate of political theory within the profession of political science, but the ideological and political relationship of political science to American liberalism, capitalism, and the war being conducted in Vietnam and against the antiwar movement within the university.

Over the years, political theorists in North America developed a sustained critique of positivism and empiricism in political science and, in the course of doing so, expanded the boundaries of political theory to include an increasingly wide range of theoretical interests and European and non-Western influences. The latter-day result for political theory is that it has become increasingly pluralistic in every possible sense, a condition that most political theorists believe to be responsible for its obvious creativity. Fred Dallmayr must be counted among the most prominent of the many theorists who critically engaged political science, a group whose best-known figures also include Sheldon Wolin, Alasdair MacIntyre, Charles Taylor, and William Connolly. Their work continues to influence theorists of my generation and those coming after.

Each of the essays in this volume speaks in different ways to the significance of Fred Dallmayr's scholarship. My contribution draws attention to a special feature of his thought: how its breadth and depth have served to clarify difficult theoretical ideas that also are made complex by the normative dimensions of the controversies of which they are a part. Like the thought of other influential thinkers in the earlier generations of political theorists I have mentioned, Dallmayr's theorizing has pushed along my own work in decisive ways. In this essay I highlight how Dallmayr's insights into Horkeimer and Adorno's *Dialectic of Enlightenment* enable me to think more clearly about a theoretical issue importantly related to a problem on which I have been working—namely, conceptualizing "aesthetic reason," a problem tied intimately to our understanding of modernity and the nature of modern democratic life. To my mind, absent Dallmayr's insights any progress on this problem I might make would have been stalled. Such intellectual debts are a great pleasure to acknowledge.

THE IDEA OF AESTHETIC REASON

Of the many works in whole or part that Theodor Adorno devotes to the concept of aesthetic rationality, it is in *Dialectic of Enlightenment,* his coauthored work with Max Horkheimer, where it begins to be fleshed out theoretically as an alternative to instrumental reason. While years before *Dialectic of Enlightenment* Adorno explicated aesthetic rationality in his 1941 essay on Arnold Schoenberg, "Schoenberg and Progress," later incorporated into *Philosophy of Modern Music,*[1] there he demonstrated that aesthetic reason ultimately becomes an extension of the logic of instrumental reason. Developments in modern music all but collapse the antagonism between art and mass culture even in those artworks, such as atonal and twelve-tone compositions, that no less than conventional art forms continue to offend tastes encouraged by mass culture. Except for a reflexive self-understanding emerging from certain modern compositional techniques that illuminate the extent to which aesthetic form has been colonized by instrumental reason, in the most advanced music the distinction between aesthetic and instrumental reason is all but obliterated.

Carrying over this argument from the earlier discussion of Schoenberg, in Adorno's *Philosophy of Modern Music* art does not articulate a form of reason that defines a positive enlightenment. Such a theoretical move, as I propose elsewhere, is what distinguishes *Dialectic of Enlightenment*.[2] Others, such as Martin Zenck[3] and Martin Jay,[4] have stressed to the contrary the consistency between the two works with respect to their common attention to the cultural hegemony of instrumental reason. Moreover, it is well known that Jürgen Habermas has maintained that in *Dialectic of Enlightenment* the totality of reason and instrumental reason are equated with only theoretically insignificant qualifications and to the neglect of the rational content of modernity.[5] Contrary to Habermas's argument that the thesis developed in Horkheimer and Adorno's *Dialectic of Enlightenment* does not direct us to the Weberian path that "leads through the inner logics of the different complexes of rationality,"[6] it can be argued that it is precisely in that work where a differentiated concept of aesthetic reason first surfaces as a rival to the conceptual imperialism of instrumental reason.[7] Without a doubt, as it appears in *Dialectic of Enlightenment* their differentiated concept of aesthetic reason is underdeveloped. It is an idea that in its fledgling stage left Horkheimer and Adorno vulnerable to Habermas's claim that they suffer the embarrassment of being entangled aporetically, thus undermining the justification of their critique of enlightenment.[8]

Nevertheless, if we take the embryonic concept of a differentiated form of aesthetic reason in *Dialectic of Enlightenment* as our analytical point of departure, we are able to recognize and better appreciate in several important ways what Adorno was trying to accomplish in his later work.

First, the primacy of the concept of aesthetic reason is foregrounded within the context of a larger theoretical project born with *Dialectic of Enlightenment*, the relation not only of instrumental reason, but also of aesthetic rationality to the process of enlightenment and modernity. All attention subsequently should be focused on Adorno's *Aesthetic Theory*.[9] Against the backdrop of the larger theoretical project it becomes apparent that it is this work that develops the concept of aesthetic reason as the basis for the rational content of modernity and for the idea of a positive enlightenment to which

Horkheimer and Adorno alluded in their earlier study.[10] Conceptualizing aesthetic reason must be counted among those issues in *Dialectic of Enlightenment* that, as Günter Figal puts it, "motivate" Adorno to write his last book, *Aesthetic Theory.*[11]

Second, though the fledgling concept of aesthetic reason in *Dialectic of Enlightenment* leads to a new appreciation of a larger theoretical project elaborated in *Aesthetic Theory,* once we proceed on that basis to flesh out the mature form of aesthetic rationality in the latter work, we are required to take two further steps. We must problematize the prejudice toward mass culture in Adorno's *Aesthetic Theory* that it is only in modern art that aesthetic rationality finds a home, and we must contest Horkheimer and Adorno's earlier conclusion that the form of rationality belonging to modern art is emasculated in mass culture. As it is developed in *Aesthetic Theory,* Adorno's concept of aesthetic rationality is so rich that many of its properties can be found in modern cultural forms in addition to art. These properties of aesthetic reason are, in fact, present throughout mass culture, which reproduces rather than effaces the integrity of aesthetic rationality in modern art to earn it the distinction Adorno reserved for unique artworks. A first line of defense for this claim can be made by looking for evidence of aesthetic rationality in film.

Finally, if aesthetic reason can be shown to have taken up residence in mass culture, the universality that aesthetic reason acquires through the increasing universality of mass culture not only would portend another, positive enlightenment in the sense in which Horkheimer and Adorno together first conceived of it. The recovery of the rational content of modernity would be at its doorstep. We are encouraged by the presence of aesthetic reason in mass culture to entertain the possibility that by establishing the universality of aesthetic reason, the universality of mass culture may place us on the threshold of the next enlightenment, an aesthetic enlightenment that would complete modernity's as yet unfinished project.

With these considerations in mind, I intend to follow the path to which *Dialectic of Enlightenment* led us by drawing out properties of the concept of aesthetic reason as it is developed in Adorno's *Aesthetic Theory.* Once essential features of aesthetic rationality have been assembled, I want to search for evidence of aesthetic reason in mass culture, exactly where in light of Horkheimer and Adorno's work we should be least likely to find it. I am extending the path begun with *Dialectic of Enlightenment* into the territory of mass culture to determine if their concept of aesthetic reason can be emancipated from what I believe to be its premature confinement to modern art in Adorno's later writings on aesthetics. Proceeding in this way offers insight into the connection between modern art, aesthetic reason, and mass culture. It also provides some indication whether this connection may hold promise regarding a deeper and as yet unrecognized historical connection between the enlightenment Horkheimer and Adorno thought of as mass deception and the concept of a positive enlightenment to which they believed it was opposed.

THE *WORK* OF ART

No sooner do we enter into Adorno's aesthetic theory than we realize he intends to make art intelligible in terms typically reserved for discussions about thinking. To speak of art is to speak of a certain kind of reasoning process that takes, as one of its several forms, the form of art. In this aesthetic form reason functions to reflect on a second form of thinking—instrumental reason. Although the aesthetic form of thinking modeled by art is qualitatively different from instrumental reason, art includes instrumental reason within it as one of two dimensions of its process of thinking. Without the part played by instrumental reason, the work of art cannot represent objects in images that constitute the artwork's appearance. The part played by the noninstrumental, reflexive features of the process of thinking belonging to art enables art to challenge the representational adequacy of artistic images to the object the image portrays. In Adorno's estimation, the *work* of the artwork, its reasoning process and specific claim to reason, is its power to represent objects and simultaneously to draw attention reflexively to the inadequacy of the representation. Artworks illuminate their own representational inadequacy by proliferating representations. Image is negated by image.

An example of this twofold power of aesthetic rationality is the series of paintings between 1892 and 1895 by Monet, representing the western façade of the Rouen Cathedral during different times of the day. As Monet paints one, ten, twenty, eventually nearly thirty paintings of the cathedral, it remains elusive, so that the series, which in principle could go on indefinitely, comes to reflect not only the cathedral being represented, but what it means to represent the cathedral. Monet's series teaches that no artwork can ever capture an object as it really is. Through the series as a whole, representation is represented reflexively as identifying an object, though identifying it incompletely as a deficit made up by yet another image. Each work of art calls forth another artwork to erase the inadequacy of every representation.

To highlight the way aesthetic rationality works in this instance, imagine, by contrast, that the Rouen artworks defined a second aesthetic strategy, one aspiring to capture completely the cathedral's objectivity, which from the works of art we earlier learned remains elusive. From Adorno's standpoint, we would say that the instrumental properties of the artworks had prevailed over the aesthetic, that instrumental reason had substituted its fixed image of the cathedral for the cathedral as it really is, that the work of art had been arrested. In Monet's artworks the cathedral had become a means through which instrumental reason created its own image of an object on which this static image is imposed. So long as its representation passes unchallenged by the production of yet another image, the fixed image pretends to have captured what eludes capture. Representation becomes semblance, image becomes illusion.

As the illustration of Adorno's concept of aesthetic rationality first revealed, on the other hand, the work of Monet's artworks to the contrary exemplifies how art disrupts the identifications it embodies in images. By dint of the work of art's process of reasoning, Monet's artworks prove their images are nonidentical with—are different from—what they represent. Nonidentity is integral to the process of aesthetic reasoning, which performs the work of art in relation to representations whose claim to identify the object is negated by the aesthetic process of reasoning. In this way aesthetic reason emancipates reason from its instrumental will to power to create the world in its own image. Art, as Romand Coles puts it, transcends relations of domination.[12] It is not art *per se,* though, that negates relations of domination, but the work of art that is performed by some artworks—great artworks—and not by all artworks in Adorno's view. I later radicalize this distinction by arguing that if the work of art—the reflexive process of aesthetic reasoning—is characteristic of some art rather than all art, it may well be characteristic of some art that is not great modernist art, which Adorno[13] (and Horkheimer independently)[14] argued served as the womb within which historically the work of art, its logic, developed. For now I want to distinguish the *work* of art from the artwork. To paraphrase Diana Coole, the work of art is exhibited by but not reducible to art.[15]

Adorno's aesthetic theory, I am proposing, conceptualizes the work of art as consisting of a twofold process of thought. Images of objects are formed by a cognitive, instrumental form of reason, by "rationality" as he says in shorthand in *Aesthetic Theory*.[16] Then, through the contribution of a noncognitive mimetic function to the work of art, about which I have more to say shortly, the identities of the objects constructed by these images are shown to be different from (nonidentical with) the objects themselves. As a reflexive process of reasoning, the cognitive power of the work of art as a whole points beyond the artwork to thematize an unbridgeable divide between our knowledge of the world and the world, between concepts and the objects to which our concepts refer. The work of art displays a respect for the object as itself different from the illusory identity an artwork's image constructs, and opposes instrumental reason's equation of image with object. In the example of aesthetic rationality offered by Monet's series of paintings, each image of the cathedral draws attention to what is missing in every other image, to the inadequacy of the representational power of instrumental reason. While Monet's series well illustrates the work of art, it also is somewhat misleading, for the work of art is integral to the individual artwork as well and primarily, and does not require a series of artworks for the work of art to be performed. Or, to anticipate myself, every artwork that performs the work of art is itself a series of artworks.

THE TWOFOLD PROCESS OF AESTHETIC REASON: RATIONALITY AND MIMESIS

As the work of art, aesthetic reason belongs to the modernist artwork after the fact, as it were, of having been differentiated out of society and developed in the form of art, as Horkheimer and Adorno made clear in *Dialectic of Enlightenment* through their analysis of the sirens episode in the *Odyssey*'s twelfth book. To ensure his crew's self-preservation while enraptured by the sirens' lure, Odysseus orders that his pleas to be released from bondage to his ship's mast be ignored. His reason like his body remaining secured in place as his ship passes the sirens, their song fading into the distance, is evidence that his receptivity to an enchanted world assumes the timeless form of art. As Horkheimer and Adorno construe this episode, "[T]he bonds with which he has irrevocably fettered himself to praxis at the same time keep the Sirens at a distance from praxis: their lure is neutralized as a mere object of contemplation, as art."[17] Displaced to art, Odysseus's *primary* orientation to the world, we are being told, is aesthetic. The artwork is the secondary form in which this aesthetic orientation appears. The artwork's neutralization of the sirens' lure described in *Dialectic of Enlightenment* is that very disavowal of magical practices we find Adorno in *Aesthetic Theory* associating with Weber's disenchantment thesis.[18] Differentiating out—*rationalizing*—a primary aesthetic relation to social reality, art marks the aesthetic orientation as "participation in rationality," as Adorno puts it, as an aesthetic form of rationality, or aesthetic reason.[19]

By highlighting Horkheimer and Adorno's conception of aesthetic reason as originally a primary orientation of subjectivity prior to its rationalization as art, or perhaps as Jane Bennett speculates in more essentialist terms, as a "primary drive,"[20] the connection of aesthetic reason to nature is drawn out. By this I mean not only the noninstrumental relation of aesthetic reason *to* external nature that theorists most often find recollected in the aesthetic elements of Horkheimer and Adorno's ideas of reconciliation, but especially nature's presence *in* aesthetic reason.

Drawing out this latter aspect of Horkheimer and Adorno's connection between aesthetic reason and nature has been controversial. Theorists at odds with their work have reduced their idea of the aesthetic realm to the sensuous side of our nature, neglecting the aesthetic realm's cognitive side. A case in point is Habermas's description of "mimesis," a central property of Horkheimer and Adorno's concept of aesthetic reason (and later of Adorno's), as "impulse."[21] Habermas's undisguised motive is to trivialize their notion of aesthetic rationality by confining it to the visceral level. Similarly, characterizing the aesthetic realm as an "other" of instrumental reason and describing its contribution to truth as "nondiscursive," as Seyla Benhabib does, impugns the cognitive power of the aesthetic dimension.[22] In the same vein Terry Eagleton, whose understanding of Adorno's aesthetic theory is otherwise quite thoughtful, describes the aesthetic dimension as an "alternative *to* thought" rather than an alternative form *of* thought, as I have maintained.[23]

Progress toward understanding the presence of nature in aesthetic reason is made by Fred Dallmayr's interpretation of Horkheimer and Adorno's use of mimesis, a perceptive reading that situates mimesis on a "quasi-sensual" or "quasi-material" level, establishing its resemblance to an anti-instrumental, reflective form of play.[24] Conceptualized in this way, Dallmayr proposes, play permeates everything, so that it assumes a universality that "recover[s] a good deal of the spirit (if not the letter) of Hegel's legacy" while at the same time "expelling the absolute on the level of the 'idea,'" an insight consistent with Horkheimer and Adorno's critique of Hegel's rationalism.[25] Though this Hegelian feature Dallmayr associates with mimesis ties it to rationality, more advanced in this regard is his attention to its *quasi*-sensual feature, which suspends aesthetic rationality between the cognitive and noncognitive, brings it into proximity with reason, and resists its reduction to "impulse," to reason's "other," to an "alternative to thought," or, in a word, to mere nature.

To fully grasp the rationality of the work of art, it is necessary to take the next step beyond the important, anti-reductionist point to which Dallmayr's interpretation brings us. The rationality of the work of art must be understood as the result of an aesthetic *process* of which the noncognitive dimension, nature in reason, is one part and not to be equated with the process in its entirety. Where the aesthetic realm is identified with the noncognitive, as when it is confined to the sensuous side of our mimetic nature, then the sphere of rationality and the aesthetic dimension are separated from the very beginning: rationality as the result of an aesthetic process is suppressed, and aesthetic rationality can be achieved only through some work of reason other than through the work of art. Albrecht Wellmer begins to see this clearly, though his insight is undone when he attempts to reconstruct Adorno's concept of aesthetic rationality within Habermas's communicative paradigm. "Rationality must combine with a mimetic principle in order to be released from its own irrationality," Wellmer explains, by which he understands correctly that *instrumental* reason is released from its irrationality when combined with a mimetic (sensuous) principle.[26] Importantly, though he does not recognize Adorno to be the architect of this argument, Wellmer recognizes its architecture, the basic elements of Adorno's argument regarding how the work of art, consisting of a twofold reflexive process of forming images instrumentally and negating images mimetically, produces aesthetic rationality. From here, however, Wellmer goes astray.

First, while Wellmer acknowledges a "'mimetic' moment within conceptual thought itself," he wrongly criticizes Adorno for failing to do so and for conceiving, instead, "of mimesis as the Other of rationality."[27] Wellmer errs by rooting Adorno's alleged failure in his allegiance to the paradigm of the philosophy of consciousness, which Wellmer, following Habermas, believes limits reason to instrumental rationality, locking subjectivity into an antagonistic relationship to the object. According to the Habermas-Wellmer critique of the philosophy of consciousness, if the totality of reason is instrumental reason, then mimesis must be something "other" than reason. Wellmer's error can be traced back to his own failure, again made in Habermas's wake, to recognize that Horkheimer and Adorno already had conceptualized mimesis as integral to reason by laying claim to a theory of rationalization that differentiated out art from social reality as an aesthetic sphere of rationality. "Reason" meant aesthetic as well as instrumental reason, and aesthetic reason included both instrumental and mimetic properties. As I indicated, this is the path to which Horkheimer and Adorno led us in *Dialectic of Enlightenment*. Following this path to Adorno's aesthetic theory and its configuration of the work of art, we encounter the fully developed version of the earlier argument, explaining why the paradigm of the philosophy of consciousness does not restrict reason to the opposition of subject and object where thinking's instrumental orientation imposes identity on the object. Art proves that the paradigm also entails an aesthetic relation between subject and object that is rational in another sense. By virtue of its mimetic capacity, a subject reasoning aesthetically understands the object to be *different* from its images of it, and nonidentity is the dissolution of instrumental reason's subject–object polarity.

Wellmer's second error is to correct Adorno's alleged separation of reason and mimesis by framing the integration of reason and the aesthetic realm within the paradigm of communicative interaction.[28] Arguing that the truth content of the artwork is expressed metaphorically through aesthetic experience that is subjective and variably interpreted among individuals, Wellmer holds that the rationality of art must be referred back to our intersubjective experience where it can be gauged according to the pragmatics of communicative interaction. Any enlightenment accruing to individuals that is leveraged by the independent form of rationality intrinsic to art, as Horkheimer and Adorno understand it, would become parasitic on the determination of rationality through communicative discourse. What is *originally* rational in their aesthetic sense becomes *derivative* for Wellmer. It is reduced to a derivation of an activity informed by aesthetic validity claims, which vary experientially for subjects and possess a rationality that becomes contingent on a communicative experience that is neither aesthetic nor mediated by pragmatic criteria that are aesthetic. Art, for Wellmer, has only a rational potential that may not necessarily be redeemed.[29]

Martin Morris likewise overlooks the rationalization thesis in *Dialectic of Enlightenment*, defining the aesthetic realm as a sphere of reason; however, he improves on Wellmer's argument through a parallel discussion of Horkheimer and Adorno's text and Adorno's later writings where the concept of aesthetic reason is elaborated. Moving between *Dialectic of Enlightenment* and Adorno's *Negative Dialectics*, in particular, Morris explicates the all-important aesthetic features of thinking and their significance for a concept of aesthetic reason, which I have referred to here as the *work* of art. In Morris's interpretation of Adorno, thinking loses its capacity to determine the difference between the idea of an object and the object itself when its connection is severed to the "immediacy of sensual and imitative life," which is to say reasoning becomes instrumental when the "central cognitive validity of aesthetic mimesis is abandoned."[30] Seeing, as Wellmer did not, that Adorno includes mimesis in thought as the property that subdues identity thinking, Morris likewise understands that instrumental reason is an "incomplete type of thought that is better understood as a moment or aspect of thought rather than equivalent to the whole of thought itself."[31] Morris properly configures thinking as a process consisting of an instrumental and mimetic dimension and the second, mimetic dimension as the one responsible for curing reason of its instrumental relation to objects. By so doing, Morris moves a crucial step closer to conceptualizing this process of thought as aesthetic reason. Some of Morris's progress in this direction, though, is lost to other of his claims.

At one extreme, he suggests that in its relation to nonidentity a noninstrumental form of reason is dependent on the "extra-rational or un-reason," implying unintentionally that aesthetic reason draws its rationality from a source other than mimesis.[32] Certainly, mimesis is not rational in the familiar instrumental sense. To allow aesthetic reason to depend on the extrarational or irrational is perplexing, however, since it begs the question how mimesis is cured of its irrationality in art or why it does not impair the rationality of aesthetic reason. It would be preferable to describe mimesis as a preform of rationality (*die Vorform von Rationalität*), as Günter Figal does,[33] or as possessing a rational potential (*Rationalitätspotential*), as does Ulrich Müller.[34] Both appear to think of mimesis as an underdeveloped form of rationality that only realizes its rational potential when bound to instrumental reason. At the other extreme, Morris presents noninstrumental reason as a "truly new way of thinking" and as an "alternative notion of enlightenment that is utopian."[35] Such valorizations serve more to place an aesthetic form of reason out of the practical reach of reason than to measure the deficiencies of instrumental rationality and in their light to justify the urgency of an alternative mode of reason.

If we understand the aesthetic realm to refer to a reflexive process of reason, Morris's claims are countered in this way. Aesthetic reason reshapes thought through mimetic activity that fastens sensuously onto what belongs to the object that its concept has not yet included. The illusory limits of the concept are made visible *only as* mimesis forces it into an engagement with what is conceptually related but not yet conceptually integrated. Because this process reaches mimetically for what lies outside the boundaries of the concept—outside of instrumental reason—but not for what lies outside of aesthetic reason as a whole, aesthetic reason is rational all the way through. And because aesthetic reason works processually to make the concept *increasingly* more complete, the movement between concept and object is repetitive. Aesthetic reason is a continuous process of reflection on the limits of concepts and is characteristic of thought that has not discarded its mimetic capacity to falsely secure the adequacy of its concepts. As reflexive thinking, aesthetic reason is neither new nor utopian, but ordinary in the sense of being intrinsic to every form of thought that calls itself into question and replaces or supplements one thought with another thought. As reflexive thinking, aesthetic reason becomes the praxis of thinking that establishes the primacy of aesthetic rationality not only over instrumental reason, but over every form of thought resting on the principle that thinking can overcome the difference between an object and its concept.

Against the idea of the "ordinariness" of aesthetic reason that I am advancing, it may be objected that Adorno privileged art and philosophy, two extraordinary forms of thought, as the two forms in modernity aesthetic reason assumed exclusively. In response, it is important to remember that Adorno privileged art and philosophy because he held these to be the expressions of a marginalized aesthetic rationality threatened with extinction by an instrumental reason that had become hegemonic. Yet the fate of aesthetic reason that Adorno and Horkheimer attributed to reification should not obscure, as it has for Habermas, their more fundamental thesis. An aesthetic form of reason intrinsic to thinking was differentiated out by a process of societal rationalization that developed the logic of aesthetic reason in the form of art. The lesson of this thesis is that when we recover aesthetic reason from the form it takes in art, we learn that every thought that is reflexive is aesthetic, and every thought that is aesthetic is rational.

Strong support for this argument is offered by Christoph Menke, whose description of Adorno's concept of "aesthetic experience" as a "two-stage process" closely resembles my characterization of Adorno's theory of the "work of art" as a "twofold process." As Menke puts it, the "two-stage description of aesthetic experience" entails an experience of the artwork "as an attempt at understanding" that which the artwork takes as its object and "as the negation of the attempt."[36] What Menke does here is to distinguish an act of understanding that by itself is "nonaesthetic," though integral to aesthetic experience, from the negation of this nonaesthetic understanding as the defining element of aesthetic experience. "Automatic acts of recognition," his term for nonaesthetic, identity (instrumental) thinking, undergo an "aesthetically experienced fate," the act of reflection on the limited understanding peculiar to instrumental reasoning and the second stage of a process of aesthetic experience that yields aesthetic pleasure.[37] If the process of aesthetic experience were to be disassembled so that its stages no longer related to one another negatively, the product of aesthetic experience—the aesthetic pleasure on which Menke has focused—would be sacrificed in the same manner as aesthetic reason, which I foregrounded, is sacrificed to an instrumental rationality that escaped reflection.

Our arguments thus are complementary rather than opposed, as they would be if founded on different sides of the conventional Cartesian dualism between mind and body, reason and sense or emotion. Menke's interest in the *pleasure* associated with aesthetic experience, and my interest in the *rationality* of the work of art, combine to pinpoint the twin products of the same relationship of negation between the same two processual elements: instrumental reason and mimesis (sensuousness). Despite the difference in our interests, from my standpoint what is most important in Menke's account is his insight that these two elements and the relationship between them form a process that *as a whole* constitutes aesthetic experience, and that aesthetic experience is the process of reflective thought. Menke agrees that each thought that is reflexive is aesthetic and each thought that is aesthetic is rational, and, he adds, pleasurable.

THE ARTWORK IN MOTION

Once again our earlier lesson is born out, this time through a closer inspection of the way theorists conceptualize the relationship, integral to the work of art, between instrumental rationality and mimesis. Aesthetic reason as reflexive thinking follows from the analysis of the work of art as a processual relationship between rationality and mimesis. Permitting the entire concept of aesthetic reason to rest on this relationship, Adorno adds in *Aesthetic Theory* that "the sentimentality and debility of almost the entire tradition of aesthetic thought . . . has suppressed the dialectics of rationality and mimesis immanent to art."[38] In rebellion against Enlightenment rationalism, the romantic tradition to which he refers stressed the sensual side of art to the virtual exclusion of the rational. Because the rebellion drew its vitality from this supposed opposition between sensuality and reason, it sabotaged any possibility of raising art to the status of a form of reason offering an alternative to Enlightenment rationality.

To avoid this danger Adorno adopts a different strategy. No matter which aesthetic category he examines, to determine the contribution of each to the conceptual development of aesthetic reason he never permits the fundamental relationship between mimesis and rationality to be severed. By considering his discussion of aesthetic form, we can measure the contribution to a concept of aesthetic reason Adorno's strategy ensures, though in addition we will discover theoretical opportunities to which Adorno was blinded by his historical situation. Since aesthetic form is likewise the form taken by aesthetic reason, the dynamics of form produced by rationality and mimesis working in tandem sets the stage for determining whether there are other cultural forms in modern art that share its aesthetic form. If there are, they then would share, as well, the same properties of aesthetic reason Adorno attributed to aesthetic form.

Perhaps there is no better way than through sculpture to illustrate Adorno's idea of how aesthetic form and its dynamics are produced by the working relationship between rationality and mimesis. More so than other art forms, in sculpture the construction of aesthetic form stands out in relief because the sensuous, mimetic dimension of art is doubly present. This is important when we recall that of the two terms that anchor Adorno's concept of aesthetic reason, if not his aesthetic theory as a whole, mimesis has been viewed more skeptically than rationality. Habermas's critique of mimesis as impulse is not the harshest indictment; Benhabib complains that mimesis is "fuzzy precisely because it cannot suggest a real alternative to relations of domination."[39] Sculpture is of great benefit to us conceptually because mimesis, rather than fuzzy, is itself palpable in the sensuous reshaping of material, such as clay or marble, and is immanent in the work of the artwork. Sculpture thus should help us clarify the contribution mimesis makes to an alternative concept of enlightenment. If we keep in mind these two manifestations of mimesis, we can better appreciate the artwork's mimetic power, which is easy to underestimate in the presence of a finished work standing motionless before us. Imagine the sheer power of the sensuous material resisting the ultimately more powerful sensuous attachment of the eyes and hands forming it, so that as the sculptor returns repeatedly to the material to re-form it over again the material gradually but ever more resembles the artist's idea. The sculpture is created through repeated movements between the artist's sensuous relation to sensuous material, on the one hand, and on the other through the emergence of a first and then successor images as the movement between sensuousness and subsequent images, mimesis and rationality, continues.

What is true for the process of *creating* the sculpture—the unbroken reciprocal motion from the sensuous to the representational—for Adorno is true of the modernist artwork itself. The modern artwork standing still is at the same time in motion, Adorno wants us to understand, a point I first have tried to explicate by drawing the analogy between the artwork in motion and the process of artistic creation. Indeed, the motion of the artwork is so basic to Adorno, he proposes, speaking figuratively, that an artwork only becomes visible when its movement comes to a standstill.[40] Immersing ourselves in the artwork reanimates its fixed image, which recedes as its motion comes into view to represent an image other than the still life that has suspended the artwork's movement in time and space. Through sculpture we can watch as our immersion in the artwork enables us to see in movement what originally we took to be motionless.

Illus. 1.
Auguste Rodin,
La Pensée,
S. 2837, courtesy
of the Musée
Rodin, Paris.

Rodin's sculpture, *Thought* (1886; illus. 1), is of a woman's head and face sitting on a pedestal of rough-hewed marble, the head covered with a simple cap drawn snugly over the hair and ears and with a facial expression that is, like quietude, free of disturbance and not otherwise pensive.

The image, in its visible, immobile state, is Cartesian, if you will: mind without body, commanding the idea that thinking occurs uninterrupted by the body. Just then, however, the body moves into focus, made present through its conspicuous absence, a presence-through-absence represented dramatically by the unsculpted marble block focusing our attention on the place where the body should be. With the body now in mind, the countenance that persisted uninterrupted is suddenly disturbed by our revised image of how the original image would newly appear if it had been joined to a body. Rodin's artwork swings us from the one extreme of an image his ini-

Illus. 2.
Auguste Rodin,
La Méditation,
Ph 1684, courtesy
of the Musée
Rodin, Paris.

tial sensuous engagement with the material produced to a second sensuous encounter that returns with a reconstructed image. An important argument is being made by the multiple images created by the processual rationality of the artwork. If "thought" is to think beyond thoughts that can be presented placidly—if thought is to think difficult thoughts, thoughts requiring labor to develop, thoughts weighed down or pushed forward by contradictions, criticism, doubt and self-doubt—thought would express all this through a mind that is *also* a body.

Thought's argument about the relation of the mind to the body is moved forward by *Meditation,* another of Rodin's sculptures reflecting on thought, which he also referred to as the *Inner Voice* (1896; illus. 2).

Meditation is represented by a female figure standing with her right leg quite straight and stiff and the left bent at the knee with its foot pressed against an elevation in the pedestal for balance. The curvaceousness of the thighs and torso are accentuated through the shoulders, which are pulled further to the right side by the head bending in the same direction down and toward the torso. Rodin impresses us with the internality of thought by breaking off the top of her knees and leaving one breast unformed, as are the arms unformed from the shoulder, so that thought emerges all the more as the body disappears or is diminished. Again, as with the previous artwork, our first image is of thought nurtured by its release from the body, though only momentarily.

Immediately we are captivated by the sensuousness of a second image that suggests thought wrapping around itself as this body wraps around itself. It was as though the body-of-thought, perhaps the emotions indistinguishable from an inner thought, were shielding itself from a world from which thought required escape to ensure its privacy. Once more the work of art swings us between an image and a sensuous reattachment to its object to produce a second image, proving the artwork to be a creation that recreates itself in different images. As the process of movement from which it derives its meaning, the artwork is in motion between sensuous attachments to an aesthetic object and its images, and the multiple images created by this motion suggest one artwork is comprised of many, the one becoming visible when the motion is arrested.

Meditation illustrates the movement between sensuousness and image more dramatically than *Thought* because the connection between mind and body to which the former artwork's image is related sensuously is present in a sensuous form, whereas in *Thought* it is present through its absence. Pursuing the same logic of analysis, for the robustness of its imagery of the mind–body nexus Rodin's *The Thinker* (1880; illus. 3) is the most poignant example of the artwork in motion.

The thinker is seated deep in thought, at first glance a figure whose mental preoccupation places him at odds with himself, his immense strength so conspicuously earning the attention we are obliged to pay to the comparatively unarticulated intellect. Then noticing how the head is not resting on but is held up by the powerful right arm, which is buoyed by the coordinated musculature of the entire body, we ponder the weight and power of a thought requiring such strength to sustain it. Finally, noting the continuous circuit running from the head to hand, through the wrist, arm, leg, torso, shoulders, and neck, we realize Rodin's *Thinker* expresses the indivisibility of mind and

Illus. 3.
Auguste Rodin,
Le Penseur,
S. 1295, courtesy
of the Musée
Rodin, Paris.

body, and the strength they represent to be uniform and indivisible. Rodin's statue moves under its own power between the mind and body to produce images of mind–body relations, each image reattaching itself sensuously to mind and body or to mind–body to evolve a different image.

Each of these examples demonstrates what Adorno called the artwork's "law of motion" he found common to modernist artworks.[41] Artworks are set into motion by a relationship of reciprocity between rationality and mimesis. Each requires the other. Rationality requires sensuous attachment to an object to furnish the sensory impressions from which reason constructs the object's image. Sensuousness requires reason to impart identity to its impressions. Adorno makes clear it is the *instrumental* form of rationality within the artwork that works in partnership with mimesis, as he speaks of the movement between them as an immanent dynamic through which "rigidification is unified with what is most intensely alive."[42] Rationality is associated with the brittleness of the image and identitarian thinking, and mimesis with what is living and the sensuous disruption of the image that forces it to relinquish and revise its identity. Foregrounding the ontological aspects of Adorno's argument, in Ullrich Schwartz's view, mimesis subdues the "delusion of the autarchy of the intellect," thinking absent reflection, which proceeds undisturbed so long as sensuousness, the somatic element of knowledge and the essential nature (*wesentlich des Subjekts als Naturwesen*) of an otherwise historical subject, has been eliminated from reason.[43] Such accounts serve to drive home the point that for Adorno reason that has dispensed with reflection—positivism, for instance—has done so by suppressing the part played in the formation of knowledge by the senses, feelings, desire, in a word by the body. Schwartz makes this point precisely by saying "everything bodily (*alles Leibliche*) is excluded from the concept of objective knowledge."[44]

If we are to weight sufficiently the motion in the artwork propelled by the work of rationality and mimesis, we cannot stress enough Adorno's insistence that rationality and mimesis function in reciprocal relation to one another. Acting as a *persistently* creative element, mimesis is not limited to the initial sensuous attachment to an object from which a first aesthetic image is constructed. Thereafter it *disrupts* the image through a renewed sensuous attachment that compels the original image to be reconstructed and to pass again through further metamorphoses. Movement between rationality and mimesis, construction and reconstruction, image and sensuous attachment, was apparent in the way the initial and subsequent images of *Thought, Meditation,* and *The Thinker* were disrupted and revised to incorporate aspects of the mind–body relation each image excluded. The modernist artwork is in perpetual motion between image and sensuous attachment to an object its representations make out to be inexhaustible, so that an antithesis between rationality and mimesis crystallizes that appears to be irresolvable (for a similar view, see Figal).[45]

Owing to its dynamic quality, the artwork in motion has no stable state of being. Ontologically, it is in the process of becoming. Epistemologically, this means that claims to truth and reason entailed by artworks' images are contested by a succession of other images presenting new claims. By means of a discursive process resembling that defended by John Stuart Mill in *On Liberty,* knowledge is advanced by the artwork through images that reflect the limits of each by representing what each omits, so that Adorno says of art's relation to knowledge that "it completes knowledge with what is excluded from knowledge."[46] Aesthetic reason's relentless assault on rationality is hardly a retreat from rationality, but supposes reason's capacity to make rationality its own achievement. And since art's dialectic of rationality and mimesis is by reason of the artwork and not by reason of the artist, its critique of knowledge claims and of rationality possesses an objectivity and autonomy prior to any political allegiance claimed for the artwork. Taking the artwork as a whole, then, the relationship between rationality and mimesis constitutes a dynamic process, the work of art that throws the artwork into motion to produce an aesthetic form of rationality distinctive for its reflection on the limits of every ontological, epistemological, and ideological position constructed by thought.

Aesthetic form becomes visible when the artwork is taken as a whole in this way. It is the "relation of the elements to each other," Adorno explains, "that constitutes form," which as the sum of these relations is the one element he allows to define the artwork.[47] By studying its form, we see that each of the artwork's elements function differently and possess different meanings than when they are examined apart from the artwork and independently of one another. Within the artwork rationality ceases to operate instrumentally as sclerotic thought that has hardened by cutting itself off from the lifeblood of its object. Sensuousness ceases to be inchoate as it infuses with impressions the image that gives them shape. Rationality and mimesis struggle together to create images, each of which challenges another image's claim to validity. Aesthetic form emerges, and here no words are more evocative than Adorno's own, from "centers of energy that strain toward the whole on the basis of a necessity that they equally perform."[48] Watching these centers (rationality and mimesis) equally perform, their necessity is a higher rationality devoted to the fullness of thought through reflection on the limitations of every thought. By formulating the connection between form and the whole of the artwork's elements in this way, Adorno opposes our practice of trying to grasp the artwork by permitting any of its elements, such as mimesis, to be equated with the whole. Aesthetic form keeps the whole of the artwork in focus so that the rationality of the artwork cannot be thought of as less than the whole, and thus as something less than rationality.

Art bears an enormous burden in Horkheimer and Adorno's work. *Dialectic of Enlightenment* contends that modernity's fate has been woven densely from a process of enlightenment that elevates instrumental reason to a universal principle of rationality. Instrumental reason has transformed nature into an object of mastery together with the nature of the agent who carried out the enlightenment project. Along its lengthy evolutionary road extending from the origins of thought to the present, enlightenment made mastery possible by developing a logic that permitted qualitative differences to be reduced to equivalencies. Continuous with this deep structure, enlightenment, at least in the West, has produced a modernity comprised of societies obedient to the same values and in pursuit of the same form of life. Uniformity in identity among all and within each is the norm dictated by the logic of equivalency, though this achievement is not the worst of it. At its extremes, which occur often enough, modernity has advanced through violence toward difference. For Horkheimer and Adorno, the Jewish Holocaust quintessentially expresses the irrational kernel of enlightenment rationality and the inevitable consequence of its logic. All other modes of thought and culture having been coordinated with a ubiquitous instrumental rationality, only art, and then only modern art, opposes this history of domination and violence by representing an alternative form of reason. Horkheimer and Adorno record the survival of a rational reason in its differentiated aesthetic form, which sheltered and nurtured the normative standpoint of their critique of modernity and of the process of enlightenment from which modernity originated. Adorno next develops the concept of aesthetic reason in his aesthetic theory, which reconstructs its anatomy from an archeology of modern art.

Now, however, we are positioned to think with Adorno against Adorno, to entertain the possibility that the principle of rationality he reserved for modern art has another and less exclusive home in mass culture. To pursue reason from modern art to modern mass culture is an enormous irony, as it is shadowed by Horkheimer and Adorno's merciless repudiation of the culture industry for "infecting everything with sameness," for having raised enlightenment's logic of equivalency to the level of mass deception.[49] Yet Adorno affords us the opportunity to engage in this pursuit with his claim that "aesthetic experience becomes living experience only by way of its object, in that instant in which artworks themselves become animate under its gaze."[50] To capture the significance of this statement in light of the preceding argument, I propose that what Adorno formulates as the artwork's law of motion, which rests art's claim to reason on its animation, is likewise operable in what we know as "motion pictures." My comparison is more than play on words. Film may not be less hospitable to aesthetic rationality than modern art, and may have the additional virtue of providing a vehicle for aesthetic reason that guarantees a ubiquity and promises a universality equal to the ubiquity and universality of instrumental reason.

Far from Heaven (2002) is set in 1950s Hartford, Connecticut during the fall season. Spectacular and breathtaking, the fall colors displayed in the opening scenes suggest nature has achieved perfection. Later in the film, the aesthetic significance of color is confirmed by its power to represent the illusion of perfection, as we learn from a conversation in a local art gallery between Kathy and Raymond, Hartford's model housewife and her "colored" gardener, as he is referred to by the city's dominant white culture. Raymond is educated and has taken his daughter to an exhibition where he is approached by Kathy, whom he asks what she thinks of modern art as they stand together in front of Miro's *Nightingale's Song at Midnight and Morning Rain*. As the narrative portrayal of this middle-class community to this point has led us to expect, Kathy answers that "it's hard to put into words, I only know what I care for and what I don't." Gently pedagogical, Raymond speculates about Miro's abstract work that modern art may have picked up where religious art left off, reducing art to its basic elements, color and shape, to connect us to divinity. To ensure that we understand that its connection to God establishes color as the representation of illusion, still later in the film an out-of-doors discussion between our two protagonists about the loveliness of a fall day establishes a seamless tie between God, color, beauty, harmony, and surface. Surface connotes illusion, color harmony, harmony beauty, and their relation to God perfection. Color establishes at the outset of the film that the principle image created by the work of this artwork is the illusion of perfect harmony, which this artwork in motion will next proceed to utterly shatter and then redeem.

As the film's narrative unfolds we learn that Kathy's husband Frank is a successful advertising executive, they are parents to a boy and girl, domesticity is made carefree by the services of their black maid, Sybil, and Kathy is featured in a local society newspaper as having it all—the perfectly attractive woman with the perfect husband, perfect home, and perfect family, all set against a perfectly vibrant setting of reds, oranges, yellows, and greens. The film's narrative unfolds quickly, for how long could the image of such an illusion be sustained? Unbeknownst to Kathy, Frank is struggling with his homosexuality, which he had repressed during their courtship and marriage, and the suffering he endures from trying to maintain his illusory heterosexual identity has been compounded by alcoholism and further complicates his relationship with Kathy.

When Kathy discovers her husband's secret, she guilelessly arranges for a psychiatric conversion, and he complies, heroically trying to preserve his marriage, family, and position against the fate that soon will overwhelm him. As Frank and his psychiatrist battle for his normality, Kathy befriends her "colored" gardener who reciprocates, sensing the same loneliness, gentleness, intelligence, and receptivity in her that he personifies. As Frank's temporary therapeutic success succumbs to his nature and his marriage collapses, Kathy and Raymond draw closer and, though never intimate, become the subject of vicious rumors that intensify the film's dissonance and force Raymond to leave Hartford for the safety of a segregated black Baltimore. Frank divorces Kathy for his lover, with whom he experiences romantic love for the first time, and Kathy apparently remains in Hartford. A brief scene at the film's conclusion finds Sybil explaining to Kathy that although the matron of the house finds it unnecessary, the tables are to be polished because it's Friday. Life as usual continues, we are being told, if not quite the same for Kathy then at least for her community, as her remaining behind in Hartford suggests, as does our recollection of her statement near the film's opening that she can't understand why she was chosen for the society pages, as she is "just like every other wife and mother." At the film's end, we are to understand, the lives of other wives and mothers and their families are yet intact, though only on the surface.

Albeit dramatically revised from the perfect harmony to which we originally were introduced, as the film ends an illusion of harmony is preserved after the opening illusion is dissolved by a series of images documenting the decay and decline transforming a way of life. Indeed, though the return home of Kathy and her children from the train station where she and Raymond bid a silent farewell is set in winter, the perfect harmony symbolized by color now devastated, in this final sequence we catch peeking out on the screen's left a sprig of dogwood blossoms that has survived the seasonal change. The illusion on which every great artwork depends has survived, so that we can imagine further motion between this new illusion and its subsequent negation. *Far from Heaven* does not allow closure, but supplants the first illusion its subsequent images contested with another we expect to be challenged in its turn. As an artwork in motion, the motion picture has taught us about the contradictions that prove the idealization of a way of life to be illusory, destructive of those implicated, unsustainable and subject to revision and reconstitution.

Moreover, the motion picture understands itself to be an artwork in motion in precisely this way. A brilliant scene depicts Kathy attending her daughter's ballet recital as several of her daughter's friends in ballet costume cling fearfully to their mothers' skirts a short distance from where Kathy and her daughter stand whispering anxiously to one another. Kathy and her daughter are positioned at the rear of the auditorium, the other mothers and daughters to their right and further to the rear, but over Kathy's and her daughter's heads to the left the stage is also visible where the ballet is in progress. The wide sweep of the camera, which pans from images of Kathy and her daughter to images (on their left) of the ballet on stage, and then back past Kathy and her daughter to images (on their right) of the mothers and daughters at the auditorium's rear, doubly illustrates the work of art in motion. Here the film shows us the artwork, represented by the ballet, offering its illusion of beauty and also the motion that is the work of art and the illusion's undoing—the image of the little ballerinas clinging to mothers who at home already have loudly voiced what Kathy threatens, integration and the end of white hegemony. The motion picture has become self-referential, an artwork reflecting on itself performing the work of art. Panning to the ballet—which startles us with its uncanny resemblance to Degas's 1878 painting *Ballet Scene*—film takes itself as an artwork moving reflexively within itself between image and its negation, illusion and reality, claims to rationality and the mimetic, sensuous attachment to life out of which new images are constructed that challenge these claims.

A second artwork in motion that reflects on middle-class life, the film *American Beauty* (1999) thematizes many of the same illusions and their underlying antagonisms critically examined in *Far from Heaven*. Lester and Carolyn once had a happy marriage and with their daughter Jane once formed a happy family, which we learn from photographs lying about their home and sporadic dialogue alluding to how they once related to one another. Marriage and parenting and family life as a whole have been emptied of their prior meaning, and hollowed-out practices, such as dining together to music intended to create an anxiety-calming ambiance, are all that remain to perpetuate the now transparent illusion that nothing in the past has changed.

Each is painfully uncomfortable with the other, and the stress of their relationships shows through every attempt they make to communicate as well as when no attempts to communicate are made at all.

Each character's personal illusions are then shattered in turn. To cope with his loneliness, Lester fantasizes about Jane's nubile adolescent friend Angela, who represents his illusion of beauty and sensuality that falls apart in a revelation of her concealed innocence when, in a desperate attempt to maintain her own illusion of not being ordinary, she offers herself to him. Adopting the imperative "to be successful you must project an image of success" from an envied business competitor with whom she commits adultery, Carolyn is crushed by the weight of the illusion of success as her exasperation at being unable to project the sought-after image reduces her to despair. Her next door neighbor Ricky Fitts, with whom she becomes involved, enables Jane to see through all the illusions burdening everyone else, a power of insight Ricky acquired by learning to use the camera, which he explains unveils the life hidden behind things. Abused, Ricky will escape his own family, which has remaining few illusions of its own, save the illusion his marine colonel father strains to protect of a son who has overcome a drug habit by modeling himself on the image his father projects of disciplined hypermasculinity, an illusion the colonel has created to hide his homosexuality.

As *American Beauty* concludes, Colonel Fitts has murdered Lester out of fear that he would compromise his masculinity by disclosing his homosexuality, which Lester learned of when the colonel, believing him to be homosexual as well, made a sexual advance toward Lester he rejected. Colonel Fitt's concluded mistakenly that Lester had been having a sexual relationship with his son, whom he exiled from his home in a rage provoked by his delusion of his son's homosexuality. With the illusions of family and marital happiness, romantic love and sexual fulfillment, success and masculinity all destroyed, the moment before Lester is shot he nevertheless is meditating happily on a photograph of himself and his family during better times. In the moment after his death, his voice-over recalls only the beauty in the world, and that its abundance is so overwhelming as to leave him barely able to take in its impressions. On the occasion of this recollection, though, beauty now includes the myriad ways in which illusions are betrayed as well as the original illusions. Beauty is composed of beauty and its other.

So the artwork has made progress beyond the original illusions by sublimating their ugly outcomes in a higher conception of beauty through which the illusions are reconstructed. Yet the new illusion is at the mercy of the same indeterminate range of contingencies as its earlier incarnations, a lesson conveyed by the powerful final contrast between the new, ambiguous ideal of beauty with the unambiguous ideal image of family life Lester carries to his death. Again, the work of art in motion moves the artwork back and forth between illusory images and life in order to reconstruct those images in light of newly formed sensuous impressions. Art's dialectic of rationality and mimesis shunts reason between the two poles of its cognitive process. And the artwork's final reflection, a far more complex illusion of beauty than the images initially portrayed by the work of art, promises motion to come. For the new, complex illusion is of the beauty of all that life contains, including death, and the camera that reveals the hidden life behind things, the cognitive power of the work of art Ricky Fitts confides to us, will eventually teach that death is not beautiful, or not only beautiful. Although we must imagine this latter motion continuing after the film ends, it is virtually in view, because we infer it from the fundamental instability this artwork has shown belongs to all illusions. After all, the film has depicted the death of beauty itself, represented by the perfect rose, the American Beauty, its every cameo appearance a sensuous dew-covered image. The artwork in motion symbolically documents its death, for the family, the perfect rose's namesake, which cultivated the American Beauty in its garden has passed on.

One final example of the work of the artwork in motion pictures will enable us to draw some conclusions about the similarities between modern art and mass culture with regard to aesthetic reason. *Pleasantville* (1998) is a fantasy about two late-modern, 1990s adolescents, David and Jennifer, who magically become characters in the reruns of a black-and-white television series that transports them back in time where they join a 1950s family living in a town that bears the name of the film. As in *Far from Heaven* and *American Beauty,* the American family is again the object of critical reflection. In Pleasantville, David and Jennifer assume the roles of Budd and Marysue, the children of Betty and George, perfect housewife and mother, father and provider, whose relationship is free of stress and distress as are the lives of every other family in a community believing the world ends at its city limits and that it is thus a world unto itself. As visitors from the future, the worldly David and Jennifer introduce expansive versions of adolescence into their new personas, and soon desire travels through the teenage ranks and into the adult population to divide the town in half. Adults and adolescents fearful of emotions and their divisive consequences are set against those who are not, with those loyal to family and community values remaining colorless in a black-and-white world while those who embrace the new ways and new values become flesh-toned and experience the world in living technicolor. Following various conflicts between the colorless and colorful, the entire town and its inhabitants are filled with color, and the community discovers the world outside to begin the next stage of its journey through modernity.

Of course, David doubling as Budd and Jennifer as Marysue tell us that the forces of progress already were latent in Pleasantville, impossible to contain because the contradictions they generate compel the town's social evolution. From the standpoint of the aesthetic form of the film, the forces of progress could be contained so long as they were confined to a poor modern artwork, a black-and-white television series able to maintain the illusion without question because it does none of the cognitive work of art possible in the color-filled modernist artwork. The television series only becomes an artwork in motion in the film, where it is thrown into motion by the film's contrast between black-and-white and color. As an artwork in motion, *Pleasantville* shatters the illusion of perfect contentment that characterized the community and family life of the 1950s for a nation that needed to justify its wartime sacrifices with idealizations of postwar existence. And together with *Far from Heaven* and especially *American Beauty*, *Pleasantville* also vindicates the idea of illusion by reconstructing it in a different form. Pleasantville's black-and-white world is replaced by one that is color-filled. The colors of this new world harmonize to portray a diverse world that achieves a more complex harmony, while this illusion is replaced in turn when David returns to his own time to discover his single parent mother crying at the dinner table over having been betrayed in a relationship by a younger man, an image of the risks entailed by postmodern inclusions of difference. *Pleasantville* is an artwork in continuous motion between representations of life and life itself. Its motion proves its representations to be illusions, images based on claims to rationality unable to stand up to the negations of its images that flow from the artwork's sensuous attachment to existence.

Pleasantville, moreover, is an artwork that understands itself to be in motion, as did *Far from Heaven* and *American Beauty*. After color and the diversity it expresses is emancipated in Pleasantville, a soda jerk who fulfills his fantasy of becoming an artist produces on the store front window a painting of his naked lover—a liberated Betty—lying on the soda fountain counter on her side surrounded by desserts the soda fountain had to offer. The artwork is primitive and powerful, as the desire it recognizes unsettles the painting as it disturbs the untroubled form of social life implied by the image of the soda fountain. Yet its portrayal of desire also represents the release of the repressed feelings of desire the soda fountain's ice cream and cake also signify. *Pleasantville* thus self-consciously represents the artwork in motion. Not only does it move between rationality and mimesis, proliferating images out of a mimetic relationship to life that subjects each image to further reflection and reconstruction, it privileges the work of art as exactly this movement between rationality and mimesis. The artwork in motion reflects on the work of art as a form of reasoning, highlighting its aesthetic features and, consistent with an aesthetic form of rationality, reflecting on every image it creates to ensure that it performs its work completely.

THE WORK OF ART IN MODERN ART AND MASS CULTURE

At the outset I proposed that Horkheimer and Adorno's *Dialectic of Enlightenment* is the point of departure for inquiring after the positive concept of enlightenment to which they committed themselves in that work. Contrary to the criticism of Habermas, Wellmer, Benhabib, and other theorists working on the communicative paradigm, Horkheimer and Adorno return us to the path through modernity first mapped by Weber in which reason is differentiated and developed in three distinct forms. If Horkheimer and Adorno do lead us to this path, it is a direction of great consequence for their work. It would mean that they did not equate the totality of reason with instrumental reason. Rather, they laid claim to a rival form of reason that held promise as an alternative to the eclipse of reason, freed them from the charge of being implicated in the aporia of performative contradiction, and served as the normative standpoint for their critique of enlightenment. In Adorno's later *Aesthetic Theory* this rival form of reason then evolved into a fully elaborated concept of aesthetic rationality that, in retrospect, delivered on the promissory of another enlightenment made in the earlier work where its possibility was remote but not extinguished. Recalling Horkheimer and Adorno's contribution as the background for my argument opens to three concluding points.

To date, Habermas's insights into the rational content of modernity are among the most productive contemporary political theorists have had to consider, and his theory of communicative interaction in important ways has been developed in opposition to Horkheimer and Adorno's critique of enlightenment. It consequently is appropriate first to compare his concept of reason in modernity with Adorno's robust variation of the concept of aesthetic reason that appeared in its fledgling form in his work with Horkheimer.

Adorno's framework for rationality in modernity differentiates aesthetic and instrumental rationality, the latter form of rationality collapsing Habermas's distinction between cognitive-instrumental and moral-ethical reason. Depending on our theoretical relationship to Habermas, Adorno's revision either captures or impoverishes modernity's alternative rationalities. At the same time, owing to the serious underdevelopment of his concept of aesthetic reason and the part it plays in communicative action, Habermas's theory is handicapped on its own terms. Without his systematic statement on the nature of aesthetic reason, it cannot finally be decided if it would remain dependent on nonaesthetic pragmatic criteria of communicative discourse, as Wellmer has argued, if it would play a symmetrical role with forms of reason in communicative interaction, or if it would assume a dominant role in relation to these rationality complexes. Such uncertainty is absent from Adorno's concept of aesthetic reason, which privileges reflexivity as its chief criterion of rationality. Designed to reflect on the limits of every claim to rationality, aesthetic reason sits in judgment to the extent implied by a concept of reflection and is not parasitic on cognitive-instrumental and moral-ethical claims to reason. By virtue of its uncompromising allegiance to reflection, aesthetic reason enjoys a primacy that must be denied to other forms of reason, which in comparison appear to be the less stalwart forms of reason defining modernity's content.

Second, though aesthetic reason in a singular way may define the rational content of modernity, it does not follow that it is sufficient to meet the philosophical burden of enlightenment. One test of the philosophical status of aesthetic reason would be to determine the extent to which it measures up to the standard-bearer concepts of enlightenment rationality, such as Mill's defense of the affinity between the pursuit of truth and unabated and deathless critique and contestation. My earlier allusion to Mill was meant to suggest this approach. Nevertheless, it is not adequate to evaluate the complete range of cultural possibilities supported by aesthetic reason. Even as Adorno conceptualized aesthetic rationality, it must be thought of as an abridged version of what modern art since *Aesthetic Theory* potentially contributes to the further theoretical development of what constitutes an aesthetic value sphere. A revaluation of aesthetic reason in view of modern art since Adorno likewise requires a more demanding test of aesthetic reason's enlightenment credentials than Mill and other enlightenment thinkers provide.

Finally, as the brunt of the argument here has maintained, what Adorno discovered about the work of art may well have found another home in mass culture, as I have begun to show with examples from film. To be sure, any project that investigates the possibility of such commonalities also must consider why, as Adorno had, much modern art failed to rise to the level of aesthetic reason, and whether similar and new shortcomings thwart the development of aesthetic reason in mass culture. Under no circumstances, though, should such an investigation be discouraged on the grounds of Adorno's own reservations about mass culture or those of mass culture's other critics. If there is one characteristic of mass culture on which its critics and defenders agree, it is that mass culture for good or evil is becoming universal and that its "universality" is not confined to the West. Mass culture's tendency to universality may foretell of the next enlightenment, a time when a positive concept of enlightenment formulated around the *work* of art—reflexivity—*in mass culture* would coincide with a global sea change in the human spirit that has not flowed since the first Enlightenment of modern times.

NOTES

With minor differences of footnote style and the inclusion of my brief introduction, this essay was published originally in the *Journal for Cultural Research* 9, no. 2 (January 2005).

1. Theodor W. Adorno, *Philosophy of Modern Music* (New York: Seabury Press, 1973), pp. 29–133. Originally published as *Philosophie der neuen Musik* (Tübingen: Mohr, 1949).

2. Morton Schoolman, "Avoiding 'Embarrassment': Aesthetic Reason and Aporetic Critique in Dialectic of Enlightenment," *Polity* 37, no. 3 (2005), pp. 335–64.

3. Martin Zenck, *Kunst als Begriffslose Erkenntnis* (Munich: Fink, 1977), p. 9.

4. Martin Jay, *The Dialectical Imagination: A History of the Frankfurt School and Institute for Social Research 1923–1950* (Boston: Little, Brown, 1973), pp. 195–96), and *Adorno* (Cambridge: Harvard University Press, 1984), p. 152.

5. Jürgen Habermas, *The Philosophical Discourse of Modernity* (Cambridge: MIT Press, 1987), pp. 113, 114.

6. Jürgen Habermas, *The Theory of Communicative Action: Reason and the Rationalization of Society I,* trans. Thomas McCarthy (Boston: Beacon Press, 1984), p. 382.

7. Schoolman, "Avoiding 'Embarrassment.'"

8. Habermas, *Philosophical Discourse of Modernity*, p. 127. See also Habermas, *Theory of Communicative Action I*, pp. 387, 382, and "Remarks on the Development of Horkheimer's Work," in *On Max Horkheimer: New Perspectives*, ed. Seyla Benhabib, Wolfgang Bonss, and John McCole (Cambridge: MIT Press, 1993).

9. Theodor Adorno, *Ästhetische Theorie* (Frankfurt: Suhrkamp, 1970). Translated into English as *Aesthetic Theory* (Minneapolis: University of Minnesota Press, 1997).

10. Max Horkheimer and Theodor Adorno, *The Dialectic of Enlightenment* (Stanford: Stanford University Press, 2002), p. xviii. Originally published as *Dialektik der Aufklarung* (Amsterdam: Querido, 1947).

11. Günter Figal, *Theodor W. Adorno: Das Naturschöne als spekulative Gedankenfigur* (Bonn: Bouvier Verlag Herbert Grundmann, 1977), p. 16.

12. Romand Coles, *Rethinking Generosity* (Ithaca: Cornell University Press, 1997), p. 115.

13. Adorno, *Aesthetic Theory*, p. 54.

14. Max Horkheimer, "Art and Mass Culture," in Horkheimier, *Critical Theory* (New York: Herder and Herder, 1972), pp. 273, 275. Originally published in *Studies in Philosophy and Social Science* 9, no. 2 (1941).

15. Diana Coole, *Politics and Negativity* (London: Routledge, 2000), p. 171.

16. Adorno, *Aesthetic Theory*, p. 55.

17. Horkheimer and Adorno, *Dialectic of Enlightenment*, p. 27.

18. Adorno, *Aesthetic Theory*, p. 54.

19. Ibid., p. 53.

20. Jane Bennett, *The Enchantment of Modern Life: Attachments, Crossings, and Ethics* (Princeton: Princeton University Press, 2001), p. 123.

21. Habermas, *The Theory of Communicative Action I*, p. 390.

22. Seyla Benhabib, *Critique, Norm, and Utopia* (New York: Columbia University Press, 1986), p. 220.

23. Terry Eagleton, *The Ideology of the Aesthetic* (Oxford: Blackwell, 1990), p. 349.

24. Fred Dallmayr, *Between Freiburg and Frankfurt: Toward a Critical Ontology* (Amherst: University of Massachusetts Press, 1991), p. 93.

25. Horkheimer and Adorno, *Dialectic of Enlightenment*, p. 18.

26. Albrecht Wellmer, *The Persistence of Modernity: Essays on Aesthetics, Ethics, and Postmodernism* (Cambridge: MIT Press, 1991), p. 4.

27. Ibid., p. 13.

28. Ibid., pp. 13–35.

29. Ibid., p. 28.

30. Martin Morris, *Rethinking the Communicative Turn: Adorno, Habermas and the Problem of Communicative Freedom* (Albany: SUNY Press, 2001), pp. 51, 53.

31. Ibid., p. 51.

32. Ibid.

33. Figal, *Theodor W. Adorno*, p. 58.

34. Ulrich Müller, *Erkenntniskritik und Negative Metaphysik bei Adorno* (Frankfurt: Athenaeum, 1988), p. 192.

35. Morris, *Rethinking the Communicative Turn*, p. 173.

36. Christoph Menke, *The Sovereignty of Art: Aesthetic Negativity in Adorno and Derrida* (Cambridge: MIT Press, 1998), p. 24.

37. Ibid., p. 13.

38. Adorno, *Aesthetic Theory*, p. 54.

39. Benhabib, *Critique, Norm, and Utopia*, p. 219.

40. Adorno, *Aesthetic Theory*, p. 176.

41. Ibid., p. 54.

42. Ibid., p. 176.

43. Ullrich Schwartz, *Rettende Kritik und antizipierte Utopie. Zum geschichtlichen Gehalt ästhetisher Erfahrung in den Theorien von Jan Mukarovsky, Walter Benjamin, und Theodor W. Adorno* (Munich: Fink, 1981), pp. 187–89.

44. Ibid., p. 188.

45. Figal, *Theodor W. Adorno*, p. 59.

46. Adorno, *Aesthetic Theory*, p. 54.

47. Ibid., pp. 40, 140.

48. Ibid., p. 178.

49. Horkheimer and Adorno, *Dialectic of Enlightenment*, p. 94.

50. Adorno, *Aesthetic Theory*, p. 176.

THREE

Multicultural Cosmopolitanism:
Remarks on the Idea
of Universal History

Thomas McCarthy

From the time of our first communication, some thirty years ago, Fred Dallmayr and I have never ceased to disagree about key foundational issues in social and political theory. Our disagreements are not haphazard, but consistent; they might be characterized roughly as stemming from the differences between his brand of hermeneutics and my brand of critical theory, or between his sources of inspiration in Hegel and Heidegger and my own in Kant and Jürgen Habermas. But they are also "reasonable disagreements" that allow for considerable "overlapping consensus" on both methodological and substantive issues. Thus we overlapped sufficiently on questions concerning the role of interpretive understanding in social inquiry to coedit an anthology on that topic very early on.[1] And I want to suggest here that we now overlap sufficiently on the idea of multicultural cosmopolitanism to make our ongoing conversation continually fruitful despite the persistent differences in our "comprehensive doctrines." Those differences do entail, however, that we follow widely diverging paths before arriving in the same region of the politico-theoretical world. And they likely also mean that we are relying on different maps of this region and of the roads leading beyond it as well. But here I confine my remarks to charting an alternative route to the sort of global and plural democracy that Dallmayr has set out in a series of recent works.[2] It is a route that leads from Kant's idea for a universal history from a cosmopolitan point of view, through Habermas's conceptions of social evolution and a postnational constellation, to a sketch of multicultural cosmopolitanism that bears strong affinities to Dallmayr's vision of "our world."

KANT and UNIVERSAL HISTORY

Though the genre of universal history to which Kant gave exemplary expression was deeply implicated in colonial domination and exploitation, it cannot simply be discarded in favor of genealogical or other broadly deconstructive modes of historical consciousness. Kant did not conjure the genre out of thin air; he was articulating the spirit of an age that was already deeply involved in capitalist globalization through conquest, colonization, settlement, and the burgeoning Atlantic slave trade. The West and East Indian Companies, for instance, and the Royal African Company had been established long before he wrote. It is, moreover, only a myth that Enlightenment thinkers were uninterested in cultural difference. Kant no less than Diderot was intensely preoccupied with it and with the problems it raised for his moral universalism.[3] What is more, his general approach to reconciling the universal and the particular became paradigmatic for liberalism in the centuries that followed: cultural diversity was reconciled with moral, religious, legal, and political universalism by way of a general account of human development, particularly of social and cultural modernization. There can be no doubt of the justice of postcolonial criticisms of this genre as offering a totalizing view of history that reduced others to more or less retarded versions of the same and thus warranted their subordination and tutelage. And given the disastrous consequences of the neocolonial theory and practice of "development" after World War II, there seems to be no positive political purpose to be served by retaining anything at all from this genre, however transformed. But I am of the view that a critical social theory of modernization is still a valuable, even irreplaceable, complement to deconstructive critiques thereof. For one thing, the growing global interdependence that gave birth to the genre of universal history at the dawn of the modern age and sustained it thereafter has since the 1970s accelerated at a mind-boggling pace. Decoupling cultures and societies from this process is no longer a viable option. Universal history, in short, is where we actually are and have been for some time. And it is out of this situation that we must think, must try to understand the social, economic, and cultural patterns and dynamics that inform it, discern the possibilities of change and openings for alternatives that lie within it, identify and engage the social forces capable of transforming it, and so on. Of course, critical social theory is not the place where all or even most of this can be done. But such theory might contribute to the sort of broad reflection on the modern world that provides badly needed background to more concrete thinking about alternative modernities, if the latter is to avoid degenerating into policy-oriented social "science" or evanescing into cultural imaginings unmoored from socioeconomic realities.

Be that as it may, all I mean to offer here are some very general remarks on the fate of developmental theory after Kant and some equally general thoughts on where that leaves us in thinking about globalization today. I shall assume the readers' familiarity with the main lines of Kant's universal history and the cosmopolitan world order in which we can rationally hope (not predict) it will eventuate, and begin with a few broad, brief, and unargued observations concerning their subsequent fate.

1. To begin with the obvious, Kant's *biologized account of racial, ethnic, and national differences* was eventually displaced by views that accentuate the historically contingent, socioculturally constructed, and usually politically motivated representations of race, ethnicity, and nationality. And with it went Kant's naturalized account of the supposedly unalterable differences in talent and temperament between various human groups, together with the basic explanatory role they played in his reading of history. This sort of account, which subsequently came to dominate the age of imperialism, was effectively displaced only in the latter half of the twentieth century.

2. At the opposite extreme, but equally obvious, the *demands of theodicy* that Kant placed on history play no role in postmetaphysical, postontotheological frames of interpretation. There is no *Endzweck* of history; it does not have to make moral-rational sense.

3. Along with theodicy goes the *teleology of nature* embedded in it. In post-Darwinian science there is no place for the purposes, plans, or designs of nature that functioned for Kant as stand-ins for Providence; evolutionary development is not the realization of a telos inherent in the nature of things. In particular, there is no way to make sense of the claim that the full development of the natural capacities of the human species is *der letzte Zweck der Natur*, the ultimate aim of nature.

4. The *teleology of history* is a more complicated matter. For postmetaphysical thinking there can be no historical puposiveness in the strict sense— no aims or designs, ultimate or final ends of history. And this means that strictly teleological modes of interpretation and forms of explanation no longer have a legitimate place in historical or social studies. On the other hand,

this does not automatically preclude broadly naturalistic approaches that retain some of the features of teleological thinking. There are, for instance, various empirical approaches to the study of human development that make no appeal to design and no claim to certainty but argue, nevertheless, for the cumulative and directional character of the processes they study. The cogency of such naturalized developmental approaches is not a matter to be decided a priori; it is, rather, a question of their comparative strengths and weaknesses as interpretive and explanatory schemes for particular domains, that is, of how they stand up in the conflict of interpretations.

5. Finally, postmetaphysical thought has renounced, on good grounds, central aspects of *Kant's subjectivistic critique of reason:* the monological character of his conception of reason and rationality; the monocultural character of his idea of humanity; the repression of nature and subordination of happiness built into his concept of moral autonomy; connected with that, his insufficiently relational—social, historical, cultural, embodied—conception of subjectivity; and, of course, the residually metaphysical aspects of his distinction between noumenal and phenomenal.

6. Hegel, to be sure, already tried to get beyond Kant's dualism and subjectivism, but the price was too high. His philosophy of world history does not so much overcome that eighteenth-century genre as outdo it—with such claims as "reason governs the world," that it is "the substance" of history and "the power" animating it, and thus the aim of philosophical inquiry into history is "to eliminate the contingent," any "external necessity" originating in "causes which are themselves no more than external circumstances."[4] Subsequent theorists of modernization as rationalization were generally unwilling to go that far. Some, however, remained close to Hegel on one point: the idea that there are *inner logics to cultural developments* that must be articulated by any adequate theory of societal transformation. Thus Max Weber was concerned to spell out the *Eigenlogik* of the cultural spheres whose rationalization he was studying; and Habermas has tried to articulate the "developmental logics" underlying the cultural learning processes he studies. But unlike Hegel, and like most social theorists since, they regard rationalization processes, whatever their inner logics, as empirically conditioned all the way down.

7. Marx, of course, led the way in this regard. Though world-historical processes of development did tend toward the full unfolding of human rational capacities, what ultimately drove them belonged rather to the "external

circumstances" that Hegel wanted to eliminate than to the internal development of the Spirit. "From the start," Marx insisted, "the 'spirit' is afflicted with the curse of being 'burdened' with matter."[5] Consequently, "life is not determined by consciousness, but consciousness by life"; so "philosophy as an independent branch of knowledge loses its medium of existence" and has to give way to the *materialist theory of history*.[6] Post-Marxian social theorists have largely agreed that "material circumstances" must be a central part of any explanation of cultural developments, as they have with the view that the power that drives historical change is not primarily that of reason but that of productive forces, political struggles, and a variety of other "material" factors. At the same time, they have distanced themselves from the residues of Hegel's dialectic in Marx's theory of history—and thus from the residual necessity and providentiality in his account of the inexorable development of productive forces and eventual arrival of a classless society.

8. This rejection of the Hegel that is still in Marx sometimes took the form of eliminating altogether the internal logic of cultural development from the explanation of societal transformations. Thus in the nineteenth-century evolutionary theories of society that proliferated in the wake of Darwin, social development was typically presented as the evolution of quasi-organic systems and reconstructed entirely from an externalist perspective. But the most influential social theorists of the late-nineteenth and twentieth centuries attempted rather to grasp the *connection between "internal" and "external" factors,* however variously conceived, than to eliminate one in favor of the other. Thus Durkheim wanted to understand the interrelations between changes in the division of labor, on the one hand, and the changing forms of sociocultural integration through norms and values, on the other; Weber wanted to connect the rationalization of worldviews to the institutionalization of instrumental rationality in the major domains of society; and Habermas has tried to construct a dual-perspective approach to society that views it both as lifeworld and as system, and connects rationalization under the former aspect to increasing complexity under the latter.

9. For our purposes, it is important to note that this type of approach explicitly seeks to distance itself from many of the most objectionable features of eighteenth-century philosophy of history and its nineteenth-century progeny. Development is not claimed to be necessary but thoroughly contingent; it is not unilinear but allows for diverse paths to the same level of development; nor is it continuous, irreversible, or even across all domains of social

life. What this type of approach does retain, however, is the idea that *some developments are cumulative and directional;* and in cultural domains this typically means that they can be rationally reconstructed as learning processes. Insofar as that idea holds up, internally reconstructible developments of rational capacities—developmental logics—will be an important part of understanding the changes in question. There may also be cumulative, directional changes in other than specifically cultural domains, for instance, in the growth of productive forces, in the scale and internal differentiation of organizations, or in the complexity and adaptive capacity of state administrations. In such cases, the type of approach in question examines the ways in which cultural learning gets transposed into social institutions.

10. It is equally important to note that this way of theorizing social and cultural development does *not* of itself commit the theorist to such *totalized notions of progress* as we find in the providential teleo-logics of the philosophy of history. Developments may occur in various domains, at different rates, and with diverse consequences. They are always shot through with contingency—for example, the empirical conditions under which a certain sort of cultural learning may occur—and ringed around with contingency—for example, the empirical circumstances that promote the institutionalization of certain cultural developments. And their significance for human well-being, however defined, will vary with the boundary conditions under which they occur. Such an approach is quite different from any scheme in which developmental advance itself serves as the basic standard of evaluation for any change, as was the case with nineteenth-century evolutionism.

11. This helps explain why theorists in this tradition, from Durkheim to Habermas, could be of quite different minds regarding *the relation of social progress to human happiness,* broadly and variously understood. Thus Weber, under the influence of Nietzsche and fin de siècle pessimism, saw modernization processes as forging an "iron cage" of instrumental rationality and resulting in losses of meaning and freedom. This diagnosis was reformulated by Max Horkheimer and Theodor Adorno during the darkest days of World War II, and it has since been repeatedly varied to comprehend the rapid advances in everything from techniques of social control to technologies of mass destruction. Habermas's version of the "glittering misery" that already worried Kant turns on the selectivity of capitalist modernization—a failure to develop and institutionalize in a balanced way all the various potentialities of cultural rationalization, which has resulted in a growing "colonization of

the lifeworld by the system." Thus the normative and evaluative standpoints that have informed developmental frameworks of interpretation have varied considerably.

12. This variability of standpoints has made *the relationship between developmental theory and political practice* hard to avoid as an explicit theme in the conflict of interpretations. In this respect developmental thinking today is closer to Kant than to the putative transcendence of the is/ought divide in Hegel and Marx or to its obliteration in social evolutionism and other varieties of allegedly scientific history. Recall that for Kant history was a domain of reflective judgment not of scientific certainty, and that universal-historical reflection was to be carried out in *praktischer Absicht*, not as an exercise in theoretical reason. This meant that general interpretations of human history, depending as they did on a course of future events that could not be theoretically predicted but only practically projected, had an intrinsic relation to practice. Of course today, in the absence of any religious or metaphysical guarantees, the historical hopes that sustain political practice are even more tenuous than Kant's.

13. Finally, it should be noted that through all the alterations and variations that take us from Enlightenment philosophies of history to contemporary theories of social and cultural development, *Eurocentrism* has remained a constant. That is, in all the major developmental theorists—from Hegel and Marx, through Durkheim and Weber, to Parsons and Habermas—the main lines of development, at least in the modern period, run through the West and from there outward to the rest of the world.

Habermas and Modernization Theory

It is against this historical background that Habermas's efforts to rearticulate a theory of modernization as rationalization should be understood. As is well known, the metatheory of reason that underpins his developmental approach takes the form of a universal pragmatics of communication. Unlike Kant's critique of reason, it is meant to be an empirical, reconstructive theory; but analogously to Kant's critique, it makes use of various form/content distinctions, seeks to disclose a number of "quasi-transcendental" structures of language-in-use, and maintains that certain idealizations are unavoidable presuppositions of linguistic interaction. The theory of communicative action that results is given a developmental twist in regard to both the life history of individuals and the universal history of the species. Ontogenetically, the acquisition of communicative competence proceeds through a series of stages of cognitive, social, linguistic, and affective development. Phylogenetically, development turns on a widening and deepening rationalization of culture and society that is, however, typically uneven and frequently pathological.

Dallmayr objects to all of this, and I readily concede that there is more than enough here to take issue with. But because I want to examine the idea of multicultural universalism, I shall simply move on without further ado. This is not as question-begging as it may at first seem, for a central feature of Habermas's account of communicative reason is that, in the final analysis, there is no possibility of rationally adjudicating competing claims to validity of various sorts—claims to truth, rightness, justice, and legitimacy, among others—apart from entering into discourse and weighing the considerations offered on the different sides of an issue. His radically discursive theory of validity means that no party to a disagreement is in an inherently privileged position to decide it; that agreements arrived at discursively can claim to be reasonable only insofar as discussion is open, inclusive, and free from domination and repression; and that no outcome of any discourse is ever final—commentary, contestation, and correction are in principle ongoing and never-ending. Now something very much like this could, I think, be endorsed, in one formulation or another, by theorists in the hermeneutic tradition generally and by Dallmayr in particular. And that is all I need to commence the line of reasoning I want to plot here.

My first point is a variation of sorts on the Hegelian theme that negativity is inherent in reflexivity. The participants in the discourse of (post)-modernity find themselves in roughly symmetrical conditions with respect to the cultural resources at their disposal. In fact, the recent course of discussion suggests that representatives of historically oppressed and marginalized groups are quite often more adept with the weapons of critique than their opposite numbers; the great virtuosos of reflexivity in our time have come disproportionately from such groups. More to the point, the capacity for critical reflection is not simply a matter of occasional ingenuity or individual virtuosity. It is bound up with social and cultural conditions that undergo historical change. In modern societies conditions are such as to provide increased institutional, cultural, and motivational support for reflective modes of argumentation and critique. Forms of specialized discourse, transmitted and developed within specialized cultural traditions and embodied in differentiated cultural institutions, present enduring possibilities of discursively thematizing various types of validity claims and of productively assimilating the results of critical reflection on them. It is, among other things, the extent to which and the manner in which modes of critical-reflective discourse have been institutionalized, and the requisite cultural and motivational conditions for them have been satisfied, that distinguishes posttraditional from traditional cultural spheres.

It goes without saying that "posttraditional" here does not mean "floating free of tradition altogether." It alludes to changes in our relations to inherited contexts of meaning and validity, schemes of interpretation and justification, patterns of socialization and identification, and the like. These changes are always matters of degree and never global in their reach, but they are not without far-reaching effects. What Habermas has referred to as the "communicative thawing" of fixed forms in ever-expanding domains of modern life increasingly exposes the authority of tradition to discursive questioning, displaces particularistic norms and values by more general and abstract ones, and replaces traditionally ascribed identities with identities that have to be constructed and reconstructed in ongoing, ever-changing situations. Customary beliefs can less and less be relied on to guarantee the reproduction of modern forms of life; context-specific norms and values are less and less adequate to the demands of social integration; concrete roles and inherited models are increasingly insufficient to secure identity. There are growing needs for discursively tested convictions, general principles of legality and morality, and highly individuated, self-directing subjects. (It has been a commonplace of sociology since Durkheim, at the latest, that greater generality of norms and values and heightened individualism are interdependent and not opposed developments.) And it is important to note that this heightening of reflexivity, generality, and individualism informs and structures the contemporary discourse of (post)modernity itself. For instance, all the various participants—postmodernist and antimodernist, as well as modernist—take for granted the possibility of reflectively questioning received beliefs and values, of gaining critical distance from inherited norms and roles, and of challenging ascribed individual and group identities. Even arguments like Alasdair MacIntyre's for the superiority of premodern traditions are not themselves traditional arguments, but the traditionalistic arguments of hyperreflexive moderns. We—participants in the discourse of (post)-modernity—can argue about these basic features of posttraditional culture only by drawing on them; and this is a good indication that they are practically unavoidable presuppositions of contemporary discourse.

A reconstruction of the pragmatics of our—the participants'—communicative situation could, then, make clear at least where our discussions have to start. And this in itself has far-reaching consequences for the discourse of (post)modernity. That discourse turns on what we, the participants, can and cannot make sense of, render plausible, justify, refute, effectively criticize, conceive of as alternatives, and so on. If there are constraining preconditions built into our discursive situation itself, they may in turn constrain the range of possible outcomes. Consider, for instance, how we relate to worldviews and forms of life marked by a comparative lack of awareness of, or openness to, alternatives to the established body of beliefs, and connected with this our defensive or avoidance reactions in the face of challenges to them. It is precisely our historically, sociologically, and anthropologically schooled view of the diversity of systems of belief and practice that informs our discourse about (post)modernity. Hence we are constrained, on pain of incoherence, to regard systems of belief that do not understand themselves as interpretations of the world, subject to error and open to revision, as deficient in that respect, as not having learned something that we know. There is, to put it plainly, no going back on the experiences of cultural change and pluralism we have had, or unlearning what we have learned from them about the variability of forms of life and views of the world. In the current discourse of (post)modernity we cannot sensibly argue against that.

There are other general presuppositions of contemporary discourse with which one might, perhaps, meaningfully take issue, but with respect to which the burden of proof on the critic is so great as to be prohibitive. Consider, for instance, the distinction we now draw between empirical-scientific questions and questions of religion, morality, or metaphysics. There is no easy way to go back on this and argue convincingly, for example, that the number, position, and composition of the planets could be decided by appeal to revelation, morals, or metaphysics. The same could be said for animistic and anthropomorphic accounts of nature, magical techniques that blur our current distinction between instrumental control over things and moral relations among persons, or attitudes toward names and naming that contravene our distinction between the symbolic power of expression and physical efficacy. In our cultural-historical situation it would be difficult if not impossible to produce a warranted denial that there has been a significant learning process underway in regard at least to our scientific understanding of nature and our technical ability to manipulate it, and that modern societies have learned to pursue the interest in prediction and control more effectively by differentiating it out from other concerns. (Practically living out that denial would, of course, be even more difficult.) But this means that from where we—the participants in the discourse of (post)modernity—must start, some differences in beliefs and practices will be more than mere differences, precisely because they can only be made sense of as the results of learning.

I have been speaking primarily of beliefs, but it is worth remarking that our assessment of norms and values cannot remain unaffected by what we regard as learning in more narrowly cognitive domains. Traditional value systems are intimately interwoven with beliefs about how the world is. That is why the learning processes associated with names like Galileo and Darwin have had such profound impacts on normative and evaluative elements of modern life. To put the point somewhat crudely, certain ethical views can be publicly justified only by appeal to beliefs that are no longer tenable. Since the reasons we regard as warranting evaluative and normative judgments have to be compatible with what we have learned in other domains, whole classes of reasons for acting are no longer available to us. In such cases it is *kinds of reasons* that have been devalued and lost their discursive weight, and not just specific claims resting on them. This is what appears to have happened, for instance, with justifications of unequal treatment by appeal to the natural inferiority and unfitness for self-rule of this race or that sex. That is to say, fundamental inequalities that could once be justified by appeals to beliefs about the world that are no longer tenable will be hard put to find substitute justifications capable of withstanding critical-reflective scrutiny. In any case, the discourse of (post)modernity itself is structured by a pragmatic presupposition of normative symmetry that requires treating all participants with equal respect. The tension between that presupposition—with its attendant train of ideas of dignity, tolerance, fairness, and so forth—and ethical views constructed around basic inequalities—whether "natural," "God-given," "time-honored," or what have you—is evident and inescapable. This too enormously increases the burden of proof on anyone who would discursively defend such views.

Though the elimination of broad classes of reasons does not by itself settle questions of right and wrong, good and bad, better and worse, the scope of reasonable disagreement gets considerably narrowed. As a result, the range of norms and values that could stand up to criticism and be upheld in free and open discussion is by no means coextensive with the spectrum of what has historically been valued or might arbitrarily be commanded. But it is also not uniquely determined. One of the things we moderns have learned about values, for instance, is that reasonable people can reasonably hold different conceptions of the good, that there is no one way of life suited to all individuals and groups, and thus that a pluralistic culture within which members can pursue—within common limits—their different ideas of the good life is the most reasonable societal arrangement. And this acknowledgment obliges us to rethink Enlightenment universalism from the perspective of multiculturalism.

The "Fact" of Social Modernity

To these sketchy remarks about the "fact" of cultural modernity, I want now to add a few equally sketchy remarks about the "fact" of social modernity. The conditions of global modernity in which all contemporary societies willy-nilly find themselves present them with an array of large-scale societal problems that they have to resolve if they want to survive—problems, for instance, concerning how to relate to an increasingly integrated global market economy; how to administer an increasingly complex and differentiated society; how to accommodate ethnic, cultural, and religious diversity in a single society; how to maintain political unity and legitimacy in the face of it; and so forth. Habermas has argued that certain modern institutions are less the results of peculiarities of Western culture than responses to societal challenges of just this sort. Consider, for instance, something that is often represented as the epitome of modern Western civilization: the entrenchment of individual rights. In *Between Facts and Norms,* Habermas follows the main line of the sociology of law in arguing that modern law must have most of the formal properties it has in order to fulfill the functions it fulfills, that there are no functional equivalents for its formality, positivity, reflexivity, individuality, actionability, and the like.[7]

The fact that modern law is based on individual rights and liberties releases legal persons from moral obligations in certain spheres of action and gives them latitude, within legally defined limits, to act on their own choices free from interference by the state or by third parties—as is required in decentralized market societies. If these rights and liberties are to have the protection of the law, they must be connected with actionable claims, such that subjects who consider their rights to have been violated may have recourse to legal remedies. At the same time, as membership in the legal communities of diverse modern societies can less and less be defined in terms of cultural or religious membership, it comes to be more and more abstractly defined in terms of the equal rights and responsibilities of citizens as legal subjects. The fact that positive law issues from the changeable decisions of a legislator loosens its ties with traditional morality and makes it suitable as a means of organizing and steering complex modern societies. This requires that the enactment, administration, and application of the law themselves be legally institutionalized; law becomes reflexive. And since modern law, as a positive, reflexive, and therefore fungible "steering medium," can no longer be legitimated solely by appeal to inherited beliefs and practices, there is a need for new forms of legitimation. That need is compounded by the facts that cultural pluralism limits the authority of any one tradition and that rights-based conceptions of citizenship increase the pressure for political participation.

One could go on in this vein. The general line of argument is that the functions and forms of modern law are tailored to one another. Because any contemporary society, whatever its cultural traditions, will find it difficult to do without the former, it will find it correspondingly difficult to do without some version of the latter. As Habermas puts the point: "[T]he decisive alternatives lie not at the cultural but at the socioeconomic level. . . . [T]he question is not whether human rights, as part of an individualistic legal order, are compatible with the transmission of one's own culture. Rather, the question is whether traditional forms of political and societal integration can be reasserted against, or must instead be adapted to, the hard-to-resist imperatives of economic modernization."[8] To the extent that individuals are guaranteed spheres of choice free from collectively binding beliefs and values, that citizenship qualifications are made independent of religious profession or cultural membership, that legislation is legitimated by procedures of enactment, and so forth, to that extent legal and political culture is being differentiated from traditional worldviews and forms of life. What further cultural changes are likely to be associated with that differentiation and its consequences is an open question.

Similar lines of thought could be elaborated for other aspects of societal modernization. And together they pose an issue that has been increasingly discussed under the rubric of "alternative" or "multiple" modernities. Charles Taylor formulates it in general terms as follows: Assuming that some degree of convergence in economic, governmental, and legal institutions and practices is an unavoidable feature of a globalized modernity, what kinds and degrees of divergence remain possible and desirable?[9] In particular, how much room do such modernizing tendencies leave for deep cultural differences? Taylor emphasizes that different starting points for the transition to modernity are likely to lead to different outcomes, and thus that new forms of modern society are likely to evince new forms of difference. This is, of course, already true of Western modernity: Swedish society is interestingly different from French or Italian society, let alone U.S. society. And yet they are too much the same to satisfy Taylor's interests in alternative modernities or, it is clear, the interests of the many other multiculturalists, including Dallmayr, who are concerned with broader and deeper differences in ideas and beliefs, outlooks and attitudes, values and identities, and practices and institutions than these societies evince.

To the question of how much and what kinds of difference we have good empirical and theoretical reasons to expect to persist, there is clearly no generally accepted answer. But one might well conjecture that it is less than Taylor and like-minded theorists hope for. He concedes that market economies and bureaucratic states are inescapable features of modern societies, and that with them come expanded spheres of instrumental action as well as increased industrialization, mobility, and urbanization. He also mentions science and technology as something all modern societies have to take on, as well as general education and mass literacy. We might add to these the legal forms I mentioned above, together with legal cultures that support them. And we might further add a host of other changes that also appear to be irresistible for modern societies: decline of the agricultural mode of life that has defined most of humanity for much of our recorded history; functional differentiation and specialization of occupational and professional life; further diversification of lifestyles, outlooks, and attitudes; increasing pluralization of belief systems, value commitments, and forms of personal and group identity; steady growth of knowledge understood as fallible and susceptible to criticism and revision; spread of mass media and of mass-mediated popular culture; and, of course, ever-deeper immersion in transnational flows of capital, commodities, technology, information, communication, and culture. We might also add changes that most participants in these discussions find desirable but concerning which the empirical tendencies are not as clear: the decline of patriarchal, racist, and ethnocentric stereotyping and role-casting, and of other "natural" hierarchies of these sorts; the inclusion, as equals, of all inhabitants of a territory in its legal and political community; and the existence of public political spheres that allow for open exchange and debate.

One could go on, but these few remarks are enough to suggest that the scope of deep divergence possible and desirable is somewhat more constricted than many multiculturalists acknowledge, especially if we take into account the very dense internal relations and causal connections between the aforementioned changes and the cultural phenomena that are too often discussed in abstraction from them.

Universalism after Multiculturalsim

Where does all this leave our discourse about universalism after multiculturalism, to which I have added considerations of developmentalism. If my claims about the "facts" of cultural and social modernity hold up, at least in general if not in all specifics, then the constraints on the multiple modernities in the process of formation may be rather more substantive than many theorists of multiculturalism seem to suppose. On the other hand, the perspective of global discourse carried on at a critical-reflective level opens up an inexhaustible horizon of possibilities for contestation and variation. From that perspective, not only claims to universal validity have to stand up to transcultural scrutiny but developmental claims as well, for they implicate claims to superiority. Representing a given cultural change as the result of a learning process implies that it offers a superior way of dealing with some domain of experience. For instance, in regard to a broad range of questions and problems, there seems to be little doubt that the history of the natural sciences and associated technologies can be represented as a progressive learning process. The same can be said, in relation to another broad range, for the history of historiography and other human studies in the modern period—at least in general, for when it comes to specifics, as we know, there is more than enough room for disagreement. However, even if the developmental interpretation of a particular cultural innovation *as such* proves to be better than competing accounts, there still remains the rather different question of what to make of it in practice, that is, of what *role* it should play in our lives, of whether and how it should be institutionalized, and the like. Thus, for instance, neither Weber nor Habermas doubts that scientifically based technologies and instrumental techniques for managing human affairs are the results of learning processes, progressive enhancements of our rational capacities to cope with certain types of problems. But, in their different ways, both are deeply critical of how those developments have been incorporated into advanced capitalist societies by way of markets and bureaucracies. Obviously, when issues of this sort are debated across a diversity of societies, with a diversity of traditions, and in a diversity of circumstances, one would expect a diversity of views; for they centrally involve matters of well-being, variously understood, and on such matters unanimity is neither likely nor, in many cases, desirable.

A related point can be made regarding "structural" or "functional" or "systemic" modifications as well. There is little doubt that certain innovations—for example, market economies, bureaucratic administrations, or, more generally, the differentiation and integration of functionally specialized subsystems of action—generally increase the power or "adaptive capacity" of complex societies. That is, they are thereby better able to cope with certain ranges of problems than societies without such innovations. However, the role they should play in a given society is certainly open to debate. Furthermore, societal developments of these sorts are open to contestation in ways that cultural developments as such are not. Wholesale critiques of cultural modernity by its inhabitants always risk incoherence or bad faith, for participants in the discourse of (post)modernity cannot but draw on it in criticizing it. There is no extramundane standpoint available to us from which we could set modern culture as a whole at a distance. By contrast, rejecting power-enhancing systemic innovations may be perfectly coherent: there need be no *conceptual* confusion involved in wanting to live without markets or bureaucracies. Of course, *in practice,* in the type of world we live in, going without developments of this systemic sort runs the risk not of incoherence, but of impotence, of being dominated and exploited by others in ways that undermine a population's well-being even more than would likely result from undertaking the transformation in question. Obviously, the choices a society faces are quite different if it is situated (today) in a nexus of neoliberal globalization dominated by great—formerly imperial—powers or, as some hope (one day), in a more law-governed, democratic, egalitarian, cosmopolitan world order.

A crucial feature, then, of disagreements regarding the role either cultural or societal innovations should play in the life of a society is that they cannot be decided simply by arguing that a certain transformation represents a developmental advance, either of "rational capacity" or of "adaptive capacity." Once the demands of theodicy and teleology are stripped from developmental schemes, such advances no longer carry the imprimatur of divine Providence, ends of nature, or even the cunning of reason. The "perfection of species capacities," for its own sake, no longer serves, as it did for Kant and most of his successors, as an ultimate sanction of historical developments, no matter how bloody. The issues under discussion in practical discourses about the desirability of adopting specific innovations have directly to do not with species perfection, but with what we judge to be in the best interests of everyone affected by those changes, including those not yet born who will have to live with the consequences of our decisions. In practice, these sorts of discussions unavoidably implicate the different values, goods, and identities of those involved, and thus can often be brought to a conclusion only through negotiation, compromise, accommodation, voting or the like—that is, through something short of consensus. Of course, one has to keep in mind that developmental advances are deemed to be such because of the enhanced capacity they bring to deal with certain ranges of real problems. And improving our ability to cope with the world bears directly on our pursuit of well-being, at least under most interpretations thereof. So judgments concerning the social development of adaptive capacities are by no means irrelevant to practical discourse, but neither are they decisive. On the other hand, cultural developments as such, in contrast to particular institutionalizations of them, normally can be decided against only by deciding for a closed society in which threats to established views from that quarter are forcibly excluded or repressed. Those who have understood the cultural developments will usually find any defense of such a society that rests on incomprehension of them unpersuasive and any defense of it that draws on them sinister.

I have been writing as if cultural and societal developments belong to two different orders of reality. But that is merely an analytical distinction and it can take us only so far. In reality, societal structures are anchored in cultural lifeworlds, and cultural practices are shaped by institutional forces. This interdependence becomes crucial to the discourse of modernization because, as we well know, structural changes have cultural presuppositions, so that if they are externally imposed or hastily adopted they often disintegrate or transmute; and they entail significant, unforeseen and often unwanted cultural side effects. On the other hand, cultural modernization can make certain traditional institutions unsustainable, at least in their traditional forms, and may make certain modern institutions unavoidable. Habermas argues that this last is the case with the democratic constitutional state—that is, that modern subjects formed in modern cultures will eventually demand basic legal protections and rights, including rights of political participation, and will increasingly refuse legitimacy to governments that deny them. In this and like cases, cultural learning and societal problemsolving converge on the same institutional changes, which reflect enhanced "rational capacity" and "adaptive capacity" at once. Consequently, they can be defended as developmental advances, as superior to what came before, both normatively and functionally. Habermas argues projectively that this is also the case with cosmopolitanism—that it is the only rationally defensible and practically effective form of world order in a globalized modernity.

HABERMAS ON COSMOPOLITICAL JUSTICE

In adopting cosmopolitical justice as the practical standpoint from which to articulate his general narrative of human development, Habermas clearly moves closer to Kant than to Hegel or Marx. Recall that for Kant the ideal of systematic unity among human beings with diverse, often conflicting interests has the form of a civil union under a rule of law that permits the greatest individual freedom compatible with a like freedom for all. By the same logic, the coexistence of the freedom of one independent state with a like freedom for all others is possible for him only under a rule of enforceable law governing relations between them. Thus practical reason requires not only that individuals abandon the lawless state of nature and enter into a law-governed commonwealth, but also that individual nations, in their external relations, "abandon a lawless state of savagery and enter into a federation of peoples in which every state, even the smallest, could expect to derive its security and right."[10] This not an empty ideal of practical reason, Kant maintained, for historical developments increasingly push us in that direction. Cultural developments, in particular, play a key role, leading to an expansion of mutual understanding across national barriers and growing agreement on basic principles. Nevertheless, Kant conceded that in his time the idea of a global civil union was impracticable and could best be approximated by a voluntary, revocable, league of nations under a law of peoples. In the meantime, the unprecedented slaughter of the twentieth century has made a mockery of even his weak faith in the capacity of classical international law and interstate treaties to preserve global peace; furthermore, the chief theoretical and practical alternative to these failed measures remains some stronger version of the legal pacifism projected in his cosmopolitan ideal. In any case, that is the practical hope animating Habermas's grand metanarrative of development.

Of course, Habermas has revised Kant's eighteenth-century understanding of that ideal to incorporate the democratic, social, and cultural concerns that have animated political struggles in the nineteenth and twentieth centuries. Thus his conception of cosmopolitical justice thematizes not only civil rights but also transnational forms of democratic participation, economic redistribution, and cultural recognition.[11] What I want to emphasize here, however, are his efforts—different from but parallel to Dallmayr's—to displace the monocultural universalism underlying Kant's construction of the cosmopolitan ideal by a multicultural universalism more sensitive to the dialectic of the universal and the particular mentioned above. The key to that displacement is recognition of the ways in which the interests, goods, values, identities, and the like embedded in different cultural contexts inextricably figure in legal and political discourse. "Law," Habermas writes, "serves as a medium for the self-organization of legal communities that maintain themselves in their social environments under particular historical conditions." As a result, "the facticity of the existing context cannot be eliminated."[12] And it is not only statutory law that is pervaded with particularity: constitutional undertakings to spell out the basic principles of government and the basic rights of citizens also express the particular cultural backgrounds and historical circumstances of founding generations. Though Habermas expressly regards basic human rights as an idea of practical-political reason that should guide every constitution-framing process, he is equally clear that any actually existing system of rights is, and can only be, a situated interpretation of that idea. "No one can credit herself with access to the system of rights in the singular, independent of the interpretations she already has historically available. 'The' system of rights does not exist in transcendental purity."[13] Furthermore, "every constitution is a living project that can endure only as an ongoing interpretation continually carried forth at all levels of the production of law."[14] And this "ongoing interpretation" is in practice an ongoing conflict of interpretations.

Even these few sketchy remarks should serve to make clear that for Habermas the rule of law in a democratic constitutional state is not a fixed essence, but an idea that has to be actualized in and through being variously interpreted and embodied in historically and culturally diverse constitutional projects. Accordingly, what he calls "constitutional patriotism" is construed broadly as allegiance to a particular constitutional tradition—that is, to a particular, ongoing, historical project of creating and renewing an association of free and equal citizens under a democratic rule of law. And if that project is itself to include space for a pluralism of worldviews and forms of life, as Habermas argues it must, then constitutional patriotism may not be wedded to monocultural or hegemonic-cultural interpretations of basic rights and principles to the exclusion, repression, or marginalization of minority perspectives. This means, of course, that we must understand the core of a constitutional tradition dynamically and dialogically—as an ongoing, legally institutionalized conflict of interpretations of basic rights and principles, procedures and practices, values and institutions. Inasmuch as these interpretations purport to be of the same constitutional tradition, and inasmuch as their proponents are and wish to remain members of the same political community, the ongoing accomplishment of sufficiently widespread agreement, for all practical purposes, concerning how persistent disagreements may be legitimately settled, at least for the time being, also seems to belong to that core.

Extending this model to the global level obviously makes these ongoing accomplishments all the more difficult. Habermas's cosmopolitan ideal calls for embodying the "same" system of basic rights in a diversity of politico-cultural settings; and that evidently raises familiar questions concerning the possibilities and limits of transcultural understanding and justification of human rights. To deal with such questions, John Rawls has famously introduced the idea of an "overlapping consensus" on a law of peoples among political societies of widely different political cultures—liberal and nonliberal, democratic and nondemocratic, egalitarian and hierarchical, secular and religious.[15] Habermas's cosmopolitan ideal does not allow for as broad a scope of variation among political cultures; it makes cosmopolitan justice turn on institutionalizing at a global level a generalized version of the same rights and principles already variously institutionalized in national constitutional traditions. Thus it requires a greater degree of convergence among legal and political cultures than does Rawls's approach, or Dallmayr's, even if one allows for the processual, practical, and situated character of negotiating cross-cultural agreements. It is in part to underwrite this possibility that Habermas propounds his general account of cultural and societal development as interconnected "rationalization processes." The positive import of the constraints thereby placed on "alternative modernities" is that the idea of a global rule of law is not as hopelessly impracticable as it might otherwise seem. Of course, it would require further developing and strengthening the cultural and institutional conditions for multicultural cosmopolitical discourse. And it would also—and especially—require leveling down the massive asymmetries in the global networks of power within which cross-cultural encounters are now situated. For all of this, developmental theory can offer no more than what Kant called a "rational hope."

The Struggle over the Universal

This conception of universal history is descended from Kant by way of Marx and a tradition of social theory infused with a peculiarly modern time consciousness. The present is understood to be weighted with the past and charged with the future, and social theory to be the meeting place of historical and utopian thought.[16] The past is no longer viewed as exemplary; the future is hoped to be better; and the present is seen as the point of possible transition from the one to the other. Thus, the theory of the present has somehow to fuse empirical-historical and political-emancipatory impulses, with each informing and limiting the other. Already in Kant, the interpretation of history from the perspective of human development had to be consistent with the findings of empirical research. Reflective judgment did not replace or override determinative judgment, but complemented and completed it. And Marx, of course, had nothing but contempt for *merely* utopian thinking. The subsequent renunciation of Marx's scientism by Western Marxists did not mean a return to utopianism; the possibilities for different futures had somehow to be seen as inherent in the historical process itself, that is, as "realistic" utopias. Habermas comes out of this tradition of interrelating theory and practice. Hence in exploring the emancipatory potentials of the present, he is concerned to draw on whatever empirical resources are available to ascertain, so far as possible, "objective" conditions, constraints, tendencies, and possibilities. Of course, appeals to realism, objectivity, and the like are under clouds of suspicion today. But they cannot be simply dumped if we want our epistemic, moral, and political judgments to make any sense at all. Rather, they have to be ongoingly reconstructed to take account of reflective critiques of received notions. I cannot defend that view here.[17] I shall merely suggest, by way of concluding, some ways in which our understanding of "objective constraints," "objective possibilities," and the like have come to differ from that of Kant, who understood objectivity in terms of validity for "consciousness in general."

Habermas has "socialized" Kant's approach in terms of his discourse theory, so that validity is tied to what could be rationally agreed to in unrestricted discourse. In the present context, this means that the testing, vindication, and rejection of claims to objectivity, universal validity, developmental superiority, and the like would have to transpire in and through universal, transcultural discourse. In fact, this applies reflexively to Habermas's own theory of communicative reason in all it parts, including his conception of validity itself. That is to say, it follows from the discourse theory of validity that it must itself be reflexively endorsed by participants in universal discourse. Of course, for that to happen, someone has first to propose and defend it *as* universally valid. Claiming validity in this way is what gets and keeps the dialectic moving, and the course the latter takes often involves an ongoing transformation of the very claims and conceptions being defended. What we have to do with here is a kind of struggle over the universal, to borrow an apt phrase from Judith Butler.[18] This kind of struggle cannot simply renounce universality, for that is what orients and structures it.

Even if this is granted in general, however, there are a number of problems specific to Habermas's approach that would require some reworking. To begin with, there is the ineradicable interpretive dimension of social and historical inquiry, stressed by Dallmayr, which makes the pursuit of objectivity there importantly different from in the natural sciences. In the absence of a general theory on which a consensus has formed within and among the relevant communities of inquiry in the human studies, the languages, and hence the facts—not to mention the general "laws"—of the human "sciences" are up for discussion. If realistic emancipatory theories have to incorporate knowledge of the general character of the social systems to which they are meant to apply, they cannot avoid getting involved in the sorts of conflict of interpretation that have marked social and political theory in the modern period. Moreover, as Dallmayr has repeatedly emphasized, interpretive approaches do not hold out the promise of a "view from nowhere," even in the qualified sense that this might be said of the natural sciences. The perspectives on the social world they offer always reflect the "somewhere," the hermeneutic situation of the interpreter. And because interpretive situations are themselves located in the stream of historical life, they bring with them evaluative as well as cognitive presuppositions. This means that our objective knowledge of the social world is value-laden in a stronger sense than is our objective knowledge of the natural world, for it reflects not only the epistemic values of a particular mode of rational inquiry, but also, and unavoidably, the values of the sociocultural locations from which it is pursued. And this suggests that claims to objectivity will also have to be defended on normative and evaluative as well as on more narrowly cognitive grounds.

Habermas is optimistic about objectivity in the restricted sphere of "morality" proper, which he privileges, but he recognizes that in the sphere of what he calls "ethics," which Dallmayr privileges, questions involving competing goods, values, identities, and the like do not admit of universal answers.[19] I have argued elsewhere that in law and politics, considerations of morality and ethics—of the right and the good—are inextricably entwined and thus that justice claims are susceptible to contestation from many of the same angles as interpretive and evaluative claims generally.[20] All of this could be summed up by saying that Habermas's theory of communicative action, with its prominent developmental component, is best understood as a *general interpretive framework* used to construct critical histories of the present, especially of capitalist modernization with its vast consequences for traditional societies—rather like Marx's historical materialism and Weber's theory of rationalization. As such, the space for reasonable disagreement it allows—no matter how "saturated" it may be with empirical findings—is more extensive and multidimensional than in the sciences of nature. This is true, in particular, for claims regarding objective constraints and possibilities, conditions and consequences. As we know very well, from policy debates for instance, such claims are strongly influenced by interpretive and evaluative standpoints that reflect political commitments; and they also involve political will, so that judgments of impossibility may be expressions of an unwillingness to take action. To acknowledge this is not, in my view, to say that there are no better and worse arguments in this area, but only that, *pace* Habermas, there will often be no single right answer.[21]

There is another host of problems attending specifically to developmental-logical claims. For one thing, at a critical-reflective level of discourse, developmental claims are a peculiarly blunt instrument with which to settle cultural disagreements. The presumed asymmetry between the developmental theorist's reflective grasp of historical cultures and the prereflective understandings of their members breaks down here. In the discourse of (post)-modernity all participants are in principle operating at the same discursive level, which means that any culture talked about is in a position to talk back—for instance, to argue with the theorist about his or her own presuppositions, procedures, standards, assessments, and so forth. In short, discursive symmetry makes any cross-cultural epistemic or evaluative assumptions essentially contestable. One thing that may well be subject to disagreement is whether a declared endpoint of development—or "end of history"—is really such or is, instead, still in need of *Aufhebung*—for instance, whether the dominant Western understandings of human rights are overly individualized and in need of rebalancing with concerns for the common good. Furthermore, even when there is more or less general agreement that a certain development is an improvement on what came before, the structural features that characterize it in developmental-logical terms will typically be of such a general and abstract nature as to allow for an indeterminate variety of concrete realizations. All of this already holds true of debates about development within Western cultures; and the considerable displacements of scholarly common sense already brought about by postcolonial theorists make clear that the transcultural expansion of discourse about development will induce yet greater dialectical movement into all "fixed, fast-frozen relations" unable to withstand critical scrutiny.

Approached in this way, universalism does not become superfluous after multiculturalism; it becomes rather an ongoing struggle over the universals we have to bring into play in structuring our common lives, an ongoing contestation and negotiation of their practical meanings and political contents. Establishing common ground in and through cross-cultural dialogue is essential for constructing the kind of cosmopolitan order that would offer an alternative to the current neoliberal desolation of entire geographic regions, economic sectors, and "superfluous" populations. And in multicultural, cosmopolitan discourse, the rule is mutual learning rather than learning on one side and assimilation on the other, as was generally taken to be the rule in monocultural, imperialist discourse. As the "objects" of the latter discourse increasingly become the subjects of the former, the universal audience ideally projected by claims to justice more and more assumes cultural reality in our global public sphere. And one may hope, along with Fred Dallmayr, that this growing global civic culture will contribute to building a cosmopolitan democracy "from below" that can contain and transform the globalization "from above" imposed by colonial and neocolonial domination.[22] This is, at least, one form that Kant's idea for a universal history from a cosmopolitan point of view may take today.

Notes

1. *Understanding and Social Inquiry* (Notre Dame, Ind.: University of Notre Dame Press, 1977). The notions of "reasonable disagreement," "overlapping consensus," and (below) "comprehensive doctrines" are, of course, borrowed (loosely) from John Rawls.

2. See Fred Dallmayr, *Beyond Orientalism* (New York: SUNY Press, 1996); *Alternative Visions: Paths in the Global Village* (Lanham, Md.: Rowman and Littlefield, 1998); and *Achieving Our World: Toward a Global and Plural Democracy* (Lanham, Md.: Rowman and Littlefield, 2001). In this essay I refer especially to the last work.

3. See Sankar Muthu, *Enlightenment against Empire* (Princeton: Princeton University Press, 2003).

4. G. W. F. Hegel, *Lectures on the Philosophy of World History: Introduction*, trans. H. B. Nisbet (Cambridge: Cambridge University Press, 1993), pp. 27–28.

5. Karl Marx, *The German Ideology,* in *The Marx–Engels Reader,* ed. Robert C. Tucker (New York: Norton, 1978), pp. 146–200, at p. 158.

6. Ibid., p. 155.

7. Jürgen Habermas, *Between Facts and Norms,* trans. W. Rehg (Cambridge: MIT Press, 1996), chaps. 1–3.

8. Jürgen Habermas, "Remarks on Legitimation through Human Rights," in Habermas, *The Postnational Constellation,* ed. and trans. Max Pensky (Cambridge: MIT Press, 2001), pp. 113–29, at p. 124.

9. See, e.g., his "Two Theories of Modernity," in *Alternative Modernities,* ed. D. P. Gaonkar (Durham: Duke University Press, 2001), pp. 172–96; and my comments thereupon, "On Reconciling Cosmopolitan Unity and National Diversity," in ibid., pp. 197–235, esp. pp. 227–35.

10. Immanuel Kant, "Idea for a Universal History with a Cosmopolitan Purpose," in *Kant: Political Writings,* ed. H. Reiss, trans. H. B. Nisbet (Cambridge: Cambridge University Press, 1991), pp. 41–53, at p. 47.

11. See, e.g., Habermas, *The Postnational Constellation.* In these respects, Habermas comes closer to the view of human rights that Dallmayr articulates in chapter 3 of *Achieving Our World,* where he criticizes the near exclusive concern with individual civil and political liberties in Western human-rights discourse and calls for a shift of emphasis in the direction of the social and economic, cultural, and collective rights required to protect underprivileged groups and populations from the depredations of neoliberal globalization. I suspect, however, that Dallmayr would go further with cultural and collective rights than would Habermas.

12. Habermas, *Between Facts and Norms,* pp. 151, 156.

13. Ibid., p. 129.

14. Ibid.

15. John Rawls, *The Law of Peoples* (Cambridge: Harvard University Press, 1999).

16. See Jürgen Habermas, "The New Obscurity," in Habermas, *The New Conservatism,* ed. and trans. S. Weber Nicholsen (Cambridge: MIT Press, 1989), pp. 48–70.

17. I have done so in part 1 of David Hoy and Thomas McCarthy, *Critical Theory* (Oxford: Blackwell, 1994).

18. See her *Excitable Speech* (New York: Routledge, 1997), p. 89.

19. See his "On the Pragmatic, the Ethical, and the Moral Employments of Practical Reason," in Habermas, *Justification and Application,* trans. C. Cronin (Cambridge: MIT Press, 1993), pp. 1–17.

20. See my "Practical Discourse: On the Relation of Morality to Politics," in McCarthy, *Ideals and Illusions* (Cambridge: MIT Press, 1991), pp. 181–99.

21. See my "Legitimacy and Diversity," in *Habermas on Law and Democracy: Critical Exchanges,* ed. M. Rosenfeld and A. Arato (Berkeley: University of California Press, 1998), pp. 115–53; and see Habermas's "Reply," pp. 390–404 of the same volume.

22. See chapter 2 of Dallmayr, *Achieving Our World.*

The Other Politics: Anthropocentrism, Power, Nihilation

Krzysztof Ziarek

The knowledge of the men of old reached the ultimate height. What was the ultimate height of knowledge? They recognized that nothing but nothing existed.

Chuang-tse

It somehow seems a misnomer to call Fred Dallmayr's work "political theory" or "political philosophy." Clearly his thought belongs to, and yet also explicitly questions, these fields of study, with their particular commitments to specific precepts of theorizing politics and their investment in various modes of philosophical reflection. What is striking and challenging about Dallmayr's approach to "political thought," or, more precisely, to the thought *of* politics, is his characteristic interest in elucidating how the very happening of being becomes political—how it both clears the space and provides the framework for what is customarily understood as politics: namely, political action and policymaking.

Reaching thus beyond both political theory and political philosophy, without surrendering their critical insights or ceding their importance, Dallmayr's thought engages the "workings" of politics in terms of different historical and cultural modes or ways of being. It is his affinity with Martin Heidegger's questioning of being, especially the concern with the political dimensions of the finite human being-in-the-world, that has made Dallmayr's thought, despite our belonging to different and often dissociated academic locales, interesting and important to me. And this has been the case since my initial encounter with Dallmayr's *Polis and Praxis* even before I had the privilege of becoming his colleague at the University of Notre Dame, and then later during the growing admiration for the breadth, thoughtfulness, and originality of Fred's more recent work, from *The Other Heidegger* to *Beyond Orientalism* and *Alternative Visions*. One of the key issues Dallmayr examines in *Beyond Orientalism* is the relation between Heidegger—and his undoing of the metaphysical tradition of the West—and Eastern thought: Indian, Buddhist, and Zen Buddhist, together with the possible implications of such an encounter for political issues in the epoch of globalization. Among a plethora of innovative ideas about a different approach to politics "between" East and West, what this dialogue makes possible is the realization of Heidegger's increasing proximity, especially in his later thought, to Eastern thinking, especially to two key notions in Eastern thought: nothingness and emptiness.[1]

Within this broader context, the remarks that follow are both prompted by and indebted to Dallmayr's innovative and rigorous thinking of a post-Heideggerian encounter with the East "beyond orientalism." This encounter, which does not mean to efface or gloss over the differences between these traditions, or to assimilate Eastern thought into European philosophy, must be carefully analyzed in relation to such key Heideggerian terms as "the event," "letting be," "*Ab-grund*," "nihilation," and "emptiness." Beyond these terminological proximities, and beyond what might appear to be merely "superficial" similarities between Heidegger's work and Eastern thinking, what renders Heidegger's thought indeed close to Eastern philosophies is its unprecedented de-anthropocentrization, even de-anthropization, of thinking and of the event. It is this specific, nonanthropic vector of Heidegger's thinking that I explore in this essay.

What Comes after "Man," or the *Entmenschung* of Thought

The attempt to refashion thinking in a nonmetaphysical and nonanthropocentric (even nonanthropic) manner—Heidegger refers to it as the *Entmenschung*—remains the most challenging and least understood aspect of Heidegger's work,[2] one that is particularly difficult to grapple with in the context of politics and political thought. This difficulty is partially due to the fact that the nonanthropocentric view demands that we look at politics not from within the broad context of human affairs and their influences on the world around us, but that we critically shift perspectives and resituate human affairs, along with ethics and politics, vis-à-vis the happening of being, thus giving the primacy of consideration to the historico-temporal character of its event. Assigning importance to being's event (*das Ereignis*) does not entail, however, ethical and historical indifference or political quietism, but implies instead a rethinking of the human, and with it of the political, from the nonanthropic vantage point of the event's nihilation, taken here to mean the abyssal (*abgründig*) emptiness of the spacing-temporalizing of history. In other words, through the prism of being one begins to think politics nonanthropocentrically, which implies starting not from social relations but from *Dasein*'s relation to the nihilating event of being.

Heidegger's recurrent use of the phrase "the other beginning" indicates in this context not simply a new way of doing politics or a different manner of political thought, and certainly not a novel political formation/regime, but a more radical and disquieting call to "begin" politics otherwise—that is, from the event of being and the human place within it. "Within" here is of crucial importance, as it implies ceding the "priority" to the event itself and enveloping human affairs from the start within the nonanthropic "sense" (*Sinn* in Heidegger's discourse) of being's history. What this implies is that not only should "human affairs" refrain from imposing their meaning onto being but that, conversely, their own sense should come from the "inhuman," nonanthropic happening of being. One could see this as indeed a "non-Western" and a nonmetaphysical manner of thinking, which strips the human of its priority and centrality in order to unconceal a different mode of being for the human, namely, *Da-sein,* or "being-there." The difference marked by *Dasein* lies in the fact that "being-there" always already responds to and concerns itself with being, *before,* as it were, attending to and construing its own being metaphysically in such terms as *anthropos,* "man," "the human." To begin politics otherwise would amount here to rethinking and critiquing politics and social relations through a cluster of nonmetaphysical and nonanthropocentric terms: the event, the *Ab-grund* (abyss), nihilation, letting be.

In this "politics," if one can still use the term here, what "comes first," as it were, is the issue of how being comes to happen. Of course, being for Heidegger is not a disembodied idea or an abstract category, but the spatio-temporalization of history, understood as the always "concrete" and "singular" occurrence of what comes to be through its ground-free—that is to say, futural and open—happening. Such a politics entails keeping constantly in play the nonanthropic—"other" and "foreign"—"sense" of being's event. And this "sense" is not a meaning at all, but rather the force of nihilation, the emptying openness of history's spatio-temporal play.

If given its due, this call to decenter man, to "dishumanize" (*entmenschen*) thinking and the world, is what is truly difficult, indeed "foreign," in Heidegger's work from the late 1930s and 1940s. It also, unfortunately, has produced numerous misreadings of Heideggerian thought as antihumanist, relativist, or mystical. When I write "dishumanizing," I want to avoid the mistaken connotations of dehumanization, readily associated with the degrading of the human. *Entmenschung* not only does not "devalue" humans but, on the contrary, for Heidegger, it unconceals their being as *Da-sein,* thus finally giving their due to the temporality, historicity, and finitude constitutive of *Dasein's* existence. In the context of Heidegger's insistence on the critical *Entmenschung* and the "uncovering" of *Dasein,* it is not enough, as has been the practice in much postmodern thought, to decenter the subject, that is, to think the "(post)subject" as fractured or split, or to see such a "posthumanist" subject in terms of the larger context of power relations operating in society. In such thinking, the anthropic still persists, whether as a split/decentered subject or as the effect of the differential unfolding of power relations.

No doubt important revisions happen as a result of such a transformation of perspectives, yet, in the context of Heidegger's claim, these changes do not go far enough insofar as they do not perform the *Entmenschung* of thought and being, and do not dispense with the residues of anthropism: "That *Being and Time* aims to do away with man and his priority in philosophy, and give its due simply to the happening of being, that with *Da-sein* it is not only the subjectivity of man but the role of man that is shattered, will be one day realized."[3] It is true that in postmodernism the subject is "split" and decentered, that it is thought of as an effect rather than an origin or a foundation, yet these revisions do not necessarily question the prevalent framework in which the anthropic remains at the center of things, where humans and their relations have priority and count the most. Despite the claims made by postmodern philosophy to its no-longer metaphysical character and ways of thinking, what often belies these statements—with exceptions, for instance, in the thought of Jean-François Lyotard, Gilles Deleuze, Jacques Derrida, or

Michel Foucault—is the recurrent centrality of the anthropic even if concealed under the proliferating analyses of culture, capital, and technology.
While ways of thinking difference, otherness, or identity have no doubt undergone radical reevaluation and politically and ethically crucial refashion-
ing, these momentous and innovative insights retain a certain anthropism
that continues to place everything within the human perspective, as is evident, for instance, in the recent wave of postmodern scholarship on ethics.[4]

What, by contrast, is quite "foreign" about Heidegger's thought is that
the transformation of the subject into *Dasein* is only a prelude to opening up,
through *Da-sein,* the thought/concern with being. Concern with being is
"originary," which means that, as *Dasein,* humans are always already concerned with being, with how being occurs, and, more specifically, with
whether it occurs as en event whose nihilating force is heeded and "watched
over," thus making it possible to keep in view the abyssal emptiness of the
spatio-temporalizing of history as the strange "ground" that stays away from
grounding (the *Ab-grund*). To perhaps oversimplify the point, the originary
concern is not with the well-being of man but with the event of being. Still
thinking metaphysically in terms of value, one would say that being here becomes more important than "man." More fittingly for the context of Heidegger's thought, being as event is more real—literally, "more in being"
(*seiender*)—than any being or entity, including humans. This is why being-
there (*Da-sein*) indicates the site where being is no longer anthropic but instead emerges as the originary concern of *Da-sein.* "Originary" here does not
signify foundational or grounding, but marks the temporal leap that in each
and every moment has always already opened *Dasein* as a relation (that is, as
Da-sein) to being. Human responsibility comes from and is bound to the
event of being, for, as *Being and Time* would have it, in their being, or rather
in "there-being" (*Da-sein*), humans are first and foremost "concerned" with
being, that is, with keeping in view—which entails also keeping their actions
in view of—the nihilation of the spatio-temporal unfolding of history. The
concern here is precisely with temporality and historicity, which in their critically emptying and futural force become determinative of all aspects of being,
including interhuman, social, and political relations.

Being-there (*Da-sein*)—keeping humans in view of the nihilation intrinsic to being—does not mean forgetting or neglecting human beings, social relations, ethics, or politics, as is often all too hastily and mistakenly
asserted about Heideggerian thought. Rather, it means a transformation of

what ethics, politics, and the human "mean" within a nonanthropic perspective. This transformation involves a decisive de-anthropomorphizing (*Entmenschung*) of humans into *Da-sein*, and thus a parallel *Entmenschung* also of ethics and politics. For Western thought, this is a staggering demand, a deeply disquieting call—as it should be, given the West's metaphysical underpinnings—to the still, and perhaps more than ever, anthropocentrically oriented Western culture. This Heideggerian call to thinking being historically, and thus nonanthopocentrically, is so disquieting because it is indeed "other"—foreign and alien—to Western thinking and its metaphysical horizons. This is why for the West this has always been the most suspicious, perhaps even dangerous and "escapist," aspect of Heideggerian thought. For the East, however, it has been the most promising opening for an Eastern–Western dialogue "beyond orientalism," as Dallmayr puts it. And it has been promising precisely by virtue of its deliberate otherness and foreignness within Western thought, because of its "alien" attempt to begin to think "otherwise" than anthropocentrically and metaphysically. Even, as was the case with the Kyoto school and its aftermath, this otherness opening Western thought from within provided an opportunity to reengage and rethink the Buddhist heritage of Eastern thought in the context of Heidegger's "destruction" of metaphysics.

The Heideggerian "destruction" is indeed an astonishing claim put on thinking: a call to *entmenschen,* to "disman" or "dishumanize" thought, being, history, and humanity too, and thus to release them from the overbearing and manipulative grasp of human categories, representations, and values. The "other" in Heidegger's phrase "the other beginning" does not mean simply another or a different beginning, but a beginning that is indeed other—foreign, alien, strange—by virtue of its nonmetaphysical and nonanthropic character. It is important to keep in mind here that Heidegger sees metaphysics as a thorough and totalizing *Vermenschung* (anthropomorphization) of all aspects of being: not only of beings but also of space, time, history, thought. It amounts also, and perhaps most significantly, to concealing *Dasein* as the "being-there" constitutive of human existence. This concealment leads to (mis)representing and solidifying *Dasein*—which refers to a happening and a relation (to being), that unfolds as part of being's event—as a (human) entity, self, or person. It forgets the abyssal happening of the event and its occurrence away from grounding, and construes human existence in relation to grounds, foundations, origins, reasons, meanings, and values.

Perhaps the main reason why this "dishumanizing" impetus of Heidegger's thought is so frequently misunderstood is because nihilation, crucial to his critique of metaphysics, is still thought of in a predominantly negative fashion. Within metaphysics, nihilation appears as nothing—and evokes nihilism—or as negation and the negative. What is "other" and "foreign" to Western thought, and what consequently renders Heidegger's work "strange" within the metaphysical tradition, is his thinking of nihilation not as negating or canceling, or even as castrating, but instead as a critical enabling. As Heidegger remarks in *Besinnung*, "The nothing is neither negation of beings nor that of beingness [*Seiendheit*], nor is it the 'privation' of being, its deprivation, which would also be annihilation, but *the nothing is the first and the highest gift of being.*"[5] In *Beiträge zur Philosophie*, he writes about nihilation as a concealed gift of being.[6] This gift is being itself, which, sending itself as event (*Ereignis*), constitutes the peculiar origin (*Ursprung*) that happens as an abyss (*Ab-grund*), characterized by its staying away from grounding. And it is concealed precisely because nihilation becomes covered over and forgotten under the "negative" connotations of negation, negativity, or worse, nihilism.

Heidegger decisively refashions nihilation away from the connotations of negativity or nihilism, seeing in it an enabling force of the "abyss" (*Ab-grund*) of being. As he puts it in *Geschichte des Seyns:* "Being is nothing / Nothing nihilates / Nihilation refuses / The refusal guards."[7] Since what it declines is power with its grasping and manipulative impetus, nihilation can, therefore, be said to desist from making, effecting, or producing. And what this refusal of making and power guards is the clearing of the in-between of spacing and temporalization. In other words, nihilation keeps opening the space-time of history, nihilating beings not into nothing understood as absence, lack, or emptiness, but into the event that happens as the spatio-temporalization of history. Despite its enabling force, nihilation becomes disfigured into negativity by the "improper" or "inauthentic," as Heidegger would say, grasping of beings in terms of "solid" and manipulable entities and categories. However, seen differently in the context of historicity and finitude, nihilation enables beings to be more in being (*seiender*), that is, more as historico-temporal happenings than as fixed or stable entities. As such an enabling, nihilation is not only intrinsic to being but constitutes its "gift," because it releases beings into their event-like occurrence, thus giving them back their proper temporality and groundless existence. Through this strange enabling, nihilation "guards" the historicity of being from disappearance into the seemingly solid and enduring forms of beings, things, and objects. It keeps beings open and transformable in relation to their intrinsically histori- cal and temporal happening, a happening that "grounds" by not admitting any grounds, essentializations, or objectifications.

By completely transforming the notion of grounding from foundation- alism to "grounding" as *Ab-grund*—as no*thing*—nihilation enables an open- ing toward otherness, an openness that is ceaselessly reopened by the very happening of the event. As Heidegger writes in *Contributions to Philosophy*, happening as nihilation, being enables and enforces otherness.[8] This other- ness enabled by nihilation cannot be subsumed into negation or opposition, but marks instead the differentiation intrinsic to the event. This differentian is grounded not in difference but in the futurity kept open by nihilation. Fur- thermore, otherness here is not a matter of identity and difference, since it is inscribed not just on the ontic level of beings and entites, but on the level of the ontological. In short, otherness is there not because there are differences but, rather, there are differences because otherness is enabled and "enforced" by the very mode in which being happens, that is, by its event. Since other- ness is intrinsic to the happening of being, it happens beyond both negation and positing, beyond representation, sublation, erasure, or exclusion. What makes this otherness so resistant to closure is the fact that it is enabled by the nihilation intrinsic to being and as such remains nondialectical without being either immediate or indeterminate.

The spatio-temporal happening here called "nihilation" eludes both di- alectical terms and historicist explanations. This is the case because the emp- tiness characteristic of the event, without ever becoming a positivity, is not something negative or a nothing. Rather, it is nothingness seen as nihilation, as emptiness that is futural and transformative. Nihilating and emptying the notions of self, identity, community, and the like, it brings into view the ra- dically temporal character of being and allows for a futural opening and transformation. The momentum of nihilation is "negative" only when it is (mis)perceived in a metaphysical way—that is, from the point of view of metaphysical concepts and constructs, from the vantage of thought that op- erates in terms of such concepts and within the boundaries prescribed by the very idea of conceptual thinking. For the nothing of nihilation is neither ne- gation nor bad infinity. Neither empty nor indeterminate, it indicates the way in which the event unfolds history as the emptying play of spacing and temporalization. In this specific sense, nihilation is beyond both dialectics, on the one hand, and positivism and historicism, on the other. This emptiness of the historical spatio-temporalizing enables transformation beyond the scope of changes and transitions possible within metaphysics. It also enables the transformation of the human into *Da-sein*, where "being-there" becomes a part, and more precisely a vector, of the event of being, without becoming its central moment or privileged point of reference. In the event, being is not referred "first" to the human; rather *Da-sein* is first "referred to" being. As *Da-sein*, the (no-longer) humans become part of the happening of being, which means that they keep in view the "sense" of being as nihilation, and think their place and role from within such nihilating history of being.

This reversal of perspectives on nihilation is what the Heideggerian "turning" (*Kehre*) signals. In other words, this turning is not just a change in Heidegger's way of thinking, a fork or a divergence from *Being and Time* to his later writings, but a turn from the anthropocentric beginning, where politics and ethics begin with the human being—human life, self, community, which, have always already assumed the "central" place[9]—to the other, foreign, nonanthropocentric beginning, where politics and ethics begin with nihilation and emptiness. Because of this reversal, ethics and politics cannot be concerned first with humans but only subsequently so, due to a realization of the narrow optics of this anthropocentric vision, amended by expansion beyond humanity, for instance, into ecoethics or ecopolitics. In the Heideggerian perspective, politics is always already a "politics of being." This means not an abstract politics of an empty, atemporal notion (of being), but a politics mindful of the nihilating vector of the event, that is, respectful of how nihilation disposes relations by emptying them, that is, opening them to the abyssal temporality of their futural happening.

It would be a fundamental misunderstanding of Heidegger's thought to suggest that this nonanthropic approach depreciates or devalues the human. It is not the case for Heidegger that the "human" is not a value, which would amount to antihumanism and would explain itself within metaphysics as an opposition to and a negation of humanism. In short, it would constitute a still metaphysical reevaluation, here a negative one (a negation), of the human as a value. Rather, for Heidegger the human is *Da-sein*, and such "being-there," because it is a ceaselessly singular temporal happening, cannot be restricted to or fixed and abstracted into values. The turning does not mean that being becomes a value higher than "man," which would result in a de-valuing/depreciation of the human—this would constitute a reading that leads to (mis)charging Heidegger's late thought with ethical and political in-difference.[10] For Heidegger, "to value" means to turn the happening of being into entities/values—to denihilate and disenable the event. One cannot value being or *Da-sein* not because they have no value, or are worthless, but be-cause valuing solidifies being and arrests the spatio-temporalizing of history, in effect concealing *Dasein*. In short, values dehistoricize being, disfiguring its nihilating occurrence into graspable, valuable, and thus manipulable "pieces": values, ideas, identities, deeds, objects—all possessions of "man" in the modern unfolding of being as power and machination.

To make the happening of being in terms of values would be to force it into a perspective where it would be seen as either something positive or as something negative. Within the perspective of value, nihilation can only ap-pear as negative, as the negation of or the opposition to what is positive. Since values operate in terms of presence, nihilation becomes equivalent to absence as the negative (value) of presence. As such, value covers over the enabling momentum of nihilation, distorting it into negativity and nothingness within the binary optics of presence/absence, or good/bad. This is why in the 1940s, Heidegger grows increasingly critical of Nietzsche, whose reevaluation of all values continues to operate within the metaphysical perspective of value, when in an anti-Platonic gesture it reverses the value of the sensible and the suprasensible. Nietzsche still thinks being as a value—as static, permanent, unchangeable—and thus devalues it vis-à-vis "becoming." Becoming is what is to be cherished, celebrated, and encouraged; it becomes the new value par excellence. Heidegger's critique shows how the reversal proposed by Nietz-sche not only fails to escape metaphysics, but in fact becomes its fulfillment by explicitly grasping being in terms of value, that is, as a negative value or a nonvalue.

In Heidegger's critique, value is part and parcel of the manipulative power characteristic of technological modernity. Making being, event, or *Da-sein* into a value, into the human, renders "being-there" unrecognizable to such an extent that *Dasein* no longer registers as a happening but becomes a being: a self, a subject, a person, or, more recently, a resource or a piece of data. This "valuation" anthropomorphizes *Da-sein*, turning its singular oc-currence as a relation to being, implied by the hyphen, into a "subject/person," and with this gesture performs a thorough *Vermenschung* of being: it instills the human into everything, effectively rendering all aspects of being anthropic. This *Vermenschung* constitutes the totalizing "making" or production of being in anthropic/anthropocentric terms. Heidegger's critique indicates that value thinking presupposes the ideas of "making/production/ power," as well as the notion of the human as essentially constituted in terms of production as producer, creator, maker, engineer, discoverer, and so forth. In short, "to produce is human." To be human means to produce (*Herstellen*) and to represent (*Vorstellen*); it means to enframe being and help turn it into the *Ge-stell,* which renders everything into part of the operations of power. To such a metaphysical slogan par excellence, Heidegger's work would juxtapose a way of thinking that could be characterized in the following way: "to think happens as *Da-sein.*" And such *Da-sein,* or being-there, is neither production, nor representation, nor power. This occurrence of *Dasein* as an alternative to the "existence" of man as a subject/producer cannot be measured in terms of gains, material, spiritual, or psychological well-being, power, rights, and so on, but should be seen as keeping open the enabling force of nihilation. Such occurrence would no longer be "human," strictly speaking; rather, it would involve a maintaining of "being-there," a deed in the "middle voice," which means a deed that happens as *Da-sein,* as the hyphen between being and the "there" of thinking. As a between, this "deed" is not a human doing or making, and it is not even at human disposal. This is why *Dasein* is not an agent but an occurrence, in which the human being participates—and in effect becomes this occurrence—through a specific way of letting it be. What allows "being-there" to happen, and thus transforms human being into *Dasein,* is the openness to nihilation and to its enabling force. Human participation is indispensable to nihilation because it is only through such an openness to nihilation that its enabling force can be released. In other words, by releasing nihilation from negativity into its enabling force, the "human" occurs as *Dasein.*

A Politics of Nihilation?

The nonmetaphysical, value-less mode of thinking that Heidegger attempts to initiate does not lead automatically to depreciating or putting aside politics, even though Heidegger himself distances his later thought from explicit political considerations. When Heidegger writes about "overcoming" metaphysics, he carefully makes clear that the overcoming does not mean leaving behind, putting aside, or depreciating. This is in part the case because Heideggerian thinking is not a value-thinking, and therefore it cannot either value or devalue metaphysics, together with the value-oriented thinking essential to it. It does, however, point to how value-thinking restricts and hardens being, forgetting the enabling and transformative momentum of nihilation. Metaphysics constitutes effectively a forgetting and thus a restricting of the nonanthropic perspective of nihilation to the optics of positing/negation and of presence/absence. Seen as human or world affairs, politics comes to be developed within this narrowed, metaphysical optics. Yet Heidegger's approach should not be misunderstood as dismissing this view of politics, but can instead be seen as making it possible to enfold this metaphysical perspective on politics, freedom, and action in a nonmetaphysical event, whose nihilating force would enable a transformation of the very idea of politics: no longer "just" a human affair, politics could become the matter of the *Stimmung,* that is, of the disposition, or "key," of relations, one which would enable them to transpire as power-free (*machtlos*). This Heideggerian move can be seen from two different angles: either as a de-anthropomorphization of the metaphysical perspective, or as a gesture of enfolding metaphysics within a "broader" perspective of being as event. Either way, it opens a new critical vantage point by immersing politics into nihilation.

In the dialectic of power and powerlessness operating within modern machination and manipulative power (*Machenschaft*), freedom comes to mean being free from oppression and injustice, and thus being empowered to act, create, and produce as a subject, a subject that is conceived as the subject of rights and freedoms. This approach presupposes the understanding of human being as a subject/person, that is, it involves the particular metaphysical machinery that renders the happening of being into discrete identities, which become, in the same gesture, both subjects (endowed with psychic life and rights) and objects (resources or data functioning as part of contemporary technicized social relations). For Heidegger, such a person/subject of rights has to be enveloped within another critical perspective, namely, the one of *Da-sein.* Happening as *Da-sein,* as being-there, the human is otherwise than a subject, and, therefore, freedom associated with the notion of subjectivity and communal existence must be rethought accordingly. From this new vantage point, freedom cannot be limited to a possession, property, or right of an individual or a communal subject, but pertains to how *Da-sein* occurs. Freedom is to be approached in terms of the between, of the hyphen spacing and holding together *Da* and *sein*. In short, freedom is to be thought on the "ontological" level, in terms of being and its event, not in terms of subjectivity, with its appropriately allocated properties and rights. Thought ontically, freedom becomes determined as a matter of the subject's "self-possession," empowerment, or control vis-à-vis social relations, operations of power, or state apparatus; but seen ontologically, it concerns the modality in which the relation of being-there takes place.

Again, this does not mean that, because of their ontic status, the problems of freedoms, rights, injustice, and oppression are no longer important, or that they become sidelined or dissolved into the supposed anonymity and neutrality of the happening of being. Rather, what Heidegger's questioning suggests is the immersion of these concerns into the perspective of the nihilating momentum of the event, and their consequent revision with regard to the emptying effect of the spatio-temporalization of history. What emerges into view within the nonanthropic perspective is the question—which constitutes the preeminent question in Heidegger's work of the late 1930s and into the 1940s—of how being unfolds and whether it becomes disposed into relations of power, with their correlative dialectic of power and powerlessness. In this context, freedom concerns not individual or collective subjectivities but the very modality in which being happens, the "key" or "pitch" (*Stimmung*) according to which relations become disposed. For in Heidegger's approach, how and as what beings or entities come to be, is determined (*bestimmt*) by the modality of relations in which beings participate and through which they acquire their standing in history. This modality is to be thought of as active, as a verb, not as a fixed or a static relation, which entails understanding freedom in terms of the key or the pitch of relations; how and what beings are—that is, whether they are free or not—depends on the modality of the relations through which these beings come to be constituted in their spatio-temporal existence. This is why, within the nonanthropic perspective of being as the event, freedom is first and foremost the question of the modality in which being happens.

For Heidegger, this question concerns primarily the problem of power, that is, the possibility that, when seen non-metaphysically, being's unfolding is not a matter of power: "In its essential ground, being is never power and, therefore, also never powerlessness. We call it the power-less (*das Macht-lose*), which does not mean that being lacks power; rather, the name indicates that being, in concert with its happening, remains disengaged, free from power."[11] Because being happens as *macht-los* or *macht-frei*—Heidegger uses both terms as equivalent to indicate power-free happening—it can never be rendered powerless (*entmachtet*). Rendering powerless is possible only within the "dialectic" of power and powerlessness. In other words, to be rendered powerless, one already has to be "power-ful," in the sense of existing within the purview of power and its multiple operations. To the extent that being becomes unbound or released from power, as the suffix *-los* indicates, it can neither be empowered nor made powerless, and this is the case because being, as the nihilating momentum of the event, remains disengaged—free from the diverse, positive and negative, investments of power.

Within metaphysics, freedom pertains to the question of the subject, and is consequently determined and shaped within the metaphysics of subjectivity. In the non-metaphysical perspective of being as the event, freedom becomes the "matter" of being, that is, of whether the very spatio-temporalizing of history remains disengaged from power. Freedom here entails letting being remain free from power, allowing it to unfold the way that it occurs, as Heidegger suggests, in accordance with its character as the event. This letting be is not passive, because it requires *Dasein* to allow nihilation to have an enabling force. Freedom thus becomes the question of whether and how *Dasein* occurs, of how being-there takes place in relation to the nihilation intrinsic to being. With regard to *Da-sein*, freedom must be seen in terms of the relation indicated by the hyphen, that is, of how being-in-the-world comports itself toward the unfolding of being, specifically, whether "being-there" occurs in such a way that the historical unfolding of the spatio-temporal play of being remains *macht-los*, that is, power-free, in its nihilating momentum. This is the case because nihilation means neither power nor powerlessness but, instead, the emptiness of the spatio-temporal expanse of being, which allows for a different modality of relations, not bound by power.

The nonanthropism of this approach consists in the shift of emphasis from subjectivity to the mode in which being occurs and according to which relations come to be disposed: freedom becomes the question of the "freedom of being." This freedom, however, is not to be construed as simply anonymous or neutral, because, when thought carefully, the freedom of being from power translates into the power-free disposition of relations, and, thus, of the power-free occurrence of beings within these relations. In other words, the freedom of being from power is the "origin" of the freedom of beings.

Again, this is to be conceived here prudently and in a very particular sense: to say that the freedom of beings (whether human or nonhuman) has its origin in being's disengagement from power, in its specific *Machtlosigkeit*, indicates that, as a power-free event, being gives power-free relations and thus secures the freedom of beings. Accordingly, freedom here means not simply freedom from injustice or oppression—without in any way depreciating their significance—but also freedom of the specific, power-free happening of being. In the same gesture, the freedom of being to happen as power-free does entail—that is, originate or spring into (in the sense of *Ursprung*)—power-free relations and, by the same token, power-free modes of being for the entities involved in them.

Because metaphysics operates in terms of power and of the *Ge-stell*—making (*machen*), representing (*vorstellen*), producing (*herstellen*)—it always already misrecognizes and distorts the power-free happening of being. As Heidegger remarks, power must always misrecognize the power-free[12] because its own perspective does not admit of anything that does not transpire or explain itself in terms of power. Within metaphysics, if something is not powerful, it has to be powerless, inactive, indifferent, without any force. Since within modern techno-metaphysics, power operates not simply as dominating or constraining but as primarily productive or creative, what is withdrawn from such essentially productive power, *das Macht-lose*, or the power-free, is "sensed" only as lack, as absence of power.[13] Even though one has to maintain a critical distinction between creative/productive power and power that dominates, manipulates, calculates, or orders, all these diverse operations effectuate power, and as such they all point—beyond the moralizing distinction between good and evil—to various facets of making or effecting. This is why it is this "effecting" character of power that needs to be transformed, and not just its dominating or oppressive operations that easily fall under the rubric of manipulation and machination. If we only criticize manipulation, we will not critique power as such, only some of its manifestations, still seen through the metaphysical prism of good and evil, of creative and manipulative/restrictive "effecting." This is the reason why the turning or *Kehre* Heidegger writes about would also have to involve a transformation of the essence of power: from producing and effecting to the middle voice of enabling, or in other words, from the metaphysical value of power as "making" (*Macht* as *machen*) to the nonmetaphysical "power" of nihilation that remains making-free and thus also power-free.[14]

To put this in the context of our discussion of nihilation, the nihilating momentum of the event does not, as it were, register metaphysically. What nihilation, understood as the enabling emptiness of the spatio-temporalizing of history, enables or lets be is precisely the power-free modality of relating. However, within the techno-metaphysical perspective of the modern West, such enabling is inevitably misrecognized as powerless, precisely because its mode of letting be—as a releasement from power—does not register within the spectrum of the operations of power, whether restrictive or creative, facilitating or oppressing. Within metaphysics and its complex operations of techno-power, the enabling force of nihilation becomes misrecognized as "nothing." For our metaphysical/technical eye, reality is constituted as actuality (*Wirklichkeit*), which entails that only what is understandable in terms of "effecting" (*Wirkung*) counts as real. As Heidegger suggests, power admits a being if and only when this being is makeable. Such "makeability" (*Machsamkeit*) consists in the fact that beings can be planned and calculated, and, when represented or made available through these specific ways of effecting, they remain producible and available at any time.[15] Only what can be (grasped as) made, produced, effected, actualized, and so forth, "really" exists. By the same token, only an action that is a species of power operating as a form of effecting—for example, making, creating, or manipulating—is real and recognized as activity.

In distinction from these various genres of effecting constitutive of the modern flows of power, nihilation "only" opens the spatio-temporalizing expanse of being, releasing its enabling and transformative emptiness. It does not create or effect the emptiness, only lets its force unfold and claim being. What follows is that nihilation, since it neither "effects" nor "produces," amounts to "nothing," that is, it is seen as inactive, ineffective, neutral, indifferent, and the like. Metaphysically speaking, emptiness is not an enabling clearing of the spacing and temporalizing event that unfolds as history, but a blankness, a void, and a nothingness. Both nihilation and emptiness get read negatively, since metaphysics can only read in positive or negative terms. Nihilation cancels, annuls, negates, voids, abolishes, invalidates, rescinds, supercedes, or discredits, and thus "discredits itself" as "negative" or empty, unless the negative becomes "subsumed" into a double negation and is repositioned and revalued as "positive." Countering such (mis)readings of nihilation, Heidegger's thought makes room for the middle voice, for the in-between that is neither active nor passive, neither powerful nor powerless, but indicates a reciprocal, participatory enabling, a mutual freeing constitutive of *Da-sein* as the relation of being-there.

Heidegger's preoccupation with freedom reaches beyond the confines of metaphysical thought, and thus political thought as well, to see freedom in terms of the freeing force of nihilation, released or kept open as *Da-sein*. In a way, for Heidegger, freedom becomes the matter of releasing the enabling momentum of nihilation to its "proper" modality of "emptiness" and away from its metaphysical mischaracterization as negative, disabling, or powerless "nothingness." Thus, Heidegger's discourse about releasement (*Gelassenheit*) and letting be is not a discourse of indifference or political quietism—though it may appear as such within the metaphysical optics of political thought—but about thinking freedom as the enabling momentum of nihilation.

"The politics of nihilation" is inevitably a misnomer, yet I retain it here in order to indicate that nihilation, since it concerns freedom from power, has critical political significance, or, better put, is of critical significance for political thought. First and foremost, it exposes and questions the anthropocentric constitution of politics and political thinking. Anthropocentrism suggests that politics takes its cues from the welfare of the human, and most of the time limits itself to this welfare. Nihilation, by contrast, takes its cue from the freedom of being from power. Yet, this freedom of being from power is not only not indifferent or insignificant to human affairs but is the "human" affair par excellence—it is its constitutive relation, its *Da-sein*. Maintaining the nihilating momentum of the event is what opens up the space of politics and releases it from power. But what is meant here by releasing from power? Nihilation "nihilates" subjectivity, self, identity, and so on, which does not mean that it negates or annuls them but, rather, that it transforms them into a modality of being that needs no grounding, that becomes ceaselessly "grounded" in a releasement from grounding, that is, in the *Abgrund*.

Nihilation thus calls for a political being that needs no grounds (in personal, family, ethnic, class, national, racial, or "human" identities), that remains, as it were, released from the ceaseless "politics" of grounding. It entails the opening of the human to *Da-sein*, and thus involves opening politics beyond the human; or, put more clearly, it keeps the "politics of nihilation" from being misrecognized and conceptualized metaphysically as a human affair, that is, as an affair that concerns and happens only or primarily for the sake of the humans. This also implies that any argument that attempts to ground politics in some way, in identity or values, has to be critiqued and transformed through the prism of nihilation. Such critique would mandate rethinking the politics nonanthropocentrically, even nonanthropically, which, in a sense, would "nihilate" the meaning of human politics, enabling it to transform itself beyond its "inauthentic," as Heidegger would say, "human" optics and values. On the other hand, this approach also indicates that politics itself needs to be given a "nihilating" momentum. This does not mean that politics would become empty, negative, or "nihilistic," or would cease to act or exist, but that, instead of being constituted in and confined to the terms of goals, identities, relations, or agendas, it would keep in view as its "larger" and nonmetaphysical perspective the enabling momentum of nihilation.

What *Da-sein* "cares" for is, first and foremost, clearing the space for the nihilating momentum of being from the metaphysical "clutter" of ideas, values, and identities. In "caring" for nihilation, *Da-sein* opens a different, nonanthropic mode of being-in-the-world and changes the optics of politics: from narrowly conceived as a human affair to "taking care" of being, and thus of all beings. The distinctiveness of the "human" for Heidegger does not lie in the fact that humans are simply most important among beings but in that their response and "responsibility" is first and foremost to "being," that is, to any and all beings, which means responsibility to how those beings *are*, to how they happen and what their modes of being are like. And this responsibility to being and all beings is "secured"—that is, kept open—by maintaining in play the nihilating momentum of history. It is again the question, but a critical one, of perspective. For Heidegger, thinking does not "begin" simply with the human but, in the other beginning—which remains deliberately strange and foreign to metaphysics—it starts with being and nihilation. For such thinking, politics too begins "otherwise": it has another beginning, not in the organization of interhuman relations, but in the politics of relation as nihilation. Our "primary" responsibility is to keep nihilation in play, and help relations unfold from and within the spatio-temporal play of nihilation. Relations to being, to world and earth, to other humans and other beings unfold in the mode of nihilating, which indicates letting what is unfold in the full play of its spatio-temporal occurrence, thus enabling it to be how and what it is.

As emptiness, nihilation opens *Da-sein*, radically and inescapably, in other words, beyond any "closure" into concepts, values, or identities that mark existence, to the spacing and temporalizing of history. In the same gesture, it opens *Dasein* to all beings that happen in(to) history, and consequently, to "all" human others. To say that what is "originary" for humans is *Da-sein* means that concern with nihilation (with being, event, and its giving), that is, being-there, is the "origin" of concern and care for humans and other beings. *Da-sein's* concern for nihilation, for maintaining nihilation as enabling and not allowing it to be misrecognized as nothingness, negativity, and void, claims and enables it to care for others and other human beings. Heidegger here forcefully critiques anthropocentric, metaphysical, theological, and moralistic explanations of the various grounds for politics and ethics. However, he does not at all suggest indifference or relativism in their place, but rather shows that it is not only possible but critically important to "ground" ethics and politics nonanthropically, namely in the care/concern for the way in which nihilation "de-grounds," that is, lets being stay away from grounding. This transformation of politics through nihilation shows how anthropocentric politics remains—how centered on humans and their power games it is—not because of a moral failure on the part of humans but as a result of the metaphysical constitution of politics and action. Without dismissing or invalidating such anthropic, and predominantly anthropocentric, politics, Heidegger offers the possibility of rethinking it beyond the optics of power, which is to say beyond the interlocking play of powerlessness, domination, and empowerment.

It is in this context that Heidegger's comments on the Greek notion of *dike* (justice) and on Nietzsche's *Gerechtigkeit* should be placed. The Greek term *dike* suggests that justice is not simply a human affair but a matter of the "fittingness" of the happening of being. *Dike* indicates the juncture, and the ways in which the junctures of relations come to be shaped or disposed. The concern with *dike* implies not just concern with justice in human affairs, but attentiveness to how being "joins" and disposes beings into relations. It means attending to whether the way being happens "fits" with the event's freedom from power and befits being's *Machtlosigkeit*. "Justice" means here the "just" fitting of relations in a manner that allows them to transpire as power-free. It is within this power-free momentum of relations that human affairs, our relations to others, receive their "proper" or "fitting" disposition. And the fitting disposition for human affairs is to remain power-free, that is, it calls for taking care to let relations transpire as power-free. The power-free here designates the nonanthropic vector of relations, that is, the "fitting" (just) momentum for ethics and politics. The transformation of politics at stake here involves a critical "deanthropization" that would give the pride of place to being—to the enabling allowed by nihilation.

NIHILATION AND AN "OTHER" HUMANISM?

Such a politics of nihilation becomes especially important today, in the epoch of globalization and rapidly intensifying transformations of techno-power. Heidegger's concern with technology is motivated not by technophobia or mistrust of technological gadgets, but by concern for *Da-sein*. Manipulative power, which lies at the essence of technology, covers over what is "specifically" human, namely *Da-sein*. In his "Letter on Humanism," Heidegger argues that being-there is more "properly" human than any humanism, that is, that it defines more fittingly being-in-the-world than any value and anthropo-oriented humanist conception, whether one thinks here of Renaissance and modern humanism, existentialism, or Marxism. This radically nihilating dimension of the "human"—its *Da-sein*—becomes covered over by the technicist disposition of relations in modernity. What it means in specific terms is that the human being becomes defined and explained in technicist notions: in terms of making, creating, producing, and power. Their important differences notwithstanding, existentialist "self-creation" of one's essence through existence, or Marxist emphasis on labor as the defining human characteristic, coincide metaphysically in explaining human "essence" technologically: in terms of creating, self-making, producing, and laboring. They both see the human in the metaphysical terms of techno-power. The "threat" involved in the *Technik*, that is, in the essence of technology, is linked to the understanding of being in modernity in terms of *Machenschaft*, that is, as machination and manipulative power. Technicity means here that relations become disposed in terms of power—as either positive or negative manifestations, and that what does not and cannot appear is the enabling force of nihilation.

What technicity occludes in the "human" is precisely *Da-sein*'s capacity and responsibility for nihilation: namely, *Da-sein*'s capacity to bring into the open and participate in the enabling momentum of nihilation without ossifying and hardening this enabling into positivity: identity, subjectivity, value, power, and so on. *Da-sein*'s task, its open, futural relation to being marked by the hyphen, is precisely to keep open the enabling potential of nihilation. Technicity belies this enabling force of nihilation: it cannot see it as positivity, since nihilation cannot be arrested or hardened into positing, and therefore either misrecognizes nihilation as nothing or, more readily, dismisses and forgets it. Within technicity, only what makes, produces, or creates—that is, only what involves power: *Macht* linked to the sense of making—can be recognized, registered, and counted as real. As a consequence, the modality of enabling specific to nihilation, its power-free letting, becomes unreadable and forgotten in technicity. This is partially due to the fact that *Da-sein*'s participation in nihilation is always in the middle voice. This participation is not active, *Da-sein* does not make nihilation happen; instead, it only "lets" nihilation unfold its enabling momentum of emptiness.

Technicity has occluded the ability to "see" this letting be as action in the middle voice, and since letting be does not claim the status of making, causing, or effecting, and thus of power, it becomes categorized as the absence of action, as inaction, passivity, and powerlessness. In short, if it does not "make," that is, instantiate power, or become effected by it, it does not exist and is, therefore, not "real." In this specific manner, technicity increasingly "threatens" to conceal *Da-sein*'s capacity and responsibility for "preserving" nihilation and its enabling force. Technicity endangers the very mode of being of humans, who, as being-in-the-world, should "take care" of nihilation, that is, keep open its alternative modality of enabling, one free of making, production, and power. This would also entail keeping open the alternative modality of relating to all beings, human and nonhuman, a modality facilitated and guided by the enabling emptiness of spatio-temporalizing. This relation is neither "technicist" nor based on the centrality of the human as producer, maker, and possessor of power, but transpires in the mode of being-there understood as a relation to being that remains futural and transformative by enabling the force of nihilation without resort to making, effecting, or power.

Yet at the same time that technicity dramatically intensifies its operations in the age of information management and genetic engineering, it also retains a trace of this other, alien and foreign, beginning of relations. By pushing manipulation and power to its extremes: global power on the macroplanetary scale, whether economic, political, or military, on the one hand, and the microscopic manipulation and reprogramming of information, on the other, technicity displays its supposed "limitlessness." But through this apparent limitlessness of making, production, and manipulation, heralding the dawn of the twenty-first century, technicity also begins to disclose the culmination of the metaphysics in machination (*Machenschaft*) and its own essence as power. By thoroughly anthropomorphizing being, by saturating it with the "human" (*vermenschen*), technicity unwittingly begins to draw attention to the "in-human": not to technology as the nonhuman other, but to the otherwise human marked by *Da-sein*.

Enabling without positivity or empowerment, nihilation without negativity or inaction: those are the vectors of *Da-sein*'s "acting" in the middle voice. This mode of acting is the exorbitant, critically "dishumanizing" question posed to the always already anthropic/anthropocentric conceptions of ethics and politics. To make it clear again, the adjective "dishumanizing" does not denote any depreciation or degradation of the human. On the contrary, the *Entmenschung*, the disanthropization of being, is the prelude to the unfolding of what appears as "properly" human in the age of technology, that is, *Da-sein*, and with it, of a *Dasein*-oriented politics and ethics. Such "politics" would no longer be a politics of identity, values, subjectivity, or power, but, in the specific sense I tried to elaborate above, of nihilation. Nihilation has the force that enables transformation through emptiness, where emptiness is not a void but the clearing, and the "clarity," extended and offered by the spatio-temporalization of the event. In the age of globalization, with the intensifying planetary powers in play and the issue of planetary (in)justice increasingly salient, this question of the enabling "politics" of nihilation both remains unheard and rises with a particular, "otherwise human," poignancy and urgency.

NOTES

1. Particularly instructive and inspiring in this regard is the chapter "*Sunyata* East and West," in which Dallmayr explores the enabling force of nothingness and emptiness in Eastern thought and Heidegger, and discusses their implications for political nonfoundationalism. See Fred Dallmayr, *Beyond Orientalism: Essays on Cross-Cultural Encounter* (Albany: SUNY Press, 1996), pp. 175–99.

2. In his insightful and careful reading in "The Ends of Man," Jacques Derrida points to a double vector of Heidegger's rethinking of "man" and "humanity" in terms of *Dasein*, or "being-there." This ambiguity arises from the fact that "being-there" refers both to *Dasein* understood as the being of humans, and to the "there" of

being, that is, the *Da* of *Sein*. This prompts Derrida to state that *Dasein*, "though *not* man, is nevertheless *nothing other* than man," and, a little later: "It remains that the thinking of Being, the thinking of the truth of Being, in the name of which Heidegger de-limits humanism and metaphysics, remains as thinking *of* man." Jacques Derrida, *Margins of Philosophy,* trans. Alan Bass (Chicago: University of Chicago Press, 1982), pp. 127, 128. Derrida's remarks fittingly describe the problematic of *Dasein* within what might be called the "first" metaphysical beginning of thought. However, one needs to take more explicitly into consideration the "turn" from the first to the other beginning, and, the impact of the radical nihilation opened up by this turn, as I try to explore it in this essay. Within the "other" beginning indicated by Heidegger from mid-1930s on, the thinking of being is no longer the thinking of being but of the event (*Ereignis*) and, as such, is not an anthropic affair. While it is true that this thinking does not transpire without the human participation, the thinking Heidegger is after occurs in the "middle" voice, as the thinking of the *Da*, of the "there" as the site of the event and the relation to being, and is not, therefore, *of* "man": neither strictly speaking *about* "man" nor *belonging to* "man," but, more appropriately, to *Dasein*'s relation to being. While within the "destruction" of metaphysics, *Dasein* can be seen as "nothing other than man," within the other beginning, it is indeed "other" than "man": it is the happening of the event. Humans participate in the "there" of this event—let it come about, so to speak—yet this site or "clearing" (*Lichtung*) is not *of* them but, rather, marks precisely the "nonanthropism" of the event.

3. Martin Heidegger, *Metaphysik und Nihilismus,* in *Gesamtausgabe,* vol. 67 (Frankfurt: Klostermann, 1999), p. 90.

4. It would be important in this context to think through whether and to what extent some of the most vocal critiques of Heidegger are prompted, without being articulated in these terms, by the residual or "habitual" anthropocentrism, and conceal a reaction to the nonanthropic impetus of Heidegger's thought. One could think here, for instance, of Theodor Adorno's insistence, against abounding, in fact, omnipresent statements by Heidegger to the contrary, that Heidegger's being is abstract, ahistorical, unmediated, "essentialist"; or of Emmanuel Levinas's or Jürgen Habermas's discomfort with the neutrality, anonymity, indifference, or quietism supposedly implied by the Heideggerian notion of "being."

5. Martin Heidegger, *Besinnung, Gesamtausgabe,* vol. 66 (Frankfurt: Klostermann, 1997), pp. 294–95.

6. Martin Heidegger, *Beiträge zur Philosophie (Vom Ereignis), Gesamtausgabe,* vol. 65 (Frankfurt: Klostermann, 1989), pp. 266–67.

7. Martin Heidegger, *Die Geschichte des Seyns, Gesamtausgabe,* vol. 69 (Frankfurt: Klostermann, 1998), p. 140.

8. "Als nichthaftes wesend ermöglicht und erzwingt es zugleich Andersheit." Heidegger, *Beiträge zur Philosophie,* p. 267.

9. This is why Heidegger often writes in the context of *Entmenschung* about the need to grant dignity (*Würdigung*) to being, in other words, to its nihilating momentum.

10. One must carefully think here how and to what extent anonymity and indifference already reflect an anthropic, if not anthropocentric, perspective. It seems that to speak of anonymity, one has to presuppose personhood and the idea of the other as a person, with the subtending "metaphysics" of the human.

11. Heidegger, *Besinnung*, pp. 192–93.

12. Ibid., p. 191.

13. Heidegger, *Die Geschichte des Seyns*, p. 64.

14. Ibid., p. 21.

15. Ibid., p. 185.

PART II.

MULTICULTURALISM AND COMPARATIVE POLITICAL THEORY

Encounters with Modernity and Tradition

Ronald J. Terchek

Fred Dallmayr has been addressing issues of modernity in a variety of ways for some time. With dexterity and intelligence, he has recently turned to non-Western encounters with modernity. In this essay, I explore the writings of Sri Aurobindo (1872–1950), particularly his interrogation of modernity, and borrow for that purpose several of the categories Dallmayr employs in his own work.[1]

Aurobindo and his contemporaries Mahatma Gandhi and Rabindranath Tagore were preeminent figures in India during the first half of the twentieth century. They came of age after the Indian Rebellion of 1857 (the "Mutiny," as it is commonly called in Britain and the United States), when the power of the raj was at its height. It was a time when Indian law, property claims, Hindu–Moslem relations, and the like were being rapidly transformed. It was also a period when modern ideas and practices spread throughout India: increasingly schools patterned their curricula after the British model, for example, and new positions began to open in a changing economy for those who could obtain the necessary (usually clerical) skills and adapt themselves to the new order of things exported by imperial Britain. Puzzling to many Indians during this period was the brute fact that a small European nation controlled the entire subcontinent. For many, the success of the raj demonstrated the ascendancy of the modern West over a tradition-bound Orient.[2] Its science and technology, its celebration of reason (of a certain sort) over tradition and religion, its wide-ranging commerce and ever-expanding ability to produce more goods, its successful military advantage, its emphasis on efficiency as a way of proceeding in all corners of life—all these and more seemed to many to validate modern claims to superiority over traditional ways of proceeding.

| It is in such a milieu that we find Aurobindo assessing the confrontations between the modern West and traditional India. For him, the supreme challenge is how India can be vitally connected to the core of its tradition, which he believes to be life-affirming and spiritual, while at the same time removing the disabilities that have accumulated over the centuries. Aurobindo simultaneously wants to take what he finds to be emancipatory from the modern West and reject what he sees as dangerous. In the end, he seeks a synthesis between tradition and modernity, a task that dominates his work. Before turning to a closer consideration of Aurobindo's efforts, I briefly take up Dallmayr's sophisticated and intelligent commentaries on modernity in his recent works on comparative political theory.

SELF-CONFIDENT MODERNITY AND MULTIPLE MODERNITIES

Modernity promotes reason and science, celebrates human rights and individual autonomy, and espouses democracy as the best form of governance. The dominant expression of modernity that has emerged in the West, what I call a "self-confident modernity," frequently takes the position that its outlooks, goals, and ways of doing thing are the only appropriate ones not only for the West, but also for the rest of the world as well because alternatives are said to be hopelessly flawed and invariably inferior. The universalizing claims of self-confident modernity leave little outside the West immune from its judgmental gaze and desire to rearrange matters according to its understanding of what needs to be done. This expression of modernity is presented as embodying the truth through its depictions of what is good, natural, and possible. It tells us which questions are relevant and which are not and where to find the right answers. However differently proponents of self-confident modernity understand the concept, they usually find that outside of its boundaries are superstition, ignorance, and prejudice.

Although modernity has become the orthodoxy of countries with developed market economies, elsewhere it has often had a much more skeptical reception and sometimes has been met with outright hostility. One reason is that its appearance has almost always been unsettling. Traditional livelihoods are often displaced, once stable agrarian societies give way to growing urban centers, and traditional ways of thinking and traditional social relations are frequently uprooted. Even as many are materially "better off" in the wake of modernity, many others are not; in fact, they are worse off. Even its beneficiaries are often dissatisfied with many features of modernity.

Frequently, critics of modernity take shelter in a "fundamentalist" version of their religious tradition to provide security and assurance in an unsettled world. Such critics hold that self-confident modernity seems bent on colonizing everyone and everything, everywhere. They generally deplore the secular character of self-confident modernity with its disdain or at least low regard for religion. And many of these critics of modernity attack what they take to be the homogenizing effects of modern production and consumption, which have become leading indicators of what is said to be good in society. In an earlier era, the self-confident expression of modernity was associated with colonialism; today, it is linked with globalization in its economic, political, and cultural expressions.

Dallmayr rejects the claim that self-confident modernity is the whole of modernity; rather he sees modernity as complex, varied in its expressions, and capable of taking on new characteristics and expressions at various times and for various people. In this view, because there is more than one modernity, we are not fated to accept a single, monolithic reading of it but can mine its many expressions to find what is and what is not valuable. As Dallmayr sees matters, "Under the influence of Herder, Hegel, and many other thinkers, modern Europe has generated a broad and highly nuanced panoply of self-images or self-interpretations—much broader than a narrow focus on liberal Enlightenment ideas might suggest."[3] Given the variety of modernities, we need not live with one we find confining, intolerant, or disabling. Dallmayr invites us to search for a generous reading of modernity, one that recognizes the important parts of its legacy, such as its ideals of critical reason, freedom, equality, and autonomy, while simultaneously leaving behind its dangerous parts, or at least challenging them.

Dallmayr interrogates modernity in order to demonstrate what is valuable and what is dangerous in the modern project. More important than the right answers—since answers evolve for Dallmayr in a dialogue and are not fixed in advance—are the right questions. His work is crowded with questions, and a sampling suggests the path he means to take:

> Are we really forced into a "no exit" situation, constrained to choose between polar opposites that may be equally unpalatable? . . . In the political domain: does the rejection or critique of liberal universalism

inevitably force us to embrace the alternative of parochialism and hateful xenophobia? Is it not possible—indeed are there not good practical and philosophical reasons—to cherish cultural and ethnic diversity while at the same time opposing the blandishments of both cosmopolitanism and local narcissism?[4]

Highlighting both the successes and failures of modernity, Dallmayr observes in *Dialogue among Civilizations* that "one can hardly deny the considerable accomplishments of the modern period: its contributions to the expansion of human knowledge and to the strengthening of civil-political liberty and personal autonomy. By hindsight, of course, it is also evident that some of these gains were bought at a price."[5]

What are some of these costs? One is what Dallmayr calls "an exodus from tradition,"[6] a topic I take up below. Another has to do with its dire effects on the world's poor. Pointing out that matters have reached "grotesque proportions," he sees growing inequalities inhibiting autonomy.[7] A third cost Dallmayr attributes to modernity is a sameness and dullness that is creeping into life as its homogenizing effects spill everywhere.

Finding that modernity is not as emancipatory as many of its defenders claim nor as bankrupt or dominating as several critics charge, Dallmayr refuses to assess modernity from either such narrowly limited perspectives. He urges "Europeans (and their friends) to be mindful both of the accomplishments of Europe—especially the modern achievements of equal liberty, rule of law, and human rights—and the temptation of cultural self-enclosure and exclusiveness." For him, a "generous construal of Europe's heritage . . . honors the modern Enlightenment as a part or facet of a complex historical narrative recalcitrant to univocal summary." Europe and the United States are not the product of some single cause, proceeding in some unbroken linear progression. Rather, they are the "outgrowth of multiple sources and strands, reaching from antiquity and the Christian Middle Ages through Renaissance and Reformation to more recent forms of 'authenticity' and everydayness—with reason and faith, religion and politics embroiled in protracted negotiations."[8]

Tradition can be a rich resource and a vehicle for assessing the effects of modernity in part, Dallmayr argues, because tradition makes room for much that is lost in modernity. It can be an effective counterweight or "antidote to the ongoing process of global standardization and Westernization, a source of resistance for non-Western societies in the grip of Western hegemony." Yet Dallmayr knows that tradition can be reactionary, parochial, or insular and that care must be taken to protect against such dangers while at the same time appreciating the self-transforming aspects of tradition.[9] Because tradition can be debilitating, cruel, arbitrary, and steeped in hierarchy, Dallmayr reminds us of why many are skeptical of it: "Probably the most serious shortcoming of the opponents of modernity . . . is their inability" to appreciate its importance in confronting the "totalizing power structures that, in most traditional societies, were monopolized by privileged elites (kings, emperors, aristocratic and priestly castes)." The emancipatory expression of modernity is, for Dallmayr, one of the positive legacies of the Enlightenment.

Dallmayr points out "a path between (Habermasian) modernity and its radical opponents (or antimodernists), a path that acknowledges the beneficial or emancipating dimensions of modernity while refusing to canonize its defects."[10] This can happen only where there is an open and frank dialogue among different voices that are not silenced by either superior power or claims to infallibility, whether such pronouncements come from tradition or modernity. To achieve this goal, Dallmayr examines non-Western writers who seek freedom and justice, reach for critical reason, and move beyond narrowly limited "either/or" constructions. These writers often see a tension between the old and new, the spiritual and the rational, but do not want to reduce these tensions to an inflexible juxtaposition of polar opposites. This was certainly a feature in the work of Aurobindo, whom I now discuss.

THE YOUNG AUROBINDO

Before turning directly to the young Aurobindo, it is helpful to give an overview of the India of his time to highlight the growing unrest in the country and the many clashes between tradition and modernity. India was awash with change throughout the nineteenth and twentieth centuries, and in the midst of this turbulent period, Sri Aurobindo would make important contributions, first as a fiery political figure and later as one of the most prominent philosophers in modern India, indeed some would say the leading philosopher of the time.[11]

Traditional India did not encounter the modern West in a single wave but in a series of contacts that over time came to touch more and more spheres of Indian life. Buttressed by its military prowess, the British during the time of the raj imposed laws covering all manner of things, ranging from property law, to the regulation of forests, to tax law, to tariffs, and to health codes. As part of this process, the Indian economy increasingly was transformed as, for example, large sections of agriculture moved from crops that served local markets and the subsistence needs of farmers and their families to crops that became part of a much broader market and, therefore, subject to significant market fluctuations. More importantly for many Indians, and Aurobindo must be counted among them, the proponents of Western modernism sought to determine how Indians thought about themselves, their traditions, their social practices, and their own governance. The British offered an account of its own superiority at the expense of Indian culture and tradition, and many Indians, Aurobindo came to believe, uncritically accepted the Westerners' side of things. Too many were willing to forsake their own traditions in order to emulate British practices. New conceptions of what is important in life (particularly money and materialism) threatened to create a homogenized India, an India no longer Indian but a replica of Britain, and a poor one at that. At the same time, however, Aurobindo came to acknowledge that there was much of value in the practices and commitments of the modern West, though he insisted that any appropriation of those values be on India's terms.

Amidst these many social changes, the Indian National Congress was founded in the late 1880s. This small, well-educated group pressed the British to introduce civil reforms, but they met with only limited effects. Indeed, the British seemed intent on strengthening their hold on the subcontinent and, in one of Britain's most daring moves, announced the partition of Bengal in 1905. This excited intense opposition in the Hindu community and Aurobindo was a major figure in the resistance. Looking back at his role, Jawaharlal Nehru recalls that during Aurobindo's active years in Indian politics, he "shone like a brilliant meteor and created a powerful impression on the youth of India. The great antipartition movement in Bengal gained much of its philosophy from him and, undoubtedly, prepared the day for the great movements led by Mahatma Gandhi."[12] During this period, Aurobindo's concerns were exclusively political; nationalism was his touchstone. For the young Aurobindo, the highest duty is to the nation, or "The Mother."

Even before he would become active in the politics of Bengal, Aurobindo was prompted to mount a vigorous attack on the Congress leadership, claiming it to be not only elitist but, more damning, beside the point in contemporary India.[13] Seeing Congress ruled by a group that has no contact with ordinary Indians, Aurobindo wants to mobilize a mass movement to oppose the British. But Congress is not up to the task, being "a middle-class organ, selfish and disingenuous in its public action and hollow in its professions of a large and disinterested patriotism."[14]

> I say of the Congress, then, this—that its aims are mistaken, that the spirit in which it proceeds towards their accomplishment is not a spirit of sincerity and whole-heartedness, and that the methods it has chosen are not the right methods, and the leaders in whom it trusts not the right sort of men to be leaders;—in brief, that we are at present the blind led, if not by the blind, at any rate by the one-eyed.[15]

Insisting that Indians challenge British imperialism, Aurobindo declares that Congress is squandering the moment.[16] Interested in minor reforms, it takes an assimilationist stance, failing to appreciate the gravity of the problem. The moderates fail to see that the British pose more than a political, economic, or military threat; for Aurobindo, the British are propagating a whole new way of thinking, one that is dehumanizing. One expression of this is the British proclivity to sanctify machinery and make efficiency and productivity their touchstones, something Aurobindo finds is a "logical absurdity. With their rigid emphasis on one single element of life, the British slur over others of equal or superior importance." As he understands matters, machinery has become not only an industrial tool but also a political one that is used to write a whole new text about what is important and what is not.[17] With their understanding of what counts, the British are seeking to transform India into something that is useful to them and, in the process, are destroying the country.

Acknowledging that the need to confront Britain is pressing, Aurobindo also claims the time is ripe because the British are vulnerable. Displaying his penchant for seeing paradox, he finds that apparent British successes often conceal their deep wounds. "Overconfident in her material success," the British fail to see their power is waning in the face of infectious ideas that they seek to appropriate only for themselves as they try to quarantine the rest of the world from demands for equality. Ironically, some of their vulnerability is a result of their being blinded by their military and political success.[18] They believe that their superior power in some spheres makes them superior in all spheres.

A little more than a decade later, the partition of Bengal shakes the political landscape. Aurobindo believes that the British are acting in a despotic way, one that will unwittingly hasten their own downfall. They "overestimate their coercive power and underestimate the power and vitality of ideas and sentiments." For him, nationalism, democracy, and liberty "are more powerful than fighting men and guns and princes and laws."[19] Not learning from the fall of "earlier despotisms," Aurobindo claims the British believe they are different: they see themselves as "stronger, more moral and virtuous, better organized."[20] But British self-confidence makes them all the more vulnerable because (as is the case so often with those who hold unaccountable power) they are not likely to be self-critical and are therefore blind to the threats they are creating around them.

Shortly before his exile, which I discuss in the following section, Aurobindo writes "The Idea of Karmayogin," in which he anticipates some of the themes that mark his later philosophical writings. In the nineteenth century, he tells us, India "aspired to political emancipation, social renovation, religious vision and rebirth, but it failed because it adopted Western motives and methods, [and] ignored the spirit, history, and destiny" of its own tradition. He warns Indians that simply removing the British and taking control of the government the raj has established means that India will fall far short of real independence. To achieve freedom, Indians first must change themselves. "It is the spirit alone that saves, and only by becoming great and free in heart can we become socially and politically great and free." With this in mind, he argues that real freedom comes only by "conquering the kingdom within, not by harnessing the forces of Nature to the service of comfort and luxury but by mastering the forces of the intellect and the spirit, by vindicating the freedom on man within as well as without."[21] In this editorial, Aurobindo moves away from his preoccupation with politics and his explicit linkage of freedom and national independence. In his earlier political writings, he address Indian humiliation and the need to rekindle Indian pride. Action, then, is tied to politics and the freedom it can deliver.

The Philosophical Writings

In 1910, already arrested once for his pro-independence activities, Aurobindo flees Calcutta and goes into exile in the French enclave of Pondicherry. There he formally announces he is leaving politics and embarking on his work in philosophy and spirituality. In his Pondicherry writings, Aurobindo frequently reaches for Hindu texts to celebrate what he takes to be its core as a way to respond to modernity as well as to what he takes to be the deficiencies of contemporary Hinduism. Like Gandhi, he castigates Hinduism as practiced for its failures, such as the persistence of untouchability and what is at times an empty ritualism, and simultaneously warns Indians about the dangers he sees residing in Western modernity. Unlike Gandhi, who hesitantly accepted selected fragments of modernity,[22] Aurobindo seeks to merge more of its central features, such as science and a particular expression of reason, with what he takes to be the spiritual core of Hinduism. In his writings at Pondicherry, we encounter such topics as action and a continued attack on fatalism; an emphasis on spirituality and transcendence; the priority of society over the state; an evolutionary outlook on history; and a call for a synthesis between the best of India with the best of the modern West. In his philosophical writings, Indian pride and action remain important but are presented in philosophical language, and politics and nationalism fade into the background, though never fully disappear.

Reason, Science, and Tradition

According to Aurobindo, one of the great achievements of the modern West concerns the power and role of reason, although he continually reminds his readers that there are many expressions of reason: some liberating, others narrowly instrumental and self-serving, and still others vehicles for domination. The best expression of reason, we are told, requires disengagement and detachment. On his account, detachment leads to critical reason, critical not only of tradition and convention, but of the story that reason is itself unfolding. Reason, for Aurobindo, is above all tied to doubt, which he believes to be essential if we are to penetrate the truth claims that come with orthodoxy, convention, and modernity.[23] Without doubt, such truth claims become frozen and each of their defects are perpetuated. With the power of critical reason, Aurobindo finds the modern age to be "a time especially when humanity got rid of much that was cruel, evil, ignorant, dark, odious, not by the power of religion, but by the awakened intelligence and of human idealism and sympathy."[24]

The knowledge that comes with disinterested reason does not necessarily lead to the same conclusion for everyone, according to Aurobindo. All those seeking to understand themselves and their relations with the world will each come to their own truths and express them in their own ways. But this does not lead to a thoroughgoing relativism for Aurobindo. He expects that disinterested reason teaches us all that materialism and possessiveness are not the ultimate ends of human beings; that is, there is something transcendent to such Western values that is a part of every life, and the ways people understand transcendence and translate it into their everyday lives reflects their individual experiences and insights.

One of the troubling expressions of reason for Aurobindo is instrumentalism. Perhaps with Hobbes and Hume in mind, particularly in light of their view that reason serves the passions, Aurobindo argues that instrumental reason is limiting and diverts us from critical reason. When we employ instrumental reason, "we limit our intellectual gain, limit our view of things, distort the truth because we cast it into the mold of some particular idea or utility and ignore or deny all that conflicts with that utility or that set idea." In this way, instrumental reason traps us into searching for ways to satisfy our personal gratifications and blinds us to other, richer possibilities, something that Aurobindo thinks that critical reason can lead us to see.[25]

Impatient with the tendency of modern reason to universalize the particular, Aurobindo rejects the boast that it can explain "the whole truth of life." Such as an imperial reach also applies to those who believe that science can uncover all of the secrets of life. Aurobindo fears that such outlooks invite science and reason to invade territories where they have no warrant. He laments, for example, that science leaves "almost every problem untouched." It cannot comprehend transcendence (except to try to refute it), it cannot explain love or duty or charity except in mechanical ways, and it cannot understand the meaning of life. When science enters into such domains and offers its own explanations, it leaves too much unattended and thus depletes such concepts of their deeper meanings. Not surprisingly, Aurobindo challenges the sweeping, unreflective applications of science that attempt to impose its findings hither and yon, whether or not they fit, as it imposes its own new orthodoxy. Because it acts without a telos or purpose, we, living in the demystified world that science has created, are left without a compass to guide us. In its pursuit of knowledge, science fragments the cosmos, breaking it "up into parts, to make more or less artificial classifications, to build systems with limited data which are contradicted, upset, or have to be continually modified by other data."[26] In this way, it contributes to an unstable world that we cannot understand. The imperial claims of modern reason and science are kindling a "revolt of the human mind against this sovereignty of the intellect."[27] Even before modernity, reason has challenged alternative ways of knowing, including tradition and religion, but now people are asking whether reason is fully up to the task of explaining who we are and what is the purpose of our existence.

When people encounter the inadequacy of rational strategies to offer convincing explanations for all questions about reality, Aurobindo expects that a frequent response is to generate new ideas or discover new facts to provide a better understanding. Often this strategy is appropriate, indeed necessary, but frequently it is beside the point. Sometimes reason has exhausted itself regarding the matter at hand or has entered domains where its resources have little to contribute. Although it can expose falsehoods and move us closer to the truth, "reason cannot arrive at any final truth." Aurobindo is particularly alarmed by efforts to create and organize "a purely rational society," something he believes cannot "come into being and, if it could . . . [it] would sterlise [sic] and petrify human existence."[28]

Aurobindo argues that we ought not allow ourselves to be rigidly controlled by ideas whether they are the product of modernism or have roots extending deep into the past. A full life, according to Aurobindo, "escapes from the formulas and systems which our reason labours to impose on it. It proclaims itself too complex, too full of infinite potentialities to by tyrannized" by arbitrary ideas, whatever their origin. He finds that "even Science and Philosophy are never entirely dispassionate and disinterested. They fall into subjection to the tyranny of their own ideas, . . . [and] they seek to impose these upon life."[29]

Self-confident modern reason is said to trump all other ways of knowing and, therefore, alternatives are taken to be defective, if not outright dangerous. This is thought to be particularly true of the knowledge that tradition conveys, which its critics see as fixed in the deadweight of the past and unable to respond, except blindly and sometimes violently, to a world in flux. Sanctified by its followers, tradition is protected against those who would scrutinize, criticize, and challenge it with an eye to replacing it with something else. But tradition is not monolithic; it is not a seamless body of ideals and practices that always cohere, and even its core principles can be buried under the debris of unearned privilege and unaccountable power. Traditions grow and change over time, sometimes for the better and sometimes for the worse, and Aurobindo holds that it is the work of the living to protect what is most valuable in a tradition against those who would weaken the expression of its principles.

Aurobindo notes that some Indians are reactionary in their responses to modernity. They accept "everything Indian as it stood and because it was Indian." For all of its shortcomings, this response nevertheless can contribute to the recovery of what is valuable in the past by resisting modern claims that tradition is inherently retrogressive. If the reactionaries are to make a real contribution, they will not seek to find refuge in the past but rather offer a "restatement" that takes account of modern conditions.[30] They should actively engage with modernity, not retreat from it, remembering that "Indian spirituality in its greatest eras . . . has not been a tired quietism or a conventional monasticism."[31] Traditions endure not because they are rigidly repeated in a world that has changed from the time of their initial appearance, but because those who seek to keep a tradition vital distinguish what is central to a tradition, what is peripheral, and what has decayed or becomes corrupted. Prepared to eliminate the latter, Aurobindo reinterprets tradition in ways, he believes, that simultaneously adhere to its core as well as speak to new conditions.

Tradition is important to Aurobindo because it moves beyond the immediate concerns of the here and now to remind us there are many things in our lives that are important. Providing a way to transcend the immediate and material, it teaches that the world does not revolve around us and that pride diminishes us. Holding that community counts, duties are important, and cooperation is essential, a lively tradition recognizes, unlike ritualized orthodoxies, that there are many routes to the transcendent and spiritual and thus privileges plurality as against conformity. By refusing to make one sphere dominate all others, traditions at their best address our multiple needs as well as ensure the integrity of the many different spheres of life.

Aurobindo does more than praise and defend his tradition, however; he also criticizes it: "The courage to defend our culture against ignorant Occidental criticism and to maintain it against the gigantic modern pressure comes first, but with it there must be courage to admit not from any European standpoint but from our own outlook the errors of our culture."[32]

Alongside critical reason and tradition, Aurobindo wants to see an idealism of a certain sort, one which "demands a constant effort of self-transcendence and the impulsion towards things unachieved and even immediately impossible." Although even idealists, poets, and artists are defeated by their efforts to have their lives continually correspond to their ideals,[33] ideals nevertheless provide us with goals that transcend concerns about security, convenience, and desire and give a deeper purpose to life than can prudence or practicality. Aurobindo wants our ideals to address what is unique in us as well as what binds us together in a community. Without ideals, anything counts, and we enter the realm of a thoroughgoing relativism that saturates the whole of life. Left without the standards that ideals provide, we have no reason to be angry or moved by injustice, harm, or domination. We then readily take the world as it is, finding ourselves accepting what it coughs up. Idealists from Socrates to Aurobindo to the present argue that there is something better than convention and urge us to break out of its clutches in order to examine and question and, when appropriate, to modify or even reject it.

Unlike many who embrace what they take to be the best of their tradition, Aurobindo analyzes his tradition, often with the resources that modernity provides. At the same time that he employs critical reason and the scientific method, he means to show their limitations and dangers. In some ways, his encounters with modernity can be thought of as "old fashioned" in that he raises broad and deep issues that are out of tune with our times, and he moves away from a narrowly framed analytical gaze that characterizes much contemporary scholarship and problemsolving. Aurobindo raises questions about the meaning of life, the validity of different modalities of knowledge, the character of people and how they might be interconnected, and the manner in which we make our way in the world. With the busy, crowded schedules scripted for modern men and women, such issues find little room for exploration or contemplation. Aurobindo resists this kind of lethargy. That there are no ready, convincing answers for everyone, he argues, does not mean that we should not interrupt our routines and ask questions that penetrate to the depths of our experience and existence. Aurobindo encourages us to be suspicious of universal claims of reason and science, but at the same time use modernism's tools to examine conventional practices, rituals, and dogmas that survive from the past.

Diversity, Freedom, and Transcendence

If people are to develop and deepen their understanding of themselves and the world, and if the worth and dignity of each individual are to be respected and protected, then freedom is necessary. For Aurobindo, freedom is not merely about making choices, although it is surely that. To restrict the meaning of freedom to choice, however, risks its becoming purely instrumental and consequently mired in the present with little attention to the past or future, particularly a shared past or future. The tendency of instrumentally inclined individuals is to ask how they can more efficiently attend to their own advantages. Freedom is much more important than this to Aurobindo, who associates it with individual growth and with opening the possibilities for intellectual, social, moral, and spiritual development. As we shall see, he seeks to nurture such growth in each of the many aspects of our lives in such a way that the importance of one feature is not exaggerated and the rest dwarfed.[34] Growth, on his reading, is something that emerges from each individual and cannot be mandated by others. Each person needs freedom both to think and act "in order that he may grow, otherwise he will remain fixed where he was, a stunted and static being."[35] This freedom is also important if people are to think critically. For Aurobindo, "[r]eason cannot do its work, act or rule if the mind of man is denied freedom to think or freedom to realise its thought by action."[36] When people are denied the freedom of thought, their prospects for growth are stalled and they become frozen in the present.

Prizing diversity, Aurobindo condemns unthinking conformity to the past, which can in effect reproduce dangerous features of earlier periods of India's history. When authority becomes rigid and despotic, its original ideals lose their animating spirit. Uniformity transforms someone who was once alive with possibiliy into something seemingly inanimate. Aurobindo recognizes this as a consequence of the stress on religious ritualism, which crushes the freedom that authentic spirituality requires.[37] Addressing people in the context of their daily lives, he encourages them to think and act in ways that make sense to them, reflecting their inner life and how it intersects with the many inheritances and experiences, aspirations, and disappointments that are a part of each person's unique life history. Therefore, no single rule can cover each individual's honest expression of who that person is.[38] Continually celebrating the diversity he finds within India, Aurobindo claims that the seemingly limitless symbols of Hinduism offer a rich variety of "suggestions" for potential paths toward spirituality: "This infinite variety is itself, as Vivekananda pertinently pointed out, a sign of a superior religious culture." Indians have recognized that spirituality "must always present itself in an endless variety of aspects."[39]

Aurobindo ties freedom closely to a diversity that is reflected in the freely chosen paths taken by men and women as individuals. This form of diversity stands in contrast to one imposed by those in power who construct a society of graded inequalities and rigid social classifications. Aurobindo believes his conception of diversity reflects what he calls the "inner person" and that person's encounters with tradition and present-day life. But again he warns of the lapse into a deadening conformity. Trapped by a single rule meant to direct the thought and behavior of everyone, the conformist does not recognize that "[a]ll men cannot follow in all things one common and invariable rule. Life is too complex to admit of the arbitrary ideal simplicity which the moralizing theorist loves. Natures differ. . . . The call of life, the call of the spirit within is not the same for everyone."[40] Aurobindo charges the conformist with declining to call on critical reason or to summon doubt in order to ask whether the present way of proceeding is, in fact, the best way.

A common danger to freedom comes from state interference into the lives of its subjects. Intruding into various aspects of the private and public spheres, the interfering state mandates certain behaviors and forbids others, using its coercive power to enforce its edicts. The dangers posed by unaccountable state power have led a wide array of modern social and political thinkers, from Locke's day to the present, to seek protection for what they take to be basic rights from an interfering state. But while it is essential for freedom, noninterference is not sufficient. Unlike most liberals, Aurobindo addresses those denials of freedom that come with domination, which has many expressions. Social, economic, and family relations, for example, potentially house expressions of domination whereby those with power in a given sphere of life wrongfully use others for their own purposes, denying them freedom in that particular sphere.[41] The good society as envisioned by Aurobindo must eliminate state interference and domination by the powerful in all its many expressions. He finds that the traditional ecclesiastical order which "suppressed liberty of thought and new ethical and social development, has to be dispossessed of its despotic authority, so that man may be mentally free." When he turns to modern expressions of domination, he argues, for example, that the "suffering, poverty, and exploitation" that comes with capitalism must "be eliminated and the wealth of the community be more equally shared by all who help to create it."[42]

For Aurobindo, an important expression of freedom in liberal societies is equality of opportunity—that everyone deserves a fair chance and that artificial barriers such as caste, class, race, religion, or gender ought not be erected to deny opportunities to some. As commonly understood in market societies such as the United States, equality of opportunity distributes rewards fairly; those with little somehow deserve what they have and those with much somehow deserve their share. Aurobindo challenges market conceptions of reward such as this and calls for something approximating equal distributions. He wants to see "so far as may be, an equal share in the advantages of the aggregate life as the right of all [who] contribute to" their community to the best "of their capacities."[43] This is a revolutionary claim not only in the India of his day with its rigid caste system, untouchability, and patriarchal domination, but also in market societies that use equality of opportunity to justify significant and substantive inequalities.

Some insist that certain people are not ready for freedom because they are prone to make mistakes. Aurobindo recognizes that errors in judgment and conduct cannot always be avoided, particularly when people face new situations and embark on new choices, no matter how thoughtful and well intentioned they are. For him, our errors should become an integral part of our education, and we should employ these lessons in ways that facilitate our growth and development. In other words, freedom ought not be available only to those who never, or almost never, err. The practice of restricting freedom in this way rests on several faulty assumptions: that we can sort out the wise from the unwise, that there is one standard of wisdom to which all must accede before they are granted their freedom, and that those prone to mistakes cannot learn from their errors and thus do not deserve to be free.[44]

The great goal of freedom for Aurobindo is the development of the whole person, culminating in a spiritualized existence. The important features of spirituality he identifies are strength, courage, and self-governance. The last of these, in Aurobindo's philosophical writings, has less to do with politics or economics, although they are not important to him. Rather, self-governance is especially an internal matter in which our biological drives or material and sensual desires do not master us but are mastered by us. This he deems possible because we have used critical reason to unshackle the many fetters that once bound us. In our quest for spirituality, then, Aurobindo encourages us to recover those elements of our tradition that teach us about detachment and transcendence, about our interconnectedness, and about our dignity and duties.

Detachment, which is central to Aurobindo's conception of spirituality, does not call for people to permanently remove themselves from the world; rather, once having detached themselves, they then return to the world and resume their lives as part of it, but with the advantage of a clearer perspective. They no longer see themselves as essentially satisfiers of utility, desire, domination, comfort, or security and recognize they have an intrinsic value in their own right as part of a pulsating, interdependent world. Aurobindo's conception of spirituality does not exclude "any of the great aims of human life, any of the great problems of our modern world, any form of human activity."[45] For this reason, spirituality encompasses the "whole being,"[46] so that those on a spiritual quest might come to hold "sacred all the different parts of man's life which correspond" to the physical, emotional, aesthetic, ethical, and intellectual properties of persons.[47]

The spirituality taught by Aurobindo infuses everyday life with its multiple needs and concerns, and applies to all the different stages of human life. As Aurobindo understands matters, spirituality is dynamic insofar as it has different expressions and meanings for different people, and even in the same person over time. One important feature that these different modes of spirituality share is a harmony of the parts, which makes it a mistake to exaggerate one aspect of any person's life or any community's sense of what is important. As Aurobindo puts it, a "want of balance gives rise to one-sided tendencies which are not properly checked, not kept in their due place, and bring about unhealthy exaggerations."[48] We need freedom not for one or another of our capacities to flourish, but for all of them to do so. To be denied the opportunity to develop the various aspects of our lives not only arrests the full flourishing of a person but also ensures that those parts that are freely pursued will never achieve their fullest potential because they can never be in harmony with the parts that are unfree and undeveloped. The denial of freedom and the lapse into mere conformity takes many forms, but what they have in common is the effort to squelch the aspirations of persons to grow and flourish.

Aurobindo believes that not only is freedom important to individual development, but that the elimination of destitution is also necessary. Claims that India's poverty provides especially fertile ground for spirituality insofar as it encourages Indians to transcend materialism, Aurobindo argues, are shallow and dangerous. What appears as spirituality in conditions of poverty "is something morbid, hectic, and exposed to perilous reactions. It is when the race has lived most richly and thought most profoundly that spirituality finds its heights and its depths and its constant and many-sided fruition."[49] The idea that poverty aids spirituality serves as a justification for domination by the rich over the poor because, on this line of reasoning, the impoverished have achieved a higher level of spirituality because of their destitution. Aurobindo argues in return that poverty is often not only personally degrading, but it empties the spirit of the impetus to grow and develop: the poor haven't the luxury of embarking on a spiritual quest, for their most pressing concern each day is with meeting their most elementary needs.

In comparing India's traditional social and political practices with modernity's sweeping claims, Aurobindo finds fault and merit in each. As for Indian traditionalism, he often condemns many of the same practices and attitudes faulted by the British, such as dogmatism, fatalism, and untouchability.[50] Aurobindo writes:

> [W]e should recognize without any sophistical denial those things in our creeds of life and social institutions which are in themselves mistaken and some of them indefensible, things weakening to our national life, degrading to our civilization, dishonouring to our culture. A flagrant example can be found in the treatment of our outcasts. There are those who would excuse it as an unavoidable error in the circumstances of the past; there are others who contend that is was the best possible solution then available. . . . The excuse was there, but it is no justification for continuance. The contention is highly disputable. A solution which condemns by segregation one-sixth of the nation to permanent ignominy, continued filth, uncleanliness of the inner and outer life and a brutal animal existence instead of lifting them out of it is no solution but rather an acceptance of weakness and a constant wound to the social

body and to its collective spiritual, intellectual, moral and material welfare.[51]

Aurobindo does not call for a fatalistic acceptance of matters as they are. The spirituality he practices, as we have seen, is not one of withdrawal but requires involvement in the world. Nor is his spirituality even remotely served by drowning in religious dogmatism and ritual. Aurobindo's conception of spirituality begins with individual freedom and the practice of critical reason to cast doubt on mandates that tell us what we must be and do.

In a secular, cynical, materialistic age, it might appear that Aurobindo's emphasis on spirituality and transcendence has little to say to us. But a case can be made that the present-day privileging of economic analyses in the study of humankind and the world around us—our political and societal structures—reveals a truncated outlook. Such an outlook makes economics the reigning ideology of our time, and Aurobindo means to challenge this hegemony. Recoiling at the dominance of economics, he urges people to strive for the full development of their body, mind, and spirit. The more we find, with William Wordsworth, that the world is too much with us, and the more we allow the present-day trend toward allowing economic analyses to script our lives, the less will we act by our own lights. There is a subtle pressure, as part of that trend, to suspend our own thinking—particularly our critical reasoning.

Struggling with Evil

In his *Essays on the Gita*, Aurobindo writes that we should look "upon war as an aspect of life and the ideal of man as a warrior."[52] Aurobindo understands the world to evolve within the context of a struggle between what he refers to as "good" and "evil." At first glance, it appears that he borrows much from the Social Darwinists such as Herbert Spencer, but any similarities prove not to be very deep or compelling. Social Darwinists tend to focus on only one aspect of life—namely, the broad economic conditions governing the raw forces of competition. Although Aurobindo accepts that competition for survival is a part of life, he holds that much contemporary competition results in the evil of domination, not freedom, and will be superseded in the future by a voluntary harmony.

One of the worst things that can happen in the face of this understanding of evil is that those who are the objects of domination decline to struggle and simply accept their condition fatalistically. They may do so because good and evil, as Aurobindo thinks of them, while always locked in combat with each other, are not entirely separate. Both the British and the Indians of his day reflected this duality in which neither the ideals of the modern West nor those of India adequately accounted for the encounter of Britain with traditional India. For Aurobindo, the pride of the British and of the modern West generally flowed from its critical rationality, science, and commitment to liberty. For its part, Hinduism could be proud of its spirituality, appreciation of both diversity and community, and simultaneous celebration of liberty and duty. But both modernism and traditional Hinduism are shackled by forces of domination, the former by colonization, industrial competition, and materialism and the latter by a rigid social system, ritualism, dogmatism, and fatalism.

Aurobindo insists that before we can find ways to improve the world, we must first see it as it really is. That means we must acknowledge not only "love and life and beauty and good" but also the dark side of life.[53] If we are to advance intellectually, socially, politically, and morally, "we can make no real step forward without a struggle, a battle between what exists and lives and what seeks to exist and live," that is, our ideals for a better future. For Aurobindo, struggle is central to life, and those without the clarity of sight to see this are themselves destined to be dominated and to forgo their own spiritual development.[54]

His reading of the *Bhagavat Gita* stresses struggle in "its two aspects, the inner struggle and the outer battle." As for the former, "the slaying of desire, ignorance, egoism is the victory." In the external world, on the other hand, the battle between good and evil often takes place, as we have seen, as a conflict between freedom and domination, and he means to challenge the latter publicly and resolutely. An important part of that struggle is detachment from our customary concerns for security, profit, and convenience in order to do what is best in the circumstances. When this happens, "personal desire and personal emotions no longer govern" individuals' behavior.[55]

We earlier saw that Aurobindo's detached person uses doubt and critical reason to analyze the world in its many aspects. That same process—questioning tradition, convention, and what sometimes passes for rationality—can also reveal what is, to use Aurobindo's language, "good" and "evil." Sometimes, the effort is relatively easy; the good shines brightly and evil stands undisguised. However, there are many instances where evil is hidden. Conformity, for example, has a numbing, corrosive effect on individuals who seem unaware of how their freedom is constricting. Or, to take another example, Aurobindo challenges the priority of economics that bears a special appeal to the materially comfortable. The soul of economic man revels in its acquisitions and is indifferent to the ways that a fixation on material well-being dwarfs those other aspects of life that are an integral part of who we are.

As we battle evil in our opponents, we often fail to notice the evil that is allied to our own cause. It often comes disguised as the "Children of Light," who appropriate such a title to themselves in their battle with the "Children of Darkness."[56] Clear about the dangers of the enemy, the Children of Light often take on their own pretensions regarding their own goodness, spawn their own domination and interference, and excuse their excesses in the name of what they take to be the supreme contest between good and evil. Because we often stand with the Children of Light and assume their posture in our conflict with an alien evil, we often blind ourselves to what we have become or are becoming. Here Aurobindo offers a cautionary tale: detachment, critical reason, and doubt are necessary not only when we encounter expressions of oppression but also when we enter the lists on behalf of our conception of the good.

To mount challenges to good and evil, Aurobindo would not only have us doubt and employ critical reason, but also turn to a tradition that has been subjected to rational scrutiny. Aurobindo believes that the failures of tradition can be repaired and that it is possible to once again be a touchstone for its highest ideals, the kind that Aurobindo frequently calls "life-affirming." Such an invigorated tradition will remind people that their lives have a meaning beyond working and consuming, and that their individual dignity is affirmed best in a cooperative society of equals. It will also remind them that, even in ordinary times, evil does not disappear once and for all but asserts itself in different guises and in many different settings. Aurobindo, often seen as a deeply spiritual writer, wants spirituality to permeate ordinary life and embarrass those who conform either to the norms of mass society or religious dogmas as well as challenge those who would employ modern rationales to dominate or interfere with others.

Conclusion

Comparative political theory is not an exercise that plucks bits and pieces from various bodies of theorizing with a view toward building a new theory or somehow showing the superiority or inadequacy of one or another theory. Rather, I contend that comparative political theory attempts to accomplish two very different things. In the first place, it seeks to enrich any particular theory by analyzing it from a fresh perspective to understand its own deepest premises, commitments, and directions, as well as potential but often unseen and unappreciated costs. In the second place, it seeks, as Fred Dallmayr does, to enter into dialogues concerning different theories and traditions, and to do so in such a way as to enrich them all. In such dialogical exercises, no participant can remain mute; each must have a place at the table and the right and interest in speaking openly and honestly. A consequence of such dialogues is the breaking-down of previously held stereotypes.

One reason to promote such a dialogue and find new paths comes with its beneficial effects on the modern West. For those who cling to modernity as the only valid voice that can speak, there is a pressing need to move from inflexible positions which can too often lead to an arrogance of power and which too readily freezes inequalities in place. Victims of a defective modernity are found not only in the non-West but also in the West with its predilection for efficiency, bureaucracy, globalization and its readiness to promote sameness. The antimodernists who would jettison the entire modern project should recognize not only that there is much good in the Enlightenment project but also that their alternative often introduces a relativism that is misplaced and dangerous.

The non-West also gains when it reminds itself that reason is not an exclusive import from the West; that in its own development reason has often been prized as has a respect for the worth of every individual, and diversity has been highly regarded and protected. Dallmayr's invitation to dialogue also recognizes that some of the best responses to change (something that cannot long be avoided) have not been withdrawal, hostility, reaction, or fatalism but a direct response, open examination, and possibly a synthesis between their tradition and modernity that non-Westerners will determine for themselves. For Dallmayr this "learning experience can only occur through mutual interrogation and interpellation, through a mode of interaction stopping short of both instant hybridization and plain surrender." A good experience will "resist both the lure of a domineering appropriation of difference—the posture of an aggressive 'logocentrism'—and the indifference through self-effacement."[57]

NOTES

1. For sensitive discussions of Aurobindo's efforts to synthesize secular and spiritual outlooks, see Dennis Dalton, *Indian Idea of Freedom* (Gurgaon: Academic Press, 1982); V. R. Mehta, *Foundations of Indian Political Thought* (New Delhi: Manohar, 1992), V. P. Varma, *The Political Philosophy of Sri Aurobindo* (Delhi: Motilal Banarsidass, 1976); and Kenneth Deutsch, "Sri Aurobindo and the Search for Political and Spiritual Perfection," in *Political Thought in Modern India*, ed. Thomas Pantham and Kenneth Deutsch (New Delhi: Sage, 1986), pp. 192–208.

2. See Edward Said, *Orientalism* (New York: Vintage Books, 1979). In Gandhi's assessment, the Indians gave India to the British; the British did not take it. See Gandhi, *Hind Swaraj*, 2d ed. (New Delhi: South Asia Books, 1998).

3. Fred Dallmayr, *Dialogue among Civilizations: Some Exemplary Voices* (New York: Palgrave Macmillan, 2002), p. 61.

4. Ibid., p. 22.

5. Ibid., p. 26. Dallmayr sides with those who challenge both "Euro-arrogance" and "Euro-denial" (ibid., p. 57). See also his *Alternative Visions: Paths in the Global Village* (Lanham, Md.: Rowman and Littlefield, 1998), p. 1.

6. Dallmayr, *Alternative Visions*, p. 247.

7. Dallmayr, *Dialogue among Civilizations*, p. 73.

8. Ibid., pp. 62, 64.

9. Dallmayr, *Alternative Visions*, pp. 247–48.

10. Dallmayr, *Dialogue among Civilizations*, p. 97.

11. See Mehta, *Foundations of Indian Political Thought*; Dalton, *Indian Idea of Freedom*.

12. Jawaharlal Nehru, foreword in Karan Singh, *Prophet of Indian Nationalism* (London: Allen and Unwin, 1963), p. 7.

13. Sri Aurobindo, "New Lamps for Old," *Indu Prakash*, August 21, 1893, pp. 14–15. Originally published as a series of articles between August and December 1893. This material is taken from Sri Aurobindo, *Bande Mataram: Early Political Writings* (Pondicherry: Sri Aurobindo Ashram, 1973). The editor writes that "the articles in this Volume are not an index of Sri Aurobindo's later views on the leading problems of the day. His views had undergone a great change with the development of his consciousness and knowledge."

14. Sri Aurobindo, "New Lamps for Old, No. 7," *Indu Prakash*, December 4, 1893. Congress at this point is seeking a variety of reforms that neither calls for Indian independence nor addresses the conditions of the vast majority of Indians.

15. Sri Aurobindo, "New Lamps for Old, No. 3," *Indu Prakash*, August 28, 1893.

16. Aurobindo insists that reforms can, at best, be only partially successful because the country is not politically independent. He tells his readers that success requires freedom—both a free mind and a free Indian state (Aurobindo, *Bande Mataram*, April 4, 1907, p. 91).

17. Sri Aurobindo, *Indu Prakash*, October 30, 1893, p. 29

18. Aurobindo, "New Lamps for Old, No. 3."

19. Aurobindo, *Bande Mataram*, June 9, 1907, p. 411.

20. Ibid., p. 413. An oppressive regime is blind to its own shortcomings. It can invent new forms of coercion but does not understand that its very use of force undermines its own rule. See Aurobindo, *Bande Mataram*, October 7, 1907, p. 558.

21. Sri Aurobindo, "The Idea of Karmayogin," *Karmayogin* [a weekly newspaper edited by Aurobindo], June 19, 1909. Taken from *The Essential Writings of Sri Aurobindo*, ed. Peter Heehs (Delhi: Oxford University Press, 1998), pp. 43–45.

22. For Gandhi's selective borrowing from modernity, see Ashis Nandy, *Traditions, Tyranny, and Utopia* (Delhi: Oxford University Press, 1987); Thomas Pantham, "On Modernity, Rationality, and Morality: Habermas and Gandhi," *Indian Journal of Social Science* 1, no. 2 (1988): 187–208; and Ronald Terchek, *Gandhi: Struggling for Autonomy* (Lanham, Md.: Rowman and Littlefield, 1998).

23. See Sri Aurobindo, "The Human Cycle," in *The Human Cycle: The Ideal of Human Unity, and War and Self-Determination* (Pondicherry: Sri Aurobindo Ashram, 1970), pp. 106, 183.

24. Ibid. p. 163.

25. Ibid., p. 98. "Reason can indeed make itself a mere servant of life; it can limit itself to the work the average normal man demands from it, content to furnish means and justifications for the interests, passions, prejudices of man and clothe them with a misleading garb of rationality" (ibid., p. 102).

26. Ibid., pp. 100–101.

27. Ibid., p. 97.

28. Ibid., pp. 112–13.

29. Ibid., pp. 99–100, 103. Reason "can in its nature be used and has always been used to justify any idea, theory of life, system of society or government . . . to which the will of man attaches itself for the moment or through the centuries" (ibid., p. 111).

30. Sri Aurobindo, *The Renaissance in India* (Pondicherry: Sri Aurobindo Ashram, 1951), p. 39.

31. Sri Aurobindo, *The Foundations of Indian Culture* (Pondicherry: Aurobindo Ashram, 1971), p. 75. "The monastic attitude implies a fear, an aversion, a distrust of life and its aspirations, and one cannot wisely guide that with which one is entirely out of sympathy" (Aurobindo, *Human Cycle*, p. 69).

32. Aurobindo, *Foundations of Indian Culture*, p. 35. See, on caste, Aurobindo, *Human Cycle*, p. 118.

33. Aurobindo, *Human Cycle*, pp. 102–3.

34. On Aurobindo's conception of freedom and harmony, see Dalton, *Indian Idea of Freedom*, chaps. 4–5, esp. pp. 101–5.

35. Aurobindo, *Human Cycle*, p. 198.

36. Ibid., p. 193.

37. Aurobindo, *Renaissance in India*, p. 24. For him, the "real sense and purpose" of religion has to do with how it helps individuals become spiritual. It is not about following orders. "Spirituality respects the freedom of the human soul because it is itself fulfilled by freedom, and the deepest meaning of freedom is the power to expand and grow towards perfection by the law of one's own Dharma" (Aurobindo, *Human Cycle*, p. 170). See Sri Aurobindo, "Ideal of Human Unity," in Aurobindo, *Human Cycle*, p. 211.

38. Aurobindo, *Foundations of Indian Culture*, p. 107

39. Ibid., p. 129. Vivekananda was a leading figure in late-nineteenth-century India who stressed the importance of having pride in a reformed Hinduism and of developing a strong sense of one's own worth and personal courage.

40. Ibid., p. 104. For an elaboration of the importance of diversity, see Aurobindo, *Ideal of Human Unity*, p. 490.

41. For an elaboration of the importance of nondomination and how it is distinguished from noninterference, see Philip Pettit, *Republicanism* (Oxford: Oxford University Press, 1997).

42. Aurobindo, *Ideal of Human Unity*, p. 359.

43. Ibid., p. 360.

44. For a further discussion on freedom and error, see Aurobindo, *Human Cycle*, p. 214.

45. Aurobindo, *The Renaissance in India*, pp. 63, 65. Also see Aurobindo, *Human Cycle*, pp. 213, 215. Elsewhere he holds that "[s]piritual freedom [and] spiritual perfection [are] not figured as a far-off intangible idea, but presented as the highest human aim towards which all must grow in the end" (Aurobindo, *Foundations of Indian Culture*, p. 107). He also claims that Hinduism gives room "for all terrestrial aims" (ibid., p. 101).

46. Aurobindo, *Renaissance in India*, p. 65.

47. Aurobindo, *Human Cycle*, p. 213.

48. Aurobindo, *Foundations of Indian Culture*, p. 174.

49. Aurobindo, *Renaissance in India*, pp. 15–16. He goes on to argue that Europeans are struck that Indian spirituality is an "illusionist denial of life." This feature of Hinduism "assumed exaggerated proportions only in the period of decline" (ibid., p. 16).

50. Aurobindo, *Foundations of Indian Culture*, p. 25.

51. Ibid., p. 35.

52. Aurobindo, *Essays on the Gita* (New York: Sri Aurobindo Library, 1950), p. 38. The *Bhagavat Gita* is a sacred text that recounts the battle between Arjuna and the forces of light with the forces of darkness. Arjuna recoils at fighting his enemies who are also his kin and teachers, even though they have deprived him of his rightful

claims. He is instructed by Krishna that he must do his duty and fight. In Gandhi's commentary on the *Bhagavat Gita*, the military struggle is metaphorical; the real struggle is nonviolent. See his *Discourses on the Gita* (Ahmedabad: Navajivan Publishing House, 1946).

53. Aurobindo, *Essays on the Gita*, pp. 38–39. Not denying the importance of Gandhi's "love force," Aurobindo finds it inadequate to the task of facing the real world today. Aurobindo's reality is a world of good and evil, a world that is evolving. Successive steps aim at an eventual harmony, but until that time evil will retain its crushing and challenging presence in the world.

In "The Morality of Boycott" (in *Bande Mataram*, 3 vols. [New Delhi: Sri Aurobindo Ashram Publishers, 1998], in volume 3), Aurobindo denies that love has a role in politics. To ask people to love their enemy is to "ignore human nature." He goes on to insist that the *Bhagavat Gita* admonishes us not to shrink from battle.

54. Aurobindo, *Essays on the Gita*, pp. 38–39, 44.

55. Ibid., pp. 156, 223.

56. See Reinhold Niebuhr, *The Children of Light and the Children of Darkness* (New York: Scribners, 1944).

57. Dallmayr, *Alternative Visions*, pp. 6–7.

SIX

Between Athens and Jerusalem (or Mecca): A Journey with Dallmayr, Strauss, Ibn Rushd, and Jabiri

Michaelle Browers

Despite their radical difference, [Athens and Jerusalem,] I feel, have been implicated with each other for some time, their walls having been breached long ago; in a sense, in the midst of Athens or her interstices, Jerusalem has always been lying in wait—not as a historical destiny, nor as a mission to be implemented, but as a hidden sense. This is why, despite an internal distance or exile and despite the "prohibition of the name," philosophers have never ceased to speak obliquely and in a roundabout way also about Jerusalem. This is also why, in the midst of the conflicts and agonies of the day, political thinkers through the ages, latter-day Athenians one and all, have continued searching for the linkage or tunnel—never quite knowing the direction, stumbling badly all along the way, tapping like blind men with a cane the rocks and curbsides for the sounds or echoes of a noiseless promise: the promised city of peace.

Fred Dallmayr

I have long been a student of Fred Dallmayr's work in continental philosophy, but have been most influenced by his recent major contributions toward opening up the academic subfield in which we both dwell—political theory—to comparative and non-Western studies, a project perhaps not much older than the scholarly work he collected as editor of the volume bearing the promising title *Border Crossings: Toward a Comparative Political Theory*.[1] No one has done as much to challenge the provincialism of political theory as Dallmayr and I will always be grateful for the space his work has opened for studies of alternative political thought. *Beyond Orientalism* (1996), *Alternative Visions* (1998) and some of the articles that were incorporated into *Achieving Our World* (2001) and *Dialogue among Civilizations* (2002), each of which encompasses various engagements with Arab and Islamic thinkers, were published as I was conceptualizing my doctoral dissertation; these works provided much of the inspiration and encouragement that led to my own study of Arab and Islamic political thought (hardly a traditional dissertation topic in political theory). I think it no exaggeration to say that Fred Dallmayr's most recent interventions in political theory go a long way toward chartering more cosmopolitan, less dichotomous journeys with individuals and schools of thought from the Muslim world.

THE STRAUSSIAN LEGACY

Certainly, Dallmayr is not the first political theorist to engage in productive encounters with thinkers in the Arab and Islamic traditions. Leo Strauss and his students (and his students' students) have done much to continue and further the study of both contemporary, but especially early, Islamic political thought and I would be remiss if I did not acknowledge their contribution and influence. At the same time, I have also been troubled by the domination of the Straussian school and its esoteric approach[2] to Islamic political thought, especially in the United States. One scholar has gone so far as to refer (disparagingly) to the esoteric approach as the "standard interpretation" of Islamic philosophy.[3] More disconcerting, perhaps, is the sense of rupture and clash that animates the Straussian approach, such that one feels pressured to choose a side—or at least to add fuel to the ongoing conflict—between the various competing dichotomies put forth: ancient and modern, Athens and Jerusalem, reason and Revelation, philosophy and theology.[4]

Even in non-Straussian readings of Islamic political thought one feels the shadow of such conflicts. One example of this is found in studies on the twelfth-century Muslim philosopher from Cordova, Ibn Rushd (1126–98), known in the West as Averroës. The first English translator of Ibn Rushd's commentary on Plato's *Republic*, Erwin Rosenthal, maintained that we should understand the *falasifa* (the medieval Muslim philosophers) as "Muslim philosophers first and followers of their masters Plato and Aristotle second."[5] In the introduction to his subsequent translation of Averroës's same commentary, Ralph Lerner asserts the opposite: rather than first and foremost a Muslim philosopher, Ibn Rushd is presented as "the faithful companion of Plato." Elevating this conclusion to an interpretive principle, Lerner concludes that "Averroës, like kindred souls before and after him, found utility, relevance, and value in Plato's *Republic* for various reasons. Not least of these was Plato's truth about lying."[6] Whereas Rosenthal concludes that Ibn Rushd identified Plato's ideal state with that suggested in Islamic law, Ralph Lerner's translation of the same work seems to be undertaken in large part to correct that view. Averroës, Lerner maintains, "denies that the *shariʿa* has any decisive superiority [over philosophy]."[7]

The debate between Straussians (such as Lerner, Charles Butterworth, Miriam Galston, among others) and non-Straussians (such as Rosenthal, Seyyed Hossein Nasr, and Henry Corbin, the latter of whom referred to Islamic philosophy as *la philosophie prophétique*) often seems to take the character of a competition in which one must choose among various clearly defined worldviews. Particular Muslim philosophers (and Jewish philosophers as well) must be seen as either in kinship with the Greeks or in kinship with the *umma* (community of believers), and the two must be seen as in tension, such that one of the kinships must be either denied, hidden from view, or appropriated by the other. There is a contemporary corollary to this side-taking in studies that feel a need to identify various modern Arab thinkers as falling on either one side or the other of a deep divide presumably separating the secular and the religious. As Strauss himself has put it: "[The Western] tradition has two roots. It consists of two heterogeneous elements, of two elements which are ultimately incompatible with each other—the Hebrew element and the Greek element. We speak, and we speak rightly, of the antagonism between Jerusalem and Athens, between faith and philosophy."[8]

It is statements such as these that lead Dallmayr to take note of a "general proclivity pervading Strauss's thought: the tendency to replace tensions or paradoxes by stark antinomies or dualisms."[9] One might locate in Dallmayr's work precisely the opposite: a tendency to reconstruct conflictual dualisms as creative tensions. David Rasmussen has noted[10] (and Dallmayr has confirmed) the significance of Dallmayr's choice of book titles as "markers of intellectual engagement and of a movement in the 'chasm' or *intermonde* along a road which was never clearly precharted,"[11] terms such as "twilight," "margins," "between," "other," and more recently "toward," "beyond," "among," "encounters," "paths," and "crossings." A common thread in *Beyond Orientalism, Alternative Visions, Border Crossings, Achieving Our World,* and *Dialogue among Civilizations* lies in the attempt to articulate "the proper modes of living and sharing together" and the "opening-up of a space or shared matrix holding the speakers silently together" amid the "alternative visions" that occupy our increasingly "global village." Perhaps Dallmayr's most profound contribution to those of us who wish to engage non-Western political thought is his efforts to find a hermeneutic—or perhaps more accurately, an "ethic"—to guide cross-cultural interactions that move beyond that of strife, competition, and contestation of the unbridgeable gulfs of the Straussian approach.

This is seen most clearly in *Beyond Orientalism* where he identifies seven "modes of cross-cultural encounter": conquest, conversion, assimilation/ acculturation, partial assimilation/cultural borrowing, liberalism/minimal engagement, conflict/class struggle, and dialogical engagement. Dallmayr characterizes the first three (conquest, conversion, assimilation) as starkly hegemonic or hierarchical.[12] The fourth, partial assimilation, takes place on a more nearly equal basis, but the "outcome," Dallmayr notes, "can be greatly varied," ranging from "the melting-pot syndrome" to "an ambivalent form of syncretism" or "a precarious type of cultural coexistence" to a "movement of genuine self-transformation." The fifth mode (liberalism/minimal engagement) tends toward isolationism; while the sixth (conflict/class struggle) he deems overly contentious and unstable. Dallmayr's mode of choice is the final one (that of dialogical engagement and interaction), which he understands as a deconstructive dialogue that respects otherness beyond assimilation. That he seeks both to articulate and to engage in this form of "dialogic interaction" is illustrated in many of Dallmayr's recent works, which carve out a space for a non-Straussian reading of Islamic thought (or any thought that exists within the context of a religious tradition), while at the same time locating the possibility of a nonconfrontational reading of faith and reason within Strauss's own work. My aim here is to retrace a path in Dallmayr's journey, in the spirit of what he has referred to as an "exercise," "a theorizing 'en route' venturing—albeit hesitantly—beyond traditional categories and philosophical benchmarks."[13] In the process of doing so, I hope to foreground aspects of the surroundings (various trees, roots, and rhizomes) along the way that guide us toward a better understanding of parallel attempts in Arab-Islamic contexts to venture beyond the traditional "benchmark" of "the secular."

TOWARD A THIRD DIMENSION: BEYOND DICHOTOMY AND FUSION

The notion of an inevitable or necessary antagonism, of incompatibility, contest, or even battle between faith and philosophy is found in a number of Strauss's works. It is not always clear whether one should consider such characterizations as descriptive, normative, or critical. At times the conflict is put forth as "the secret of the vitality of the West," sometimes the source of and other times the result of "the crisis of modernity"—although according to a more Nietzschian worldview such assessments need not be seen as at odds. As a description of the modern situation, Strauss is more ambiguous. In "Progress or Return?" he asserts that the "radical disagreement today is frequently played down, and this playing down has a certain superficial justification, for the whole history of the West presents itself at first glance as an attempt to harmonize, or to synthesize, the Bible and Greek philosophy."[14] Yet, later in the same essay, Strauss maintains that each of the two "antagonists"—philosophy and the Bible—"has tried for millennia to refute the other [and this] effort is continued in our day, and in fact it is taking on a new intensity after some decades of indifference."[15]

Amid Strauss's famous elaborations of this ongoing battle between Athens and Jerusalem, Dallmayr, in his "Leo Strauss Peregrinus," manages to uncover a more fruitful "process of mutual questioning and contestation," one that "simultaneously preserve[s] the integrity of their [ancients' and moderns'] respective positions."[16] Dallmayr does so by focusing less on Strauss's delineation of the two opponents and more on those spaces where there are intimations of their interaction, sharing, and engagement. According to Strauss, "every disagreement . . . presupposes a disagreement about something and must agree as to the importance of that something." In the case of the Bible and Greek philosophy, the two share "perfect agreement" in regard to their "rejection" of various elements of modernity and "regarding the importance of morality, regarding the content of morality, and regarding its ultimate insufficiency." However, "they disagree as regards the basis of morality."[17] Strauss goes on to specify a further, related "common ground" that exists between the "two roots": "the problem of divine law."[18] Both Athens and Jerusalem, philosophy and religion (Judaism and Islam, at least), are based in laws, the laws of the cosmos or the revealed law—they are both based in the world or the "always already" of "being." At the end of the essay, rather than advocating a clear choice between the two sides, Strauss concludes that the answer lies "between the two codes," amid their "fundamental tension." While "no one can be both a philosopher and theologian," neither can one "transcend the conflict" or "pretend to be a synthesis": we can and must "live that conflict." Although Strauss suggests that this involves being "either one or the other" in some sense, he also suggests that it is not enough to choose a side. Each side must remain "open to the challenge" of the other.[19]

Dallmayr highlights this strand in Strauss's work while continuing to worry that his alternative rationalism tends toward the theoretical or contemplative in such a way that it "corroborates and reinforces the divorce or gulf between philosophy and politics." "By portraying politics as an external bulwark shielding private reflection," Dallmayr notes that "[Strauss's] treatment (wittingly or unwittingly) raises added doubts regarding the 'very possibility' of political thought as a viable philosophical enterprise."[20]

In an assessment of the modern age that echoes the Straussian theme, Dallmayr acknowledges that "as many times before in human history, reason and faith are at loggerheads today." He is, however, quick to add that "what is frequently neglected . . . is the contextual character of the topic—the aspect that there is a third dimension operative in the reason–faith relation. This dimension is the domain of politics or political praxis, a domain powerfully molding the character of the relation."[21] Rather than viewing this domain as extrinsic or antithetical to philosophical contemplation, as a result of either its mundane or recalcitrant character, Dallmayr calls attention to the philosopher's ontological status, as one who already "lives that conflict," such that one's participation can never be truly esoteric. There is no vantage point outside that of his rootedness in his own being. To clarify the character of that third dimension and how it reflects the relationship between reason and faith, Athens and Jerusalem, Dallmayr like Strauss turns to the work of an early Islamic philosopher, Ibn Rushd. It is characteristic of Dallmayr's opus that he turns to those most sensitive and seemingly most distantiated ideas and thinkers in order to not confirm or reinforce existing bifurcations and separations, but to arrive at a perspective of the "other," "which sees 'difference' as harboring a linkage devoid of fusion or synthesis."[22]

FROM SIBLING RIVALRY TO A POLITICAL PRAXIS OF COMPANIONSHIP IN IBN RUSHD

In regard to reading Islamic thought (or any thought with a relation to a religious tradition), Dallmayr suggests a hermeneutic that involves considering the possibility that philosophy and Revelation are not in a zero-sum contest that determines whether "philosophy, which means to be the queen, must be made the handmaid of revelation or vice versa,"[23] but rather whether there is the possibility of "relatedness without synthesis."[24] In the words of Ibn Rushd, "philosophy (al-hikma) is the companion (sahiba) and milk-sister (al-ukht al-radhi'a) of religion (al-shari'a)." They are "companions by nature (al-mustahibatan bil-tab') and lovers by essence and instinct (al-mutahabbatan bil-jawhar wa al-ghariza)."[25] A milk-sister forms her relation by nursing at the breast of the same woman as another, who becomes her "milk-sister" or "milk-brother." According to Islamic law, those so bound are subject to the same laws prohibiting marriage regardless of their lack of biological bond.

Ibn Rushd understood philosophy and Revelation to exist within a fundamental bond, as they draw nourishment from the same source. Reason and Revelation neither contradict nor replace each other, nor can one be reduced to or explained in terms of the other. In Ibn Rushd's view, whoever holds otherwise does not truly understand the nature of either. He further affirms the productive, even necessary role of philosophy within Islam: "Reflect, then, O people of perception" (Qur'an 59:2) and contemplate "the kingdom of heaven and earth and the things which God hath created" (Qur'an 7:184). The Qur'an also admonishes: "Will they, then, not consider the camels, how they were created? And heaven, how it was raised up?" (Qur'an 88:17–18).[26] Thus, Ibn Rushd arrives at his answer to the question of "whether the study of philosophy and logic is allowed by the Law, or prohibited, or commanded either by way of recommendation or as obligatory" from a study of "the standpoint of the study of the Law."[27] In locating a public defense of philosophy within the principles of the shari'a, Ibn Rushd demonstrates, in Dallmayr's words, a "commitment to a shared horizon of praxis."[28]

It is the socially embedded character of both philosophy and religion, along with the need for a particular character of the social, that binds the two. That is not to deny the existence of conflict. Throughout his works, Ibn Rushd remains critical of the theologians (*mutakallimun*) who would deny philosophy, as well as those philosophers who do harm to religion, often expressing great anguish and scolding them for their sibling rivalries. "For our soul is in the utmost sorrow and pain," he proclaims, "on account of the evil fancies and perverted beliefs which have infiltrated this religion, and particularly such afflictions as have happened to it at the hand of would-be philosophers. For the injuries from a friend are more severe than injuries from an enemy," especially injuries between two that "are companions by nature and lovers by essence and instinct."[29] But if we can understand Ibn Rushd himself as neither aiming to reconcile reason and Revelation, nor to alienate one or the other—rather than as a philosopher apart, caught in the midst of a necessarily and incessantly conflictual relationship that forces him to choose between reason and Revelation, philosophy and theology, Athens and Mecca—it becomes possible to understand Ibn Rushd as a thinker who remains both culturally situated and who, in his wisdom, is able to extend beyond his situatedness. Such an understanding of Ibn Rushd and the relation between reason and Revelation are reflected in more recent Arab-Islamic political thought as well.

Journeying beyond the Secular/Religious Divide with Jabiri

Just as Western studies of Ibn Rushd are at odds over whether to consider him a philosopher or a Muslim first and foremost, many Western analysts are forever trying to categorize contemporary Arab thinkers as either secular or Islamic. Yet, some thinkers resist being categorized in this way. One such example is provided by the Moroccan philosopher Muhammad 'Abid al-Jabiri (b. 1936). Jabiri has been attributed with espousing a "Latin Averroism" with the paradoxical aims of "striv[ing] to secularize thought and separate state and religion," while at the same time "leaving room for the religious legitimation of scientific thinking," which, to at least one author, is taken as "a concession to the Islamists."[30] Jabiri has been characterized as socialist, Islamic leftist, Islamic modernist, and liberal modernist (the latter by me) and accused of Eurocentrism and conservatism, among other things. I am told he has also been referred to as the "Arab Allan Bloom." He is perhaps best known in Morocco, however, for the articles he writes for the newspaper al-Ittihad al-ishtiraki, which is published by the Socialist Union of Popular Forces Party. For his part, Jabiri resists narrowly characterizing himself and his work, and has taken particular care not to be indentified with secularism. On a number of occasions, Jabiri has maintained that efforts to position oneself and one's opponents under the banner of "secularism" or "Islamism" are a way of avoiding other, more pressing concerns.

> The question of secularism in the Arab world is a false question (masala muzayyafa), insofar as it expresses real needs by reference to categories which do not correspond to them: the need for independence within a single national identity, the need for a democracy which protects the rights of minorities and the need for the rational practice of political action. All of these are objective—even reasonable and necessary—needs in the Arab world. However, they lose their justification and necessity when expressed through the use of dubious slogans like "secularism."[31]

Democracy, according to Jabiri's formulation, consists of the protection of rights, both individual and collective rights; and rationalism entails a political practice based on logical and ethical standards, "rather than on identity, fanaticism, or fickleness." Thus, the exclusion of Islam from politics is neither democratic nor rational.[32]

"Islam," Jabiri argues, "is not a church that we can separate from the state."[33] While at first glance this position might be seen to echo those Islamists who maintain Islam is both a religion and a state (Islam din wa dawla), it is quite clear that Jabiri means something else. He maintains that it is a historical fact that Islam formed Arabs into a religion and a state. But it is also a fact, he says, that the state and its form were not designated in the text of the Qur'an or the accounts (hadith) of the Prophet. Rather, the form of the state was decided on by Muslims. What Jabiri means in asserting that "Islam is not a church that we can separate from the state" is that just as historically the Arab constituted the "matter of Islam," so too Islam is part of the "spirit" of the Arab. As such, Islam becomes a basis for the Arab community: "the spiritual Islam for the Arab Muslims and the civilizational Islam for all Arabs—Muslims or non-Muslim."[34]

Secularism is clearly a particularly vexing and contested concept, and not only in Muslim contexts. For many Arab thinkers, secularism is tied to state modernization projects that first emerged during the *Nahda* (Arab Renaissance or Enlightenment) period, which in the nineteenth century first attempted to address what was perceived to be the "backwardness" of the Arab and Islamic world when seen in light of the modern West. In this context, secularism was often intended to support state development projects and, in many cases, "did not seek to separate religion from politics" so much as it sought "to subjugate religion" and other social forces to political control.[35] Echoing a question earlier posed by the Muslim modernist and Arab *Nahda* thinker Amir Shakib Arslan (1869–1946) Jabiri asks: "Why did the Muslims fall behind while the others—the West in particular—advanced?"[36] This immediately prompts the further query: "How do we catch up?"[37] The same questions that drove the *Nahda* still animate contemporary calls for a renewal (*tajdid*) of this project, but the questions must be addressed in a fundamentally different way, based on new principles appropriate for the currently existing reality.

For many thinkers, much of the general sense of crisis (*azma*) that today pervades the Arab context can be traced back to the failure of the *Nahda* project and the autocratic states it left in its wake. Amondo Salvatore characterizes this sense of crisis in the writings of Jabiri and other Arab intellectuals as a profound uneasiness emerging from a feeling of disjuncture reached when one's fundamental framework of reference (the Arab-Islamic heritage, *al-turath*) is no longer capable of sustaining the claims of distinctions normally allowed by the framework or the demands of one's historical situation.[38] The crisis, Jabiri argues, is something that is experienced at the level of consciousness, as a form of cultural disorder in which the individual becomes increasingly unable to relate social and political ideas and values to his or her life situation.[39] He maintains that the crisis is also apparent at the level of the current political, social, and economic reality where societal institutions and structures are increasingly experienced as fetters denying the individual the opportunity to grow and to realize his or her potential. Many Arab thinkers, including Jabiri, diagnose the problem particularly as a "crisis of democracy" (*azmat al-dimuqratiyya*) the symptoms of which are exhibited in the apathy, alienation, and passivity on the part of the masses, as well as in the limited participation and the repressive practices at the level of the state.[40]

The understanding of crisis articulated in Arab political thought corresponds in many ways to what Strauss refers to as "the crisis of our time" or the "crisis of modernity."[41] This crisis, which has its origins in the wholesale forgetting of the teachings of the ancients, requires not only a return to the ancients, but a reexamination of the nature and origins of modernity. Clearly, Strauss and Jabiri situate themselves and their respective societies vis-à-vis the crisis differently. Strauss locates a rupture of "moral orientation" in modern secularism's accent on anthropocentric, subject-centered desires and wants. Much of Jabiri's concern is with deconstructing the referential authority of an ahistorical Islamic heritage that "Arab reason" (al-'aql al-'arabi) is said to rely on.[42] Following Ibn Rushd, Jabiri maintains that there exists a correspondence (tawafuq), not harmonization (tawfiq), between religion and reason, and that the two shall always remain distinct. While some have found within Jabiri's critique a rationalism that they have characterized as "secular," Jabiri does not refer to it as such; rather, he calls it "objective."

Another main "referential authority" Jabiri seeks to deconstruct is the Western Enlightenment and the secular Marxist and liberal ideologies to which it gave birth. Implicit in Jabiri's question regarding how best to appropriate this heritage is another query concerning how to remain authentic in a way that engages both the Arab-Islamic heritage and Western modernity, as well as addresses contemporary reality. It is clear that Jabiri is trying to carve out a space that is not dominated by either fundamentalism or secularism, both of which he understands to embody ideological perspectives. According to Salvatore, from the point of view of thinkers such as Jabiri, "modernity entails the double dimension of a subject which is transculturally embedded in a Western-centered age, i.e., contemporary to it (al-mu'asara), but also involved in a potentially universal, although still Western-based, process of qualitative search for the new (al-hadatha)."[43] Arab modernity can entail neither an unproblematic adoption of Western modernity nor a wholesale opposition to it. Jabiri often uses the two terms together (al-hadatha wa al-mu'asara, modernity and contemporaneity) to designate "modernity" as such, drawing attention to the fact that addressing both Western modernity and Arab contemporaneity—that is, addressing both Western hegemony and the pressing questions of their time—are necessary facets of an Arab project of modernity.

Certainly many Arab intellectuals experience the crisis as a call for them to choose between "the seduction of Western thought, with its superiority in the economic, scientific, technological, and military spheres," and "the classical 'golden' period of the Arab-Islamic Empire," or alternatively, to engage in some form of "eclectism that combined what was seen as positive in both of the two models."[44] In Jabiri's view, dichotomizations between Western secularism and Islam, or between the traditional heritage and modernity, amount to "false problematics" (*mushkilat muzayyafa*). Rather than suggesting that Islam awaits or is in need of secularization, he asserts the mutual interpenetration of Islam and secularism, as well as the modernity of contemporary Arab societies. Thus, it is not the adoption (or capitulation) to Western secular modernity that is the most salient issue, but rather the reappropriation (*imtilak*) of the critical Islamic rationalism that Jabiri associates with the neglected tradition of Ibn Rushd and others—that is a reclaiming "from within" (*min al-dakhil*) that recognizes the already intimate and intertwined relationship between the various strands that are too often put at odds.

I understand the stance being negotiated by the Moroccan philosopher to have parallels with Dallmayr's engagement with Strauss, as well as to suggest a perspective on secularism that has been perhaps more fully articulated by William Connolly in one of his most recent works *Why I Am Not a Secularist*. According to Connolly, secularism constitutes the "wish to provide an authoritative and self-sufficient public space equipped to regulate and limit 'religious' disputes in public life."[45] But as secularism comes to see itself as that authority, it contributes to the same sort of intolerance and limitations that secularists fear from religious fundamentalists. Connolly sees secularism as "a political settlement," and thus one that can be reworked into a new settlement that opens up new conditions of being.[46] One need only consider the sensitive issue of the ban against the Muslim *hijab* (as well as Jewish skullcaps and large Christian crosses) in France's public schools. The ban was enacted under the French doctrine of *laicité*, which has come to mean the barring of religion from the public arena in order to guarantee the equality of all citizens before the law, regardless of their particular beliefs. Many perceive the ban as reflecting more a phobia of Islam than the protection of equal rights, and criticize it for singling out and alienating French Muslims and, hence, for fundamentally conflicting with the goal of integration.

In contrast to the Rushdian metaphor of "milk-sisters" who take sustenance from the same source, Connolly's preferred image is that of the rhizome, an image he takes from Gilles Deleuze, which is a structure consisting of a system of various tubers, stems, and filaments, "connected by multiple notes," yet lacking any single or main taproot from which they all feed. Connolly wishes this to shed light on what he refers to as "deep pluralism," in which we are connected to others in a variety of ways, organizing ourselves into a complex array of partially overlapping and intersecting assemblages, without the need for a common center—a "democratic ethos of engagement across multidimensional lines of difference" that is "jointed to a sensibility that affirms the ambiguity of being and the deep contingency of things."[47] In the end, there are problems with any metaphor that tends to conceive of the components as entities. Ibn Rushd's milk-sisters cannot be equated with philosopher and theologian any more perfectly than can individuals make up the tubers of even the most complex rhizome. But there is again an important difference of emphasis or accent. Both Revelation and philosophy contain inner tensions in addition to those tensions without. Jabiri and Dallmayr—and perhaps Dallmayr's Strauss—still seek to locate not a common center or a single root (like a tree with various branches), nor a jointed eclecticism that draws from several sources, but the recognition of a shared ground of political praxis from which we all draw—one more conducive to "mediation, reconciliation, and friendship"[48] and less susceptible to "decline into warring fragments when some of its constituencies insist upon sinking deep, exclusionary roots, disabling possibilities for the formation of democratic assemblages."[49] To return to the example of French *laicité*, the attunement Dallmayr suggests might encourage a recognition of the fact that both opposition to and support of the ban is fought on a shared ground of political praxis—let alone over the bodies of young schoolgirls—and inspire a "continued searching for the linkage or tunnel" among citizens who have "been implicated with each other for some time." Whether in the Middle East or Europe one hopes, with Fred Dallmayr, that the invocation of Ibn Rushd will persist as a signal for "the yearning for a tolerantly open, yet morally responsible society, a society in which reason and faith, respect for humans and for the divine are balanced (not collapsed) in a carefully calibrated way."[50]

NOTES

1. Fred Dallmayr, ed., *Border Crossings: Toward a Comparative Political Theory* (Lanham, Md.: Lexington Books, 1999).

2. I take the "esoteric approach" to be one that identifies different levels of meaning addressed to different levels of readers. In Strauss's works, this esotericism is understood as a necessary way for philosophers to communicate truths that might run afoul of existing (religious) authorities or disrupt the (religious) beliefs that maintain civil peace and order. See Leo Strauss, *Persecution and the Art of Writing* (Glencoe, Ill.: Free Press, 1952).

3. Oliver Leaman, "Does the Interpretation of Islamic Philosophy Rest on a Mistake?" *International Journal of Middle East Studies* 12 (1980): 525.

4. Certainly this conflict of interpretation does not originate with Strauss. Leaman points out that "the esoteric interpretation is in fact a reaction against an older type of interpretation, according to which the *falasifa* managed or thought they managed, by and large, to reconcile Islam and philosophy, and their writings showed how this feat could be accomplished. This type of interpretation was itself a reaction to the earlier view (largely based on the nature of Averroism in medieval Christian Europe) that the *falasifa* were rationalists who rejected the values and beliefs of the community of Islam in favour of what they had learnt from Aristotle and Greek logic." Oliver Leaman, *An Introduction to Classical Islamic Philosophy* (Cambridge: Cambridge University Press, 2002), p. 213.

5. Erwin I. J. Rosenthal, *Political Thought in Medieval Islam* (Cambridge: Cambridge University Press, 1962), p. 4. See also Erwin I. J. Rosenthal, *Averroës' Commentary on Plato's Republic* (Cambridge: Cambridge University Press, 1966).

6. Ralph Lerner, *Averroës on Plato's Republic* (Ithaca: Cornell University Press, 1974), p. xxvii.

7. Rosenthal, *Averroës' Commentary,* p. 14; Lerner, *Averroës on Plato's Republic,* p. xvii.

8. Leo Strauss, "Thucydides: The Meaning of Political History," in *The Rebirth of Classical Rationalism: An Introduction to the Thought of Leo Strauss, Essays and Lectures by Leo Strauss,* ed. Thomas L. Pangle (Chicago: Chicago University Press, 1989), p. 72.

9. Fred Dallmayr, "Politics against Philosophy: Strauss and Drury," *Political Theory* 15, no. 3 (1987): 332.

10. David M. Rasmussen, "Fred Dallmayr: The Odyssey of Reconciling Reason," *Human Studies* 21 (1998): 274.

11. Fred Dallmayr, "A Response to Friends," *Human Studies* 21 (1998): 297.

12. Fred Dallmayr, *Beyond Orientalism: Essays on Cross-Cultural Encounter* (Albany: SUNY Press, 1996), pp. 3–37.

13. Fred Dallmayr, *Polis and Praxis: Exercises in Contemporary Political Theory* (Cambridge: MIT Press, 1984), p. 11.

14. Leo Strauss, "Progress or Return?" in *Rebirth of Classical Political Rationalism,* p. 245.

15. Ibid., p. 260.

16. Fred Dallmayr, "Leo Strauss Peregrinus," *Social Research* 61, no. 4 (1994): 877–906. Although, here too, Dallmayr critically reflects on Strauss's tendency to

grant preference "to disjuncture over juncture, to dichotomous rupture or antinomy over reciprocity and correlation," and to assert "philosophical ambiguities and unresolved paradoxes (where 'ambiguity' is not equivalent to a fruitful tension)."

17. Strauss, "Progress or Return?" p. 246.

18. Ibid., p. 248.

19. Ibid., p. 270.

20. Dallmayr, *Polis and Praxis*, p. 36.

21. Fred Dallmayr, *Dialogue among Civilizations: Some Exemplary Voices* (New York: Palgrave Macmillan, 2002), p. 122.

22. Ibid., p. 3.

23. Leo Strauss, *Natural Right and History* (Chicago: University of Chicago Press, 1953), pp. 74–75.

24. Dallmayr, *Dialogue among Civilizations*, p. 125.

25. Ibn Rushd, *Fasl al-maqal fima bayn al-hikma wa al-shari'a min al-ittisal* (The Decisive Treatise regarding the Relationship between Philosophy and the Law), ed. Muhammad 'Imara (Cairo: Dar al-ma'rif, 1972), p. 67.

26. *The Qur'an: A Modern English Version*, trans. Majid Fakhri; Ibn Rushd, *Fasl al-maqal*, pp. 22–23.

27. *Averroës on the Harmony of Religion and Philosophy*, trans. George F. Hourani (London: Luzac, 1961), p. 44.

28. Dallmayr, *Dialogue among Civilizations*, p. 128.

29. *Averroës on the Harmony of Religion and Philosophy*, p. 68.

30. Anke von Kügelgen, "A Call for Rationalism: 'Arab Averroists' in the Twentieth Century," *Alif* 16 (1996): 98, 117.

31. Muhammad 'Abid al-Jabiri, *al-Din wa al-dawla wa tatbiq al-shar'ia* (Religion, the State, and the Application of Islamic Law) (Beirut: Center for Arab Unity Studies, 1996), p. 113. These lines are also found in his "Badal al-'almaniyya: al-dimuqratiyya wa al-'aqlaniyya" (The Alternative of Secularism: Democracy and Rationalism), *al-yawm al-sabi'* p. 224 (August 22, 1988), and "al-'almaniyya wa al-Islam: islam laysat kanisa likay nufasilahu 'an al-dawla" (Secularism and Islam: Islam Is Not a Church That We Can Separate from the State), in Jabiri and Hasan Hanafi, *Hiwar al-mashriq al-maghrib: talih silsila al-rudud wa al-munaqashat* (East-West Dialogue: Followed by a Series of Replies and Debates) (Casablanca: Dar al-tubqal, 1990), p. 46.

32. Jabiri, "al-'almaniyya wa al-Islam," p. 46.

33. Ibid., p. 45.

34. Ibid., pp. 45–46.

35. Vali Nasr, "Lessons from the Muslim World," *Daedalus* 132, no. 3 (2003): 67–72.

36. Shakib Arslan, *Why Did the Muslims Fall Behind While the Others Advanced?* (limadha ta'akhkhara al-muslimun wa limadha taqaddama ghayruhum) (Beirut: Dar maktabat al-hayah, 1965).

37. Muhammad 'Abid al-Jabiri, "Ishkaliyyat al-asala wa al-mu'asara fi al-fikr al-'arabi al-hadith wa al-mu'asir: sira tabaqi am mushkil thaqafi?" (The Problematic of

Authenticity and Contemporaneity in Modern and Contemporary Arab Political Thought: A Class Struggle or Cultural Problem?), in *al-Turath wa tahaddiyya al-'asr fi al-watan al-'arabi: al-asala wa al-mu'asara* (The Heritage and the Challenges of the Age in the Arab World: Authenticity and Contemporaneity), ed. al-Sayyid Yasin (Beirut: Center for Arab Unity Studies, 1984), p. 35. Jabiri uses the term *nanhadu* here, meaning "to catch up" or "to stand up," which has the same root as *nahda*.

38. Amando Salvatore, "The Rational Authentication of *turath* in Contemporary Arab Thought: Muhammad al-Jabiri and Hasan Hanafi," *Muslim World* 85, no. 3/4 (1995): 191–214.

39. Muhammad 'Abid al-Jabiri, Interview with author, Rabat, Morocco (November 1996). See also Muhammad 'Abid al-Jabiri, *Ishkaliyyat al-fikr al-'arabi al-mu'asir* (Problematics of Contemporary Arab Thought) (Beirut: Center for Arab Unity Studies, 1989).

40. See Khalid al-Nasr, "Azmat al-dimuqratiyya fi al-watan al-'arabi" (The Crisis of Democracy in the Arab World), in *al-Dimuqratiyya wa al-huquq al-insan fi al-watan al-'arabi* (Democracy and Human Rights in the Arab World), ed. 'Ali al-Din Hilal (Beirut: Center for Arab Unity Studies, 1983), pp. 25–61.

41. Leo Strauss, "The Crisis of Our Time," in *The Predicament of Modern Politics,* ed. Harold J. Spaeth (Detroit: University of Detroit Press, 1964), p. 41.

42. See, e.g., Muhammad 'Abid al-Jabiri, *Takwin al-aql al-'arabi* (The Formation of Arab Reason) (Beirut: Dar al-tali'a, 1984).

43. Armando Salvatore, *Islam and the Political Discourse of Modernity* (Reading, UK: Ithaca Press, 1997), p. 226.

44. Walid Hamarnehi, introduction to Mohamed 'Abed al-Jabri, *Arab-Islamic Philosophy: A Contemporary Critique,* trans. Aziz Abbassi (Austin: University of Texas Press, 1999), p. x.

45. William Connolly, *Why I Am Not a Secularist* (Minneapolis: University of Minnesota Press, 1999), p. 5.

46. Ibid., p. 36.

47. Ibid., p. 186.

48. Dallmayr, "A Response to Friends," p. 306.

49. William Connolly, *The Ethos of Pluralization* (Minneapolis: University of Minnesota Press, 1995), p. 94.

50. Dallmayr, *Dialogue among Civilizations,* p. 146.

SEVEN

Letting Being Be: Cross-Cultural Encounters in a University Setting

Neve Gordon

Lies will flow from my lips, but there may perhaps be some truth mixed up with them; it is for you to seek out this truth and decide whether any part of it is worth keeping. If not you will of course throw the whole of it in the wastepaper basket and forget all about it.

Virginia Woolf

"To Be Removed beyond the Reach of Mixture"

It was still unclear whether the student had cheated. Following the professor's complaint, I had asked the department secretary to invite her to come to my office, and she was now waiting outside my door. I was a bit tense as usual when sorting out such uncomfortable matters. For the past two years I have headed the departmental curriculum committee, which is responsible, among other things, for dealing with special student requests and a wide range of disciplinary issues. On this occasion one of my colleagues suspected that her student had copied the final paper in the course "Minorities in Democracies." The student in question was a young Bedouin woman from a village unrecognized by the Israeli government. The professor was familiar with her work and confident that the student had not written the paper. "It was not her style," she told me, "the level of analysis, the fact that most of the bibliography was in English—and the student can hardly read English—the length of the paper (which was twice as long as the one requested), as well as a series of other details all suggested that someone else wrote the paper, probably for a different class."

I arrived at the office about an hour earlier than the scheduled meeting in order to go over the material. I skimmed through the student's paper, which was on Thomas Jefferson's views regarding slavery. It was indeed well written and seemed very interesting in its analysis of the standpoint of the dominant elite toward an oppressed minority. The bibliography was impressive, particularly considering that the student was a sophomore. I logged on to the internet and found that many of the items appearing in her bibliography are not available in our library. I then took *The Portable Thomas Jefferson* from my shelf and started perusing it. I read a few passages from Jefferson's letters and then looked at some paragraphs from "The Public Papers," and, finally I found myself reading from "The Notes on the State of Virginia."

Somewhere in the middle of the essay, while discussing the issue of slavery, Jefferson asks his readers: "Why not retain and incorporate the blacks into the state, and thus save the expense of supplying, by importation of settlers, the vacancies they will leave?"[1] While Jefferson goes on to argue against the incorporation of blacks in American society, his question intrigued me. Over two hundred years have passed since the essay was written, and here I was sitting in my office on a different continent, a Jewish man in an Israeli university, and it struck me that even though the context was totally different, the question was still relevant. The Bedouins, I thought to myself, are, in some sense, Israel's blacks.

They are the indigenous population of the Israeli desert, the Negev, where my university is located.[2] This Bedouin community consists of roughly 130,000 people. Before the establishment of the State of Israel, approximately 70,000 Bedouins lived in the area, but following the 1948 war only 12,000 or so remained; the rest fled or were expelled to Jordan and Egypt. Under the directives of Israel's first premier David Ben-Gurion—after whom my university is named—those who remained in Israel were uprooted from the lands they had inhabited and were concentrated in the northeastern part of the Negev (a mostly barren area) known as the "Sayag" zone or "enclosure zone." The more fertile western part of the Negev was reserved for Jewish settlement.[3] Until 1966, the Bedouins were subjected to harsh military rule, their movement was restricted, and they did not enjoy basic political and social rights.

Throughout the 1950s and until the mid 1960s, a considerable portion of their ancestral lands was confiscated and registered as state land. In the 1970s, about half the Bedouin population was moved once again by the Israeli government, this time into seven townships. The idea was to concentrate the Bedouin population within a small area that comprises only a small percentage of their original tribal lands, the land from which they had been expelled. These Bedouins were forced to give up their land rights in order to be granted the dubious privilege of living in overcrowded townships.[4]

The remaining half of the Bedouin population was unwilling to give up their property rights and is now scattered across the Negev in forty-five villages that have never been recognized by the state. Israel makes life in these unrecognized villages unbearable through harsh enforcement of planning and construction laws. For the "crime" of illegal construction, the Israeli government demolishes houses and imposes criminal sanctions. Moreover, the state does not connect these villages to electricity grids, running water, sewage system, or telephone services. There are no paved roads leading to the unrecognized Bedouin villages. As a result, emergency services cannot reach them quickly, and access to other basic services—health, education, and welfare—is difficult and limited.[5]

As I browsed through Jefferson's essay, I glanced at the bulletin board where I had pinned a small map of the unrecognized Bedouin villages. I wanted to see the exact location of the village the student who was now waiting outside my door called home. I had received the map in the mail a few years ago as a gift from the *unrecognized* regional council of the *unrecognized* villages (since the villages have not been recognized by the Israeli government, the government has also been unwilling to recognize their elected council). In the cover letter attached to the map, the head of the council had pointed out that the unrecognized population suffers from an extremely high unemployment rate: approximately 60 percent for men and 85 percent for women. The population is characterized by grinding poverty, a high rate of infant mortality, few skilled laborers, and a high crime rate. Moreover, approximately 40 percent of Bedouin children drop out of school, and only 6 percent of those who actually graduate pass matriculation exams that allow them to apply to university. The student who handed in the paper on Jefferson was part of that 6 percent; she was one of the 147 Bedouin women—out of approximately one hundred thousand students—pursuing an academic degree in an Israeli university.[6]

Even though her village is no more than ten miles away from a major Jewish city, it may very well be that the first time she actually had a serious conversation with a Jew was at the university. Israeli society, after all, is extremely segregated; Jews and Bedouins (including almost all Palestinians) live in separate towns or at the very least in different neighborhoods, and it is unusual for their children to go to school together or mix in any way.[7] While Jews and Bedouins come into contact at the university, the segregation between the two groups continues and one seldom encounters Jewish and Bedouins students sitting together in the cafeteria or library; it is even rarer for a Jew and Bedouin to become friends. While a university degree surely facilitates the integration of Bedouins into Israeli society, the truth of it is that the university does very little, if anything, to undo the Palestinian and Bedouin citizens' mark as other, and in many ways reproduces it.

Although it was already two minutes after our scheduled appointment, I decided to take my time and to think about the matter a bit longer. I sensed that some kind of parallel could be drawn between the question that Jefferson raised about the incorporation of blacks into American society and the current situation of Bedouins in Israel. After all, cultural, social, political, and legal recognition of social groups is a form of incorporation and acceptance, whereas nonrecognition excludes a people and violates their basic rights. Insofar as our identity is formed by recognition, nonrecognition, in and of itself, should be considered a form of abuse.[8] The same governments that were unwilling to recognize the student's village or her representatives absorbed in the 1990s over a million Jewish immigrants from the former Soviet Union.[9] Unlike the Bedouins, the Jewish immigrants were given a stipend for a number of years, many of them were offered jobs, and the government provided them with grants and relatively good mortgages to buy apartments in different Israeli cities. Almost all of them now enjoy a higher standard of living than the indigenous Bedouin population.

Since the establishment of the State of Israel, all the governments had followed Jefferson's advice against incorporating the other into the state. In "The Notes on the State of Virginia," Jefferson suggests that the differences between whites and blacks cannot be overcome. He maintains that alongside the political differences between the two peoples, there are also important "physical and moral" differences:

The first difference which strikes us is that of color. Whether the black of the negro resides in the reticular membrane between the skin and the scarf-skin, or in the scarf-skin itself, whether it proceeds from the color of the blood, the color of the bile, or from that of some other secretion, the difference is fixed in nature, and is as real as if its seat and cause were better known to us. . . . Add to these, flowing hair, a more elegant symmetry of form, their own judgments in favor of the whites, declared by their preferences of them. . . . The circumstances of superior beauty, is thought worthy attention in the propagation of our horses, dogs and other domestic animals; why not in that of man? Besides those of color, figure and hair, there are other physical distinctions proving a difference of race. . . . They seem to require less sleep. A black after hard labor through the day, will be induced by the slightest amusements to sit up till midnight, or later, though knowing he must be out with the first of dawn of the morning. . . . They are more ardent after their female: but love seems with them to be more an eager desire, than a tender delicate mixture of sentiment and sensation. Their griefs are transient.[10]

Jefferson goes on to maintain that the "unfortunate difference of color, and perhaps of faculty, is a powerful obstacle to the emancipation of these people." He therefore recommends to his contemporaries that, when freed, the black person "is to be removed beyond the reach of mixture."[11]

"Removed beyond the reach of mixture," I repeated to myself the chilling phrase. In Israel, the term "transfer"—we use the English word in Hebrew—has been employed to denote a similar idea. The term has several meanings in the Israeli context.[12] Most prominently, transfer means physically moving the Palestinians from one geographical area to another, uprooting and expelling them from their ancestral lands and homes. There are, of course, various formulations for how the transfer of the Palestinian population should be carried out, ranging from the aggressive version proposed by former Minister Avigdor Lieberman, through the "soft" version of "voluntary transfer" promulgated by the right-wing party Moledet, all the way to the idea of abrogating the political rights of the Palestinians and transferring them from their land and homes only if political circumstances call for such action, as suggested by former Minister Efraim Eitam.[13] The unrecognized Bedouins are also constantly under threat of being transferred from their

unrecognized villages and moved into new townships that the government is planning to build.[14] The idea is to take over their land.

The term "transfer" also has political connotations: denying a people the right to participate in politics by not allowing the group's representatives to run for office, or by refusing to interview them in the media and in this way exclude them from the public arena. Finally, transfer refers to the exclusion of minorities from the dominant culture, through numerous forms of segregation. A Jew and a Muslim, for example, cannot get married in Israel since the orthodox religious authorities must approve all weddings. There is no way to *legally mix,* at least not if people choose to preserve their differences. "Was it coincidental then that the student handed in a paper dealing with Jefferson's views concerning slavery?" I asked myself as I opened the office door.

THE FIRST ENCOUNTER

Amal sat down in the blue chair, directly under the picture of Mahatma Gandhi.[15] She was wearing a scarf around her head, but not the Hijab, the traditional Muslim dress. This suggested that she was not a devout Muslim, but rather someone who follows the traditions and customs of her community. I could sense that she was anxious and asked whether she knew why she had been invited to see me. She did not. I pointed to the paper that was lying on the table and asked whether she had written it. I could tell that she was taken aback.

"Of course," she said, "I wrote it."

"Are you sure," I asked.

"Yes," she replied.

I proceeded to ask her questions about the paper, both substantial questions about issues discussed in the paper as well as questions about the bibliography. To my dismay, Amal was unable to answer any of my questions. It was clear that she was under a lot of pressure, as any student in her situation would be. After a few minutes, I asked her why she could not answer the questions: if she had actually written the paper, then presumably she should know what she meant by certain phrases in it. Despite her inability to answer, Amal insisted that she wrote the paper, adding, though, that a cousin who had returned after completing his academic studies in the United States had assisted her.

"He helped me," she said.

I then tried to clarify the distinction between assistance in writing a paper and actually having someone else write it. But Amal was adamant that her cousin had not written it for her; he, she continued to claim, had only assisted her. I pressed on, "How is it then that you cannot answer any of my questions about the contents of the paper?" Her head tilted down, and she shrugged her shoulders. For about a minute, both of us were silent. I did not know what to do and decided to suspend my decision, asking her to come see me the following week. I told her, however, that the minimal disciplinary measure for copying was failure in the course.

After Amal left, I thought about our brief encounter. I was quite certain that Amal had been sincere. I was also convinced, though, that she had not written the paper. While this ostensible contradiction bothered me, even more troublesome was a mounting sensation that the meeting was a reproduction of a colonial experience. The power differential between us was enormous, and certainly could not be reduced to the differences between a professor and his student. Here I was, a Jew living in a Jewish state, whereas Amal is part of the Muslim minority. While both of us are citizens, I am a member of the ethnic group controlling the state, and she a member of the group dispossessed by that same state. She is a Bedouin, one unrecognized, and her community is considered to be at the bottom of the social hierarchy within the Muslim minority inside Israel. As a young woman, she is at the very base of this hierarchy. Considering that she comes from an extremely oppressive, patriarchical community—in her community every year women are murdered for not dressing modestly or for sleeping with a man outside of wedlock—the gender difference between us was particularly pronounced.[16] The fact that a man was confronting her—regardless of my ethnicity and professional position—surely had some bearing on the encounter. Finally, I am a member of the middle class, while Amal comes from an extremely poor family. I am a Westerner, my parents are academics, I was educated in the United States, I speak and write English, and I feel comfortable in a university setting. I embody many of the hegemonic norms connected to this institution. Amal, by contrast, is the first member of her family to attend university, her parents are illiterate, Hebrew is her second language, and she hardly speaks English, the language needed for research. The university is in many ways foreign to her; she is a stranger in this environment; she does not have a feel for the game, the university is not part of her *habitus*.[17]

As I continued to mull over the meeting with Amal, I was confident that she too sensed some of these differences, and perhaps several others. I wanted my decision to be moral but was uncertain about how to address the issue. I was aware of many of the structural disadvantages that Amal had to confront in her day-to-day existence, realizing that any Bedouin woman who managed to reach the university had already accomplished a great feat. But structural disadvantages did not, in my view, excuse cheating; making such allowances, I thought, would be counterproductive both for her and to her community.

CROSS-CULTURAL UNDERSTANDING

Often in such situations, I refer to my own role models. Since the cross-cultural dimension of the encounter was, in my mind, the confusing part, I pulled out Fred Dallmayr's book *Beyond Orientalism*, where he discusses the conditions of possibility of such an encounter. Even though I did not remember the book very well, it was clear from my pencil marks that I had read it carefully. I decided to reread the chapter "Heidegger, Bhakti, and Vedanta," in an attempt to find a clue about what to say to Amal when she returned.

Dallmayr's essay begins with a number of straightforward questions: "How can we or should we approach the other, especially an other belonging to a distant world, to a radically different culture? Are we always condemned to misunderstand, seeing that our approach necessarily departs from our own life world and our taken-for-granted assumptions and prejudgments? . . . How can we properly gain understanding?"[18] In an attempt to address these questions, Dallmayr turns to Heidegger: "Heidegger's *Being and Time*, in particular, was at pains to show that human existence or *Dasien* does not fit into the schema of modern epistemology with its stress on the distinction between subject and object, knower and known. Instead of privileging consciousness or self-consciousness, Heidegger center-staged *Dasein*'s openness to being . . . ."[19]

"*Dasein*'s openness to being . . . ." These words took me back almost a decade to a seminar I had with Dallmayr during my first semester as a graduate student at the University of Notre Dame. The title of the seminar was, if I remember correctly, "Martin Heidegger: Theory and Praxis." We examined the ethical implications of Heidegger's philosophy in order to explore whether a connection could be drawn between his theory and his collaboration with Nazism. It was an intimate class, about eight of us crammed into a small room, and each week we sat for three hours around a table carefully reading texts such as *Being and Time*, *The Letter on Humanism*, *What is Metaphysics?*, and *The Question concerning Technology*. Sitting in my office nearly ten years later, I now recalled, with a trace of jealousy, the strong sense of intellectual energy Dallmayr brought to his classes; he disturbed us, challenged our worldviews, and encouraged us to think critically; indeed, he wanted us to stretch our minds, because for him "thinking accomplishes the relation of Being to the essence of man."[20]

For much of the Heidegger seminar, Dallmayr concentrated on laying bare the meaning of being and Heidegger's notion of *Dasein's* openness to being. He wanted us, his students, to understand. Understanding, I slowly learned and came to accept, "involves not an intentional strategy but rather participation in an ongoing interplay of questioning, an interplay which implies not an attempt at mastery but a willingness to give oneself over 'to the *Sache*.'"[21] It is this kind of understanding, I thought to myself, that I must engage in before reaching a decision regarding Amal; it is this kind of understanding that is implied in Heidegger's emphasis on *Dasein's* openness to being.

Dallmayr deals more directly with understanding in another chapter in *Beyond Orientalism* titled "Gadamer, Derrida, and the Hermeneutics of Difference." This essay goes directly to the point, stressing at the outset the significance of "good will" to understanding. Dallmayr suggests, following Hans-Georg Gadamer, that one should develop a "disinclination to let rupture or estrangement have the last word," and he highlights the importance of being attentive to the "said" as well as to the "unsaid."[22] Amal, I thought to myself, did not say very much during our encounter, except for insisting that she did not copy the paper. Perhaps something important was left unsaid; perhaps I did not allow her to express herself.

Echoing Gadamer's analysis of the poet Paul Celan, Dallmayr maintains that the common source of exegetic failure resides in unwillingness (or lack of good will) to face up to the text's appeal: "[S]uch unwillingness surfaces in the imposition of extrinsic frameworks or criteria and more generally in the obstinate clinging to private feelings," which remain captive to subjectivism and therefore cannot attain an understanding of the other.[23] Recollecting yet again the conversation with Amal, it now became clear to me that I had inserted a series of frameworks into the encounter, notably the Western emphasis on individualism—the university's dedication to and insistence on individual work. I was in a sense captivated by my own subjectivism and therefore it was not coincidental that informing the encounter was the idea that for the paper to be Amal's she must have written it alone; this was the underlying assumption throughout the meeting. Could it be that, for Amal, writing a paper with her cousin, or even sitting with him while he did most of the work, meant that the paper was also hers? Did she and I have different conceptions of what authorship of a paper meant? How does one attain ownership of an essay?

John Stuart Mill's acknowledgment in *On Liberty*, which I sometimes teach in my introduction to political theory course, underscores some of the ambiguities underlying these kinds of questions. Not everyone has noticed that in the acknowledgment Mill insists that his partner Harriet Taylor was the "inspirer" and "in part the author" of the work.[24] In his autobiography he adds: "The [*sic*] *Liberty* was more directly and literally our joint production than anything else which bears my name, for there was no sentence of it that was not several times gone through by us together, turned over in many ways, and carefully weeded of any faults, either in thought or expression, that we detected in it. . . . The whole mode of thinking of which the book was the expression, was emphatically hers."[25] If Mill, whom I admire, was undeterred from assuming sole authorship over *On Liberty*, which, according to his own testimony, was written with Taylor, was I justified in assuming that Amal had transgressed a universal code? But perhaps I was trying too hard to understand Amal. Perhaps my attempt to undo the ostensible contradiction between my sensation that Amal was telling the truth and that she, nonetheless, had not written the paper was counterproductive. Why, after all, had Amal been unable to answer any of my questions regarding the paper's contents?

In his essay on Gadamer, Dallmayr highlights the importance of deferral and distance for thought. He claims that alongside good will and a concerted attempt to refrain from imposing extrinsic frameworks and criteria on the other, one should also exercise self-critique and self-decentering. Since self-critique and deferral of thought take time, I decided to suspend my decision regarding Amal to allow myself enough time to meditate about the different issues at hand.

YUSEF

I looked at my watch and realized that I had to rush off to teach the introduction to political theory class. As is usually the case in courses with large enrollments, students gathered after class to ask me specific questions about their assignments, the readings, or some philosophical issue they had not understood. When I finished responding, Salim came up to me and inquired whether I had a minute or two. I asked him to accompany me back to my office.

Salim is a Palestinian citizen of Israel, whose family lives in a village in the north. I knew him by name since he had taken my introductory class the year before and had failed. Reading the classics is difficult for all first-year students, but it is particularly difficult for Palestinians, since Hebrew is not their mother tongue. Almost every year a few Palestinian students fail the course, and I usually get to know them from time spent with them during office hours.

"You remember Yusef?" Salim asked as we entered the elevator.

"Of course," I answered, "he was in my office last week."

"Well . . . eh . . . he's dead," Salim said.

My heart missed a beat. "What do you mean?" I asked.

"They found him dead in his apartment late last night," he answered, just as we reached my office. I opened the office door and we both walked in. I was in utter shock. It was not only that one of the department's students had died; there was more to it, more perhaps than Salim knew. I was not sure whether I should share the information, but, since the two had been friends, I decided to tell Salim about my last encounter with Yusef.

Yusef had come to see me the week before, not as his teacher, but as the head of the curriculum committee. He wanted permission to hand in a seminar paper late. Since the university has very strict regulations about incompletes, I asked him whether he had a good excuse. I had had a few conversations with Yusef the year before, and I knew he was among the leaders of the Arab Student Committee on campus, and that he dedicated many hours to political activism, this in addition to his part-time job as a teacher. He too was a Palestinian from northern Israel, from a town called Taibeh, and had one more semester before completing his studies. During our meeting, I inquired whether his inability to turn the paper in on time was due to his political activism. I still remember how when he replied "Yes" his eyes squinted a little as if smiling at me, and then he added "and no."

Yusef proceeded to tell me about his activism, about a political rally he was trying to organize, and then went on to describe how the Israeli police, together with secret service agents, had come to his apartment at night and how they had taken the hard drive from his computer. They had also taken him to the station and interrogated him for several hours, but later released him. The seminar paper, he said, like all his other materials, was on the hard drive, which he still hoped the security services would return.

Yusef's story was not new to me. Since the eruption of the second *Intifada,* the police and secret services had arrested and interrogated many Palestinian students. Some of the department's students had already approached me asking permission to hand in papers late due to police interrogations. Incidents such as these never make the press, and most of the Jewish faculty members, not to mention students, are unaware of these arrests. The Palestinians tend not to share these experiences for fear of being branded as enemies. But even though Yusef's story was familiar, it still managed to unnerve me at the time. I recounted the essentials to Salim, who, as it turned out, knew about the arrest and the confiscation of the hard drive.

"They found him inside his apartment," Salim said, as he stood up to leave. "He was lying on the floor with his bag by his side, as if he was preparing to leave the house to go to the university. The door was locked from the inside, with the key still inside the cylinder."

"I guess he won't need the hard drive," Salim added sarcastically as he walked out of my office.

I immediately called the Physicians for Human Rights, a group based in Tel Aviv, and told one of the staff members about Yusef. I asked whether they could send an independent pathologist to the autopsy. I wanted answers. I wanted to know whether Yusef's death was related to his arrest, if he was targeted because of his activism. I was shaken and didn't know what to do.

LETTING BEING BE

A week had passed since I learned about Yusef's death. An autopsy had been carried out, witnessed by an independent pathologist. The cause of death, the physicians' group reported, was unclear. There was, however, according to the report, no evidence of foul play. Several friends of Yusef had come to see me during the week to inquire whether the university would award him a B.A. even though he had not completed his studies. They thought it would be a nice gesture, something that might alleviate, if only a little, his parents' pain. I passed the request on to the university administration, but received a negative response. I never realized that I would be dealing with such issues when I took on the role of heading the department's curriculum committee; I didn't realize it would be so difficult.

| I was now waiting for Amal, trying to figure out what to say to her during our next meeting. I knew there is no prescription for how one should venture into such encounters, not least because cross-cultural meetings are often particularly complicated.[26] I decided to return to Dallmayr, this time to his essay "Heidegger on Ethics and Justice" in *The Other Heidegger*. In many ways, this essay encapsulates the conclusions of Dallmayr's 1994 seminar on Heidegger. Towards the end of the chapter, Dallmayr writes:

> The writings discussed above [*Beiträge zur Philosophie, Schelling's Treatise on the Essence of Human Freedom, Letter on Humanism,* and the "Anaximander Fragment"] clearly have manifold implications for ethics as well as for social and political thought; they also help to correct one-sided polemical dismissals of Heidegger as a Nazi ideologist or persistent apologist for fascism. In my view, these writings can actually be read as an indictment of Nazism to the extent that the latter aimed at an imperial dominion of the world based on racial-biological grounds. As presented in the "Anaximander Fragment," juncture and hence justice is the readiness *to let others be* and to attend to them with considerate care.[27]

"Letting Being be" is, in a sense, Heidegger's ethics. This short phrase, I thought, encapsulates two crucial dimensions that were pertinent to my deliberations regarding Amal, one relating to action and the other to being. While I concur with Heidegger that we "are still far from pondering the essence of action decisively enough," the phrase "letting Being be" manages, nonetheless, to reveal something extremely important about action. It succeeds in creating a bond between two concepts that in most philosophical writings dealing with ethics are presented as polar opposites: passivity and activity.[28] In order to let Being *be* one must be passive, while in order to *let* Being be one must be active. Heidegger's ability to unite the two, while not collapsing one to the other, is a crucial insight. On the one hand, by letting Being *be* one helps maintain the integrity of the other. Letting Being *be* implies that one should not appropriate the other, relate to the other as a means, or project an external framework or a worldview on the other. Rather, one must let the other be in the other's otherness. On the other hand, *letting* Being be involves an active commitment toward the other. One must actively enable the other to be, help create the conditions that ensure the other's being, and actively resist the other's appropriation or oppression. If the other is an oppressor, then one must struggle against the oppression since oppression in and of itself is an act of not letting Being be. In class, Dallmayr often described the unity of this seeming duality as a middle ground, a path between activity and passivity, which allows the two to reside *together*. It is precisely this middle ground, I thought, that needs to be pursued during my meeting with Amal.

The idea that passivity and activity can coincide simultaneously within action is, to be sure, informed by Heidegger's conception of being. In other words, the very possibility of the overlapping of activity and passivity presupposes being, in the Heideggerian sense. In order to explain the meaning of being, Dallmayr once asked us to think of the person we felt we knew most, someone we loved and had shared our life with. He told us that he and his wife Ilse had been living together for a number of decades, they were married before most of us, his students, had been born. He then explained that, even though they have been sharing their lives for years, it was clear to him that he could never fully know her. Being, he explained, can never be fully defined or captured ontologically, for it always withdraws, always remains partially concealed. Therefore any attempt to render it permanent—to essentialize it, reduce it, or negate it—is a distortion of being. Being, ontologically speaking, is always more than one can make of it; it is overdetermined; it always maintains difference.

In *The Other Heidegger,* Dallmayr explains that difference does not mean the difference between two objects that are present-at-hand, but "the central point is to see being itself as difference (*Unterscheidung*): as the play of absence and presence, concealment and disclosure, and particularly as the generative potency letting the difference happen (*Ereignis*)."[29] *Letting* difference happen, I thought to myself, in both its ontological and normative senses, destabilizes Jefferson's recommendation to remove the other beyond the reach of mixture. The other, like the self, is always already a "mixture," and therefore all justifications for removing people beyond the reach of mixture become untenable. Moreover, Heidegger's insistence that difference exists within being and therefore also within identity is crucial for undercutting the logocentric suppositions informing Jefferson's writings, suppositions that are not merely bent on "incorporating and submerging otherness in the vortex of selfhood," but on violently removing and erasing otherness.[30]

Heidegger also stresses being's quality of revealing itself. More precisely, being is in itself a clearing (*Lichtung*), and humans are able to engage in the disclosure of being due to this clearing. In *Being and Time,* he explains that *Dasein*

> *as* Being-in-the-world is cleared [*gelichtet*] in itself, not through any other entity, but in such a way that it *is* itself the clearing. Only for an entity which is existentially cleared in this way does that which is present-at-hand become accessible in the light or hidden in the dark. By its very nature, *Dasein* brings its "there" along with it. If it lacks its "there," it is not factically the entity which is essentially *Dasein;* indeed, it is not this entity at all. *Dasein is its disclosedness.*[31]

For Heidegger, accordingly, existence is disclosure; being is an affirmation of plurality; and humans are par excellence "*the* site which being requires in order to disclose itself." In a different context, Heidegger stresses that it is the particular quality of humans to wonder and to question, to open the self to otherness, to constitute "the site of openness, the there."[32] If only I can follow these insights, I said to myself.

THE SECOND ENCOUNTER

Amal entered my office. I felt that in our last conversation she was merely responding to my allegations and had made up my mind that this time I would let her lead the conversation. I would only reach a decision after she expressed herself, after she said what she had to say. I could immediately tell that she was trying with all her strength to hold herself together. After she sat down, I asked her why she was so upset. Unable to hold back any longer, Amal began to cry. I thought she was preparing to say something about the paper, but then, to my surprise, she said: "I am nineteen years old, four months pregnant, and I don't have anything to look forward to. I don't know if you can understand . . . but life is not easy for me."

I waited a moment and then asked her what she meant. We both sat silent for what seemed to be a few minutes before she spoke:

"When I was sixteen my father reached an agreement with one of his cousins; together they decided that I would get engaged to be married to this cousin's son who is a few years older than I am. And so within a few months we were engaged. I didn't know him, but as time passed I learned that he not only slept around, but he was also a petty thief. I decided that I would not marry him; I would not ruin my life. So about a year ago, not long before we were to be married, I approached my father and told him that I was unwilling to go through with the ceremony. Although he was very upset, my mother and I managed to convince him, and ultimately the engagement was broken off. I don't know if you realize, but for us the engagement and not the wedding is the legally binding ceremony, and, in order to break off an engagement, one has to go to the courts and get what you would call a divorce.

"After I broke off the engagement my father told me that no one would marry me, and that I had, in a sense, been violated. I had not slept with the man, but because I broke off the engagement I was deemed unworthy in my father's eyes. He then went on to tell me that he had arranged with another cousin, who was already married and was sixteen years older than I am, that I would be his second wife. 'At this point, the best you can hope for is to be someone's second wife,' he said. This is my father, this is how he thinks.

"To make a long story short, all my attempts to try to change my father's decision failed and about half a year ago, this older cousin and I were married. The only condition that I managed to negotiate before the wedding was that my new husband would allow me to complete my studies. Two months after the ceremony, I got pregnant, and, a month after that, he started beating me. Finally, I decided to run away to my parents' house, and I have been living with them for the past month. I am pregnant, I am the second wife of an abusive husband, whom I don't like, not to mention love, and I am only nineteen. That's why I was crying."

Being, Politics, and Cross-Cultural Encounters

It was, I believe, the advice I received from my mentors that helped create the space that allowed Amal to feel comfortable enough to share with me the difficulties she was facing. I wanted to think that I had followed Dallmayr's interpretation of Heidegger's notion of letting Being *be*, specifically in its more passive sense. But now, I also needed to practice the more active dimension, the idea that one must *let* Being be. *Letting*, I thought, has to be carried out with care. One must recognize, however, that it is not simply a theoretical issue; being surely cannot be attended to if one remains focused on metaphysical questions, since the actual political, social, economic—and in this case also academic—context must be taken into account as well. Though, of course, one's theoretical framework always informs one's understanding of the context.

In his book *Dialogue among Civilizations*, Dallmayr stresses the need to draw the connections between ostensibly different fields—philosophical, political, social, economic, and so forth—by underscoring some of the problematics underlying traditional Western metaphysics. He accentuates Western metaphysics' assortment of polar oppositions as along a continuum—"oppositions that typically [are] tilted so as to favor one side of the paired terms"—and points out some of the repercussions they have in a global context:

> In its social or societal implications, this metaphysical focus entailed a number of predictable consequences, especially the growing division of society into a rational elite of experts—who increasingly became the managers of economic, technical, and administrative affairs—and the vast masses of less educated workers and artisans attached to the idiom of ordinary common sense. On the inter-societal and inter-civilizational level, the same focus gave rise to the distinction between rationally

advanced and rationally backward societies, between so-called developed and underdeveloped (or developing) countries; in large measure, this distinction coincided with that between Occident and Orient, with the former assigning to the latter its status and significance in the global context—a practice that came to be known as "Orientalism."[33]

It is in passages like these that Dallmayr adds a crucial dimension to his mentors, notably people like Heidegger, for he manages to translate the latter's nuanced and often convoluted philosophy into concrete political terms. Heidegger, as Dallmayr has often argued, was unable to draw the correct political conclusions from his own philosophy. One of Dallmayr's important contributions to contemporary political thought, and to my own thinking, has been his ability to draw practical conclusions from "high theory." I have employed his insights not only in class and at the university, but also in my day-to-day endeavors in Israel/Palestine, particularly as a member of a group called *Ta'ayush*, meaning Arab-Jewish partnership.

Alongside his ability to lay bare and elucidate the practical implications of complex theoretical claims, over the past fifteen years Dallmayr has set out to create a cross-cultural dialogue of political theory. This cross-cultural dialogue is, I believe, needed now—as we all become members of a "global village"—more than ever. In his attempt to lay the grounds for such a dialogue, Dallmayr has repeatedly argued against the tendency of Western philosophy to "privilege universal maxims over contingent phenomena, generally valid insights over local vernacular experiences."[34] As Dallmayr has shown, when one takes into account the contingent phenomena and the local vernacular experiences, then the process through which one reaches decisions changes.

When Yusef asked to hand in his paper late, my decision to grant him permission was obviously informed by my theoretical and political orientation. The "universal maxim" forbids submitting seminar papers after a given date, and although there are a number of exceptions to this university regulation, being arrested by the security services and having your computer's hard drive confiscated is not on the list. People treated in such a way are not only rendered suspicious, but are usually identified as enemies of the state. If I had adopted the "generally valid insights" (in this case the security forces' view) over the "local vernacular experiences," then my decision would probably have been different. I was following Dallmayr's suggestion not to automatically accept the pervasive interpretation of differences between people, which, in this specific situation, were mostly informed by a nationalism that aims at creating homogenous, permanent, and stable identities, and also conflicting ones. Within the Israeli context such a difference is employed to produce hierarchies and disparity, not least because being a Jew in Israel provides one with privileges not enjoyed by Palestinian citizens. One's role, according to Dallmayr, is neither to ignore such differences nor to accept them, but rather to challenge them, undo them, and give them a different meaning.

Although this is not the place to discuss nationalism and its implications for cross-cultural dialogue, my attempt to *let Yusef be* included using a certain academic and philosophic rationality that was poised against the rationality of the state. Following Dallmayr's advice, I did not aim to erase all the differences between us, but I was unwilling to adopt the difference created by the state. Perhaps my approach had to do with Benedict Anderson's idea that nations are imagined communities whose being is not essential and can never be fully determined, an insight that coincides with Heidegger's ontology.[35] But probably it had more to do with the fact that Yusef challenged me. He did so simply by sharing his "local vernacular experiences," thus initiating a cross-cultural dialogue. I listened to his account that not only exposed how he was harassed by the security forces, but also revealed how privileged I am as a Jew in Israel.

The encounter with Amal was even more challenging, since my meetings with her were much more complex. In her case, even more so than Yusef's, the encounter uncovered the extent of my privilege and she forced me to face a variety of mechanisms of oppression, some of which I was also complicit in and with. Both Yusef and Amal expanded my understanding of the ways through which the other has been excluded from social and political life in Israel. In Amal's case I was overwhelmed by the oppressive forces that had taken over so many aspects of her life. What amazed me most about her story was her resilience, her persistent attempt, against all odds, to challenge her family and the communal system, and to try to create a meaningful life for herself. The fact that she was still not totally imprisoned by her family and could frequent the university supplied her with some kind of consolation. She told me that she enjoyed her studies, particularly the course on minorities in democracies; she also confided being apprehensive about completing her studies and being stuck in the village. She did not want to be removed beyond the reach of mixture.

I asked her to rewrite the paper about Jefferson and submit it again, using bibliographic sources in Hebrew. I wanted to believe that this solution was my very modest way of following Dallmayr's advice and *letting* her being be.

Amal gave birth to a baby girl. Although she successfully completed the course "Minorities in Democracies," her husband has violated the marital agreement and is not allowing her to complete her undergraduate degree. She is now confined to the village.

NOTES

For their comments and suggestions, I would like to thank Lauren Basson, Louise Bethlehem, Tracy Levy, Catherine Rottenberg, and Jacinda Swanson.

1. Thomas Jefferson, *The Portable Thomas Jefferson*, ed. Merrill D. Peterson (New York: Penguin Books, 1985), p. 186.

2. As an indigenous population, the Bedouins are in many ways more similar to Native Americans, but since the student's paper dealt with Jefferson's attitude towards blacks and slaves, this essay will draw out some of the similarities the Israeli Bedouins have with blacks. One should note that many of the younger Bedouins living in Israel identify as Palestinians rather than Bedouins and consider themselves an integral part of the Palestinian people.

3. Naama Yeshuvi, *The Bedouins in Israel: A Special Report* (Jerusalem: Association for Civil Rights in Israel, 1998).

4. Jonathan Cook, "Bedouin Transfer," *Middle East Report Online,* May 10, 2003. See also Oren Yiftachel, "The Shrinking Space of Citizenship: Ethnocratic Politics in Israel," *Middle East Report* 223 (Summer 2002).

5. U.N. Covenant on Economic, Social and Cultural Rights, Information Sheet No. 3, "Land and Housing Rights—Palestinian Citizens of Israel," May 2003; Yeshuvi, *The Bedouins in Israel.*

6. Data regarding the social and economic conditions of the unrecognized Bedouins are available at www.arabhra.org/rcuv/. For data regarding Bedouin attendance in Israeli universities, see the Center for Bedouin Studies and Development at Ben-Gurion University, available at www.bgu.ac.il/bedouin/.

7. Currently, many of the Bedouins identify as Palestinians. For studies on segregation in Israel, see Oren Yiftachel, "'Ethnocracy': The Politics of Judaizing Israel/Palestine," *Constellations* 6, no. 3 (1999): 364–90. See also Ghazi Falah, "Living Together Apart: Residential Segregation in Mixed Arab-Jewish Cities in Israel," *Urban Studies* 33, no. 6 (1996): 827–57.

8. Charles Taylor, *Multiculturalism: Examining The Politics of Recognition*, ed. Amy Gutmann (Princeton: Princeton University Press, 1994), p. 64.

9. It is often suggested that up to one-third of these immigrants are actually not Jewish. See Baruch Kimmerling, "Jurisdiction in an Immigrant-Settler Society: The 'Jewish and Democratic State,'" *Comparative Political Studies* 35, no. 10 (December 2002): 1123–24.

10. Jefferson, *Portable Thomas Jefferson*, pp. 186–87.

11. Ibid., p. 193.

12. Robert Blecher, "Living on the Edge: The Threat of Transfer in Israel Palestine," *Middle East Report* 225 (Winter 2002).

13. Oren Yiftachel and Neve Gordon, "Caving In?" *In These Times*, May 24, 2002.

14. See "Adalah to PM Sharon: The Government's Five-Year Plan for the Arab Bedouin in the Naqab Is Discriminatory and Illegal," News Update, Adalah: The Legal Center for Arab Minority Rights in Israel, May 8, 2003. Available at www.adalah. org/eng/pressreleases/pr.php?file=03_05_08.

15. I have, of course, changed the names of all the students mentioned in this essay.

16. Manar Hassan, "HaPolitika Shel HaKavod [The Politics of Honor]," in *Min, Migdar, Politika* [*Sex, Gender, Politics*], ed. Dafna Yizraeli et al. (Tel Aviv: Hakibbutz Hameuchad, 1999), pp. 267–306.

17. Pierre Bourdieu, *In Other Words: Essays Towards a Reflexive Sociology* (Stanford: Stanford University Press, 1994).

18. Fred Dallmayr, *Beyond Orientalism: Essays on Cross-Cultural Encounter* (New York: SUNY Press, 1996), p. 89.

19. Ibid., p. 93.

20. Martin Heidegger, "Letter on Humanism," in *Basic Writings*, ed. David Farrell Krell (San Francisco: HarperCollins, 1993), p. 217.

21. Dallmayr, *Beyond Orientalism*, p. 97.

22. Ibid., pp. 44–45.

23. Ibid., p. 46. There are several problems with Dallmayr's analysis of Gadamer in his essay, including the implied adoption of Gadamer's distinction between extrinsic and intrinsic frameworks, a distinction that privileges the intrinsic over the extrinsic. More disturbing, though, is Dallmayr's uncritical adoption of Gadamer's claim that Europe is an example of "historical 'cohabitation with otherness in a narrow space'; experienced as a constant challenge among European peoples, this cohabitation implies a lesson for humanity at large, for an evolving ecumenical world culture" (p. 53). Gadamer is erasing here much of modern European history, most notably the Holocaust.

24. John Stuart Mill, *On Liberty and Other Essays* (Oxford: Oxford University Press, 1991).

25. John Stuart Mill, *Autobiography of John Stuart Mill* (New York: Columbia University Press, 1960), pp. 176–77.

26. Martin Buber, *I and Thou,* trans. Walter Kaufman (New York: Scribners, 1970), p. 126.

27. Fred Dallmayr, *The Other Heidegger* (Ithaca: Cornell University Press, 1993), p. 125 (italics added).

28. Heidegger, "Letter on Humanism," p. 217.

29. Dallmayr, *The Other Heidegger,* p. 101.

30. Dallmayr, *Beyond Orientalism,* p. 48.

31. Martin Heidegger, *Being and Time,* trans. John Macquarrie and Edward Robinson (Oxford: Basil Blackwell, 1988), p. 171.

32. Martin Heidegger, *An Introduction to Metaphysics,* trans. Ralph Manheim (New Haven: Yale University Press, 1987), p. 205.

33. Dallmayr, *Dialogue among Civilizations: Some Exemplary Voices* (New York: Palgrave Macmillan, 2002), p. 33.

34. Ibid., p. 33.

35. Benedict Anderson, *Imagined Communities* (London: Verso Press, 1983).

EIGHT

Mestizo Democracy: Lateral Universality
Begins at Home

John Francis Burke

In recent years, comparative political theory has sought to "cross borders" separating political theories in various settings throughout the world. Indeed, the pertinence of this undertaking has become all the more imperative with the spread of economic globalization. The question before us is not whether globalization is going to ensue, but in what manner. Will we have an unchecked neoliberal globalization or will we have what Richard Falk and Jeremy Breecher have termed a "globalization from below" that tries to ensure as much democratic participation as possible in the fundamental political and economic decisions that determine the destinies of communities?[1]

Indeed, in the 1990s, texts such as Benjamin Barber's *Jihad v. McWorld* seemingly foretold a growing sense of conflict between the economic globalization of the world dominated by the developed nations, primarily those of Western Europe and the United States, and supposedly parochial cultural frameworks from the developing world.[2] The events of 9/11 and their aftermath have only exacerbated such flashpoints. Thus, compounding the consideration of the pros and cons of globalization is the challenge of the increasing intersection between peoples, cultures, and nation-states.

In turn, philosophically, comparative political theory engages these developments in terms of the relationship between the universal and particulars. How does one move "between" a universalism that shows no respect for the variety of particular cultures and civilizations—a unity of uniformity—and a preoccupation with particulars that can become so anarchic that no sense of unity is possible? A universalism that shows no respect or deference to differences simply becomes a form of assimilation that reduces human beings to a common economic denominator—hence, "McWorld." A particularism that shields cultural identity from penetration by other cultures breeds the type of climate for the intense parochial loyalties that surfaced with a vengeance in 9/11. Seemingly, the escalation of conflict on the transnational level in the twenty-first century does not seem to hold out much hope for a "unity-in-diversity."

These sobering events, though, are all the more reason why we need to pursue Maurice Merleau-Ponty's *lateral* universality—perceiving "what is ours as alien as what was alien as our own."[3] Rather than rendering civilizations or cultures as possessions that inherently culminate in either a tyrannical universalism or anarchical particularisms, we need to depict the lateral and mutually enriching intersections of civilizations and cultures that facilitate the pursuit of a democratic unity-in-diversity on the regional, national, and transnational level.

Fred Dallmayr in particular has developed at great length and depth the "parameters, preconditions, and implications" of "dialogue among civilizations" through concrete "intra- and inter-civilization . . . encounters."[4] Perhaps more than any scholar in the Western world today, Dallmayr's textual dialogues between the Western tradition and thinkers and poets from China, India, Islam, and Latin America have charted the possibility of a "global and plural democracy" that moves beyond the prevailing "either-or" to embody a lateral universality.[5] However, two concerns differentiate my approach from Dallmayr's work and from cognate contributions in comparative political theory.

First, American scholars need not go very far in terms of pursuing comparative political theory. The prevailing temptation is to compare works in Western political theory and literature with those of Islamic, Hindu, Buddhist, and Confucian civilizations. The "comparative" dimension is seemingly some exotic "other" that can be compared to the canonical Western texts. But the reality is that these seemingly exotic civilizations are increasingly part of the U.S. and European cultural landscape. As Susan Wolf pinpoints, one does not have to go to Africa, Asia, or Latin America to encounter the other, for there are salient African American, Asian American, Latino, and Native American writers in the United States that are part-and-parcel of the U.S. experience.[6]

Second, in comparative political theory there tends to be a poetic sensibility that stresses the harmonious and consensual dimension of politics, not the agonal and conflictual dimensions. I am reminded of the Aesop fable in which the animals are gathered and the rabbit waxes discursively about how they need to bond and work in a cooperative fashion, in response to which the lion pointedly asks: "Why Mr. Rabbit, where are your claws?" If treatises such as Samuel Huntington's *The Clash of Civilizations* go too far in accenting transnational conflicts, the temptation in comparative political theory is to dwell too exclusively on the edifying dimension of cultural intersections.[7]

In view of these two concerns, in this essay I examine the pursuit of unity-in-diversity in terms of the dynamic of *mestizaje*—the historic and rapidly accelerating mixing of cultures in the U.S. Southwest. The geographic border between the United States and Mexico is the longest in the world between a developed and a developing nation. The legacy of the North American Free Trade Agreement over the past decade makes this border the frontline for the debate over globalization. Rather then turning our attention "abroad," it makes sense to examine this most immediate case of the repercussions of both multiculturalism and globalization. In turn, I temper any sanguine rendering of unity-in-diversity with sensibility for the agonal side of plurality.

Not unlike Fred Dallmayr, my presentation comprises three sections. Initially, I illustrate how Huntington's and Victor Davis Hansen's xenophobic diatribes on the growing Latino presence in the United States render multicultural and transnational intersections in terms of the "either/or" of assimilation (universalism) or separatism (particularism). In the second section, I suggest how the legacy of *mestizaje,* as rendered by U.S. Latino theologians and tempered by the work of the poet Gloria Anzaldúa, elicits instead a vision of unity-in-diversity consonant with the focus on hybridity in comparative political theory. In the final section, I address how this constructive recasting of Augustine's radical yet pessimistic rendering of plurality must nevertheless come to grips with the moral ambiguity of the strategic dimensions of politics.

PROPHETS OF DOOM

Over the past decade, numerous commentators have warned us about the impending peril that multiculturalism, and in particular the growing Latino presence, poses to U.S. American culture.[8] Of late, Huntington in a *Foreign*

Affairs essay titled "The Hispanic Challenge" and Hansen in his text *Mexifornia* have further developed this nativist motif.[9] Both authors plead for a revitalization of long-standing U.S. political culture so as to avoid being drawn into a deleterious hybrid of Latin American and U.S. American mores.

The roots of Huntington's despair lie in his previous work, *The Clash of Civilizations*. There he argues that nine key civilizations comprise the post-Cold War world: Western, Latin American, African, Islamic, Sinic, Hindu, Orthodox, Buddhist, and Japanese. Contrary to those who suggest that globalization in an economic sense will steadily "Westernize" the less developed world, Huntington contends that the resources and forces of modernization are being adapted by non-Western civilizations without contaminating their cultures.[10] This modernization, he contends, is fueling the resurgence of Islamic civilization and an increasing preponderance of Asian civilization in global politics. Such acquisition of technology, he notes, rather than building bridges, heightens the prospect of clashes between civilizations.

In this emerging multipolar world, Huntington maintains Western civilization can sustain its dominance by consolidating the linkages between Europe, North America, South America, and Japan; restricting the military development of the Islamic and the other Asian civilizations; enhancing Western technological and military superiority; and being circumspect about Western inventions in other civilizations. In a multicivilization politics, he concludes the revitalization of Western civilization is imperative for the survival of the United States and its European allies.

Although Huntington disparages any particular civilization that projects itself as universal, reminiscent of Michael Walzer he suggests that each particular civilization has its own "thick" morality, but there remains a "thin" universal morality that is "common to most civilizations" and serves as a basis for civilized discourse.[11] The closest Huntington comes, however, to articulating anything resembling a lateral, constructive integration of civilizations is his "*commonalities* rule" that "people in all civilizations should search for and attempt to expand the values, institutions, and practices they have in common with peoples of other civilizations."[12]

Ultimately, Huntington's argument remains a multicivilization rendering of the long-standing realist disposition in international relations theory: "Cold peace, cold war, trade war, quasi war, uneasy peace, troubled relations, intense rivalry, competitive coexistence, arms races: these phrases are probable descriptions of relations between entities from different civilizations.

Trust and friendship will be rare."[13] He does not envision the emergence of a transnational politics that could effect democratic syntheses between civilizations. Instead, his sympathies ultimately lie with sustaining Western power and interests in this conflict.

If in *The Clash of Civilizations* Huntington at least claims that no civilization has moral superiority, his U.S.-centric chauvinism becomes completely transparent in "The Hispanic Challenge." Specifically, he unabashedly defends the essential "Anglo-Protestant" values of the United States that he argues must be protected from the Latino wave now engulfing the country:

> Key elements of that culture include the English language; Christianity; religious commitment; English concepts of the rule of law, including the responsibility of rulers and the rights of individuals; and dissenting Protestant values of individualism, the work ethic, and the belief that humans have the ability and duty to try to create a heaven on earth, "a city on a hill."[14]

By contrast, the following Latino values, he contends, are detrimental to this heritage:

- the reality of immense social and economic poverty in Latin America;
- a concept of time too attached to history and the past, as opposed to the future;
- a mistrust of people beyond family networks;
- little self-reliance and ambition;
- no confidence in education; and
- poverty as a virtue that guarantees access to the next life.[15]

These values supposedly constitute a perilous threat, for as previously articulated in *The Clash of Civilizations,* Huntington emphasizes that Mexican immigration to the United States is distinct from that of previous groups. First, in contrast to immigrants from other continents who have to traverse an ocean to enter the United States, Mexicans can literally walk across the border and are able to sustain ties to communities both north and south of the boundary. Second, most Mexican immigrants still reside in the U.S. Southwest—an area that historically had been part of Mexico and thus forms "a continuous Mexican society stretching from Yucatan to Colorado."[16]

Third, Mexican immigrants have shown that they are more resilient than most immigrant groups in terms of sustaining their cultural identity and resisting assimilation.[17] He reinforces these findings with a smattering of statistics in "The Hispanic Presence" that suggest Latinos are not assimilating into the United States by the third generation.

This growing reality, he concludes, threatens whether "the United States [shall] remain a country with a single national language and a core Anglo-Protestant culture."[18] Whereas in *The Clash of Civilizations* Huntington remained confident that Western civilization could remain very competitive in the *external* world of foreign affairs, in "The Hispanic Challenge" he sees the growing impact of Latinos as a serious *internal* assault on the future viability of U.S. political culture.

Similarly, Hansen in *Mexifornia* bemoans the disappearance of the educational and cultural values by which he was shaped a half-century ago, a loss he ascribes to both the onslaught of Latino immigration and the U.S. and California public policies that have accelerated this trend. Most of his narrative focuses on concrete illustrations of how many Latino immigrants find themselves in a country that increasingly is a deleterious hybrid of Mexico and the United States.

Just as Huntington accents the bedrock Protestant values that undergird U.S. culture, Hansen questions the sensibility of scholars and political activists who celebrate the differences between the constitutive groups of the United States. Especially in the wake of the 9/11 assault on the United States, he finds it ludicrous that separatism should be accented over assimilation—he has the Chicano movement particularly in mind—or that the law should be treated as a matter only relevant to "ephemeral circumstances" and "particular interests."[19]

In terms of public policy and educational programs, Hansen maintains that "de facto open borders, bilingual education, new state welfare programs, the affirmation of a hyphenated identity, a sweeping revisionism in southwestern American history—has either failed to ensure economic parity or thwarted the processes of assimilation."[20] Consequently, in his estimation, undocumented aliens endure a lifestyle in the United States characterized by homicide, alcoholism, and other travails. As much as they earn far more money in the United States than they ever could in Mexico, he maintains they will never make enough to achieve a middle-class lifestyle.

Hansen is particularly incensed that this second-class citizenship is actually reinforced by educators who push Chicano studies and bilingual education. Instead of teaching students in Spanish and socializing them into cultural struggles, Hansen contends strongly that Mexican immigrants would be much better served by "broad classes in history, logic, philosophy, Western civilization, literature, and classics."[21]

In his estimation, California's cultural and educational landscape in which he was socialized during the 1950s and 1960s was far superior to the subsequent politicized advocacy of separatism and relativism. Prior to the cultural upheavals of the 1960s, he contends every student was treated as an individual, not as a cultural type, and was given the tools for success in a hardworking, competitive United States. Hansen echoes Huntington's emphasis on the bedrock Protestant values essential for both the self-improvement of immigrants and the sustenance of U.S. culture.

To reverse the spread of "Mexifornia," Hansen concludes we must have much more rigorous policing of the U.S./Mexican border and cease misbegotten separatist educational pedagogies and political outlooks. In this fashion, a smaller pool of immigrants would thereby have a better chance to assimilate into long-standing U.S. mores. Nevertheless, he fears what is emerging is a hybrid civilization that marginalizes Latinos in mediocre public schools and synthesizes the worst of both Mexican and U.S. cultures. Amid this despair, he takes solace in the fact that U.S. consumer culture captivates many young Latinos and thus provides an escape from the fatalism of their cultural past.[22]

Huntington's and Hansen's respective polemical defenses of traditional U.S. political culture conveniently overlook its deleterious side. Huntington does not acknowledge that the U.S. liberal democracy enslaved the African American race for at least two centuries (and virtually for a third), obliterated the Native American peoples who preceded the European settlers, and militarily seized what had been the northern third of Mexico. Indeed, religiously tinged notions such as "the city on a hill," "an errand in the wilderness," and "manifest destiny" provided the normative justification for the annihilation and subjugation of nonwhites. Similarly, segregated schools on the basis of race and de facto second-class citizenship for African Americans and Latinos characterized Hansen's "good old days." This white, Anglo-Saxon Protestant hegemony is hardly one many people of color would be eager to restore and its repressive legacy still lingers in many political, social, and economic networks.

At the outset of the 1960 presidential campaign, *Commonweal,* in addressing the "Catholic issue," forthrightly pinpointed that the underlying issue was whether the United States was going to shift from being a white, Anglo-Saxon Protestant nation with a tradition of toleration of other faiths and outlooks to being a genuinely pluralistic country, whose long-standing Waspish heritage would be just one of many equal and vital cultural contributors.[23] Indeed, Robert Bellah points out that over the past half-century, there have been a number of such cultural salvos entailing the inclusion of previously marginalized groups, but not at the price of having to strip their cultural identities.[24] Put otherwise, by Bettia Martinez, Huntington and Hansen are among the "premise-keepers" of the tradition whose merit and moral standing is called into question by these civil rights and cultural movements.[25]

Huntington and Hansen remain stuck in an assimilation/separatist conceptual divide. In other words, the only alternatives in relationships between diverse cultures is either to assimilate to the dominant group or conversely to accent tightly scripted separate groups whose relationship with each other is quite agonal. Huntington's plural civilizations are fundamentally in contest with each other. When he focuses on just one political culture, as in "The Hispanic Challenge," then the imperative becomes to assimilate to the dominant norms, lest the country be rent apart by a domestic "clash of cultures." Although Hansen addresses at greater depth the mixing of cultures in California, the outcome seemingly defiles the integrity of the contributing cultures. Neither Huntington nor Hansen engages the possibility that culture need not be something that defines one from someone or something else, but instead can be an intersubjective relationship in which diverse entities intersect and transform each other in lateral, constructive terms.

Indeed, as Edward Said points out, this tendency to stress either a comprehensive harmonious order or an agonal struggle between separate cultures or civilizations has its roots in the imperialist and subsequent colonial independence movements of the nineteenth and twentieth centuries. Ethnic and cultural nationalisms constitute a resistance to the imperial colonial power, not unlike Hansen's rendering of the Chicano movement. However, Said emphasizes that the composition of cultures and civilizations is a much more complicated affair in which multiple and varied traditions continually intersect.[26]

Having acknowledged that cultures and civilizations are comprised of a "radical hybridity," it becomes imperative to articulate an ethical and political vision that moves beyond the conflict intrinsic to a "us vs. them" rendering of "clashes" between civilizations.[27] Put otherwise by Said: "[U]nless we emphasize and maximize the spirit of cooperation and humanistic exchange—and here I speak not simply of uniformed delight or of amateurish enthusiasm for the exotic, but rather of profound existential commitment and labor on behalf of the other—we are going to end up superficially and stridently banging the drum for 'our' culture in opposition to all others."[28] He continues that transnational cooperation in the environmental movement, scientific research, the pursuit of universal human rights, and ethical/political outlooks emphasizing mutual sharing rather than "racial, gender, or class dominance" across borders offers some hope.[29]

Similarly, Dallmayr illustrates, through his textual dialogues both between Western thinkers and between thinkers from diverse civilizations, the possibility of moving in-between the tendency to focus on either universalism—an abstract cosmopolis void of concrete substance—or a parochial, xenophobic polis that leaves little room for eliciting a universal or transcendent sense of community.[30] Dallmayr takes Merleau-Ponty's emphasis on the "tensional intersection of meaning and non-meaning, of culture and nature, immanence and transcendence, and of self and other" and develops the prospect of just, peaceful mediations between the local and the global and in turn between diverse civilizations.[31]

In turn, he stresses that to realize peaceful dialogical relationships between peoples, we must be at peace "with ourselves, with nature, and with the divine." Dallmayr's pursuit of lateral universalism again moves "in-between" the premodern disposition to be fixated on a transcendent order and the postmodern inability to acknowledge the relevance of the transcendant, especially of a spiritual or theological orientation. Through his encounters with Islamic and Asian spiritualities, he refreshes the Western tradition with a concern for the divine that was imprudently abandoned in the West with the onset of the positivist side of modernity.

Ironically, in contrast to the assimilation/separatist divide that leads Huntington and Hansen to portray the growing Latino presence in the

United States in perilous terms, U.S. Latino theologians have been developing the spiritual, ethical, and political import of *mestizaje,* or the mixing of cultures in the Latino heritage. In transcendental terms, their exegesis of the intersection of diverse spiritualities in the Latino heritage is a kindred spirit to Dallmayr's pluralistic eliciting of the divine. In lateral terms, the cultural hermeneutical integration of multiple traditions in *mestizaje* concretely illustrates how to move beyond the assimilation/separatist divide in a manner consonant with Said's cooperative projection of hybridity and Dallmayr's global universalism that ensues through mutual, equal, lateral dialogues.

AN ETHOS OF CROSSING BORDERS

Historically, *mestizaje* refers to the mixing of the African, indigenous, and Spanish peoples in the Spanish conquest of the Americas.[32] *Una raza nueva*— a new race—emerges from this intersection—the *mestizos.* For instance, to be Mexican is to be part of a culture that is part African, part indigenous (the native tribes), and part Spanish, yet one that did not exist prior to the mixing of these groups in the sixteenth century. In turn, a subsequent *mestizaje* ensues in the U.S. Southwest over the past two centuries as Mexican and Native American peoples intersect with the colonists from the United States. Although most Latinos have come to the U.S. Southwest subsequent to the U.S.-Mexico War, they have come to a region whose Native American, Spanish, and Mexican cultural legacies precede the U.S. expansion.

The normative ethos of "crossing borders" and "mixing and matching identities" embodied in *mestizaje* has largely emerged during the past century. In the 1920s, José Vasconcelos, the great Mexican philosopher and educator, moves beyond just biological racial mixing to elicit from the Latin American experience *la raza cósmica*—the cosmic race. Vasconcelos aesthetically seeks to integrate cultures in a heterogeneous fashion that does not culminate in one culture dominating all others. He articulates *la raza cósmica* as an antithesis to petty nationalism, the explicit racism of Nazism, and the spreading materialistic and positivist perspective he sees being projected by the United States.[33] Unfortunately, Vasconcelos's retention of a Eurocentric "civilizing" of other cultures ultimately undermines his articulation of *la raza cósmica* as an aesthetic reconciliation of the universal and the particular.

Nevertheless, Vasconcelos's articulation of cultural mixing that transcends the cultural hegemonies of the nation-state system appeals to groups that have been marginalized by modernity. For instance, the Chicano movement accents the experience of a people whose identity, though shaped by both U.S. and Mexican national identities, transcends the limitations of narrow nationalist scripting.[34] In contrast to Vasconcelos's philosophical musings, Mexican Americans and other U.S. Latinos find themselves literally caught between cultures. Reflecting on growing up in San Antonio, the Mexican American theologian relates that he "was *not just* U.S.-American and *not just* Mexican but fully both and exclusively neither."[35] Hence, U.S. Latino culture is mutually shaped by long-standing indigenous, Latin American, and U.S. American legacies, yet reflects none of them in their entirety. Distinct from the assimilation and separatist outlooks that render culture as a *possession* that defines one from what one is not, *mestizaje* accents the transformations of cultures in *relation* to each other.

Unlike the so-called melting pot in U.S. culture, which essentially assimilates newcomers to the predominant European American mores, in *mestizaje* there is a dynamic conflation of cultures that generates a new culture in which aspects of the contributing cultures can still be identified. Conversely, in contrast to the separatist motifs of cultural movements—largely in reaction to the melting pot—*mestizaje*, especially as rearticulated by U.S. Latino theologians, suggests a dynamic integration of cultures that unlike Huntington's and Hansen's engagements of multiculturalism and transnationalism does not culminate either in uniformity or divisiveness.

Theologian Fernando Segovia argues that the Latino experience is "a radical sense of mixture and otherness, *mescolanza* and *otredad*, both unsettling and liberating at the same time."[36] "Barriers of exclusion" are thus antithetical to a *mestizo* politics.[37] Instead, the focus is on welcoming the stranger, not just as a measure of hospitality, but as essential to the mutual well being of the political community and its members.

Justo González clarifies this ethos of "crossing borders" with his distinction between "frontier" and "border" mentalities. A frontier mentality, as "manifested" by the U.S. westward expansion, distinguishes between civilization and the uncivilized aliens that lie "beyond the pale." As the civilization extends its boundaries, the aliens must be exterminated or assimilated—the plight of the U.S. indigenous tribes. By contrast, a border mentality emphasizes the ebb and flow of cultures across boundaries with mutual enrichment but without any one culture in permanent ascendancy.[38] Although the Spanish conquest of the Americas entails extermination of indigenous peoples, much more mixing of the European and indigenous cultures ensues than through the U.S. "manifest destiny." This Mesoamerican legacy for mixing cultures without culminating in uniformity animates the imaginations and lives of many U.S. Latinos as well as U.S. Southwest culture.[39] As much as borders remain part-and-parcel of human existence, according to Elizondo "they don't have to divide or separate. They can be privileged meeting places."[40]

The principal symbolic example of *mestizaje* in U.S. Latino theology is Our Lady of Guadalupe, who appeared to Juan Diego, a peasant, at Tepeyac in Mexico in 1531. Prior to Guadalupe, the Spaniards had met with little success in their Christian evangelizing. Her visage meshes the Virgin Mary and the Nahuatl (indigenous) spiritual entity *Tonantzin*. The blooming of roses and flowers out of season, the exquisite singing of birds, and the beautiful combination of colors adorning her attire do not simply highlight the event, but communicate the aesthetic orientation of the indigenous grasp of reality and knowledge. Though she appears as a native, Elizondo contends, Guadalupe sheds *Tonantzin's* malicious side.

Furthermore, Juan Diego becomes an empowered person, as Elizondo notes, through Guadalupe's treatment of him as a dignified human being, in contrast to the derogatory way the Spanish had been treating indigenous people. Indigenous conversions to Christianity could not ensue until this spirituality was grasped and embraced in indigenous terms. Opposing the assimilationist presumption that one had to become European in culture in order to become Christian, Elizondo contends that the Guadalupe event offers a lateral, not hierarchical, combination of cultures that is stronger than the original singular cultures; a relational, concrete, aesthetic portrait of truth; and a universal respect for others in their differences.

In contrast to such sanguinity about "crossing borders," Mexican American poet Gloria Anzaldúa draws our attention to the agonal dimension of such intersections: "The coming of two self-consistent but habitually incompatible frames of reference causes *un choque*, a cultural collision."[41] She is especially incisive regarding the long-standing repression of supposed misfits and outcasts within Mexican and Mexican American culture, especially in terms of gender and sexual preference. As much as the stress on extended family and person-to-person relationships in Mexican and Mexican American culture have much to offer a world in which each of us feels atomized and forever short on time, she counters these cultural traits have not allowed individuality or deviance. If a woman does not marry and have any children, for instance, then she is a failure.[42] Essentially, "[m]en make the rules and laws, women transmit them."[43]

Furthermore, Anzaldúa maintains that key feminine figures in Mexican culture—Guadalupe/*Tonantzin, La Chingada/Malinche,* and *La Llorona*— have been manipulated by political and religious authorities to make people subservient. Like Elizondo, Anzaldúa interprets Guadalupe as connected to *Tonantzin.* However, she argues, the Spanish recast the good and bad sides of *Tonantzin* into Guadalupe/Virgin María the pure virgin and *Coatlicue* the *puta* or whore.[44] The powerful symbolism of Our Lady of Guadalupe "as the virgin mother who has not abandoned us," she concludes, has been used by the church to make Mexicans "docile and enduring."[45] In like fashion, she contends that *La Chingada*—"the raped mother whom we have abandoned"—has made "us ashamed of our Indian side," and that *La Llorona*— "the mother who seeks her lost children"—has "made us long suffering people."[46]

Fully acknowledging that the original *mestizaje* in Mexico was begat by conquest, Anzaldúa nevertheless evinces an inclusive consciousness that intrinsically deals with contradictions, ambiguity, and combining opposites. Ultimately, for Anzaldúa, Mexican and Mexican American identity emerges as a way of being that transcends borders: "Being Mexican is a state of soul— not one of mind, not one of citizenship, neither eagle nor serpent, but both. And like the ocean, neither animal respects borders."[47]

In turn, Anzaldúa's accent on the vitality of indigenous culture and spirituality can be engaged in a way that does not just disparage or reject the European or Catholic Christian legacy in Latin America. Specifically, Latino popular religion is the principal locus in which African, European, and indigenous spiritualities effect a spiritual *mestizaje.* As Orlando Espín observes, Latino popular religion manifests a holistic "sacral world view" that synthesizes African (brought by slaves), medieval Spanish, and indigenous spiritual practices.[48] In turn, Espín provocatively claims that this medieval Spanish outlook precedes the Council of Trent and therefore is not characterized by the more rigid, doctrinaire Catholicism that emerges post-Trent.[49] Much like the conventional derogatory characterizations of *mestizos* as "half-breeds" or "mongrels," this popular religiosity has been disparaged as unsophisticated and uncivilized, if not heretical. However, the inclusiveness and people-centered spirituality manifested in popular religion potentially offers a democratic politics.

Admittedly, dwelling on aesthetic and affective sensibilities—whether by way of the exegesis of Guadalupe, Vasconcelos's *la raza cósmica*, Anzaldúa's poetry, or the heartfelt practices of popular religion—can lead to an anesthetization from politics. As opposed to an apolitical fascination with *flor y canto*—flower and song—the aesthetic, affective rationality elicited by U.S. Latino theologians focuses on engendering communities that overcome the hegemonic practices, especially of class, that presently thwart the capacity of the poor and the marginalized to participate fully in social, economic, and political decision-making forums: "The coming of the kin-dom of God has to do with a coming together of peoples, with no one being excluded and at the expense of no one."[50] As accented by Arturo Bañuelas, a fiesta is not just a party but a festive anticipation of a new universalism in which all peoples can engage each other as equals.[51] U.S. Latino theology recasts the Hegelian-Marxist legacy in liberation theology in terms of the cultural hermeneutical intersection of African, European, indigenous, and other cultures in the Americas.

| The preceding exegesis of *mestizaje* as an ethos of "crossing borders" has several implications for democratic theory. First, this deliberation uncovers a long-standing heritage from the U.S. Southwest that from its inception has been wrestling with unity-in-diversity. Political transformations are more easily effected through vivid cherished substantive traditions. As such, this legacy of mixing and matching cultural identities has much to offer when it comes to enabling the growing, not diminishing, cornucopia of cultures in the United States to mutually effect a unity-in-diversity without having to shed their heritages as the price of participation.

Second, contrary to many postmodern philosophers, these Latino scholars are able to reconcile a vision of the transcendent with their engagement of cultural differences. In contrast to the historic Eurocentrism of Christianity, in U.S. Latino theology African, European, and indigenous perspectives are on much more equal and interdependent terms. In opposition to unity as uniformity à la Huntington/Hansen, the focus is on achieving unity through lateral combinations of diverse cultures. Rethinking the relationship of the universal to the particular in this manner facilitates public discourse regarding a substantive common good and the relevance of transcendent truth without either rejecting difference or celebrating difference at the expense of the transcendent.

Third, this openness to "crossing borders" and to welcoming the "other" is vital for realizing a much more inclusive moral consensus in the United States. As much as the United States generally has been a Judeo-Christian nation, the spiritual landscape today in the United States includes Islam, Buddhism, Hinduism, an array of other traditions coming from the non-Western world, and secularism. For at least five centuries, though, Latinos have been wrestling with the intersection of African, European, and indigenous spiritualities. In addition to transforming liberation theology in a cultural hermeneutical fashion, *mestizo* spirituality moves beyond the Reformation–Counter Reformation debate to engender inclusive and hospitable intersections of spiritual traditions. This is indispensable for both negotiating the genuinely pluralistic yet democratic nation projected by *Commonweal* in 1960 and also navigating the rapidly growing global nexus between Western and non-Western spiritualities.

Fourth, and finally, the emphasis of a *mestizo* democracy on the marginalized and those deemed outcasts by the so-called mainstream never lets us forget that engendering mutual, lateral multicultural relationships is fundamentally about deconstructing the hegemonies that enable some groups to have distinct advantages over others when it comes to accessing key social, economic, and political decision-making forums. A *mestizo* democracy is not just a fashionable interchange of cultures. Given the growing gaps between the rich and the poor, both in the United States and between the developed and the developing world, a *mestizo* democracy entails overcoming inequality of political, economic, and social opportunities, especially if such disparity has a cultural, linguistic, racial, or religious hue.

There is no doubt that Latinos and other marginalized groups have frequently endured repression when caught between cultures. With full recognition of the conquest that sullies the original *mestizaje* in Latin America, U.S. Latino theologians evoke a political theology that acknowledges, challenges, and then strives to extirpate this conqueror/conquered dynamic. Indeed, moving beyond "either/or" whether in terms of culture, language, race, religion, or other categories entails conflicts and contradictions. *Mestizaje*, as praxis, conventionally castigated as engendering "half-breeds," actually embodies the possibility of inclusive, lateral, albeit at times agonal, multicultural relations.

By understanding cultural identity as an ongoing fluid combination of multiple cultures, rather than as a possession to be either kept in isolation from other cultures or superimposed on them, *mestizaje* moves beyond the assimilation/separatist dyad that is at the heart of Huntington's and Hansen's analyses. Cultures can engage each other laterally and engender new cultures that are distinct in their own right. Contrary to separatists, *mestizaje* suggests culture is not a possession to be "pickled." Counter to the static universal identity of assimilationists, *mestizaje* affirms plurality as intrinsic to cultural formation. A *mestizo* democracy is not concerned with preserving cultural enclaves or assimilating immigrants or colonized peoples into a hegemonic universality. Instead, it embraces pluralism, ambiguity, and difference in a way that eschews sterile uniformity without culminating in an anarchic relativism.

| Given that political theory has become preoccupied with "difference" over the past three decades, it makes sense to move beyond the boundaries of European and European American political theory to engage a heritage that for more than five centuries has been wrestling with the encounter between African, indigenous, and European perspectives. In vivid contrast to the prevailing *zeitgeist* of Huntington's clash of civilizations and Hansen's xenophobic rendering of hybridity, a *mestizo* democracy focuses on effecting multicultural and transnational democracies in which unity and diversity, community and individuality, and the universal and particulars are integral, not antithetical to each other.

The Augustinian Connection and the Strategic Dimension of Politics

In contrast, then, to Huntington's claim that the plurality intrinsic to the human condition inevitably set cultures and civilizations in conflict with each other, a *mestizo* democracy suggests that this plurality also offers the possibility of a richer collective life through the intersection of diverse cultures and civilizations. In this regard, the articulation of "unity-in-diversity" by the U.S. Latino theologians through the legacy of *mestizaje* is very much a synthesis of the Augustinian accent on plurality and disorder with the Thomistic accent on community and order. Moreover, Augustine's articulation of plurality accents the strategic dimension of politics that any sober, practical engagement of lateral transnational relationships must come to terms with.

The ineluctable differences between human beings, according to Augustine, makes for a politics characterized by strife and conflicts. For Augustine, as Jean Bethke Elshtain notes, the distances, differences, and antagonisms between human beings grow as one moves beyond the unity of immediate communal networks: "*From one* creates a fragile but real ontology of peace, or relative peacefulness. Bonds of affection tied human beings from the start. Bonds of kinship and affection bound them further. The more these relationship are dispersed, finally encompassing the globe, the more difficult it is to repair this fundamental kinship or sociality in order to strike a blow for peace and against war."[52] Seemingly, a fundamental "otherness" characterizes the human condition and defies cozy attempts at engendering unity.

For this reason, Augustine contends, elaborate deliberations on justice are pointless because the ambitions of human beings will always undermine their realization. Although we might catch glimpses of the "City of God" in this life, it will never be fully realized in the sinful "City of Man." Therefore, the best one can hope for politically in this life are regimes that provide a relative peace and order.

In the twentieth century, Reinhold Niebuhr updated this Augustinian sensibility with the notion that group life compounds the tendency toward ambition and willfulness found in individuals. Again, given this reality of strife and antagonism, he claims that we must pursue a low-expectation politics through balance of power schemes both between political groups within nations and between nation-states in transnational politics. Niebuhr's agonal politics informs Hans Morgenthau's realist outlook on international relations and, by extension, Huntington's "clash of civilizations."[53]

Aquinas's political theory, in contrast to Augustine's, is much more optimistic regarding the goodness and sense of substantive community that can be realized in human associations, for they are natural but imperfect reflections of God's goodness—there is a sacramental quality both to the world and nature.[54] Therefore, contrary to Augustinian thought, it is felt possible to discuss and pursue justice and the common good beyond just providing a relative peace and security.

Unfortunately, Aquinas's articulation of a good, just order remains firmly ensconced in medieval conceptions of hierarchy and cosmological order. His preference for kingship reflects a broader sensibility that the pluralistic components of the political and social order all have their natural role in harmony within "the great chain of Being."[55] Regardless of his intentions, Aquinas's rational articulation of an organic politics justifies the inequality of station not only in medieval Europe, but also in Latin America from the colonial period to the present. As much as there is a more substantive concern for preserving community in Latin American as opposed to U.S. American culture, it is also a community life rife with inequality and lacking in upward mobility. In this regard, Huntington's and Hansen's criticisms of Latin American culture have some merit.

A generation ago, Jacques Maritain and John Courtney Murray, attempted to synthesize Thomism with the pluralism manifested in twentieth-century liberal democracy—especially through their respective notions of a "practical consensus" and the "growing end."[56] Indeed, Maritain's thought had a great influence on the Christian Democratic parties in Latin America in the mid-twentieth century. In turn, Murray committed himself to fortifying a reason that could engender unity amid diversity and set back the "barbarians," as James Bacik put it, that "replace dialogue with monologue, reason with passion, and civility with harsh rhetoric."[57] At the same time, neo-Scholastic arguments continue to favor unity over diversity and order over disorder.[58] More importantly, they do not come to grips with the radical sense of alterity grasped by Augustine and highlighted in postmodern and postcolonial outlooks.[59]

Indeed, the postmodern tendency to emphasize variegated, criss-crossing identities, to debunk metanarratives, and to resist power structures that dominate not so much from the outside, but through the shaping of personal consciousness and institutional mores, defies cozy, harmonious articulations of democratic order. In turn, postcolonial discourses dealing with the complexity of moving beyond "master–slave" and "conqueror–conquered" relationships are crucial for understanding the politics of not only the developing world, but especially the developed world, as the peoples of the former increasingly characterize the latter.

Consequently, whereas Murray in 1960 was optimistic that dialogue could ensue between Catholics, Jews, and Protestants because of the truths held in common across the Judeo-Christian tradition, today the myriad of moral and ethical perspectives that constitute the United States alone call into question whether there can ever be any shared "truths" except in a hegemonic manner. If anything, the distances between perspectives enunciated by Augustine have become more salient. Therefore, when scholars such as Enrique Dussel or Calvin Schrag pursue, respectively, "transmodern" or "transversal" politics, they do so with full recognition of the hermeneutical accent on the other in postmodern and postcolonial discourses.[60]

In this light, a *mestizo* democracy, following the lead of the U.S. Latino theologians, takes the Thomistic articulation of a substantive common good through human associations and distills it in terms of the Augustinian focus on plurality. Akin to postcolonialism, this Latino ethos of "crossing borders" as the product of a double conquest—by Spain and then the United States—strives to overcome hierarchical, "conqueror-conquered" relationships. Akin to postmodernism, it accents hybridity, especially in terms of meshing diverse spiritualities, and challenges hegemonic institutional structures and processes. Unlike some postmodern perspectives though, this ethos of "crossing borders" emphasizes the integration of cultures both in terms of a substantive sense of community and a regard for the transcendent. Pursuing the "kin-dom of God" may move beyond hierarchical power relationships, but it does not succumb to the temptations of celebrating resistance and differences for their own sake or relegating transcendental concerns to the dustbin of metaphysics. The pursuit of a *mestizo* spirituality and politics, thus, is sensitive to the Augustinian articulation of plurality without appropriating his pessimistic conclusions regarding the City of Man.

The challenge remains, however, to effect a unity-in-diversity that engages the agonal and ambiguous character, not just of ontological plurality, but of the strategic dimension of politics. Political theories founded too exclusively on friendship or congenial, harmonious relationships as the basis for effecting multicultural or transnational politics accent communicative action at the expense of strategic action.[61] Politics is not just between friends, and more often than not is between interlocutors who, if not enemies, have very disparate interests and motivations.[62] In this regard, Huntington's and to a lesser extent Hansen's realist disposition has some merit despite the bombast that characterizes their analyses. What strategies and tactics are used to bring about mutual communication and understanding between diverse peoples as equals, and might they on occasion sully being morally pristine?

Early in this essay I mentioned Merleau-Ponty's notion of a lateral universality in relationship to multicultural and transnational undertakings, but we need to supplement this important notion with his reflections on what he terms the "serious humanism" found in Machiavelli.[63] As much as Machiavelli is maligned for emphasizing the strife intrinsic to history and politics "as a relationship of men rather than principles," Merleau-Ponty is quick to ask whether in reality there "is anything more certain?"[64] Therefore, he concludes it is not just the principles of politics that are crucial, but "what forces, which men, are going to apply them."[65] As Mary Dietz amplifies, this undertaking is not simply a matter of applying means to preordained ends, for there is "an entanglement of, if not a complementarity between strategic and communicative action."[66]

First, those pursuing laterally collaborative inclusive politics will encounter adversaries who will not hesitate to resort to violence rather than collaborative discourse in pursuit of their objectives. For example, the notion of "interbeing" as expressed by the Buddhist monk Thich Nhat Hanh has become popular in peace studies and in comparative political theory.[67] In "interbeing" one experiences a deep, intersubjective harmonious relationship not only with other human beings, but also with nature. At the same time, Hanh also provides the example of five disciples who during the Vietnam War were confronted and then executed by a small militia because they were part of Hanh's School of Youth for Social Service. Although the disciples practiced a nonviolent "engaged Buddhism," the militia for the moment at least prevailed.[68]

Second, as realized by Martin Luther King and the Southern Christian Leadership Conference (SCLC), effective nonviolent engagement of oppressive political, social, and economic structures can entail provoking violence on the part of the oppressor. At the outset of the U.S. civil rights movement, King, influenced by Gandhi's spirituality of nonviolent resistance, strove to win over the heart and mind of the oppressor through an appeal to the righteousness of the civil rights cause. Yet, King and the SCLC came to learn that they had to target cities in which they would be able to provoke violent retaliation by local law enforcement authorities, which would then bring coverage by the national and international media of their cause. This broader coverage would in turn put pressure on the federal government to take decisive action. Indeed, the protests staged at Birmingham, Alabama (1963) and Selma, Alabama (1965) lead respectively to enactment of the Civil Rights Act of 1964 and the Voting Rights Act of 1965. A just cause was brought about through strategies that entailed a "nonviolent" movement provoking violence.[69]

Therefore whether it be Elizondo's "universality of love, compassion, and mutual aid,"[70] Hanh's "inter-being," or Dallmayr's lateral dialogues, what are the strategies that will lead to a just "unity-in-diversity"? Indeed, Dallmayr contends that in pragmatic terms, dialogue among civilizations "offers the only viable alternative to military confrontation with its ever-present danger of nuclear holocaust and global self-destruction."[71] Yet, Dallmayr, who otherwise so deftly moves in-between antinomies such as "universal–particular" and "self–other," in this case establishes an "either-or" between lateral dialogues and military conquests because he insufficiently engages the intertwining between strategic and communicative action, and especially between both force and power and violence and non-violence.

Consequently, achieving inclusive multicultural democracies, whether national or transnational, entails strategies and tactics that not only elicit an "ethos of crossing borders" but also effectively navigate the ambiguous character of political morality stressed by Machiavelli. As understood by Emmanuel Mounier, public action takes place along a continuum from the political pole to the prophetic pole. The prophetic pole, "which lives by meditation and spiritual valour," eventually becomes too dogmatic or abstract to bring about effective action unless it has some awareness of the practical, if not manipulative side of public life.[72] The political pole, "which lives by arrangements and compromises," quickly becomes preoccupied with material and technical success if it does not maintain a concern for values, be they philosophical or spiritual.[73] "Integral action" between the poles, although it entails "dirtying one's hands," seeks rather than abandons the realization of values.[74] This "fidelity in disconcerting circumstances" reflects the same realization on the parts of King and the SCLC that no amount of spirituality will excuse one from the need to manipulate conflict for just, moral ends.[75]

A *mestizo* democracy, in contrast to the dire portraits of the growing U.S. Latino presence painted by Huntington and Hansen, elicits a constructive integration of cultures that moves between the "either/or" of assimilation and separatism. Democracy, as Fred Dallmayr, Ernesto Laclau, and Chantal Mouffe emphasize, entails the persistent renegotiation of "the multiplicity of social logics" that lie "between the logic of complete identity and that of pure difference."[76] Nevertheless, unless those of us articulating lateral engagements of multiculturalism or transnationalism also wrestle with strategic politics, Augustine's dour articulation of the agonal dimension of the human condition, which preoccupies Huntington and Hansen, too easily carries the day.

Notes

1. Richard Falk, "The World Order between Inter-State Law," in *Cosmopolitan Democracy*, ed. Daniele Archibugi and David Held (Cambridge, Mass.: Polity Press, 1995), pp. 163–79; Jeremy Breecher, "Popular Movements and Economic Globalization," in *Borderless Borders: U.S. Latinos, Latin Americans, and the Paradox of Independence*, ed. Frank Bonilla et al. (Philadelphia: Temple University Press, 1998), pp. 185–93.

2. Benjamin Barber, *Jihad v. McWorld* (New York: Times Books, 1995).

3. Maurice Merleau-Ponty, "From Mauss to Claude Lévi-Strauss," in *Signs*, trans. Richard C. McClearly (Evanston, Ill.: Northwestern University Press, 1964), p. 120.

4. Fred Dallmayr, *Dialogue among Civilizations: Some Exemplary Voices* (New York: Palgrave Macmillan, 2002), p. 2.

5. Fred Dallmayr, *Achieving Our World: Toward A Global and Plural Democracy* (Lanham, Md.: Rowman and Littlefield, 2001).

6. Susan Wolf, "Comment," in *Multiculturalism: Examining the Politics of Recognition*, ed. Amy Gutmann (Princeton: Princeton University Press, 1994), p. 81.

7. Samuel P. Huntington, *The Clash of Civilizations and the Remaking of World Order* (New York: Touchstone, 1996).

8. See, e.g., Peter Brimelow, *Alien Nation: Common Sense about America's Immigration Disaster* (New York: Routledge, 1995); Patrick Buchanan, *The Death of the West: How Dying Populations and Immigrant Invasions Imperil Our Culture and Civilization* (New York: St. Martin's Press, 2002); Georgie Anne Geyer, *Americans No More* (New York: Atlantic Monthly Press, 1996); Chilton Williamson Jr., *The Immigration Mystique: America's False Consciousness* (New York: Basic Books, 1996).

9. Samuel P. Huntington, "The Hispanic Challenge," *Foreign Policy* 83, no. 2 (March–April 2004): 30–45; Victor David Hansen, *Mexifornia: A State of Becoming* (San Francisco: Encounter Books, 2003).

10. Huntington, *The Clash of Civilizations*, p. 78.

11. Ibid., pp. 318–20.

12. Ibid., p. 320.

13. Ibid., p. 207.

14. Huntington, "The Hispanic Challenge," pp. 31–32.

15. Ibid., p. 44.

16. Huntington, *The Clash of Civilizations*, p. 206.

17. Ibid., p. 206.

18. Huntington, "The Hispanic Challenge," p. 32.

19. Hansen, *Mexifornia*, p. xi.

20. Ibid., p. 6.

21. Ibid., p. 77.

22. Ibid., pp. 141, 149–50.

23. "Catholics and the Presidency," *Commonweal* 71 (January 1, 1960): 384.

24. Robert N. Bellah et al., *The Good Society* (New York: Vintage Books, 1992), p. 300.

25. Bettia Martinez used the term during her remarks at a plenary session at the interdisciplinary conference "Hispanics: Cultural Locations," University of San Francisco, October 1997.

26. Edward W. Said, "The Clash of Definitions," in *Comparative Political Culture in the Age of Globalization: An Introductory Anthology*, ed. Hwa Yol Jung (New York: Lexington Books, 2002), pp. 368–70.

27. Ibid., p. 378.

28. Ibid., p. 375.

29. Ibid., p. 380.

30. Fred Dallmayr, "Polis and Cosmopolis," in *Comparative Political Culture in the Age of Globalization: An Introductory Anthology*, ed. Hwa Yol Jung (New York: Lexington Books, 2002), pp. 419–42.

31. Dallmayr, "Polis and Cosmopolis," p. 435.

32. Many of the ideas expressed in this section have been adapted from their more extensive presentation in chapters two and three of my *Mestizo Democracy: A Politics of Crossing Borders* (College Station: University of Texas A&M Press, 2002).

33. José Vasconcelos, *The Cosmic Race: A Bilingual Edition,* trans. Didier T. Jaén (Baltimore: Baltimore University Press, 1997).

34. Joseba Gabilondo, "Afterword to the 1997 Edition," in ibid., p. 100.

35. Virgilio Elizondo, *The Future Is Mestizo: Life Where Cultures Meet* (Bloomington, Ind.: Meyer-Stone, 1988), p. 26.

36. Fernando F. Segovia, "Two Places and No Place on Which to Stand: Mixture and Otherness in Hispanic American Theology," in *Mestizo Christianity: Theology from the Latino Perspective,* ed. Arturo J. Bañuelas (New York: Orbis, 1995), p. 31.

37. Arturo J. Bañuelas, "U.S. Hispanic Theology: An Initial Assessment," in *Mestizo Christianity,* ed. Bañuelas, p. 59.

38. Justo L. González, *Santa Biblia: The Bible Through Hispanic Eyes* (Nashville: Abingdon, 1996), p. 85.

39. Duncan Earle, "The Borders of Mesoamerica," *Texas Journal of Ideas, History, and Culture* 20 (Fall-Winter 1997): 61.

40. Elizondo quoted in Rosemary Johnston, "Theologians Ponder Meaning of Borders," *National Catholic Reporter* 33 (July 4, 1997): 11.

41. Gloria Anzaldúa, *Borderlands/La Frontera: The New Mestiza* (San Francisco: Aunt Lute, 1987), 78.

42. Ibid., pp. 17–18.

43. Ibid., p. 16.

44. Ibid., pp. 27–28.

45. Ibid., p. 31.

46. Ibid., 30–31.

47. Ibid., p. 62.

48. Orlando Espín, *The Faith of the People: Theological Reflections on Popular Catholicism* (Maryknoll, N.Y.: Orbis, 1997), pp. 122–24.

49. Ibid., p. 127.

50. Ada María Isasi-Díaz, *Mujerista Theology: A Theology for the Twenty-First Century* (Maryknoll, N.Y.: Orbis, 1996), pp. 65–66.

51. Bañuelas, "U.S. Hispanic Theology," p. 77.

52. Jean Bethke Elshtain, *Augustine and the Limits of Politics* (Notre Dame, Ind.: University of Notre Dame Press, 1995), p. 103.

53. William T. Bluhm, *Theories of the Political System: Classics of Political Thought and Modern Political Analysis*, 3d ed. (Englewood Cliffs, N.J.: Prentice-Hall, 1978), pp. 149–60.

54. Andrew Greeley, *The Catholic Myth: The Behavior and Belief of American Catholics* (New York: Charles Scribner's Sons, 1990), p. 45; Andrew Greeley, *The Catholic Imagination* (Berkeley: University of California Press, 2000), p. 5.

55. Dionysius the Areopagite, "The Celestial Hierarchy" and "The Ecclesiastical Hierarchy," in *St. Thomas Aquinas on Politics and Ethics*, ed. Paul Sigmund (New York: Norton, 1988), pp. 108–11.

56. See John Francis Burke, "Cultivating Community through Diversity: An Inductive, Hermeneutical Approach to Pluralism in Catholic Social Thought," *Journal for Peace and Justice Studies* 5, no. 1 (1993): 19–21.

57. James Bacik, *Contemporary Theologians* (Chicago: Thomas More Press, 1989), p. 141.

58. Scholars such as Philip Land are indeed recasting this static disposition of Aquinas's thought by integrating Thomism's more inductive practical wisdom with Karl Rahner's anthropology of love that is grounded in such Heideggerian notions as "being-in-the-world" and historicity. Nevertheless, neo-Scholasticism retains a static, deductive, manual-like portrait of moral and political life. Philip Land, *Catholic Social Teaching: As I Have Lived, Loathed, and Loved It* (Chicago: Loyola University Press, 1994), pp. 110–11, 118–19, 206–8.

59. Admittedly, William Connolly contends Augustine propagates a confessional outlook that brings closure to political contestation through its reliance on faith and transcendence. William Connolly, *The Augustinian Imperative: A Reflection on The Politics of Morality* (Newbury Park, Calif.: Sage Publications, 1993). Actually, the Christian voluntarism initiated by Augustine, stressing the will over the intellect, eventually leads to the sense of freedom expressed in existentialism and the sense of contest in postmodernism. The genealogy of the politics of plurality leads from Augustine to post-Nietzschean perspectives.

60. Enrique Dussel, *The Invention of the Americas: Eclipse of "the Other" and the Myth of Modernity*, trans. Michael D. Barber (New York: Continuum, 1995); Calvin O.

Schrag, "Hermeneutical Circles, Rhetorical Triangles, and Transversal Diagonals," in *Comparative Political Culture in the Age of Globalization: An Introductory Anthology,* ed. Hwa Yol Jung (New York: Lexington Books, 2002), pp. 381–96.

61. Mary Dietz, "Working in Half-Truth: Habermas, Machiavelli, and the Milieu Proper to Politics," in *Turning Operations: Feminism, Arendt, and Politics* (New York: Routledge, 2002), pp. 141–60.

62. For examples of a politics oriented by dialogical realization of friendship, see Fred Dallmayr, *Achieving Our World,* pp. 104–5; Fred Dallmayr, *Dialogue among Civilizations,* pp. 45–46.

63. Maurice Merleau-Ponty, "A Note on Machiavelli," in *Signs,* trans. Richard C. McClearly (Evanston, Ill.: Northwestern University Press, 1964), p. 223.

64. Ibid., p. 219.

65. Ibid., p. 200.

66. Dietz, "Working in Half-Truth, p. 155.

67. Thich Nhat Hanh, "The Order of Interbeing," in *Comparative Political Culture in the Age of Globalization: An Introductory Anthology,* ed. Hwa Yol Jung (New York: Lexington Books, 2002), pp. 205–11.

68. Thich Nhat Hanh, *Creating True Peace: Ending Violence in Yourself, Your Family, Your Community and the World* (New York: Free Press, 2003), p. 107. Hanh subsequently indicates that persistent "practice of love and mindfulness after each attack [on the member of the school] eventually moved the hearts of the killers and they stopped trying to kill us." The question remains how feasible it is that such spiritual practices would ensue on the scale necessary to deter if not eliminate war between peoples and nation-states.

69. David Garrow, *Protest at Selma: Martin Luther King Jr. and the Voting Rights Act of 1965* (New Haven: Yale University Press, 1978), pp. 133–60, 212–36.

70. Virgilio Elizondo, *Guadalupe: Mother of the New Creation* (Maryknoll, N.Y.: Orbis, 1997), p. 134.

71. Dallmayr, *Dialogue among Civilizations,* p. 13.

72. Emmanuel Mounier, *Personalism,* trans. Philip Mairet (Notre Dame, Ind.: University of Notre Dame Press, 1952), p. 91.

73. Ibid., p. 91.

74. Ibid., pp. 94, 92.

75. Ibid., p. 93.

76. Dallmayr quoting Laclau and Mouffe in Fred Dallmayr, "Polis and Cosmopolis," in *Comparative Political Culture in the Age of Globalization,* ed. Hwa Yol Jung, p. 437.

NINE

Transversality and Comparative Political Theory: A Tribute to Fred Dallmayr's Work

Hwa Yol Jung

There is no possible point of view from which the world can appear an absolutely single fact.

William James

Thought is informed by the *trans*-versal rather than the universal.

Calvin O. Schrag

The solution to the problem of identity: Get lost.

Norman O. Brown

What is your aim in philosophy? To shew the fly the way out of the fly-bottle.

Ludwig Wittgenstein

This volume is an occasion to honor Fred Dallmayr's intellectual achievements. For my part, I shall focus on his latest and most timely venture into comparative political theory in the age of global and even planetary politics, what he would now readily call the cosmopolis.[1] In the history of Western thought, he is one of those few who echo Diogenes's advocacy of cosmopolitan citizenship beyond the confines of polis-building of Socrates, Plato, and Aristotle. Dallmayr's most recent venture casts a new light on comparative political theory as an extension of his past intellectual itinerary. He is the first among practitioners of comparative political theory in his career as an intercontinental globetrotter. It is this aspect that should be cherished and celebrated by like-minded friends. What is philosophizing if not the cleared space enabling the writing that makes friends and keeps friendship alive and intact until the end of their lives?[2] To put it simply, philosophizing engages in the cultivation of friendship as well as humanity. For humanity begins at home: the intimate circle of friends.

"Globalization" is a mixed blessing: there are its contents and discontents. One thing is certain, however: it has the air of inescapability in the migration and exchange of ideas throughout the world where what really matters is how to make it cosmopolitan rather than predatory. As everything is a matter of communication, the late Canadian communication theorist Marshall McLuhan fashioned the avant-garde buzzword of the world as "a global village" in describing the shrinking world with the "tribal" sense of communicative intimacy in the age of electronic media that supersedes the Gutenberg era of printing technology in the West—particularly television as its exemplar, which his faithful followers update by "digitalizing" it. By way of media or communication technology, McLuhan had an unerring sense of the flow and rhythm of history since the preliterate or Homeric culture of ancient Greece. His disputed slogan "the medium is the message" scales history as much as communication theory.

THE MISSIONARY POSITION: EUROPE ON TOP

The Enlightenment is the soul of mainstream Western modernity. Its legacy continues today. Some speak of modernity as an unfinished project, a second modernity, even the modernization of modernity, or the second coming of Enlightenment itself. They have an unflinching faith in it as the absolute end of history. Enlightenment's unbridled optimism is alleged to promote and crown the Promethean progress of humanity based on the cultivation and universalization of pure and applied reason. Kant, who had a dim view of non-Europe (especially Africa), spelled out the civilizing mission of Enlightenment in the clearest and simplest term: to sanctify the autonomous benefits of reason in rescuing and emancipating humanity—perhaps more accurately European humanity—from its self-incurred immaturity. In so doing, he institutionalized the major agenda of European modernity whose rationality was never seriously challenged until the auspicious advent of post-modernity in Friedrich Nietzsche, Martin Heidegger, Jean-François Lyotard, Michel Foucault, Gilles Deleuze, Emmanuel Levinas, Jacques Derrida, and others in the twentieth century. While privileging and valorizing the authority of reason for allegedly human progress and emancipation, European modernity unfortunately overlooks, marginalizes, and disempowers the (reason's) "other," whether it be the Orient (or so-called non-West), body, woman, or nature at the altar of Enlightenment's reason. Orient, body, woman, and nature are not isolated at random but are interconnected issues: most interestingly, it is no accident that Orient, body, and nature are invariably genderized as feminine, while their counterparts—Occident, mind, and culture—are masculine or "malestream" categories.[3]

The institution of Western thought called "Eurocentrism" as well as the practice of imperialism is that habitus of mind that privileges Europe or the West as the cultural, technological, political, economic, and moral *capital* of the entire globe. "Modernization" is nothing but the all-encompassing catch-word given to the totalizing and hegemonizing process of this Eurocentric phenomenon. As the astute interpreter and critic of modernity Zygmunt Bauman relates:

> From at least the seventeenth century and well into the twentieth, the writing elite of Western Europe and its footholds on other continents considered its own way of life as a radical break in universal history. Virtually unchallenged faith in the superiority of its own mode over all alternative forms of life—contemporaneous or past—allowed it to take itself as the reference point for the interpretation of the *telos* of history. This was a novelty in the experience of objective time; for most of the history of Christian Europe, time-reckoning was organized around a fixed point in the slowly receding past. Now, . . . Europe set the reference point of objective time in motion, attaching it firmly to its own thrust towards colonizing the future in the same way as it had colonized the surrounding space.[4]

Indeed, this Eurocentric idea of colonizing the future gives new meaning to the conception of modernity as an unfinished project or the end of history.

"Oriental despotism" as a political subspecies of Eurocentrism in practice is said to be as old as "Herodotus's epic account of the struggle of free Greece against Persia's King of Kings."[5] In the political history of Western modernity, it gripped the fancy of some of its best and brightest minds: John Stuart Mill, Rousseau, Montesquieu, Hegel, Marx, and Karl Wittfogel, the last of whom wrote in 1957 the controversial book *Oriental Despotism*,[6] based on the simple theme of hydraulic dynamics in which the term "oriental" is synonymous with undeveloped or underdeveloped non-European. For Hegel, who compared to Kant is pallid and subtle, "Oriental despotism" meant the most servile stage of world history. Marx—following Hegel—recast it in economic or materialistic terms by standing the dialectics on its feet rather than on its head: "the Asiatic mode of production," which is the most underdeveloped form of economic life. Marx hoped for working out "class essentialism" and transformed it into the soteriology of the proletariat as "universal class," the idea of which is given way to or replaced by ethnicity in the world of multiculturalism. In the end, unfortunately, he was unable to free himself from the reign of Hegel's essentialized logic of identity.

Eurocentrism persists in the study of comparative politics today and manifests itself in different forms. In his watershed article "Interpretation and the Sciences of Man,"[7] which preceded his recent politics of recognition in the world of multiculturalism, Charles Taylor accused the American allegedly value-neutral science of comparative politics—particularly the influential theory of Gabriel Almond—of Eurocentrism by placing the "Atlantic type of polity at the summit of human political development." The "normalized" appellation "Third World" itself creates the Eurocentric ideology of ranking Asia, Africa, and Latin America as "underdeveloped"—euphemistically called "developing"—by placing them on the lowest scale of economic development and thus as inferior to the "First World" of Euro-American regions.

THE TAO OF TRANSVERSALITY

There is nothing trite about emphasizing that all understanding, all thinking, is more or less comparative, that is, intertextual. Comparison is the source for discovering the limits of one's discourse in light of the other, which is not one but always plural. In his contribution to the inauguration of comparative literature—"Comparative Literature, At Last!," a slogan worth emulating in political theory—Jonathan Culler prods his literary colleagues "to abandon its traditional Eurocentrism and turn global."[8] The literary critic Rey Chow argues that the study of the non-West is strongly justified in exploring and questioning the limits of Western discourse.[9] It is instructive for aspiring comparative political theorists to learn from literary comparativists about how to fashion a "world literature" since comparative political theory is at best in its infancy.

A few words of caution: understanding the other (the "foreign" other in particular), as anthropology as well as psychoanalysis has shown, is a difficult and demanding undertaking if for no other reason than that the other as a moving target is always other than itself. Indeed, the other is the "black hole" of all understanding, all conceptualization, and all relationships. At a moment of frustration and despair, the existential phenomenologist Jean-Paul Sartre faced a real moment of his black hole: "Hell is other people." Furthermore, comparativists should be aware of Akira Kurosawa's film *Rashomon*, which presents four different but equally plausible accounts of the same murder. The film raises a red flag for intercultural understandings. There is also the intriguing question of John Hu or Hu Ruowang—the first Chinese on record to travel to the West.[10] He sailed to France from Canton (Guagdon) in 1722. Like the *Rashomon* tale, the question of Hu has an intriguing plot. Because of his "strange" (foreign) behavior that astonished the Parisians, Hu was finally committed to the famous lunatic asylum of Charenton (Sha-langdon) in 1723 and remained there until 1726, when he was ordered by the French government to return to China. Setting aside for a moment the Foucauldian question of insanity as a sociocultural mechanism of control in the age of reason, the relevance of the Hu question here is whether he was committed to the asylum because he was "really mad" or perceived to be mad to the "foreign" Parisians because he was utterly "alien" to them. Either way, the question of Hu poses the scandalous difficulty of translating the dynamic chiasmata of intercultural perception, misperception, and even imperception.[11]

"Transversality" is a key word in the existential phenomenology of Calvin O. Schrag as he seeks to discover a "diagonal"[12] pathway in resolving the deadlock between Western modernity and postmodernity.[13] Sitting in a philosophical cockpit, as it were, it is a balancing act of navigating through the stormy space between the dichotomous poles of the modernist obsession with identity and universalism, on the one hand, and the postmodernist exhaustive drive for difference and pluralism, on the other. Transversality actively seeks a transformation. It is, according to Schrag, the recognition of difference that keeps open "the prospect for invention, intervention, transgression, re-creation, etc."[14] It looks for "convergence without coincidence"— to use his repeatedly emphasized expression. Thus, it broadens the "in between" for the sake of the "beyond."

Transversality is primarily a derivative concept of geometry. Schrag exacts *l'esprit de finesse* by way of a geometric configuration: in addition to the two diagonals crossing or intersecting each other at the epicenter of any rectangle, there are also the hermeneutical "circle" and the rhetorical "triangle." Insofar as it is a negotiated or compromised "middle voice," transversality touches the soul and heart of Buddhism. By way of the "middle voice" of transversality, he means to subvert and transgress particularly the dichotomy between "the Scylla of a hegemonic unification" (a "vacuous universalism") on the one hand, and the "the Charybdis of a chaotic pluralism" ("an anarchic historicism") on the other. The newly emerging face of transversality may be likened to the famous wooden statue of Buddha at a Zen temple in Kyoto, whose face marks a new dawn of awakening (*satori*) or signals the beginning of a new regime of ontology, ethics, politics, and culture. From the crack in the middle of the old face of the Buddha's statue, there emerges an interstitial, liminal face that signifies a new transfiguration and transvaluation of the existing world. The icon of the emerging new face symbolizes the arrival of *Maitreya* (the "future Enlightened One") or Middle Way—the third enabling term of transversality that is destined to navigate the difficult waters of intercultural border crossings. We are warned not to take it as a middle point between two poles. Rather, it breaks through bipolarity (modernity and postmodernity, nature and society, mind and body, femininity and masculinity, and East and West). What is important here is the fact that transversality is the paradigmatic rendition of overcoming bipolarity itself. The bipolar solids melt into the air of transversality, as it were.[15]

As disenchantment calls for transcendence, transversality is used here as a deconstructive concept.[16] It first dismantles or unpacks the status quo and then goes beyond what is given, received, or established by constructing a new formation of concepts. It, in short, attempts to challenge the assumed transparency of truth as universal and overcome the limits of universality as the Eurocentric canon of truth in Western modernity. It means to decenter Europe as the site of "universal truth" whose "identitarian" and "unitarian" motivation fails to take into account the world of multiculturalism. The pluralist Johann Gottfried Herder challenges: "I find myself unable to comprehend how reason can be presented so universally as the single summit and purpose of all human culture, all happiness, all good. Is the whole body just one big eye?"[17] The French philosopher and sinologist François Jullien calls the effort of this decentering Eurocentrism or Western modernity—with Kant in mind—"a new 'Copernican reversal.'" He contends that in "shaking up" Western modernity, China becomes a "philosophical tool," that is, he uses Chinese thought to interrogate Western philosophy and to liberate it from its own "mental cage." Most radically, he wishes to replace the very concept of "truth" itself with that of "intelligibility" because "truth" is bound up with the history of Western philosophy. Jullien puts Foucault to test in order to vindicate the Eurocentric "legislation" of truth for all global humanity.[18] In his 1978 visit to Japan, the vintage Foucault remarked that as the warp of knowledge and the woof of political power are interwoven as one fabric, European imperialism and the era of Western philosophy together come to an end. Foucault is not alone in conjecturing that philosophy of the future must be born "outside Europe" or in the "meetings and impacts" between Europe and non-Europe.[19]

Long before Foucault and Jullien, Maurice Merleau-Ponty would speak of the "lateral universal" and the lateral continuity of all humanity both "primitive" and "civilized" across history. He is unmistakably a consummate transversalist *avant la lettre*. The lateral universal is for him a new paradigm for worldmaking as well as philosophy. "Lateral" rather than "vertical" thinking is paradigmatic in that instead of digging the same hole deeper and deeper in which there is no exit in sight, it digs a new hole in another place.[20] For Merleau-Ponty, all history is not only contemporaneous and written in the present tense but also an open notebook in which a new future can be inscribed. It is unfortunate, I think, that his deconstructive effort for comparative philosophy and his sensitivity to the global scope of philosophy have escaped the attention of comparativists and specialists alike. This inattention is likely due to the same tendencies that inform our Eurocentric propensity and orientation in philosophy.

Merleau-Ponty's deconstructive effort in philosophy, in comparative philosophy, is evidenced in his critique of Hegel's Eurocentrism.[21] He charges that Hegel arbitrarily drew "a geographical frontier between philosophy and non-philosophy," that is between the West and the East.[22] Philosophy, Merleau-Ponty goes on to argue, is destined to examine its own idea of truth again and again because truth is "a treasure scattered about in human life prior to all philosophy and not divided among doctrines." If so, Western philosophy is compelled to reexamine not only its own idea of truth but also related matters and institutions such as science, economy, politics, and technology. Besides philosophy's own constant vigilance on what it is doing, Merleau-Ponty's phenomenological orientation demands its attention to the ethnography of the sociocultural life-worlds without which philosophy is a vacuous if not fatal abstraction.

The way of ethnography's "thick" description practiced by Marcel Mauss and Claude Lévi-Strauss, who also taught at the Collège de France, provides Merleau-Ponty with the idea of the lateral continuity of humanity between the "primitive" and the "civilized," that is, with the incessant ethnographic testing of the self by the other and the other by the self, which has a "diacritical value" for humanity's coexistence and its planetary solidarity. Ethnography redeems Western narcissism precisely because it is the human science of understanding the "foreign other." Merleau-Ponty contends that while for Hegel philosophical truth as absolute and universal knowledge is notarized and certified by the Occidental seal of approval alone, the Oriental past must also have an honored place in the famed hall of philosophies to celebrate its hitherto "secret, muted contribution to philosophy." He writes resolutely: "Indian and Chinese philosophies have tried not so much to dominate existence as to be the echo or the sounding board of our relationship to being. Western philosophy can learn from them to rediscover the relationships to being and an initial option which gave it birth, and to estimate the possibilities we have shut ourselves off from in becoming 'Westerners' and perhaps reopen them." "If Western thought is what it claims to be," he challenges further, "it must prove it by understanding all 'life-worlds'" as multiple geosociocultural realities.[23]

Thus Merleau-Ponty suggests that in contrast to the "overarching universal" of objective sciences or, we might add, Western metaphysics, the "lateral universal" is acquired through ethnographical experience as the way of "learning to see what is ours as alien and what was alien as our own." His lateral universal is a passport, as it were, that allows us to cross borders between diverse cultures, enter the zone of intersections and discover cross-cultural connections and convergences. While the European geophilosophical politics of identity claims its validity as universal truth, the lateral universal takes into account "local knowledge" prior to planetary knowledge (dubbed by some as "glocalization") and allows the hermeneutical autonomy of the other who may very well be right. Indeed, Merleau-Ponty's lateral universal is contextualized as an open-ended and promiscuous web of temporal and spatial (that is, chronotopic) interlacings.

The (Eurocentric) universalist has failed to seriously take into account the question of diversity or multiplicity in the world of multiculturalism. He is still entangled in the cobweb of absolute universal truth and cultural relativism. As difference marks multiplicity and all relationships, Heidegger's *Differenz* as *Unter/schied* edifies our discussion here because it plays and feeds on the coupled meaning of the words that connects, preserves, and promotes both difference and the relational in one breath.[24] In *Differenz* as *Unterschied*, the other is neither assimilated/incorporated nor erased/segregated: the integrity of the other is well preserved. Here we would be remiss if, in light of Merleau-Ponty's above-mentioned "lateral universal" including a critique of Hegel's Eurocentrism, we fail to recognize the seminal contribution of the Caribbean francophone Édouard Glissant to the making of the transversal world. Educated in philosophy and ethnography in France, he is a philosopher, a poet, and a novelist whose "poetics of relation" shaped Caribbean (*antillais*) discourse on "diversality" and "*créolité*" (creoleness).[25]

In the first place, Glissant has an uncanny convergence in the name of transversality with Merleau-Ponty in his critique of Hegel when he articulates without equivocation that transversal relation means to replace "the old concept of the universal." "Thinking about One," Glissant puts it concisely, "is not thinking about All."[26] Speaking of Hegel's conception of history, he writes:

> History is a highly functional fantasy of the West, originating at precisely the time when it alone "made" the history of the world. If Hegel relegated African peoples to the ahistorical, Amerindian peoples to the prehistorical, in order to reserve History for European people exclusively, it appears that it is not because these African or American peoples "have entered History" that we can conclude today that such a hierarchical conception of "the march of History" is no longer relevant.[27]

Glissant unpacks Hegel's history by dissolving it as irrelevant or passé in the postcolonial world of diverse cultures that rejects "the linear, hierarchical vision of a single History."[28]

In the second place and more importantly, transversality is proposed and constructed by Glissant in opposition to and as a replacement for universality. For him, transversality is the "poetics" of cross-cultural encounters. It is the way of crossing and going beyond (that is, to "creolize") ethnic, lingual, and cultural boundaries. It is indeed the site of hybridity. As Glissant himself puts it, transversality is "the site of converging paths" or the "convergence that frees us from uniformity."[29] The British postcolonial theorist Robert J. C. Young, who regards Eurocentrism as a "white mythology," makes an interesting and unusually astute observation that "[p]ostcolonialism is neither western nor non-western, but a dialectical product of interaction between the two, articulating new counterpoints of insurgency from the long-running power struggles that predate and post-date colonialism."[30] It may be said that the postcolonial mind works like a double helix. More specifically, Paul Gilroy's reputed thesis[31] of "the black Atlantic" is in favor of hybridity or "double consciousness" that sums up the transcultural intermix of African and European things.[32] Hybridity is a converging middle path of "multiple, interconnecting axes of affiliation and differentiation."[33] In the final analysis, Gilroy's "black Atlantic" is constructed quintessentially as "a counter-culture of modernity."[34]

The so-called recognition or acknowledgment of difference, which is not one but many, is not the final but only the first step in the making of hybridity. In *Éloge de la Créolité* (In Praise of Creoleness)[35]—a Caribbean manifesto purposely written bilingually—"diversality" (*la diversalité*) in opposition to universality is defined as "the conscious harmonization of preserved diversities" (*l'harmonisation consciente des diversités preservées*). When harmonization is understood musically, it enriches the totality and even coloration of "diversality" when two or more tones are put together (that is, orchestrated): there emerges harmonization (or symphony) in which each individual tone is not lost but preserved. But when two colors are mixed together, there is no harmony but another color. In the name of "a polyphonic harmony," "diversality" frowns on "the obsessional concern with the Universal." The above-mentioned Caribbean or "creolized" manifesto begins with the sentence: "Neither Europeans, nor Africans, nor Asians, we proclaim ourselves Creoles" (*Ni Europeens, ni Africains, ni Asiatiques, nous nous proclamons Créoles*). The Creole (as hybrid) is neither unitarian nor separatist, but is likened to a hybrid butterfly who frees himself/herself by breaking off from an "ethnocentrist cocoon." Glissant himself describes the principium of creoleness as the end of "diversality":

Diversity, which is neither chaos nor sterility, means the human spirit's striving for a cross-cultural relationship, without universalist transcendence. Diversity needs the presence of peoples, no longer as objects to be swallowed up, but with the intention of creating a new relationship. Sameness requires fixed Being, Diversity establishes Becoming. Just as Sameness began with expansionist plunder in the West, Diversity came to light through the political and armed resistance of peoples. As Sameness rises *within* the fascination with the individual, Diversity is spread *through* the dynamism of communities. As the Other is a source of temptation of Sameness, Wholeness is the demand of Diversity. You cannot become Trinidadian or Quebecois, if you are not; but it is from now on true that if Trinidad and Quebec did not exist as accepted components of Diversity, something would be missing from the body of world culture—that today we would feel that loss. In other words, if it was necessary for Sameness to be revealed in the solitude of individual Being, it is now imperative that Diversity should "pass" through whole communities and peoples. Sameness is sublimated difference; Diversity is accepted difference.[36]

In the formulation of hybridity as the site of transversality based on un-reifiable and unerasable difference in the world of multiculturalism, the dialogical acquires new meanings. In the first place, it is an indispensable element in the harmonics of multiple relationships. Its failure signals the end of hybridity, multiculturalism, and transversality itself.[37] Thus the dialogical is coeval with the unending process of "Becoming." Not unlike the Chinese *yin-yang* logic of correlation, in which everything is said to be changing except change itself, "Becoming" has to go on: the dialogical of multiple differences knows no final ending—no Hegelian and Marxian dialectical or identitarian synthesis that may be identified with the identity of identity and difference. For Hegel, the dialectical consummates in the State (sectarian nation-state or perhaps unitarian world-state) as the march of the Divine in history, whereas for Marx the dialectical is perfected in "class essentialism," which favors the utopian and soteriological dream of the proletariats' becoming one "universal class."

For the Russian literary theorist Mikhail Bakhtin,[38] on the other hand, everything ends when dialogue ends. Thus dialogue cannot and must not come to an end. Merleau-Ponty, too, speaks of the "hyperdialectic" that is "unstable" or on a constant move. It is the dialectic without the conceptual "trap" of synthesis which is capable of "[envisaging] the plurality of the relationships" or transversing "the spatial and temporal multiplicity of the actual" (*la multiplicité spatiale et temporelle de l'actuel*) without restriction. The hyperdialectic is not the denial per se of "the idea of surpassing that reassembles" (*l'idée du dépassement qui rassemble*), but only of synthesis. Furthermore, the dialogical context for Bakhtin knows no limits. Even past meanings are forever unstable and undecidable. They may be retrieved and renewed for the present. The indeterminacy of Bakhtin's dialogical principle applies to backtracking as well as foretracking. In the end, dialogue is "unfinalizable" (Bakhtin's own term) or "nondialectizable" (Gilles Deleuze's expression).[39] Bakhtin could not agree more with William Faulkner's epigram that "the past is never dead, it's not even past." The spirit of Bakhtin's dialogical principle is best expressed in a Zen *koan:* "When you get to the top of the mountain, keep climbing."

In the second place, Hans-Georg Gadamer, whose influence permeates the writings of Dallmayr particularly on his cosmopolitan effort—declares that the very soul of hermeneutics is the idea that the other may be right, in other words, it is heterocentric. Two monologues do not make one dialogue because dialogue is not a series of self-righteous monologues. In dialogue we must listen to what the other has to say: dialogue is a "boustrophedonic"[40] process of speaking and listening. The heterocentric orientation of dialogue or the primacy of the other in dialogue entails an ethical imperative, the ethics of responsibility that was stipulated by Ludwig Feuerbach in his philosophy of the future—a Copernican revolution in social thought where what Copernicus is to Ptolemy, the other is to the self. Emmanuel Levinas is forthright in declaring: "When I speak of [ethics as] first philosophy, I am referring to a philosophy of dialogue that cannot not be an ethics. Even the philosophy that questions the meaning of being does so on the basis of the encounter with the other."[41] It is worth emphasizing repeatedly that ethics is always heterocentric or other-directed and that a self-centered ethics is no ethics at all. Hannah Arendt's discussion of Adolf Eichmann's "banality of evil" is often misguided and misunderstood because banality properly understood as the source of evil is for Arendt one's inability to think and perform in terms and for the sake of the other. Ultimately, evil (banal or otherwise) is committed because we do not take responsibility seriously.[42] No ethics is complete without responsibility.

Geophilosophy: An Addendum to Dallmayr's New Vision

Dallmayr's vision of philosophy involves the creation and advancement of the cosmopolis in the age of globalization by breaking down existing conceptual barriers. Therefore, it is not at all contrary to his new endeavor to flavor it with the spice of geophilosophical ideas. Being transcultural and transdisciplinary, geophilosophy goes hand in hand with transversality, which is in itself a derivative of measuring the earth (that is, geometry). Global warming and nuclear pollution, for example, know no boundaries separating nation or species. For their solution, we need the unprecedented effort of transnational cooperation that is at once cultural, religious, political, economic, scientific, and technological. In a nutshell, geophilosophy is our ultimate concern for sustaining all life on earth. There is indeed a greater sense of urgency than ever before in human history.

Hannah Arendt begins her magnum opus *The Human Condition* (1958) with the fundamental premise that "[t]he earth is the very quintessence of the human condition, and earthly nature, for all we know, may be unique in the universe in providing human beings with a habitat in which they can move and breathe without effort and without artifice."[43] Geophilosophy is an all-encompassing philosophical inquiry into the nature of Interbeing—both interhuman and interspecific—as if the whole earth really matters. It negotiates "culture" and "nature," which are perhaps two of the most complex and controversial key words in human language and history. It is predicated on the regulative principle of Interbeing in which nothing exists in isolation, everything is connected to everything else in the cosmos. Interbeing is "otherwise than Being": in the beginning was Interbeing, which precedes all matters of Being. As such the death of nature signifies the death of humanity, not the other way round—the formula that neither Descartes nor Francis Bacon imagined in their undaunted pursuit of the mastery and possession of nature for the sole purpose of unabashed *philanthropia*. The so-called death of nature begins with *philanthropia* in Western modernity and the widespread propagation of modernization as a global process. For Gilles Deleuze and Félix Guattari, the eminent domain of their newly coined term "geophilosophy" is the whole earth, which is not just one element among others but is that all-encompassing element that "brings all the elements *in a single embrace*."[44] Geophilosophy may thus be called "ecocentric." The Norwegian philosopher Arne Naess speaks of "deep ecology," which is at once prescriptive/ethical and descriptive/scientific. The normative discipline of political philosophy is regarded as an integral part of deep ecology.[45] Without geophilosophy, cosmopolitan philosophy is incomplete.

Risk, according to the German sociologist Ulrich Beck, is a modern European phenomenon. What is radically new or paradigmatic in the contemporary world, however, is that risk has become global, that is, it deterritorizes national boundaries. In sum, the scope of risk society has become truly global or planetary. Beck speaks of "the inescapability of the transnational dynamic." "A cosmopolitan sociology," he contends, "posits globality as the experience of a deterritorized culture."[46] He is willing to abandon the universal in favor of the cosmopolitan since cosmopolitanism recognizes multiplicity, whereas universal "globalism" denies it.[47]

For Beck, the recognition of multiplicity is something good, whereas its denial is something bad. However, he rejects the radical paradigm shift of postmodernism because he has misgivings about its concern with "what is *not* the case" and its silence about "what *is* the case."[48] What is needed is not to replace European modernity but to "reform" it in creating "a second modernity." "Modernity has not vanished," declares Beck, "we are not past it."[49] Despite his quarrel with postmodernism, what should be noted in Beck's conception of cosmopolitan or global sociology is the recognition of multiculturalism and the acceptance of the phenomenon of globalization as a topic of sociological inquiry. In his cosmopolitan sociology, geophilosophy converges with the aim of globalization: the former transverses with the latter in their mutual emphasis on interconnectedness. Beck sloganizes the thesis that "smog is democratic," whereas "poverty is hierarchical."[50] To be sure, the scope of risk society has definitely been globalized. Global or transnational risks such as Chernobyl and HIV/AIDS dissolve and invalidate the received distinction between society and nature on the one hand, and between the body and society on the other. Intercorporeality, however, is always a precondition for sociality. Sociality is ensouled but first and foremost fully embodied: it is intercorporeal. The disembodied body is incapable of socializing with the other.

Epilogue

This essay is written in the pioneering spirit of Fred Dallmayr's vision of cosmopolitanism in the age of globalization. The goal of globalization or planetarization is to achieve cosmopolitanism for and across all humanity. In the pluralization of the world, a multiplicity of cultures *across* time and space is underscored in his cosmopolitanism. However, he is well aware of the fact that the mere recognition or acknowledgment of cultural differences would be only the first but not the final step toward achieving cosmopolitan humanity. His cosmopolitanism would reject, as Goethe would, Kipling's separatist approach of "East is East" and "West is West" with the added baggage of "white man's burden." Nor would it accept Samuel Huntington's irreconcilable "clash of civilizations" based on the chauvinistic "essentialization" of each civilization involving the reification of its own difference from the rest (for example, "occidentalizing" Occidental civilization and "orientalizing" Oriental civilization, each of which is not one but many). Nor would it be receptive to Francis Fukuyama's thesis of the "end of history," which is tantamount to valorizing the "one world" or an "empire" of Western neoliberalism that denies the basic assumptions of multiculturalism.

Transversality lays the groundwork for pursuing comparative political theory that has yet to heed in earnest Nietzsche's prophetic dictum over a century ago regarding the arrival of "the age of comparison." It holds, I submit, the secret key unlocking the gateway to comparative political theory by defenestrating the unitarian politics of identity in support of the pluralistic politics of difference, which is neither erased nor reified but dialogized. Reified difference results inevitably in what we might call the "agonistic model" of multiculturalism, in which difference is assumed to be irreconcilable for the sake of transversal relationships. Dialogized difference is a middle path between consummate consensus and total dissensus. Without it, hybridity or cosmopolitanism is unthinkable. Transversality as the site of hybridity[51] or cosmopolitanism is an ideal type or heuristic construction to answer what transpires when it deterritorizes national and cultural boundaries, that is, when it allows (diagonal) border-crossings. In the end, transversality in the name of hybridity is capable of dissolving the long-embattled argument concerning the facile dichotomy between universal absolutism and cultural relativism, modernity and postmodernity, commensurability and incommensurability, globalism and nationalism, history and nature, mind and body, and above all East and West. It indeed shows this dichotomy the way out of its bottle.

Notes

1. Dallmayr edits the Lexington Books series "Global Encounters: Studies in Comparative Political Theory." The first volume of the series he edited is titled *Border Crossings: Toward a Comparative Political Theory* (Lanham, Md.: Lexington Books, 1999). For the theme of Orientalism, globalization, and achieving humanity, see particularly his books *Beyond Orientalism: Essays on Cross-Cultural Encounter* (Albany: SUNY Press, 1996); *Alternative Visions: Paths in the Global Village* (Lanham, Md.: Rowman and Littlefield, 1998); *Achieving Our World: Toward a Global and Plural Democracy* (Lanham, Md.: Rowman and Littlefield, 2001); *Dialogue among Civilizations: Some Exemplary Voices* (London: Palgrave/Macmillan, 2002); and *Peace Talks—Who Will Listen?* (Notre Dame, Ind: University of Notre Dame Press, 2004).

2. This is a modification of Jean Paul's claim that "[p]hilosophy is the ability to make friends through the medium of a written text." Quoted in Paul Rabinow, *Anthropos Today* (Princeton: Princeton University Press, 2003), pp. 1, 80–81.

3. See my "Enlightenment and the Question of the Other: A Postmodern Audition," *Human Studies* 25 (2002): 297–306.

4. Zygmunt Bauman, *Legislators and Interpreters* (Cambridge, UK: Polity Press, 1987), p. 110.

5. Martin Malia, *Russia under Western Eyes* (Cambridge: Harvard University Press, 1999), p. 6.

6. Karl Wittfogel, *Oriental Despotism* (New Haven: Yale University Press, 1957).

7. Charles Taylor, "Interpretation and the Sciences of Man," *Review of Metaphysics* 25 (1971): 3–51.

8. Jonathan Culler, "Comparative Literature, At Last!" in *Comparative Literature in the Age of Multiculturalism,* ed. Charles Bernheimer (Baltimore: Johns Hopkins University Press, 1995), pp. 117–21.

9. Rey Chow, "In the Name of Comparative Literature," in *Comparative Literature in the Age of Multiculturalism,* ed. Charles Bernheimer (Baltimore: Johns Hopkins University Press, 1995), pp. 107–16.

10. See Jonathan D. Spence, *The Question of Hu* (New York: Knopf, 1988).

11. Zygmunt Bauman makes an interesting point when he writes: "The main point about civility is . . . the ability to interact with strangers without holding their strangeness against them and without pressing to surrender it or to renounce some or all the traits that have made them strangers in the first place." *Liquid Modernity* (Cambridge, UK: Polity Press, 2000), pp. 104–5.

12. It is interesting to note that David Farrell Krell sketches *das Geviert* envisioned by Heidegger in the pictogram of a rectangle that connects sky, earth, gods, and mortals with two diagonal lines having Being at its epicenter: the crossing of Being is not a crossing out (*Durchstreichung*) but a crossing through (*Durchkreuzen*).

See my "Heidegger's Way with Sinitic Thinking," in *Heidegger and Asian Thought,* ed. Graham Parkes (Honolulu: University of Hawaii Press, 1987), pp. 217–44, at p. 243 n. 27.

13. Schrag's conception of transversality begins in earnest in *The Resources of Rationality: A Response to the Postmodern Challenge* (Bloomington: Indiana University Press, 1992). For my appropriation of Schrag's transversality for the study of comparative culture, see "The *Tao* of Transversality as a Global Approach to Truth: A Metacommentary on Calvin O. Schrag," *Man and World* 28 (1995): 11–31.

14. *Experiences between Philosophy and Communication: Engaging the Philosophical Contributions of Calvin O. Schrag,* ed. Ramsey Eric Ramsey and David James Miller (Albany: SUNY Press, 2003), p. 26.

15. Abe Masao writes: "The Middle Way . . . should not be taken as a middle point between two poles. On the contrary, the Middle Way breaks through dipolarity; it is the overcoming of dipolarity itself." *Zen and Western Thought,* ed. William R. LaFleur (Honolulu: University of Hawaii Press, 1985), p. 157. The Kyoto school of philosophy should be noted for its transversal or hybrid attempt to incorporate East and West in the writings of Nishida Kitaro, Tanabe Hajime, Nishitani Keiji (whose thought is compared by Dallmayr with Heidegger's), and Suzuki Daisets Teitaro (whose mode of philosophizing is even the envy of Heidegger). This alone justifies Japan as a transversal or hybrid culture.

16. It is worth mentioning in passing the lengthy work of Wolfgang Welsch on "transversal reason" (*transversale Vernunft*) in part 2 of *Vernunft* (Frankfurt: Suhrkamp, 1995), whose detailed analysis is beyond the scope of this essay. Transversal reason is another defense of reason against its "death" in contemporary thought, particularly in postmodern philosophy. As "a faculty of transitions," it is a defense against "the abandonment of reason in favor of a multitude of rationalities." It is that metarationality that is concerned with the diverse paradigms of rationality and evaluates their interrelationships. It is doubtful that, despite his gallant effort, there is a breakthrough in Welsch's transversal reason beyond the confines of Eurocentrism. Postcolonial reason is untouched by Welsch's transversal reason. Whose rationality is it, anyway? Moreover, Welsch's critique of postmodernism would stand to reason if postmodern is the defense of "unreason." Lyotard's critique of the logic of Hegel's rationalism, for example, is intact when Lyotard writes: "All that is real is rational, all that is rational is real: 'Auschwitz' refutes the speculative doctrine. At least this crime, which is real, is not rational." See *The Postmodern Explained,* ed. Julian Pefanis and Morgan Thomas, trans. Don Barry, Bernadette Maher, Julian Pefanis, Virginia Spate, and Morgan Thomas (Minneapolis: University of Minnesota Press, 1992), p. 29. Two short summations of Welsch's transversal reason are available in English: "Reason and Transition: On the Concept of Transversal Reason," available at www2.uni-jena. de/welsch/Papers/reasTrans.html; and "Rationality and Reason," in *Criticism and Defense of Rationality in Contemporary Philosophy,* ed. Dane R. Gordon and Józef Niznik (Atlanta: Rodopi, 1998), pp. 17–31.

17. *J. G. Herder on Social and Political Culture,* ed. and trans. F. M. Barnard (Cambridge: Cambridge University Press, 1969), p. 199. The eye as in the "mind's eye"

is a metaphor or symbol for cerebral activity. Mainstream modern Western philosophy (Cartesianism in particular) is ocularcentric or panoptic. In this respect, Herder's use of the "eye" in this query is well chosen.

18. See François Jullien, "Did Philosophers Have to Become Fixated on Truth?" (trans. Janet Lloyd), *Critical Inquiry* 28 (2002): 803–24; "'China as Philosophical Tool,'" *Diogenes* 50 (2003): 15–21; and (with Thierry Marchaisse), *Penser d'un Dehors (la Chine): Entretiens d'Extrême-Occident* (Paris: Seuil, 2000).

19. See "Michel Foucault and Zen: A Stay in a Zen Temple (1978)" (trans. Richard Townsend), in *Religion and Culture*, ed. Jeremy R. Carrette (New York: Routledge, 1999), pp. 110–14.

20. See Edward de Bono, *New Think* (New York: Basic Books, 1968).

21. See "Everywhere and Nowhere," in *Signs*, trans. Richard C. McCleary (Evanston, Ill.: Northwestern University Press, 1964), pp. 121–58. Charles Taylor, whose theme of recognition and multiculturalism drew worldwide attention, regards Merleau-Ponty as one of the great twentieth-century deconstructors. See "Heidegger on the Connection between Nihilism, Art, Technology, and Politics," in *The Cambridge Companion to Heidegger*, ed. Charles Guignon (New York: Cambridge University Press, 1993), p. 334 n. 2.

22. Cf. Edward W. Said, *Culture and Imperialism* (New York: Knopf, 1993), p. 317: "We can no longer afford conceptions of history that stress linear development or Hegelian transcendence, any more than we can accept geographical or territorial assumptions that assign centrality to the Atlantic world and congenital and even delinquent peripherality to non-Western regions."

23. "Everywhere and Nowhere," p. 139. Now political theorists began to realize that the study of politics cannot ignore the broad context of the sociocultural lifeworld. See, e.g., Seyla Benhabib, *The Claims of Culture: Equality and Diversity in the Global Era* (Princeton: Princeton University Press, 2002); *Cultural Studies and Political Theory*, ed. Jodi Dean (Ithaca: Cornell University Press, 2000).

24. In *Intersecting Voices* (Princeton: Princeton University Press, 1997), the American feminist political theorist Iris Marion Young uses the expression "asymmetrical reciprocity" to describe when the other's difference is respected and used as a "resource" for enlarging the circle of human relationships (see esp. pp. 38–59).

25. I stumbled across Glissant in 2003 while reading Walter D. Mignolo's "Rethinking the Colonial Model," in *Rethinking Literary Theory: A Dialogue in Theory*, ed. Linda Hutcheon and Mario J. Valdés (New York: Oxford University Press, 2002), pp. 155–93. In reading Glissant's work, I came to the realization that he has an important niche in constructing transversality as a critique of Eurocentric universalism or as trans(uni)versalism. Particularly, he represents a critique of Eurocentric universalism from the model of postcolonialism along with poststructuralism and deconstructionism. They together constitute what I would broadly call postmodernism as a philosophical movement. The Caribbean—a cluster of small islands surrounded by sea—provides an ideal model of ethnic, lingual, and cultural diversity and a haven of hybridity.

26. *Poetics of Relation,* trans. Betsy Wing (Ann Arbor: University of Michigan Press, 1997), pp. 33, 49.

27. Édouard Glissant, *Caribbean Discourse: Selected Essays,* trans. J. Michael Dash (Charlottesville: University Press of Virginia, 1989), p. 64.

28. Ibid., p. 66.

29. Ibid., pp. 66, 67.

30. *Postcolonialism: An Historical Introduction* (Oxford: Blackwell, 2001), p. 68. Said makes an important and well-chosen point: "Imperialism consolidated the mixture of cultures and identities on a global scale. But its worst and most paradoxical gift was to allow people to believe that they were only, mainly, exclusively, White, or Black, or Western, or Oriental." Said, *Culture and Imperialism,* p. 336. In his magnum opus *Phenomenology of Perception* (New York: Routledge, 1978), Merleau-Ponty observes that T. E. Lawrence—the famed author of *The Seven Pillars of Wisdom*—is a hybrid man or "the man who could see things through the veils at once of two customs, two educations, two environments" (pp. 187–88 n.1).

31. Paul Gilroy, *The Black Atlantic: Modernity and Double Consciousness* (Cambridge: Harvard University Press, 1993).

32. Rita Felski, *The Gender of Modernity* (Cambridge: Harvard University Press, 1995), p. 212.

33. Quoted in John Jervis, *Transgressing the Modern* (Oxford: Blackwell, 1999), p. 198.

34. Felski, *Gender of Modernity,* p. 212.

35. Jean Bernabé, Patrick Chamoiseau, and Raphaël Confiant, *Éloge de la Créolité* (In Praise of Creoleness) (Paris: Gallimard, 1989 and Baltimore: Johns Hopkins University Press, 1990).

36. Glissant, *Caribbean Discourse,* p. 98.

37. For Schrag, transversality is a movement "beyond the dialogic": it is "not a dialogical understanding, which is why it also needs to be beyond hermeneutics since hermeneutics is fundamentally dialogical" (*Experiences between Philosophy and Communication,* pp. 24–25). Here Schrag has particularly in mind Hans-Georg Gadamer's philosophical hermeneutics. What the dialogical is to the "in-between," transversality is to the "beyond." Schrag has "a friendly *Auseinandersetzung*"—to use his own expression—with Gadamer. Although transversality is not identical with dialogical thinking, there is no reason why the method of dialogue should be bracketed off from achieving hybridity or the "fusion" of cultural horizons. To be sure, Gadamer's hermeneutical insights can be extended to comparative political theory. As his hermeneutics stands as it is, it has yet to break through its Eurocentric shell.

38. See my "Bakhtin's Dialogical Body Politics," in *Phenomenology, Body Politics and the Future of Communication Theory* (Cresskill, N.J.: Hampton Press, forthcoming).

39. See John Rajchman, *The Deleuze Connections* (Cambridge: MIT Press, 2000), p. 50. Speaking of Robert Musil, Italo Calvino wisely observes that the very notion of multiplicity in a tangled web of relationships signifies our "inability to find

an ending." Italo Calvino, *Six Memos for the Next Millennium* (Cambridge: Harvard University Press, 1988), p. 110.

40. In Greek etymology, "boustrophedonic" refers to "turn[ing] [*strophe*] back and forth, as an ox [*bous*] ploughs a field." See J. Hillis Miller and Manuel Asensi, *Black Holes: J. Hillis Miller; or, Boustrophedonic Reading* (Stanford: Stanford University Press, 1999), p. ix.

41. Emmanuel Levinas, *Alterity and Transcendence*, trans. Michael B. Smith (New York: Columbia University Press, 1999), p. 97.

42. See my "Responsibility as First Ethics: Macmurray and Levinas," in *John Macmurray: Critical Perspectives*, ed. David Fergusson and Nigel Dower (New York: Peter Lang, 2002), pp. 173–88; and my "Difference and Responsibility," in *Phänomenologie der Natur*, a special issue of *Phänomenologische Forschungen*, ed. Kah Kyung Cho and Young-Ho Lee (Freiburg: Karl Alber, 1999), pp. 129–66.

43. Second ed. (Chicago: University of Chicago, Press, 1998), p. 2.

44. Gilles Deleuze and Félix Guattari, *What Is Philosophy?* trans. Hugh Tomlinson and Graham Burchell (New York: Columbia University Press, 1994), p. 85. For further details of the connection between transversality and geophilosophy, see my "Transversality and Geophilosophy in the Age of Globalization," in *Calvin O. Schrag and the Task of Philosophy after Postmodernity*, ed. Martin Beck Matuštík and William L. McBride (Evanston, Ill.: Northwestern University Press, 2002), pp. 74–90.

45. Arne Naess, "The Shallow and the Deep, Long-Range Ecology Movement: A Summary," *Inquiry* 16 (1973): 99.

46. Ulrich Beck and Johannes Willms, *Conversations with Ulrich Beck*, trans. Michael Pollak (Cambridge, UK: Polity, 2000), p. 38.

47. Beck writes: "[T]he Enlightenment concept of cosmopolitanism has to be freed from its origins in imperial universalism, such as we find in Kant and many others. It has to be opened up to the recognition of multiplicity. It has to become the core of the concept" (ibid., p. 183).

48. Ibid., p. 25.

49. Ibid., p. 29. Beck continues in contentious language: "I am afraid I am somewhat sick of the 'post-ism,' 'de-ism,' and 'beyond-ism' of our times. . . . Modernity is a problem in need of a solution for which Europe bears a special responsibility. Europe invented it, even if it did borrow crucial bits from other cultures. . . . What we need is a fundamental self-critique, a redefinition—we might even say a reformation—of modernity and modern society. Modernity needs to be re-formed in the fullest sense on a global level" (ibid., p. 25). On account of geophilosophical configurations alone, that is, on account of the ecological crisis alone, which is truly a modern advent, it is doubtful that "reformed modernity" or "a second modernity" is capable of showing anthropocentrism the way out of its bottle. The intimation is that since all living creatures are earth dwellers in sharing and belonging to the same earth, it stands to reason to argue that our sense of humanity and compassion should be extended to nonhuman others. This requires, I think, a radical break or discontinuity with rather than a reformation of Western modernity. What if modernity has

become in Beck's own expression—a "zombie category" in the world of all forms of multiplicity? We must attempt to fit concepts into reality rather than reality into concepts.

50. Ibid., p. 130.

51. If we wish to taste hybridity in food, try the following list of Asian "delicacies": the squid pizza, the curry doughnut, the bean-paste Danish, the kimchee burger, the green tea milkshake, the BST (bacon, seaweed, and tomato) sandwich, and so on. See T. R. Reid, *Confucius Lives Next Door* (New York: Random House, 1999), p. 30. If you like burgers but not kimchee, Danishes but not bean-paste, milkshakes but not green tea, or bacon and tomatos but not seaweed then you must be an agonist or essentialist but not a dialogist! On the other hand, the Whiteheadian Charles Hartshorne once remarked that kimchee, which is spicy, heavily red-peppered Korean pickled cabbage, would dominate and thus destroy all the other flavors. That is to say, kimchee is predatory or a predatory empire builder that destroys the world as social or multiflavored reality. While recently reading Desmond Morris's *The Human Animal* ([New York: Crown, 1994], pp. 26–27), I came across the fascinating traveling gesture of fig (*fica*)—a slang term in Italian for the female genitalia—which when we were youngsters we learned to use as a gesture of sexual insult during the Japanese occupation of Korea. In fact, the fig gesture originally traveled from Europe to Japan with the Portuguese or the first Europeans in the mid-sixteenth century. Morris comments that the Portuguese must have traded gestures as well as goods on their expeditious visits to Japan. To his amazement he discovered the fig gesture signifying protection while visiting a geisha house in Kyoto for the purpose of academic research, not of *asobi*.

Part III.

Globalism and Cosmopolitics

New Ways of Being Selves in the World: Fred Dallmayr's Search for a Political Theory of Compassion

Franke Wilmer

The distinction between political theory and international relations theory—the "inside/outside" question—is neither self-evident nor, increasingly, does it seem even very useful to many of us interested in international relations theory. What may be some of the more interesting questions of normative political theory are now also the most relevant questions to understanding international relations or world politics, particularly those dealing with what kind of citizens we ought to be, especially in a pluralistic social space of increasing proximity and encounter with alterity and Otherness.

By "political theory" I mean that body of writing and thinking that reflects on and attempts to understand political life within particular historical contexts, even as the reflection itself (as well as the reflector) links those contexts to a concept of the past while simultaneously projecting contemporaneous insights onto some imagined future, some idea of how the trajectory of present political life will or ought to unfold in future. "International relations theory" refers to a cacophonic discourse about relations between polities regarded as accountable to no external authority, and to the political life produced by such relations. By some accounts, this discourse dates to historical narratives describing relations among Greek city-states, and by others to roughly the same period in which the European or Westphalian state formed. But the level and scope of that discourse dramatically increased during the twentieth century.

From Plato, Socrates, the Cynics, and Sophists to Machiavelli, Hobbes, Rousseau, and Mill, and more recently to Marx, Arendt, Heidegger, Foucault,

and Derrida, the scope and boundaries of the polities on which these thinkers reflected varied greatly—city-states, empires, principalities, nation-states,
nationalistic states, modern and postmodern states, interdependent polities,
mutually constituted polities, and polities within a geographic region that to
a particular thinker represented "the world." Today we seek relevance and
insight in their work as we reflect on political life within the boundaries of
sovereign states, aware now that both "sovereignty" and "state" are social
constructs.

MORALITY, ETHICS, AND POLITICS

The claim that a distinction between political life inside and outside of the
state is artificial is not new.[1] It is in this space of margins, nexuses, and modest harmonies that—as a traveler from international relations in search of a
theoretical framework to investigate the moral agency of political subjects
whose exclusionary identities rationalized harming Others—I met the traveling political theorist whose work this volume celebrates.

Fred Dallmayr has traveled more extensively, lingered longer, and reflected more fully in more places along the way than I have. But he carries
with him a bounty of intellectual riches. "Political theorists," he once said
with a self-effacing giggle, "do nothing but write about other political theorists!" "Ah, but then one must *read* all those other political theorists," I
thought, "as well as all of the theorists who write about them. And then find
something *new* to say." It is my good fortune that Dallmayr's path led him to
bring the fruit of his efforts as a theorist to bear on questions that are a central concern in my own work. This shared inquiry can be expressed something like this: Is civility in a pluralistic, globalized social world possible or
necessary at this historical juncture? Is the way human "beingness," its subjectivity and moral agency, is currently articulated within a set of discursive
practices emanating from the cultural and historical space of "the West" sufficient to the cultivation of global civility or global citizenship? My definition
of civility is minimal; it is reciprocity of moral obligation. I honor all the
rights for others that I wish to claim for myself and I understand my position
in relation to others to be within a community of reciprocal obligations.

Since I refer in this essay to both ethics and morality, it is helpful at the
outset to distinguish how I understand them. In keeping with Dallmayr's

usage, morality and morals refer to a normative principle or set of principles, while ethics refers to actual conduct. An ethical agent is thus an agent capable of behavior that can be judged as right or wrong according to normative principles within a community of moral agents.

While morality pertains to abstract principles that transcend particular behaviors, that does not mean that I believe in the existence of objective, universal, and fixed normative principles. I suggest instead, for example, an "ethic of reciprocity," that is, behavior directed by the moral principle of reciprocity, and an "ethic of compassion," as guidelines for exercising agency in a particular situation. I further elaborate what I think are the most useful insights into the question of global ethics and morality suggested by Dallmayr's work and its implication for "new ways of being selves in the world." I conclude with a very brief discussion of its consequences for several themes that have been important in my own inquiry—international human rights, the nexus between politics and identity, and the possibility of a civil world society.

The Self and Its Discontents in Western Political Theory

From my perspective, Dallmayr's inquiry falls roughly into three periods that reflect his penchant for examining the potential of interstices, whether philosophical, political, or cultural. In the first he explores intersections between political theory, philosophy, and social science, culminating in the publication of such texts as *Polis and Praxis: Exercises in Contemporary Political Theory* (1984), *Critical Encounters: Between Philosophy and Politics* (1987), and *Margins of Political Discourse* (1989). Even here he takes up the question of subjectivity and ethics and asks whether and how an ethical subject might emerge in the aftermath of modernity or, alternatively, in the aftermath of the postmodern critique of modernity, a theme Dallmayr would pursue with greater focus during the early 1990s.

During the next period he searches for insights into and the possibility of a postmodern ethical subject by rereading philosophers of modernity (Hegel, Heidegger, the Frankfurt school), examining the "unthought" within their thinking in an effort to identify alternative paths to a subjectivity through which political freedom can be reconciled with socially responsible ethics. The third theme to develop in Dallmayr's work is, like the other two, essentially a political practice in which he decenters his own perspective as a subject and engages Other (non-Western) thinkers in cross-cultural dialogues in an effort to transcend both theoretical and philosophical orientations limited by ethnocentric nearsightedness.

These excursions, including the edited volume on comparative political theory *Border Crossings* (1999) along with a series of collaborative projects, also led to the publication of several books in which he revisits old and new favorite political philosophers with a focus on the theme of democratizing globalization as the ultimate frontier in applied postmodern ethical subjectivity.[2] Among these are four that inquire into the possibility of restructuring the power relations among civilizational voices—*Beyond Orientalism* (1996), *Alternative Visions* (1998), *Achieving Our World* (2001), and his most recent *Dialogue among Civilizations* (2002). In these four books Dallmayr's interpretations of political thought are brought to bear on the problem of ethical subjectivity in a globalizing and pluralistic world. Thus, like so many others searching for an ethics of being human in the world, Dallmayr's quest has led him to an encounter with the necessity of rethinking boundaries— boundaries of selfhood, beingness, polity, society, nations, and states. Dallmayr's work speaks to the search for new understandings of what it means to be human in a world of such unprecedented change that seems to be accompanied by an explosive, pluralistic, and radically decentered social restructuring.

Recent debates in social theory—debates about which Dallmayr's early work had much to say—problematized subjectivity by unmasking the reliance of objectivity on the impossibility of escaping the subjective position. Claims regarding the existence of an objective reality on which a universal truth may be grounded are suspect to the extent that they presuppose the absence of subjectivity on the part of the observer. Not only has this premise been called into question by what some call "postmodern science," but it also creates two problems for social theorists. First, to the extent that philosophy was conceived as a search for a single, fixed, universal, and *essential* truth, the impossibility of objectivity is said to have ended that search, replacing it with an acknowledgment of multiple truths posited by multiple subjectivities, which are historically (temporally) and culturally (spatially) contextualized, and an interrogation into the production of meaning, systems of meaning, and their consequences.

The second problem, the "relativity versus universality" issue, follows from the first: Does accepting multiple subjectivities necessarily render all ethical positions equally worthy, or equally unworthy, since none can be judged from any position other than one's own subjectivity? Does adopting a postmodern perspective necessarily mean that the "moral-political order totally relinquishes its ethical foundation?"[3] What, in other words, are the possibilities for ethics in the absence of a single, fixed, and universal truth given the plurality of subjects and, therefore, perspectives? These two problems are related in that there is no purpose in examining the consequences of various systems of meaning unless one judges some consequences more and others less desirable, though the criteria need not be moral (a distinction between right and wrong behavior). Both question the role of ethics in public life, an issue that arises from the fact that the alleged "death of the subject/author," the impossibility of objectivity, the certainty of multiplicity, and the inescapability of pluralism have effectively decentered authority in social relations. Humpty-Dumpty cannot be put back together again.

This critique of subjectivity is frequently cast as a critique (or in Derridian terminology, "deconstruction") of the Cartesian "self/subject" or *cogito*, though some critics see more continuity than others.[4] Modernity, often associated with Descartes's articulation of the subject, is not only the metaphysical foundation on which objectivity rests, but it produced a certain kind of modern subject, or "self": a unified and solid being that is either/both the wielder of power or knocked about incessantly by it. It exists because it thinks; or, because it is capable of self-consciousness, it concludes that it *must* exist. *Cogito ergo sum.* (If I stop thinking, as Zizek says, will I cease to exist?)[5]

Some argue that this postmodern critique of the Cartesian self has developed into a full-blown "philosophy of subjectivity."[6] Dallmayr has inquired persistently into this debate, seeking, as earlier essayists put it, "the unthought" in our thinking,[7] or as suggested by this volume, pathways between poles of contestation, but always with an overriding concern for the role of ethics in human beingness and human relations. This is a concern I share, and while Dallmayr seems to focus on the ethics of individual humans in their relations with one another, my concern has centered more on the ethics that guide policies that permit or provoke injurious behavior, behavior I regard as immoral: genocide, ethnic cleansing, ethnocide,[8] racial discrimination, and human rights violations in general.

I take seriously the claim that how we understand the self is historically contingent, that the metaphysics of modernity produced not only a world-view that framed the quest for (and use of) knowledge of the material world, but also an understanding of the self and what it means to be a human being within the world viewed in that "modern" way. Who are the subjects who have these worldviews and how do these "viewing agents" understand themselves as subjects? If, as the claim of postmodernity suggests, we currently live in a moment of historical disjuncture, a point where an old view is disintegrating and a new view emerging, then what are its implications for how we understand ourselves as subjects in the world? Are we on the verge (or in need) of finding new ways of being selves in the world, and if so, how will that alter our relations with one another?

OUR WORLD, OUR SELVES

One of the most pressing issues of our time, in my view, is the simultaneous rise in both local and global interdependence and vulnerability to a level that I believe renders earlier views of security obsolete. It is not only that technologies of mass destruction and injury are ubiquitous, but also that our vulnerabilities transform the most ordinary things like box cutters and pilots licenses into the means (or weapons) of perpetrating mass destruction. By mentioning two of the weapons used in the attacks against the World Trade Center and U.S. Pentagon on September 11, 2001, I do not mean to suggest that the vulnerabilities revealed by those attacks are either unique or exceptional other than in scope and the extent to which they were unexpected. But they reveal more than specific vulnerabilities to particular strategies of attack: they are a testimony to the radical decentering of power in a world of unprecedented interdependence and vulnerability from which, in my view, we cannot (or not without tremendous human costs) retreat.

The central problem here is how to be secure—safe from injury—in a world of such decentered power, interdependence, and mutual vulnerability? Let me suggest two images. In one the world is populated by billiard-ball "selves." They are solid, impenetrable, and unconnected. They roll about bumping into one another, but they do not connect and they remain relatively unchanged by all the bumping, except for moving from one place to another. Imagine that they move of their own volition. This is a "bump or be bumped" world. If we define security as "freedom from being bumped," then we need only devise some enforceable system of restraint, perhaps punishment for violations, and we will have a secure world. Security can be achieved through coercion or cooperation, or both (depending, among other things, on how the billiard balls understand what it means to be a billiard ball!). If there are significant differences in size and capability, there may be clearly dominant balls that in turn may determine the shape and terms of order, mostly likely in ways that most benefit them. If they are of roughly equal size, then politics will become even more interesting. They may bargain, collude, and form alliances, perhaps even stratify and allocate resources and values on the basis of capability. Whether they will achieve a stable, long-term solution to the security problem or not, only game theorists know.

The second image is of a closed human chain, say a hundred individuals, all holding hands and unable to let go. Leadership training workshops often include an exercise like this. The chain is all tangled up and people are twisted around and atop one another. Anytime one person tugs, others are moved, creating a "chain" reaction. No one can prevent such reactions once one person decides to give a tug. To be secure, to reduce involuntary tugging and its consequences, they must collaborate and must work together climbing over and through one another's connected arms until they form an untangled circle. Someone may have a good idea about how to get there, but others must be convinced to listen and give the plan a try. It cannot be imposed. Size and capability do not matter. If the plan progresses them toward their goal of greater freedom, harmony, and security, then it is a good plan.

I think of the world in which the Cartesian self developed as a billiard-ball world, and the world today as made up of one tremendous human chain. The two images illustrate the differences between a world conceived as consisting of more or less autonomous selves who can use power either to bump one another around or to create a system of order in which "unauthorized bumping" is the exception, and a world of interconnected, interdependent, and mutually vulnerable selves who must understand the inevitability of their impact on one another and learn to cooperate their way to a relatively peaceful solution that maximizes both their freedom and security in light of the inescapability of their interconnectedness.

Is the self-understanding that has persisted since Descartes useful for ethical inquiries in a world of radically decentered power? Power has been progressively decentered since roughly the time of the Enlightenment and populist revolutions in Europe. We have attempted to adapt and adjust systems of authority to this shift, though not necessarily as a conscious intention. We have shown an increasing distrust for institutional authority—first the church and later the state—and increasingly regard such trust to be progressively optional or discretionary. The "unthought" in our thinking about emancipation and freedom is the necessity of restraining ourselves through more informal, unseen, and local social processes. But as power in some ways has more local, there has also been an increase in the scope and penetration of institutional authority at the local level, though I agree, as Foucault suggests, that this totalization of authority was or is not necessarily intentional. Power, as Foucault argues, is a set of relations that produce selves, and as the set of relations change, so the selves it produces also change.

The Cartesian self was conjured by a set of power relations that essentialized subjects on/against whom institutions could act coercively. The Cartesian self is an objectified target of institutional power. In seeking objective knowledge of the world, it denies its own inescapable subjectivity. Cartesian selves seek knowledge in order to control the material world, and reproduce power relations in the form of institutions to control human subjects. The move from an essential, knowable, and fixed truth/self to decentered, spatially and temporally contingent, pluralism of truths/selves has not, as some critics would have it, left contemporary humans without a moral compass. Socrates' question "How shall we live" is still a matter of great concern to modern and postmodern thinkers alike.

AN ETHICS OF HUMAN RELATIONSHIP

For contemporary philosophers and political theorists like Foucault and Derrida, who are critical of epistemologies based on subjectivity and predicated on the assumption of a discoverable, objective foundation (truth) on which universal ethics can be grounded, the question of ethics has shifted from an ethics grounded in a single and unchanging "truth" to one that arises out of relationship. As a result, self–Other relations have become the primary terrain on which questions of ethics are currently engaged. "This form of ethical transcendence is not the transcendence of an ahistorical ego or principle," say David Campbell and Michael Shapiro. Rather, in summarizing the position taken by contributors to their edited book *Moral Spaces,* they write:

[I]t is transcendence in the sense that alterity, being's other, is an ines-capable condition produced by *difference* rather than ontology. . . . In consequence, rather than being concerned with a *theory of ethics,* the contributors to this volume are motivated by the *ethical relation* in which our responsibility to the other is the basis for reflection. . . . Eschewing hierarchical constructions of moral value, they focus instead on the al-ways already ethical situation integral to the habitus of experience.[9]

Although hierarchical oppositions are suspect to the extent that they produce relations of domination and subordination, the structuring of moral struggles within the framework of dualism still appears to be common across both cultural and historical time and space.[10] This motif can be found in cul-tural narratives, literatures, religious beliefs and practices, and many of the social processes surrounding identity development and maintenance. Such struggles reflect themes of good and evil conceived as transcendent forces of duality, themes of catharsis and undoing, of paradox, contradiction, yearn-ings for connection and completion, and encounters with otherness.

If we take these struggles as one kind of widely shared human dilemma, there are nevertheless a variety of responses to and ways of culturally mediat-ing the struggle. Dualism, for example, can mean any of the following: the foundational structure of the social world; an effect of human consciousness within time and space; an illusion inescapable once one enters the world of language and social relations; the building block of all material reality; po-larity; opposition; a Manichean worldview; an unnecessary limitation on human perception; a necessary tension that makes perception possible; forces of good and evil external to human agency; and/or forces of good and evil in-herent in human nature, and the prerequisite for oppositional hierarchies. Dualism is a theme (one of many), not a verifiable material fact, and it is a pervasive theme in human social life, though its meaning varies depending on cultural and historical contexts. The co-constitution of being and alterity is yet another way of reflecting on the relationship between duality and con-nection.

However our struggles with and around the emotional poles of dualism are culturally mediated, it still seems reasonable to assert that such struggles in general are a pervasive and inescapable element of the human condition. Insofar as psychoanalytic theory provides an account of the apparent uni-versality of humans and human cultures wrestling with dualism, it may illuminate our efforts to evaluate more and less constructive mediations, cultural understandings of the self and a social world of selves more inclined toward peaceful, nonviolent, and civil relations among selves. The cross-cultural research reported in Shinobu Kitayama and Hazel Rose Markus's *Emotion and Culture*,[11] for instance, which begins with the premise that emotions are "socially produced," examines the critical role played by culture and culturally structured meaning in shaping the self and its emotional experiences.

From a Kleinian perspective, the self and its emotional capacity is constituted by the coming into our consciousness the existence of our own agency, our own boundaries, and thus, inescapably, the agency and boundaries of others—or the first Other, our primary caretaker.[12] Because this occurs at a time when we are also most vulnerable (and therefore dependent on the Other for all of our survival needs), the experience has a tremendously traumatic potential. We experience no anxieties when our needs are met, but rather when they are not. In fact, it is the discomfort of unmet needs that makes us aware of the Other's agency—and ability to withhold or deny the satisfaction of our needs. All of this sets in motion the emotional struggles around attachment and separation, love and hate, pleasure and pain, and selfness and Otherness. Under the Kleinian model, therefore, a healthy maturation involves learning that both the self and Others are capable of producing pleasure and pain, capable of caring for and harming Others, and capable of love and hate. Resolution of the paradox that a single Other can be both a source of pleasure (needs satisfaction) and pain (denial of needs satisfaction)—that a single self can experience contradictory feelings of attachment and anger toward Others—leads to emotional maturity and psychic integration.

According to this view, our relations with Others are shaped by the emotional potentialities that emerge with selfhood—attachment, rejection, love, hate, and guilt (for feeling anger toward a loved Other), for example. We experience Others both as "objects" of and repositories for these feelings. An immature self will experience a "bad" me who hates and rages, and a "good" me who loves and cares for the Other. An immature self fails to achieve integration, and experiences a social world populated by distinctly "good" and "bad" selves, a reflection of the structure of the immature psyche. One important question raised by a Kleinian analysis is whether emotional integration is "achieved" and then "fixed," or is tentative and vulnerable to digression, particularly in response to stress and trauma. One view is that these emotional possibilities combine to constitute "positions," including maladaptive or pathological positions, that reflect a more or less integrated self. I find the "positions" view more compelling, but go a step further—I propose that some cultures, some worldviews, do a better job of providing tools (in the form of cultural beliefs and social practices) that make psychic integration more likely and even more secure when confronted with stress and trauma (though culture is not the only mediating factor). I further assert that since culture and social practice are *historically* situated, particular cultures in particular times can do a better (or worse) job of facilitating psychic integration and emotional maturity.

For instance, a culture (or worldview) might understand the source of dualism and dualistic perceptions as originating within the self, as an inescapable internal struggle between "civilization and its discontents" that must first and always be addressed through self-reflection and self-knowledge. Such a culture might encourage self-criticism, self-examination, and skepticism toward encounters with Others that appear to be or are emotionally experienced simply in terms of our own victimization. Individuals might be encouraged to question their own agency in constructing polarized relationships with easily identifiable perpetrators and victims. Would such a culture produce selves more likely to engage in the resolution of conflicts or in "constructive engagement" with interpersonal conflict? Would the selves nurtured in such a culture be less likely to form identities reliant on negative constructions of Otherness, and therefore less likely to become entangled in cycles of conflict and violence? Would these selves experience *difference* differently, with greater tolerance, understanding, and appreciation? The relationship between dualism and understandings of selfhood has tremendous significance for human relations, whether within, between, across, or beyond particular polities and social groups. It is also a subject on which both political theory and international relations have had much to say. The question of identity construction and its local and global political consequences links political theory and international relations to the theories and practices of psychoanalysis, from Freud to Lacan. Identity is what the self is made of in the social sense, and yet identity itself is a paradox for identity *requires* both sameness and Otherness; it is the location of the self. Without identity, there is no self, and yet identity is predicated on the perception of both sameness and difference *across a field of selves.*

That human beings provide better treatment to those they regard as the "same" as themselves than they do to those regarded as "different" (on no other basis than their sameness/difference) seems to be a ubiquitous, if not universal, social phenomenon. Social psychologists refer to this as the "in-group" and "out-group" distinction. We feel not only attachment and loyalty toward those in our in-group, but an obligation to regard them with moral preference, to conform to the group's expectations about what constitutes morally acceptable behavior. Philosopher Charles Taylor claims that "to know who you [*are*] is to be oriented in a moral space."[13] There are, in other words, different orientations toward Otherness. "I" still regard those in "my" in-group as Others, but a different sort of Others than those "I" regard as constituting an out-group.

This moral preference for sameness, about which I have more to say in the next section, may simply be narcissistic. We "see ourselves" in those we regard as the same. Or perhaps we actually regard them as a desired (but missing) part of ourselves. Whether we regard Others has residing inside the boundaries of our constituted selves or as having their own boundaries and agency equal to ours is a crucial and very complex issue that can only be touched on here. How we regard the Other's boundaries and agency in relation to our own can have very different consequences for our ethical stance toward the Other. I can imagine, for example, three different scenarios of "Other regarding." There certainly may be more and even these three cannot be fully explored here, but they serve to illustrate the potential of "relationship grounded" ethics.

In the first scenario we "see something of ourselves" in an Other—a single Other who is different but also the same. The self acknowledges and respects the Other's agency while delighting in the Other's difference, which enables the self to empathize with the Other while transcending the self through the experience of companionship. Derrida's "distancing of the Other" and Foucault's nonhierarchical basis for ethical relations through respect for Otherness,[14] reveal possibilities to regard the Other as an actual part of the self, as *within* the boundaries of the self.

In the second scenario we regard or experience the Other as a desired part of ourselves, a part with which we wish to achieve or experience a unity of ourself that in turn produces a sense (or sensation) of wholeness, completion, or self-transcendence. The boundaries of the Other are regarded as permeable and not fixed in place. As an object of desire, the self wishes, in this scenario to experience a unity with the Other in ways in which the boundaries of Otherness seem, however temporarily, to dissolve.

This way of experiencing the Other clearly pertains to sexuality, though it need not be only sexual or sexually actualized. It can be driven to "merge" or identify with an Other we regard as embodying desirable attributes. The desire to attach to an Other perceived as a part of the self one feels incapable or less capable of "being" may be expressed as infatuation, idealization, idolatry, role modeling, or simply enjoying a warm conversation with an admired friend or mentor. Perhaps sublime devotion as described by mystics and other devotees is another manifestation of the desire to achieve unity with an idealized Other.

The third scenario seeks the inclusion of the Other within the boundaries of our own self while failing to acknowledge or perceive the Other's agency. I suppose it can be "permissive" boundary dissolving and take the form of pleasure between intimates. It can be an experience or sensation that the separation of the self and the object of intimacy dissolves, though one would think of this as temporary, relative, and perceptual. The failure to acknowledge the Other's agency, however, is a different matter. That failure may merely be the relatively innocuous and fleeting breach of normal social practices that is interpreted as a violation of the agency of the Other, such as verbal interruptions, though it should be emphasized that these are socially determined. But it can also be quite a bit more sinister, even lethal, when one's understanding of agency and perception of boundaries are muddled by emotional disorders, as it may be for a pathological personality. An immature and unintegrated self who perceives an Other as an unwanted, "evil" part of the self may try to expel or annihilate the evil part through a destructive act.

Let me say in closing this section that I do not believe that the distinctions between the first and second, or second and third scenarios of experiencing Otherness are always so clear. We may experience the same Other in all three ways, or different Others differently. Perpetrators of violence can also be individuals who act out violence against one person but tenderly care for another. We may believe we are respecting and preserving the integrity of the Other's boundaries or agency when we are in fact attempting to "lose" ourselves in some moment of unification (a first and second scenario case ambiguity). We may be delusional about whether our own agency is being violated, or we may believe we are acting out of kinship or common humanity when in fact we are seeking to eliminate the Other's existence through forced assimilation, absorption, or *consumption* of the Other. An "ethic of relation" raises issues of identity, ambiguity, empathy, domination, agency, equality of agency, encounter, and more. If one accepts that we currently live in an historical era characterized by an unprecedented scope of interdependence and mutual vulnerability, then what sort of self will enable us to live in the world more peacefully?

NEW WAYS OF BEING SELVES: THE DIALECTICAL SELF

Dallmayr has immersed himself in philosophical thinking in search of alternative ways of understanding or conceptualizing the self. The self Dallmayr seems to be looking for—what I call a "dialectical self"—is first and overall an ethical self, a central and enduring concern of philosophy and political theory, but one that, according to an orthodox view of international relations, has no place in international politics. By insisting that ethical conduct remain a central concern, Dallmayr puts himself in the center of contemporary debates about the consequences of attacks on subjectivity as the premise of modern science and humanism. According to the critical postmodern view, ethics cannot be grounded in the outcome of a search for fixed and universal truth, but that does not mean either that the search for transcendental ethics or into the role of ethics in political life must be abandoned.

The Cartesian self, *cogito*, the modern self, was also ethical, but only "inside" the community of similar selves—or selves bound by a social contract, a contract they were not born into but "freely" entered into, giving up some autonomy in exchange for securing the remainder. "Outside" was populated by Others to whom those inside had no ethical or moral obligation; it was a space devoid of morality. In contrast, a dialectical self is ethical because it is born into a nexus of transactions and relationships and its existence is inextricably linked to Others in a world of complex, overlapping, intersecting, and interdependent agents and identities. We experience sameness and difference in a variety of ways with the same and different Others. Inside and Outside are relative; Otherness and humanity are correlative.

Accepting the decenteredness of all selves also decenters a dialectical self. From this follows not only an ability to honor the equal agency of Others, but a recognition of the limitations of one's own subjectivity. Only through encounter with otherness can the limits of one's subjectivity be transcended. Relationship makes self-transcendence possible.

A dialectical self also is open-ended, like Robert Jay Lifton's "protean self." It does not resist change, but embraces it. It does not attempt to close and fix its identity in time and space, but rather is pluralistic, the locus of the experiences that shape it "always in flux and subject to the moment-by-moment negotiations of social interaction.[15] I saw a Hindu painting once in which fifty or so portraits were arranged in an arc, appearing to be fifty different people. Looking from left to right, my host explained that these were fifty different faces of one person, from infancy to old age. The painting expressed a conception of the self as pluralistic, situated in time.

A dialectical self is supple enough to accommodate ambiguity, to be "the same and different at the same time." An excellent study of Native American patriotism demonstrated how identities constituted in part by historical experiences of victimization could also accommodate identification with those whose identities were bound to the same experiences as perpetrators; how, in other words, someone could be Ojibway where being Ojibway meant, in part, historically being the target of policies intended to destroy "Ojibway-ness," and *also* be American when that meant being at one historical time the perpetrator of those policies.[16] Identity in a post-Cartesian world can be hybrid, pluralistic, overlapping, layered, or intersecting.

This does not mean that identities can or should be appropriated, however, since that would violate respect for Otherness. The dialectical self is empathetically compassionate, and makes an effort to understand the experience of Others whose identities have been the target of projects aimed at their elimination, assimilation, or appropriation. *An ethic of compassion directs us to respect the boundaries of Otherness.* Similarly, a dialectical self is anti-dogmatic, recognizing that the logic of dogmatism leads to oppositional hierarchies intolerant of difference, and in the extreme rationalizes violent campaigns to dominate or destroy Others.

Finally, the dialectical self indicated by Dallmayr's search is experiential, transformative, and progressive. It experiences itself, with its intentions, feelings, and consciousness, while making the effort to empathize with the intentions, feelings, and consciousness of Others and is transformed by that effort. It is not only an agent, not only a target, but is self-aware as an intentional agent. It is not only a victim, but aware of itself in the relationship between victim and perpetrator. It is perpetually shaped and reshaped by experience, not only as either a subject or object, but by being both. By synthesizing experience it is living and moving and changing, and by synthesizing and transforming it becomes progressive, moving from more fragmented to more integrated with maturity.

In the spirit of being a post-Cartesian, dialectical self, Dallmayr's own search has led him into rich intellectual relationships with Others from whom he has learned much without appropriating Otherness. His own excursions encourage a promising and respectful "dialogue across civilizations."

Dialectical Selves, Identity, and Human Rights

The contrast between a self whose identity and self-understanding is dialectical, contingent, and experiential and a self that is solid, fixed, and autonomous highlights the way subjectivity is mediated not only by culture but also by history, or rather by historical narratives that shape social space. The dialectical self is a perpetual work in progress, dependent on and interdependent with other selves. Its contingency, however, does not relieve it of moral agency; rather it reorients ethical responsibility along the lines of what Michael Shapiro has called an "ethic of encounter."[17] Just as individual rights and a politics of freedom and personal autonomy structured power relations and authoritative uses of power during the historical rise of modernity and with it the Cartesian self, so I believe will the reconfiguration of selves in dialectical terms posit international human rights as the *provocateur* that restructures and decenters power relations in the present and coming era.

Human rights in a postmodern world of dialectical selves extend beyond the rights of individuals confronted by the coercive power of the state. If identity—what it means to be a person—is understood as inherently relational, then there can be no selfhood outside of relationship. Thus *human* rights are the rights of *humanity,* and a violation of the human rights of any one human is a violation of an indivisible humanity. Everyone's humanity is diminished by an assault on any human.

Desmund Tutu and other African intellectuals have thought and written about *ubuntu,* an indigenous African concept that structures their understanding of human relations and civic responsibility.[18] *Ubuntu* may well capture the kind of self–Other relationship Fred Dallmayr has searched for and I have tried to begin outline here. While visiting South Africa in 2000, *ubuntu* came up in conversations with virtually every person I spoke with when questions of politics, reconciliation, or human rights were raised. Though worded differently, their definitions were consistent. *Ubuntu* means "my humanity depends on and can only be realized through my relationship with others." It is more than humanism, however. It is "the achievement of absolute dependence on God and neighbour in such a way that the eventuality of human identity is discovered therein."[19] But *ubuntu* also refers to the mutuality and interdependence of personal rights with social obligations. One can be without *ubuntu*, for example, which means to be unfaithful to one's social obligations. Everyone with whom I spoke was also very clear that *ubuntu* is not restricted to "others who are like me." As the ethical basis for national reconciliation, it did not prescribe forgiveness, though Tutu certainly advocated it. In the context of South African reconciliation, it meant simply that one was obligated to engage constructively with others because the fulfillment of one's humanity depended on it.

GLOBAL CIVIL SOCIETY AS A MORAL COMMUNITY

Can an ethic of reciprocity and an ethic of empathy be globalized? Elsewhere I have discussed the concept of a "moral community," a community in which relations are based on reciprocity of rights and respect. But a moral community also functions as an in-group in the sociological sense, which is yet another way of approaching the self–Other problem we encounter in plural societies. The question is whether it will ever be possible for us to understand world society as a kind of moral community, particularly since so many societies as moral communities seem contingent on shared identity.

This brings us squarely into a confrontation with the questions about the relationship between identity, polity, and civility. Are there ways to construct identities that do not rely on a negative regard for Otherness? Are there ways to construct identities supple enough to accommodate the apparent paradox of "being the same and different at the same time?" This is, I believe, where Fred Dallmayr's work takes us. It is clear that political leaders the world over often play the ethnic, religious, or national identity card as a means of arousing emotions for the purpose of political mobilization—and not only these identities, but any identity that relies on exclusion and condemnation of Others. They do so because it works. But *why* does it work? I have argued that it works, at least in part, because it resonates with a certain construction of the self in light of the emotional poles around which human identity develops, and that this "certain construction" is culturally and historically contingent.

I have only offered two very brief examples of cases where self–Other relations show evidence of being more "dialectical" than "Cartesian"—Ojibway patriotism and African *ubuntu*. The contributors to Parkin's *Anthropology of Evil* and Kitayama and Markus's *Emotion and Culture* indicate many more possibilities. Cultural mediations matter. That is good news and bad news, because if modernity is understood not only as a worldview, but a cultural mediation, then one consequence of "globalizing" could be to displace local variations in the structuring of the self, variations that may in fact already be more compatible with the dialectical self. The globalization of modernity may be implicated in the rise of nationalism and ethnic conflicts, not their antidote. We also have an opportunity at this historical (dis)juncture to understand our common *humanity* as an identity; we can acknowledge the centrality of our multiple and experiential subjectivities, and our selves as the only boundary constituting the "inside/outside" nexus. The opportunity inheres in our reflection on *what it means to be human, what it means to be a person*. We can approach one another and delight in our differences, the overlapping, intersecting, and perpetually in motion identities that constitute the selves we encounter as Others, while at the same time recognizing the sameness of our humanity.

NOTES

1. R. B. J. Walker, *Inside/Outside: International Relations as Political Theory* (Cambridge: Cambridge University Press, 1993), passim.

2. These were with G. N. Devi in *Between Tradition and Modernity: India's Search for Identity* (1998); with Ananta Kumar Giri in *Conversations and Transformations: Toward a New Ethic of Self and Society* (2002); and with José Rosales in *Beyond Nationalism? Sovereignty and Citizenship* (2002).

3. Emmanuel Levinas and Richard Kearney, "Dialogue with Emmanuel Levinas," in *Face to Face with Levinas*, ed. R. A. Cohen (Albany: SUNY Press, 1986).

4. For example, see Richard Tarnas, *The Passion of the Western Mind: Understanding Ideas That Have Shaped Our World View* (New York: Ballantine Books, 1991).

5. Slavoj Zizek, "Introduction," in *Cogito and the Unconscious,* ed. Slavoj Zizek (Durham: Duke University Press, 1998), p. 2.

6. Ibid.

7. Stephen K. White, ed., *Life World and Politics: Between Modernity and Post-modernity: Essays in Honor of Fred R. Dallmayr* (Notre Dame, Ind.: University of Notre Dame Press, 1989).

8. "Ethnocide" refers to policies aimed at destroying the culture of and material basis for a community, such as those enacted against indigenous peoples. See Franke Wilmer, *The Indigenous Voice in World Politics* (Newbury Park, Calif.: Sage, 1993), passim.

9. David Campbell and Michael Shapiro, "Introduction," in *Moral Spaces: Rethinking Ethics and World Politics,* ed. David Campbell and Michael Shapiro (Minneapolis: University of Minnesota Press, 1999), p. x.

10. David Parkin, ed., *The Anthropology of Evil* (Oxford: Blackwell, 1985).

11. Shinobu Kitayama and Hazel Rose Markus, *Emotion and Culture: Empirical Studies of Mutual Influence* (Washington, D.C.: American Psychological Association, 1994).

12. C. Fred Alford, *Melanie Klein and Critical Social Theory* (New Haven: Yale University Press, 1989); see also Franke Wilmer, *The Social Construction of Man, the State, and War* (New York: Routledge, 2002).

13. Charles Taylor, *Sources of the Self: The Making of Modern Identities* (Cambridge: Harvard University Press, 1989), p. 13.

14. See Dallmayr's chapter "Distancing the Other: Jacques Derrida on Friendship," in Fred Dallmayr, *Achieving Our World: Toward a Global and Plural Democracy* (Lanham, Md., Rowman and Littlefield, 2001), pp. 147–70.

15. Geoffrey M. White, "Affecting Culture: Emotion and Morality in Everyday Life," in *Emotion and Culture: Empirical Studies of Mutual Influence,* ed. Shinobu Kitayama and Hazel Rose Markus (Washington, D.C.: American Psychological Association, 1994), p. 237.

16. Diane Duffy, "An Attitudinal Study of Native American Patriotism," presented at the International Society for Political Psychology in Krakow, Poland, July 22, 1997.

17. Michael J. Shapiro, "The Ethics of Encounter: Unreading, Unmapping the Imperium," in *Moral Spaces: Rethinking Ethics and World Politics,* ed. David Campbell and Michael Shapiro (Minneapolis: University of Minnesota Press, 1999), p. 2.

18. M. J. Battle and D. M. Tutu, *Reconciliation: The Ubuntu Theology of Desmond Tutu.* (Cleveland: Pilgrim Press, 1997); M. J. Bhengu, *Ubuntu: The Essence of Democracy* (Hudson, N.Y.: Anthroposophic Press, 1998); and Leonard Hulley, Louise Kretzschmar, and Luke Lungile Pato, eds., *Archbishop Tutu: Prophetic Witness in South Africa* (Capetown: Human and Rousseau, 1996).

19. Hulley, Kretzschmar, and Pato, eds., *Archbishop Tutu,* p. 93.

ELEVEN

Cosmopolitanism and Its Problems

Chantal Mouffe

Among contemporary political theorists Fred Dallmayr occupies a special place for his long-standing engagement with non-Western thought and his insistence that we have much to learn from other cultures. This is why, when asked to write an essay in his honor for this volume, I chose to present some thoughts concerning the current debate about cosmopolitanism. In my view, the main shortcoming of cosmopolitan theorists is that they envisage the unification of the world along the lines of the universalization of the West. This is precisely the kind of universalism that Dallmayr has repeatedly warned us against. For instance, in an article titled "Cosmopolitanism: Moral and Political,"[1] he examines the proposals for a universal or global ethics put forward by theologians and philosophers in order to assess their claim that we are ready for the adoption of a cosmopolitan ethics. According to Hans Küng, there is a real urgency for globalization not to be limited to political, economic, and cultural domains, but to also become a normative enterprise. Indeed, he asserts that "[t]he one world in which we live has a chance of survival only if there is no longer any room in it for spheres of differing, contradictory and even antagonistic ethics. This one world needs one basic ethics."[2] Küng is a Roman Catholic theologian, but many contemporary philosophers like Jürgen Habermas, Karl-Otto Apel, and John Rawls are also in search of a universal ethics. Dallmayr gives particular attention to the work of Martha Nussbaum and her attempt to revive ancient Stoic cosmopolitanism, bringing to light the debt that Kant's ideas in *Perpetual Peace* owed to this tradition. In her view, this Stoic/Kantian tradition is particularly relevant for our globalized world because it transcends local contexts and particular interests and emphasizes the rational core shared by people at all times and in all places. While giving his support to Nussbaum's defense of a cosmopolitan moral education, Dallmayr indicates that, by defining reason as the universal human "essence," her approach does not recognize the distinct otherness of fellow beings and marginalizes the real differences among them as nonessential. He also worries about the sidelining of politics by morality that is found in that form of cosmopolitanism, and he agrees with Peter Euben who has criticized Nussbaum for putting forward a moral critique from which political analysis is missing, noting that this can easily lead to a Stoic-like accommodation to existing powers.[3]

In this essay, following in the steps of Dallmayr—although making some claims that he would likely not endorse—I discuss other ideas regarding cosmopolitanism. I focus my attention on the proposals made by a variety of political theorists who argue that, with the end of the bipolar world order, the time has come for the establishment of a cosmopolitan democracy. The theorists associated with this trend assert that, with the dissolution of the West's communist enemy, antagonisms are a thing of the past and that, in times of globalization, the cosmopolitan ideal formulated by Kant and a few others in the nineteenth century is more relevant than ever. They believe that the conditions now exist for realizing the unity of human societies on a global scale by way of the worldwide implementation of liberal democracy. Against such a view I contend, drawing on the work of Carl Schmitt, that we need to acknowledge the pluralist character of the world and that we should work toward the establishment of a multipolar world order.

Cosmopolitical Democracy

There are many different versions of the project of cosmopolitan democracy in political theory, but here I limit myself to the version that Daniele Archibugi calls "cosmopolitical" and that he has been elaborating jointly with David Held since the 1995 publication of their coedited book *Cosmopolitan Democracy*.[4] Archibugi defines their project in the following way:

> Cosmopolitical democracy is based on the assumption that important objectives—control of the use of force, respect for human rights, self-determination—will be obtained only through the extension and development of democracy. It differs from the general approach to cosmopolitanism in that it does not merely call for global responsibility but actually attempts to apply the principles of democracy internationally.

For such problems as the protection of the environment, the regulation of migration and the use of natural resources to be subjected to necessary democratic control, democracy must transcend the border of single states and assert itself on global level.[5]

The cosmopolitical perspective asserts that there is no reason why, now that the democratic form of government is recognized worldwide as the only legitimate one, the principles and rules of democracy should stop at the borders of a political community. This calls for the creation of new global institutions. Indeed, it would be a mistake to believe that a set of democratic states automatically entails a democratic globalism. Global democracy cannot be envisaged as the direct result of democracy within states; it requires the creation of special procedures and institutions that would add another level of political representation to the already existing one. Moreover, it is not a matter of simply transposing the democratic model as conceived at the level of the state to a world scale. Archibugi and Held do not advocate the end of nation-states and they assert that a global level of representation could coexist with the already constituted states that would keep some of their political and administrative functions. According to Archibugi, "unlike the many world-federalist projects to which it is indebted, cosmopolitan democracy aims to boost the management of human affairs at a planetary level not so much by replacing existing states as by granting more powers to existing institutions and creating new ones."[6] The time has come to imagine new forms of democracy derived from the universal rights of global citizens, and he suggests that moving from national to global democracy is akin to the conceptual revolution during the eighteenth century that provided the impetus for the passage from direct to representative democracy.

Such a revolution in part would consist in the creation of international institutions empowering individuals to have an influence on global affairs, independently of the situation in their own countries. The input of individuals throughout the world—regardless of their national origin, their class, their gender, and so on—should be considered a direct form of representation at world level. How is that to be accomplished? Part of the answer is provided by David Held, who proposes that the following measures be implemented: the U.N. Security Council should be reformed to become more representative and a second U.N. chamber created jointly with regional parliaments. The authority of international courts should be extended to enforce a cluster of key rights—civil, political, economic, and social—and a new International Human Rights Court should be established. Finally, an effective and accountable international military force should be instituted to intervene against states that repeatedly violate those rights. In the long term, Held envisages a more radical shift toward global democratic governance with the formation of an authoritative assembly of all democratic states and agencies with the authority to decide all important global issues dealing with the environment, health, alimentation, economy, war, and other such matters. In his view, there should be a permanent shift favoring greater authority on the part of global institutions rather than on the part of nation-states' coercive military capacities as the best way to avoid war as a means of resolving conflict.[7]

Another important aspect of Held's cosmopolitan framework is the entrenchment of democratic rights and obligations in national and international law. Here the aim is "to create the basis of a common structure of political action as constituting the elements of a democratic public law."[8] However, to be effective in the context of globalization, such democratic law must be internationalized, it must be transformed into a cosmopolitan democratic law. Held argues that the aim of all democrats should be to establish a cosmopolitan community, that is, a transnational structure of political action, a community of all democratic communities. Discussing the consequences of such a transnational community for the nation-state, he declares that it will "wither away," not in the sense that it will become redundant, but in the sense that

> states can no longer be, and can no longer be regarded as, the sole centers of legitimate power within their own borders, as is already the case in diverse settings. States need to be articulated with, and relocated within, an overarching democratic law. Within this framework, the laws and rules of the nation state would be but one focus for legal development, political reflection and mobilization. For this framework would respecify and reconstitute the meaning and limits of sovereign authority. Particular power centers and authority systems would enjoy legitimacy only to the extent that they upheld and enacted democratic law.[9]

I do not mean to question the noble intentions of the diverse advocates of democratic cosmopolitanism. But I do argue that, as in the case of the cosmopolitanism examined by Dallmayr, albeit in a different way, the political dimension is missing and that there are many reasons to be more than skeptical about the democratizing impact of this cosmopolitical approach. To begin with, as David Chandler has argued, serious problems arise from the attempt to extend the concept of rights beyond the nation-state without a mechanism that would allow for making those new rights accountable to their subjects.[10] Cosmopolitan rights, he says, are fictitious because they are beyond the control of their subjects—that is, the global citizen can only be represented through global civil society, which acts outside the representative framework of liberal democracy. They are necessarily dependent on the advocacy of the agency of civil society institutions. The danger of those rights without subjects is that they may be used to undermine existing democratic rights of self-government, as when civil society institutions challenge national sovereignty in the name of "global concern."

The cosmopolitical approach puts more emphasis on the legitimating function of human rights than on their democratic exercise, and Chandler rightly sees the cosmopolitan construction of the global citizen as an attempt to privilege morality over politics. He notes, in this regard, that "cosmopolitan theorists reflect broader political trends towards the privileging of advocacy rights over the representational democracy of the ballot box. Political activity is increasingly undertaken outside the traditional political parties and is becoming a sphere dominated by advocacy groups and single issues campaigns who do not seek to garner votes but to lobby or gain publicity for their claims."[11] And he concludes that the new rights of cosmopolitan citizens are a chimera because they are moral claims, not democratic rights that could be exercised.

There is an even more serious problem, however, which is that, in exchange for those fictitious new rights, the cosmopolitan approach ends up sacrificing the old rights of sovereignty. By justifying the right of international institutions to undermine sovereignty in order to uphold cosmopolitan law, it denies the democratic rights of self-government for the citizens of many countries. Chandler points out that "[c]osmopolitan regulation is in fact based on the concept of sovereign inequality, that not all states should be equally involved in the establishment and adjudication of international law. Ironically, the new cosmopolitan forms of justice and rights protection involve law-making and law-enforcement, legitimized from an increasingly partial, and explicitly Western perspective."[12]

Remember, further, how Held presents his cosmopolitan community as a community of "all democratic states." But who decides which states are democratic, and on which criteria? No doubt it is the Western conception of democracy that will be used. It is telling that Held does not see that as a problem. Indeed, when examining how democratic law should be enforced, he asserts that "cosmopolitan democratic law could be promulgated and defended by those democratic states and civil societies that are able to muster the necessary political judgment and to learn how political practices and institutions must change and adapt in the new regional and global circumstances."[13] It is therefore far from clear how the cosmopolitan framework could increase the possibility of self-government for global citizens. The implementation of a cosmopolitan order would in fact result in the imposition of the liberal democratic model on the whole world, thus bringing more people directly under the control of the West. And one can only agree with Chandler when he declares that "[r]ather than furthering democracy, the premature declaration of a framework of universal cosmopolitan rights can, in fact, result in rights that people did have being further restricted."[14]

WHICH GOVERNANCE?

The nonpolitical character of the cosmopolitan perspective is clearly brought to the fore when we examine one of its central concepts—namely, "governance." Pointing out the differences between "government" and "governance," Nadia Urbinati notes:

> Governance entails an explicit reference to "mechanisms" or "organized" and "coordinated activities" appropriate to the solution of some specific problems. Unlike government, governance refers to "policies" rather than "politics" because it is not a binding decision-making structure. Its recipients are not "the people" as a collective political subject, but "the population" that can be affected by global issues such as the environment, migration or the use of natural resources.[15]

Speaking of global governance tells us a lot about the type of actor the cosmopolitans see as being active in their model. The central feature of global governance is the negotiation among a diversity of interest groups, each of which seek to push forward their proposals in a nonadversarial way. This implies a conception of politics as resolution of technical problems, not active engagement of citizens exercising their democratic rights thanks to an agonistic confrontation about conflicting hegemonic projects. To be sure, some of those interest groups are motivated by ethical concerns, but their approach is not a properly political one. Their aim is to reach a compromise or a rational consensus, not to challenge the prevailing hegemony. Such a perspective, no doubt, chimes with the liberal understanding of politics and fits perfectly the consensual vocabulary dominant today. But in what sense can this form of governance still be considered democratic?

Robert Dahl clearly answers that it cannot, and he criticizes the celebration of international organizations by cosmopolitan advocates who see them as a further step in the long march of the democratic idea from the polis to the cosmos. For Dahl, this is a view of democracy that leaves aside the fact that all decisions, even those made by democratic governments, are disadvantageous to some people: "If the trade-offs in advantages and disadvantages were identical for everyone, judgments involved in making collective decisions would be roughly equivalent to those involved in making individual decisions: but the trade-offs are not the same for everyone."[16] Costs and benefits are therefore distributed unevenly and the central question remains who should determine that distribution and on what criteria. Hence the importance for those decisions to be open to contestation. If this is already difficult at the national level, it becomes almost intractable when one considers the case of an hypothetical international demos where great differences exist in the magnitude of the population and the power of the different states.

Dahl argues that insofar as we accept that democracy is a system of popular control over governmental policies and decisions, we must also conclude that international decisionmaking cannot be democratic. This does not consist in seeing international organizations as undesirable and negating their usefulness. But, he claims, there is "no reason to clothe international organizations in the mantle of democracy simply in order to provide them with greater legitimacy."[17] He proposes instead to treat them as "bureaucratic bargaining systems" that might be necessary but whose costs to democracy should be acknowledged and taken into account when decisions are made about ceding them important national powers.

Mary Kaldor is also skeptical of the idea that democratic procedures could be reenacted at the global level. But, contrary to Dahl, she endorses the cosmopolitan project and suggests an ingenious solution to the problems just canvassed: to envisage global civil society as a functional equivalent to democracy. According to Kaldor, once we acknowledge that the central issue in parliamentary democracy has always been one of deliberation, not representation, the difficulties linked to the establishment of a global representative democracy can be ignored. Participation in a global civil society could replace representation by providing a place for deliberation about the range of issues affecting people in different aspects of their lives. Besides the privilege that it attributes to advocacy groups, the problem with such an idea is that mere deliberation without the moment of decision and the mechanisms to enforce those decisions means very little. In the interests of adapting the notion of democracy to the changes brought about by globalization, her proposal risks depriving it of one of its important dimensions. To be sure, Kaldor defends an activist conception of civil society and she stresses the need for a redistribution of power. But according to her, civil society is the locus of a type of governance based on consent, a consent that is generated through politics conceived as "social bargaining." She believes in the possibility of "a genuinely free conversation, a rational critical dialogue," and is convinced that "through access, openness and debate, policy makers are more likely to act as an Hegelian universal class, in the interests of the human community."[18]

As should be clear by now, the central problem with the diverse forms of cosmopolitanism is that they all postulate, albeit in different guises, the availability of a form of consensual governance transcending the political, conflict, and negativity. The cosmopolitan project has therefore to deny the hegemonic dimension of politics. In fact, several cosmopolitan theorists explicitly state that their aim is to envisage a politics "beyond hegemony." Such an approach overlooks the fact that since power relations are constitutive of the social, every order is *by necessity* an hegemonic order. To believe in the possibility of a cosmopolitan democracy with cosmopolitan citizens having the same rights and obligations, a constituency that would coincide with "humanity," is a dangerous illusion. If such a project were ever realized, it could only signify the world hegemony of a dominant power that had successfully imposed its conception of the world on the entire planet and that, identifying its interests with those of humanity, would treat any disagreement as an illegitimate challenge to its "rational" leadership.

Toward a Multipolar World Order

Contrary to what the cosmopolitans claim, the end of the bipolar order of the Cold War, far from having opened the way for a cosmopolitan democracy, has led to the emergence of new global antagonisms. I submit that it is within the context of the unipolar world, resulting from the collapse of the Soviet Union and the unchallenged hegemony of the United States, that one can make sense of the recent wave of international terrorism, a situation that could easily usher in a new type of war—a sort of global civil war. The absence of a real pluralism in the international arena makes it impossible to find legitimate forms of dissension, which is why, when antagonisms emerge, they take extreme forms. It is therefore the lack of political channels for challenging the hegemony of neoliberal globalization that explains in part the proliferation of discourses and practices of radical negation of the current order. Hence the need to envisage an alternative to the universalist insistence that antagonisms can be eliminated thanks to the unification of the world and the establishment of a cosmopolitan democracy.

I suggest we heed Carl Schmitt when he reminds us that the "political world is a pluriverse, not a universe."[19] I know that to mention Schmitt will evoke negative reactions from all those who claim that his allegiance to Nazism disqualifies his thought. But I am convinced that it would be a mistake not to take seriously his critique of liberal universalism, whose pretension of offering the true and only legitimate political system he saw as a source of serious antagonisms

For a start, Schmitt brings to light how liberal universalism has used the concept of "humanity" as an ideological weapon of imperialist expansion and indicates how humanitarian ethics can become a vehicle of economic imperialism. In *The Concept of the Political,* he points out that "[w]hen a state fights its political enemy in the name of humanity, it is not a war for the sake of humanity, but a war wherein a particular state seeks to usurp a universal concept against its military opponent. At the expense of its opponent, it tries to identify itself with humanity in the same way as one can misuse peace, justice, progress and civilization in order to claim these as one's own and to deny the same to the enemy."[20] This explains, in his view, why wars waged in the name of humanity have historically been particularly inhuman: once the enemy is understood as an outlaw of humanity, all means to defeat it are justified. Although written in the 1920s this warning, far from having lost its relevance, is more pertinent than ever almost a century later.

Indeed, Schmitt foresaw the dangers entailed by the establishment of a unipolar world order and he was acutely aware that any attempt to impose a particular model worldwide would have dire consequences. After World War II, he reflected on the decline of the political in its modern form and the loss by the state of its monopoly of the political. This was linked in his view to the dissolution of the *Jus Publicum Europaeum*, the interstate European law that for three centuries had made possible what, in his 1950 book *Der Nomos der Erde*, he called *"eine Hegung des Krieges"* (a confining of war).[21] He was concerned by this loss of monopoly because he feared that the decline of the state was creating the conditions for a new form of politics—an "international civil war."

How to avoid such a prospect? What kind of order could replace the *Jus Publicum Europaeum?* Those questions are at the center of Schmitt's scholarly work as reflected in several writings of the 1950s and early 1960s in which he discussed the possibility of a new *"nomos* of the earth." In an essay from 1952,[22] he examined how the dualism created by the Cold War and the polarization between capitalism and communism could evolve and put forward several possible scenarios. He was skeptical that such a dualism was only the prelude to a final unification of the world, one that resulted from the total victory of one of the antagonists. Rather, he believed that the end of bipolarity was more likely to lead to a new equilibrium, this time under the hegemony of the United States.

But Schmitt also envisaged the possibility of a third process of evolution that would bring about a dynamics of pluralization whose outcome could establish a new global order based on the existence of several autonomous regional blocs. This would provide the conditions for an equilibrium of forces among various large spaces, instituting among them a new system of international law. Such a system would present similarities with the old *Jus Publicum Europaeum*, except that in this case, it would be truly global and not only Europeocentric. This pluralist evolution was clearly the one Schmitt favored. He thought that by establishing a "true pluralism," a multipolar world order would provide the institutions necessary to manage conflicts. In that way one could avoid the negative consequences resulting from the pseudo-universalism arising from the generalization of one single system. He was aware, however, that such a pseudo-universalism was a much more likely outcome than the pluralism he advocated. And, unfortunately, this is been borne out by developments since the collapse of Soviet communism.

No doubt Schmitt's reflections were motivated by very different concerns than those which inform my critique of cosmopolitanism. And yet I think they provide very important insights to understand the problems that we are facing today. For instance, they can help us grasp the conditions of emergence of the new forms of terrorism. As Jean-François Kervégan has suggested, Schmitt allows us to approach the question of terrorism in a different way than the dominant approach, which prefers to see terrorist acts as the work of isolated groups of fanatics.[23] Taking our bearings from his work, we can see terrorism as the product of a new configuration of the political that is characteristic of the type of world order being implemented around the hegemony of a single hyperpower. There is no doubt a correlation between the overwhelming power of the United States and the proliferation of terrorist attacks. Of course in no way do I want to pretend that this is the only explanation. Terrorism has always existed and it is due to a multiplicity of factors. But it tends to flourish in circumstances in which there are no political channels for the expression of grievances. It is therefore not a coincidence that, since the end of the Cold War, with the untrammeled imposition of a neoliberal model of globalization under U.S. dominance, we have witnessed a significant increase in terrorist attacks. Indeed, the possibilities of maintaining sociopolitical models different from the Western ones have been drastically reduced. Even liberal cosmopolitans like Richard Falk and Andrew Strauss acknowledge the link between terrorism and the present world order when they write:

> [W]ith the possibility of direct and formalized participation in the international system foreclosed, frustrated individuals and groups (especially when their government are viewed as illegitimate and hostile) have been turning to various modes of civic resistance, both peaceful and violent. Global terrorism is at the violent end of this spectrum of transnational protest, and its apparent agenda may be mainly driven by religious, ideological and regional goals rather than by resistance directly linked to globalization. But is extremist alienation is partly, at the very least, an

indirect result of globalizing impacts that may be transmuted in the political unconscious of those so afflicted into grievances associated with cultural injustices.[24]

Falk and Strauss believe that the solution to our present predicament lies in a "democratic transnationalism," the core of which would consist of a Global Parliamentary Assembly (GPA) providing a global institutional voice for the people of the world.[25] They present the mission of such an assembly—whose powers should always be exercised according to the Universal Declaration of Human Rights—as contributing to the democratization of global policy, not only in its formulation but also in its implementation. We need, they say, an international framework capable of democratically accommodating the growing institutionalization of civic politics. The GPA could provide the beginnings of a democratic form of accountability for the institutional system.

Falk and Strauss propose a version of cosmopolitanism that relies mainly on the role of civil society and sees the state as the central problem. It asserts that citizens groups and business and financial elites are beginning to recognize that they have a common interest in mounting a challenge to states, which should cease to act as their representatives in the international arena. According to them, many of the leading figures in world business, like those who meet at Davos, have an enlightened sense of their long term interests and are very sympathetic to the idea of democratizing the international system. The organized networks of global civil society and business should therefore be able to impose their democratizing projects onto the reluctant governments. The objective would be to establish a global institutional democratic structure enabling the people of the world to bypass the states and have a meaningful voice in global governance, thereby creating a peaceful global order.

While agreeing with Falk and Strauss on the importance of establishing an institutional framework that would allow for the expression of grievances, I find their solution completely inadequate. It is not only that their hope in the enlightened self-interest of the business elites is thoroughly unconvincing. My main quarrel with their proposal is that they can only envisage democracy at the world level as the globalization of the Western model. Their "global civil society" is composed of citizens, visualized as liberal individuals, fighting to defend their rights against threatened encroachment by the state. This is a typically liberal vision that is apparently insensitive to different cultural traditions and takes the individual "Western style" as the highest form of achievement. Now, it is precisely against the imposition of such a model of society that we are currently witnessing strong resistances.

Instead of thinking along cosmopolitan lines, we should adopt the perspective of Massimo Cacciari, who advocates the establishment of an international system of law based on the idea of regional poles and cultural identities federated among themselves in the recognition of their full autonomy. Cacciari is indeed right to warn us that "[w]e are facing decisive years—and the authentic decision is the decision between a universal empire and a global federalism."[26] It is high time to acknowledge the pluralist character of the world and to relinquish the Eurocentric tenet that modernization can only take place through Westernization. To envisage a pluralistic world order constructed around a certain number of great spaces and genuine cultural poles is, I believe, what could make possible the politics suggested by Dallmayr when he says in *Alternative Visions* that "our global world requires a large-scale 'politics of recognition.' . . . Such a politics is bound to involve worldwide struggle and antagonism; hopefully it can advance beyond a harsh 'clash of civilizations' to borrow Samuel Huntington's phrase—in the direction of a mutual learning process among cultures."[27]

NOTES

1. Fred Dallmayr, "Cosmopolitanism: Moral and Political," *Political Theory* 31, no. 3 (June 2003).
2. Hans Küng, quoted in ibid., p. 424.
3. Cf. J. Peter Euben, "Polis, Globalization, and Citizenship of Place," in his *Platonic Noise* (Princeton: Princeton University Press, 2003).
4. Daniele Archibugi and David Held, ed., *Cosmopolitan Democracy: An Agenda for a New World Order* (Cambridge, UK: Polity Press, 1995).
5. Daniele Archibugi, "Cosmopolitical Democracy," in *Debating Cosmopolitics*, ed. Daniele Archibugi (London: Verso, 2003), p. 7.
6. Daniele Archibugi, "Demos and Cosmopolis," in *Debating Cosmopolitics*, ed. Daniele Archibugi (London: Verso, 2003), p. 262.
7. David Held, "Democracy and the New International Order," in Archibugi and Held, eds., *Cosmopolitan Democracy*, p. 111.

8. David Held, "The Transformation of Political Community: Rethinking Democracy in the Context of Globalization," in *Democracy's Edges*, ed. I. Shapiro and C. Hacker-Cordón (Cambridge: Cambridge University Press, 1999), p. 105.

9. Ibid., p. 106.

10. David Chandler, "New Rights for Old? Cosmopolitan Citizenship and the Critique of State Sovereignty," *Political Studies* 51 (2003): 332–49.

11. Ibid., p. 340.

12. Ibid., p. 343.

13. David Held, *Democracy and the Global Order* (Cambridge, UK: Polity Press, 1995), p. 232.

14. Chandler, "New Rights for Old?" p. 347.

15. Nadia Urbinati, *Mill on Democracy: From the Athenian Polis to Representative Government* (Chicago: University of Chicago Press, 2002), p. 80.

16. Robert Dahl, "Can International Organizations Be Democratic? A Skeptical View," in *Democracy's Edges*, ed. I. Shapiro and C. Hacker-Cordón (Cambridge: Cambridge University Press, 1999), p. 25.

17. Ibid., p. 32.

18. Mary Kaldor, *Global Civil Society: An Answer to War* (Cambridge, UK: Polity Press, 2003), p. 108.

19. Carl Schmitt, *The Concept of the Political* (New Brunswick: Rutgers University Press, 1976), p. 53.

20. Ibid., p. 54.

21. Carl Schmitt, *Der Nomos der Erde im Völkerrecht des Jus Publicum Europaeum* (Berlin: Duncker and Humblot, 1997).

22. Carl Schmitt, "Die Einheit der Welt," in *Merkur* 6, no. 1 (1952).

23. Jean-François Kervégan, "Ami ou Ennemi?" in *La guerre des dieux*, special issue of *Le Nouvel Observateur*, January 2002.

24. Richard Falk and Andrew Strauss, "The Deeper Challenges of Global Terrorism: A Democratizing Response," in *Debating Cosmopolitics*, ed. Daniele Archibugi (London: Verso, 2003), p. 206.

25. Richard Falk and Andrew Strauss, "Towards Global Parliament," *Foreign Affairs* (January–February 2001).

26. Massimo Cacciari, "Digressioni su impero e tre Rome," in *Europa politica*, ed. H. Friese et al. (Rome: Manifestolibri, 2002), p. 38.

27. Fred Dallmayr, *Alternative Visions: Toward a Global and Plural Democracy* (Lanham, Md.: Rowman and Littlefield, 1998, p. 268.

TWELVE

Civility and Dialogue in
the Cosmopolitan Consensus
on Rights

David Ingram

Fred Dallmayr has built his reputation as a political theorist par excellence on the basis of his remarkable ability to mediate opposed voices. As he informs us in one of his most recent collection of essays, *Dialogue among Civilizations*,[1] the search for reconciliation and wholeness driving this endeavor is undertaken in a spirit of friendship and love—the same spirit, I might add, that he has extended to all who have sought his company in dialogue.

Today I hope to pay tribute to my mentor by undertaking a meditation on his recent work on international relations. In keeping with the dialogical ecumenism that informs his approach to these matters, I am inspired by the conviction that friendship and love can become the guiding threads linking nations in a mutually edifying and mutually transformative dialogue. This conviction may strike some realists as utopian. Perhaps it is. Yet given the urgency of achieving a global community based on respect for human rights, such a conviction may be more realistic than the realists among us think.

Indeed, if there is a sustained argument underlying Dallmayr's recent work, it is that the unilateralism currently advocated by neoconservatives is dangerously unrealistic. Witness the recent conduct of the Bush administration. Driving its disastrous intervention in the Middle East is a Manichean ideology that views the world through the polarizing lens of "us" versus "them"—where "them" variously refers to "terrorists," "Old Europeans," or simply those who do not agree with the administration. Oppositional thinking of this sort has been given even deeper philosophical credence by Samuel

Huntington, whose now-famous "clash of civilizations" thesis postulates what appears to be an almost metaphysical divide separating "the West" from "the rest."[2] In its most unqualified form, this thesis holds that the legacy of modern Enlightenment—science, technology, capitalism, the rule of law, democracy, and respect for individual rights—is a unique possession of European-based civilization that finds little or no resonance in non-Western—principally Asian, African, and Middle Eastern—civilizations. Given the terrorist threat against Western civilization emanating from a Muslim world mired in religious "fundamentalism," this line of argument seems destined to issue in an apocalyptic call to arms, with the West—led by the United States—having little choice but to impose its way of life on the rest of the world, using all available economic, geopolitical, and military assets at its disposal.

Dallmayr devotes considerable effort to dismantling this argument. He insists that it makes no sense to oppose Western and non-Western civilizations because neither one is unitary or self-contained. Western Civilization presents a complex tapestry of Judeo-Christian, Graeco-Roman, and—thanks to an on-going process of globalization extending back centuries—non-Western civilizations (chief among them Islamic), each of which is itself composed of various contrasting threads. So despite claims by thinkers like Huntington, there is no bright line dividing "us" from "them."

The argument against cultural divisiveness applies to all forms of oppositional thinking. The oppositions between reason and religion, culture and nature, and theory and practice that is still commonplace among many intellectuals of the European Enlightenment prevent us from appreciating the interlocking integrity of life, which Dallmayr defines as a life lived in common with other human beings, nature, and the transcendent source of meaning and purpose we call God.

When applied to cultural divides, oppositional thinking sometimes encourages a "live and let live attitude." A belief in "cultural relativism," or the view that no meaningful engagement with the other is really possible, can lead people of different cultural allegiances to ignore one another. Although there is nothing intrinsically wrong with that—tolerance is better than intolerance—it does not ameliorate the chief source of long-term mistrust that can eventually lead to nonmeaningful engagements of a violent sort. When "otherness" is viewed as a threat that broaches no meaningful engagement, the options for nonmeaningful engagement are stark, ranging from ethnic cleansing and genocide to forced religious conversion. Something like the latter seems to be at play in the Middle East, where ideological fundamentalists—evangelicals, neoconservatives, and neoliberals—aim to assimilate the Muslim "other" to "our" way of life, the one true and God-ordained path marked out by the American hegemon.

It is this concern that has led Dallmayr to seek in the concept of dialogue the basis for a nonhegemonic civil relationship. As he notes, civility recalls the original meaning of civilization, conceived as an urbane life of equality and mutual respect. Dialogue is nothing if not a mutual effort to reach understanding through the productive point and counterpoint of question and answer, a process that demands recognizing and even preserving the unassimilated otherness of one's interlocutor.

What chiefly interests me in Dallmayr's vision of a civilized world are precisely the limits and possibilities of dialogue as a basis for resolving the sorts of global disagreements that can lead to hegemonic politics. More precisely, I here propose to explore the kinds of transformations that dialogue must undergo in order to underwrite that cosmopolitan consensus on rights without which mutual respect among persons and peoples is unthinkable.

Following Dallmayr, I begin with the premise that such a consensus cannot rest on a vacuous appeal to reason. Perhaps each of us is endowed with a sufficiently similar faculty of reason to agree on the basic moral rules against wrongfully harming others (for example, do not kill, do not steal, do not enslave), but then we still have to define in concrete terms what, precisely, wrongful killing, taking, and enslaving are. For rights—even human rights—are not intended to be only vague moral guidelines that direct our inner conscience. They are also intended to be legally enforceable. And like all legally enforceable rights, they must be well defined in order to provide fair warning. The precise limits of our freedom cannot be known by any one person reasoning alone. They can only be known by all of us reasoning together. Such dialogic reasoning is exemplified in the kind of negotiation we find in democratic legislatures, negotiations involving persons who hold very different notions of legal reasonableness.

Negotiations can assume many different forms. Sometimes they involve exchanging favors. But negotiations regarding the reasonableness of specific definitions of rights will necessarily engage our moral beliefs about what human beings are and how they should be. In short, such negotiations will take the form of dialogue in which persons mainly seek to understand one another and themselves.

But what kind of dialogue? It is tempting to think that the primary aim of dialogue is agreement. If so, this aim might then be construed as requiring interlocutors to limit the sorts of things they say. Following thinkers like John Rawls,[3] we might propose that dialogue be conducted with certain "gag rules" in place to require that any proposed definition of a given right be neutral with respect to irreconcilable religious and ideological beliefs. The problem with this approach is that it obstructs the very means (dialogue) required to negotiate reasonable terms of right and wrong behavior. The less dialogue there is, the more we are forced to rely on our private intuitions of reasonableness. No doubt there will be some overlap among these intuitions sufficient to establish a consensus on basic moral rules, but that, as we have seen, is not enough.

Following Dallmayr, I argue that the kind of dialogue needed to reach agreement on a definite, legally enforceable schedule of rights must permit the expression of religious and ideological viewpoints that might not be shared by all. This sounds paradoxical, since if these viewpoints are not shared by all—and, given the tendency of dialogue to generate differences of opinion as well as agreements, cannot be shared by all—it seems inconceivable that we could ever reach agreement on a definite, legally enforceable schedule of rights. But the paradox is more apparent than real. For we ought not to prejudge the degree to which interlocutors in dialogue modify their different viewpoints in order to allow for greater convergence of opinion on the details that matter—in this case, the specific liberties, protections, and entitlements that are owed to any person.

Obviously, such convergence of opinion cannot be expected to happen all at once. Dialogue is a process, and like all processes, must traverse various stages. Here I share Dallmayr's view that dialogue—at least at the outset—cannot be narrowly tailored to the task of argumentatively redeeming contentious claims in the manner proposed by Jürgen Habermas.[4] The formal requirements stipulated by Habermas—for instance, that the interlocutors do not assign equivocal meanings to the terms of dialogue, and that they seek to reach agreement on a singularly unique and true justification for some single claim—are too unrealistic and in any case only apply to academic settings in which almost all the hard work of dialogue has already been accomplished. Only at the very end of the dialogical process might we expect close agreement on something like a univocal definition of rights, which in any case does not require our agreeing on their singularly unique and true justification.

Prior to reaching this stage of argumentation, interlocutors must have already learned to respect and trust one another, despite their deep differences. Here we return to Dallmayr's insistence (which he shares with Hans-Georg Gadamer) that the primary aim of dialogue is the furtherance of mutual understanding, not the resolution of arguments and disagreements. Dialogue must be conducted in a spirit of friendship, love, mutual respect, and asymmetrical deference to vulnerable others. But even this kind of dialogue must evolve through preparatory modes of communication, beginning with strategic negotiations that seek limited forms of mutual understanding.

In short, I propose to supplement Dallmayr's (and by extension, Habermas's) understanding of civil dialogue by returning to Rawls. The way to "jump start" dialogue between adversaries who do not trust or understand one another is by narrowing the terms of dialogue to what all can superficially agree on. At this initial stage, removing contestable points from the table of discussion—including imposing "gag rules"—can pave the way for a mutual acknowledgment of agreements, however superficial these may be. Merely acknowledging the other as a strategic player in a fair game of negotiation—for instance, working on timetables and frameworks for bargaining—can begin to generate trust and mutual respect where none previously existed.

After beginning with this highly formalized and limited form of negotiation, dialogue can gradually grow into more expansive forms of mutual understanding, in which—possibly—consensus on a concrete definition of rights can be argumentatively articulated. In any case, full dialogue is never merely argumentative, since it always presupposes a deeper mutual understanding of differences. Ultimately, it implies a felt attunement to the holistic integrity of one's own and others' lives as mutually complementing and enriching one another, in communication with both nature and spirit.

Classical Top-Down Universalism

In a recent essay, "Cosmopolitanism: Moral and Political,"[5] Dallmayr criticizes attempts to found human rights in a priori moral reason. What these attempts have in common is a "top-down" universalism of the sort that is commonly associated with the natural law tradition. Citing well-known criticisms of this tradition by Hegel and others, Dallmayr notes that the universalism of natural law approaches is purchased at a rather steep price. Invoking a sharp dichotomy between universal reason and particular custom, natural law theorists leaves us with little more than empty platitudes, such as Thomas Aquinas's "seek good and avoid evil," that restate the basic message contained in the Golden Rule. In order to guide and motivate action, this rule must be concretely interpreted and applied.

At this juncture—where theory meets practice—a priori reason cedes authority to a posteriori political judgment. Hence the question posed by Dallmayr: "Who [in the debate about the correct meaning of human rights] has the right of interpretation [and] in the case of conflict, who is entitled to rule between different interpretations?"[6] The appeal to reason in settling this debate seems disingenuous when it is reason itself that is being contested. Indeed, such an appeal invites the philosopher to elevate his or her own parochial understanding to the exalted status of the universal. Here arises the danger of imposing one's subjective opinion on others "in the name of reason," an imposition that delivers the legislation and adjudication of human rights "over into hegemonic and quasi-imperial powers." Perhaps this explains why, when President Bush claims to be liberating Iraqis in the name of universal values of freedom, equality, and democracy, many of them wonder whether this declamation—enforced by Proconsul Paul Bremer and the occupying "peace keeping" forces at the point of a gun—is not at bottom an affirmation of a peculiarly American kind of freedom, equality, and democracy.

Abstract ethical universalism is morally deficient for another reason as well: because it extends "recognition to fellow human beings only in the respect in which they are identical with ourselves"—namely, as possessors of one and the same exalted reason and humanity—it demands sameness of treatment for each and every individual, regardless of differences.[7] But of course differences matter. Many of Iraq's Shiites and Sunni's who feel they are under a divine command to invest the governing order with spiritual purposes do not believe in a strict separation of religion and state. Many of them also condemn a free-market capitalist system, which they think glorifies materialism at the expense of spiritual values and celebrates the selfish greed of individuals above the needs of the community.

According to Dallmayr, the only way to check the abuses associated with top-down universalism is by conceiving ethical reasoning as a political—more precisely, dialogical—enterprise. Even if we allow that general moral support for human rights and other universal norms must draw inspiration from personal philosophical and religious convictions about nature, God, and reason, we must still insist that any legally enforceable schedule of rights be an outcome (to paraphrase Habermas) to which all affected could freely consent, simply because it was the outcome of a fair and informed democratic dialogue.

RAWLS AND DIALOGICAL CIVILITY

Here is not the place to discuss the kinds of changes in the United Nations General Assembly and in the world at large that would have to be implemented in order for global democracy to become an institutional reality. Dallmayr himself notes that inequalities between nations and between individuals with respect to power, wealth, and knowledge will have to be remedied in order for the dialogue between nations and between individuals to be fully inclusive and reciprocal.[8] However, these proposals do not address the kind of civility with which global dialogue should be conducted.

Rawls has suggested that the dialogical civility appropriate between heads of state should mirror the ideal of civility characteristic of liberal democracies.[9] This ideal has a long history, being forged during several centuries of European religious warfare, during which time it became evident that reasonable people will inevitably disagree about the deepest sources of meaning and value underlying their civil commitments. In Rawls's opinion, reason itself creates a pluralism of incommensurable philosophical and religious doctrines whose comprehensive scope—reaching down to the very prediscursive habits and understandings against which all our practical reasoning is foregrounded—resists discursive resolution.

Under circumstances of reasonable pluralism, the most that can be expected in the way of a dialogical consensus on human rights, Rawls concludes, will be a rather thin set of guidelines proscribing, on one hand, slavery, serfdom, forced occupation, and unequal treatment in criminal prosecution and mandating, and on the other hand, freedom of conscience and religion, freedom to own personal property, and freedom from insecurity and want.[10] Liberal and democratic rights that proscribe gender discrimination and religious favoritism and mandate equal voting rights are not among the rights included in Rawls's list of human rights, since many reasonable Muslims (among others) will not consent to them.[11]

Corresponding to the "fact" of incommensurability in Rawls's account of dialogical consensus is a rarified notion of dialogical civility urging us to desist from appealing to reasons peculiar to our comprehensive doctrines that cannot in principle be shared by all our fellow world citizens. To appeal to these nonshareable reasons risks imposing on our fellow world citizens policies and rationales that violate their deepest moral and religious commitments. But that is no way to implement a legitimate schedule of human rights. Better that we stick with the shallow common ground we already share, even if it means that controversial demands such as gender equality are left out of our schedule of rights.

It does not take much to see that the model of civil dialogue advanced by Rawls barely gets us much further than the older natural law tradition. True, Rawls's appeal to toleration, pluralism, and other values of political liberalism respectful of cultural differences does not—unlike its natural law counterpart—claim to be true in any deep metaphysical sense, and in that respect appears to be entirely agnostic with respect to comprehensive doctrines regarding nature and God. Indeed, for Rawls it is not important that a schedule of human rights be given a deep moral foundation that all persons will accept, but that it be accepted by them for deeply held moral reasons of one sort or another. Yet despite Rawls's disclaimers to the contrary, appealing to such an "overlapping consensus"—or agreement on conclusions based on radically divergent premises—has all the signs of a monological, natural law deduction based on a priori moral reason. Once again we are brought back to the question posed by Dallmayr regarding top-down ethical universalism in general: What entitles Rawls to stipulate which rights reasonable people will agree on and which they will not? Can't this be determined only dialogically by those affected?

There are several other difficulties with Rawls's conception of dialogical consensus and dialogical civility. He assumes that there exists a common core of scientific beliefs that all reasonable persons will accept, which is certainly disputable, especially when the science in question—sociology—lacks the paradigmatic status of natural science. He further assumes that an overlapping consensus can be the basis for mutual trust—and not merely a strategic modus vivendi. But if we do not engage our most deep-seated religious and philosophical convictions in dialogue for fear of offending our interlocutors, how can they be sure that our deepest reasons for committing ourselves to this schedule of rights are moral ones? Leaving aside the fact that trustworthy agreements must ultimately be cemented by deeds, without knowing that the reasons why you (a citizen of an illiberal Islamic theocracy) and I (a citizen of a liberal democracy) agree are both deeply justifiable for roughly the same reasons, I have no grounds for trusting you. For all I know, your religious faith in rights could be trumped by fundamentalist ardor; for all you know, my secular support for the same could be trumped by economic greed.

HABERMASIAN CIVILITY AND CONSENSUS

Last but not least, Rawls's conceptions of overlapping consensus and dialogical civility leave no room for developing an enforceable schedule of rights. Abstract rights of the sort provided by such conceptions are subject to widely divergent interpretation. Although some flexibility in the interpretation of rights is desirable—especially when considering the diverse cultural and historical circumstances in which different peoples find themselves—too much is not.

Habermas's conception of consensus and dialogical civility strikes a better balance, in my opinion. It departs from the Gadamerian notion that language and culture designate transcendental conditions of possible understanding that—similar to a horizon of vision—open up as well as limit experience. Conceived as enabling conditions, such comprehensive modes of being are not as incommensurable as Rawls thinks. Indeed, if Donald Davidson is right, incommensurability itself is incoherent.[12] We could never know that two distinct languages were radically incommensurable—or incapable of communicating with another—unless we had already successfully translated both into our language, thereby rendering them commensurable. Therefore, the possibility for consensus—and the determination of what cannot (and should not) be discussed for lack of it—can be discerned only from within dialogue, in which all languages are commensurable.

A notion of dialogical civility that permits the discussion of what initially appear to be "irreconcilable differences" can thus contribute to making such differences less irreconcilable. No doubt, participants in dialogue will still decide that some differences—at least for the time being—are irreconcilable and should therefore be "bracketed." But they will also decide that some differences they originally thought were irreconcilable are not so irreconcilable, given what each of them now knows about the others. We can therefore imagine a robust multicultural dialogue gradually producing a global consensus on the concrete meaning of rights, including which rights are necessary and basic and which have priority.

Toward a Robust Dialogical Civility

Of course, dialogue does not guarantee that such a consensus will emerge. As Rawls rightly notes, rational discussion can just as easily lead to dissension. But without a robust conception of dialogue and dialogical civility, consensus on an enforceable and progressively evolving schedule of rights is impossible. That said, we now need to examine the formal conditions of dialogical civility that would bestow legitimacy on such a consensus, were it to exist. As is well known, Habermas proposes a number of formal dialogical rules that would have to be satisfied in order for consensus to be considered fully legitimate. Some of these rules specify a model of dialogical civility. These include (and here I paraphrase freely) the inclusion of all persons affected; the provision of equal chances to speak; a primary orientation toward agreement on the validity of claims rather than toward the winning of arguments; freedom from external and internal constraints that preclude openness to alternative points of view; and a robust and expansive conception of what counts as a reason, coupled with an equally robust and expansive desire to question even the most basic of assumptions.

Habermas concedes that these formal rules impose utopian expectations on interlocutors. Yet however ideally desirable they might be, it is far from clear whether they should be rigorously adhered to here and now, given current inequalities and constraints. Formulated as formal (procedural) rights that apply to everyone in the same way, they ignore obvious differences in the opportunities and capabilities of persons to participate dialogically. For example, if the criterion of inclusion is intended to include only those who can talk to one another civilly, then some people affected by the outcome of dialogue will surely be excluded from participating in it. Privileging academic discourse as exemplifying civility, for instance, will result in excluding most people, perhaps.

Again, the insistence on equal speech rights seems misplaced when some of the participants have already been privileged in exercising their speech rights. Why shouldn't members of dominant or oppressor groups be obligated to listen more to the as yet unheard voices of vulnerable, marginalized, and oppressed peoples? Since no language is neutral or innocent with respect to the points of view it privileges, allowing marginalized and oppressed groups to exercise asymmetrical opportunities to speak might enable them to combat the kinds of injustices that Jean-François Lyotard calls "differends."[13] These injustices occur whenever the dominant lingua franca prevents the expression of a different point of view or understanding of things. Thus, to take one example, labor is defined by the dominant economic and legal paradigm as a commodity to be purchased by owners of capital in exchange for a wage. According to this paradigm, workers have little right to determine the conditions under which their labor is deployed, since they have "freely" contracted to hand it over to capitalists to be used as they see fit. By contrast, if one conceives of labor as "life's need and the realization of life," as Marx put it, then very different rights come into play. For one cannot allow another to dictate one's needs and the conditions for fulfilling them any more than one can sell oneself into slavery.

Linguistic differends reveal that language is never a completely neutral medium of discourse. That being so, any rule of logic that presumes that interlocutors must assign univocal meanings to words only encourages differends. Insisting that all interlocutors mean the same thing by "labor"—which seems to be the implication of Habermas's highly idealized conception of argumentative dialogue—would make sense only in a world in which the opposed standpoints of worker and capitalist had been overcome. For this reason, equivocal usage is a normal and reasonable condition of dialogue—at least up until the moment when social changes have made possible a more univocal—and hopefully more equitable—standpoint for all potential interlocutors.

Habermas's view that rational dialogue essentially requires raising and criticizing claims that demand justification and resolution is equally problematic. To begin with, the model of Socratic dialogue invoked here is too limiting. Many people engage in dialogue in order to express themselves and to understand others. Such expression and understanding need not—and normally does not—consist in the raising of discrete claims that call for a distinctive method of justification (as when we use the scientific method to justify the truth of a factual assertion). Rather, it consists in entering into ways of life in which the entire range of beliefs and practices—cognitive, evaluative, and affective—condition one another holistically.

Ways of life can be expressed and understood only by entering into them as whole narratives that aspire to integrity even while remaining ruptured and incomplete. But the kind of dialogical attunement appropriate to this kind of experience is probing and listening—questioning that does not seek justification and answering that does not aim to provide it. In the words of Dallmayr (citing Charles Taylor)[14]:

> What these comments bring to view is a mode of communication no longer tailored to rational validity claims, but open to vernacular experiences. In a slightly sharpened formulation, one might speak here of a "thick conversation" or a "thick dialogue," that is, a communicative interchange willing to delve into the rich fabric of different lifeworlds and cultures. The appeal in such exchanges is no longer merely to the rational-cognitive capacity of participants, but rather to the full range of their situated humanity, including their hopes, aspirations, moral and spiritual convictions, as well as their agonies and frustrations.[15]

Dialogue as Existential Engagement

Dialogue in the sense described above facilitates a mutual understanding of different ways of life and their respective notions of well-being. Dialogue cannot be reduced to a narrow debate on the meaning and justification of claims, but it can facilitate it. Take the debate on human rights, for example. Human rights designate minimal thresholds of human flourishing below which human life loses its dignity and value. Such minimal thresholds refer to human capabilities that have a teleological dimension. So construed, human rights not only protect but also develop human capabilities and human goods, in all their rich diversity.

If this is so, then every criticism of a rights violation is also implicitly a criticism of human alienation—that is, a critique of humans alienated from nature and society, and from themselves. The critique of alienation, however, cannot be undertaken in the dialogue of argumentation as Habermas has defined it, because happiness does not designate a discrete sphere of validity—like factual truth and normative justice—that can be redeemed by appeal to a single criterion of rational justification (be it a scientific method or legal deduction). On the contrary, happiness refers to the felicitous balance and integration of all of life's moments that comes with realizing the full scope of one's human capabilities. Happiness and its antithesis—alienation—are thus "judged" by feeling as much as by reason. In short, to criticize the alienation created by a certain system of rights—or the lack thereof—is not to criticize the truth or falsity of an empirical description, the rightness and wrongness of a norm, or even the pleasantness or unpleasantness of an aesthetic experience. It is rather to criticize the peculiar disequilibria affecting a complex interweaving of norms, environments, and institutions—economic, political, social, and cultural—and their impact on the realization of human capabilities.

In sum, the definition of human rights—which entails a deep understanding of our complex, multifaceted, and evolving humanity—must proceed within an ongoing dialogue in which humanity itself is collectively interrogated vis-à-vis its transcendent presuppositions, both natural and spiritual (or divine). All three dimensions of existence intersect within the space opened up by human beings in dialogue with themselves about who they are and who they want to be.

THREE STAGES OF DIALOGUE

I propose that we think of dialogue as a process that traverses three main stages progressively advancing toward the ideal of full trust and friendship. In the context of our present discussion about human rights, the hope is that as global dialogue progresses, the peoples of the world will achieve a transformative understanding of their own inextricable community with nature and the higher spiritual aspirations they share with one another. In this manner, respect for individual rights and equality will go hand-in-hand with a respect for the rights of nature and human community.

The first stage of dialogue might look very much like Rawls's model of restrained dialogue. This stage assumes that people who mistrust one another have already understood the need to tolerate and negotiate with one another out of strategic necessity. Prior to dialogue, there must be a negotiated settlement of conflict establishing the most superficial terms of nonengagement with the other—something like a "live and let live" modus vivendi of the sort that eventually obtained between Protestants and Catholics after the Peace of Westphalia, and that still needs to be worked out between Palestinians and Israelis in the Middle East. Such a modus vivendi cannot survive for long without a more solid, moral basis of trust. Perhaps Hobbesian game theory might explain how an insipient form of trust might emerge. Over time—as understanding develops—we learn a little more about each other, enough for mutual respect to emerge. Only then does dialogue really happen. But the risk of disagreement is still so great—and the stakes for failing to agree so high—that the participants in dialogue might well agree to "table" certain differences for the sake of reaching consensus on a very general and necessarily superficial schedule of rights.

The second stage of dialogue involves mutually understanding one another in a more holistic way. Gadamer's notion of a "fusion of horizons"—a somewhat misleading expression—comes closest to what I have in mind. In the course of understanding the other as other, we come to enlarge our horizon of what counts as meaningful and valid.[16] This kind of understanding is not necessarily symmetrical. Gadamer, for instance, mentions that we defer to the authority of tradition when trying to understand it. Whether he is right about this is certainly open to question,[17] but the general point is that the burden of mutual understanding may fall more on one party than the other—and rightly so. Whites, for instance, have a greater duty to understand the standpoint of blacks, who continue to be unjustly marginalized in American society.

As Gadamer understands it, the "fusion of horizons" that accompanies genuine understanding indicates a mutual broadening and interpenetration of standpoints, not a one-sided assimilation of one into the other or their compression into a single standpoint without remainder of difference. Despite Gadamer's own tendency to link mutual understanding of differences with an orientation toward reaching agreement on some transcendent truth (the German word *Verständigung* conveys both mutual understanding and mutual agreement), the real thrust of his meaning is the preservation and transformation of differences in a higher "synthesis" in which they are more fully perfected and realized. Gadamer uses the Hegelian expression *Aufhebung* to capture this dialectical movement. For example, reading different interpretations of the same text does not cancel their differences. Instead it produces an expanded horizon of understanding in terms of which their mutual complementarity can be seen. Merely understanding them in relation to one another, against the background of an enlarged horizon (totality), changes and deepens (realizes) their distinctive meanings.

The third and final stage of dialogue is in some sense a continuation of the second. At a certain point, once a sufficient level of mutual understanding has been reached, the stage has been set for a concerted effort at mutual transformation oriented toward agreement on some substantive matter. This effort might well take the form of rational argumentation in Habermas's sense, in which claims and justifications are advanced. The important thing to note, however, is that the argumentative hashing out of definitions and justifications vis-à-vis specific rights proposals cannot proceed without there being at the same time a progressive exploration (and generation) of further differences, all in accordance with a Dallmayrean spirit of love and friendship.

The Global Human Rights Dialogue

Let me conclude with some illustrations of how this model applies to resolving multicultural differences regarding human rights.[18] Some of the most important differences concern whether the principal bearers of rights are individuals taken in the abstract or individuals taken in their capacity as members of groups. Other important differences concern the designation and definition of human capabilities to be protected and realized. Almost everyone agrees that freedom is one such capacity, but what do we mean by that?

To take just one example, the individual freedom to choose and act in accordance with one's religious beliefs without interference by others is itself enabled by participation in a collective—specifically religious—form of life. It is also enabled by enjoying the protection of the state, having an education, and having positive access to countless other resources and opportunities. What counts as a "baseline" set of necessary resources and opportunities will doubtless vary depending on how a given culture relates human nature to the cosmos and to the sacral source of meaning and value. The point is to engage different cultural sensibilities in dialogue with one another in ways that will enrich and deepen our understanding of the limits and possibilities of human realization.

Three examples drawn from the human rights dialogue between East and West illustrate how this can happen. The first example illustrates the way in which Eastern religion and Western rationalism can combine to create a new respect for environmental rights. Such rights seem paradoxical because they protect our domination of nature by limiting it. Affirming neither the active agency (autonomy) nor the passive dependency (heteronomy) of individuals vis-à-vis nature, they aim at affirming something in-between that designates the complementary interrelationship between these opposed terms. Following the thought of theologian Raimon Panikkar,[19] Dallmayr believes that this "cosmotheandric" perspective (which Panikkar designates by the word "ontonomy") indicates a new phase in the secularization of religion:

> What is coming into view in our age—partly as a result of secularisation—is the perspective of a "theandric" or "cosmotheandric" ontonomy that stresses the integral connection between the divine, the human, and nature (or cosmos). What this outlook opposes above all are traditional metaphysical dualisms or dichotomies. . . . Human beings in this view are considered neither as sovereign agents nor as passive victims of authority but rather as participants in the ongoing disclosure or epiphany of "being," in the effort of a "consecratio mundi" pervading the deepest strands of reality.[20]

To paraphrase Panikkar and Dallmayr, the secularization of religion brings about a corresponding sacralization of being (human and natural) in which "hunger, injustice, the exploitation of man and earth, intolerance, totalitarian movements, war, the denial of human rights, colonialism and neo-colonialism" are perceived to be religious problems, or problems concerning the transcendent holistic integrity of life itself.[21] This is one lesson that the West, with its egocentric will to power, can learn from Buddhist liberation theology. For Dallmayr, citing the Indian philosopher D. P. Chattopadhyaya, "freedom's aporetic status does not yield to a cognitive-theoretical solution offered in a spectatorial stance; if at all, its enigma can only be resolved in a participatory stance or mode of public action—though an action which is not willfully self-centered but rather self-transcending."[22] In sum, it can only be hoped that the anthropocentric individualism of Western humanism and the cosmocentric ecologism of Eastern Reform Buddhism can mutually enlarge and elevate one another in supporting norms of nonviolence, individual responsibility, and democracy capable of combating predatory globalization.[23]

The second example that illustrates the potential of an East–West dialogue on human rights is China's embrace of the Universal Declaration of Human Rights after having formerly denounced it as bourgeois ideology. What we see in this embrace is another important attempt at integrating Western individualism with Eastern holism, but this time the focus is on integrating individual freedom and communal duty. The result is a concept of human rights that has been shorn of any reference to proprietary individualism. Roger Ames notes that the Chinese word for human rights (*ch'uan-li*) has a nonlegalistic meaning that, in Confucian ethics, resonates more with ritual customs of proper behavior.[24] Embedded in the correlative notion of human nature (*jen hsing*), right is what enables the individual to realize his or her proper nature as a part of—rather than in opposition to—a community. Contrary to Western natural law tradition, Chinese custom sees rights as conventions, or ad hoc negotiated agreements that facilitate the carrying out of differential roles. Accommodating differences means that "equality" is conceived differently, often in terms of a balancing of privileges and duties over a lifetime (one's duties as a child are balanced by one's privileges as a parent). China's many constitutions reflect this conventional wisdom. Instead of seeking to settle universally valid ideals once and for all, they aim to maintain harmonious relations under ever-changing and diverse circumstances. Hence, rather than instantiating abstract principles of conflict resolution based on the notion of a social contract between self-interested persons and potential adversaries, they propose concrete substantive policies for mutual self-realization. The emphasis on local context and community means that democratic deliberation will find greater purchase at that level—in peasant and worker collectives—than at the national level.

The Chinese interpretation of human rights no doubt leaves much to be desired (by purchasing flexibility at the cost of sacrificing determinacy, it makes the meaning and enforcement of rights less certain and thereby subject to greater judicial and administrative discretion). But it teaches us at least one important lesson: that individual freedom is dependent on and limited by communal integrity. Too, it teaches us that equal justice—and equal rights—need not require treating everyone in exactly the same way, in total indifference to their different positions within society.

This last point leads directly to my third and final example: the differential treatment accorded to men and women in Islamic society. Few deny that giving equal rights to women is important for global well-being; as Amartya Sen has argued,[25] societies that go beyond minimal decency and empower women to vote, run for political office, receive and use education, and own and manage property (such as the Indian state of Kerala) show the simplest, most effective and most acceptable way to ease the kind of overpopulation that drives immigration.

The treatment of women under Islam, however, seems difficult to reconcile with the Western model of human rights. Under Islam, women are indeed ascribed equal dignity and worth, but in their limited capacity as domestic caregivers and political subordinates. Abdullahi Ahmed An-Na'im has written eloquently of the difficulties involved in implementing equal rights for women in Islamic countries.[26] The justification for and interpretation of human rights is framed by *Shari'a,* or divine law, which does not grant full equality to women and non-Muslims. Women enjoy full rights to own and dispose of property and to conclude contracts. They are guaranteed specific inheritance shares and other familial rights. However, whereas men are granted up to four wives and are entitled to divorce them at will, women are restricted to one husband and can seek divorce only under very limited conditions. Women receive only half an inheritance share and less compensation for criminal bodily harm. Women are generally judged incompetent to testify in criminal proceedings and their testimony is worth half of a man's in civil proceedings. *Shari'a* holds that men are guardians of women and may beat them "lightly" if they become "unruly." Meanwhile, women may not hold offices of authority over men. (Incidentally, non-Muslims living in traditional Islamic societies are also denied full rights. While they are secured their basic property, security, and civil rights, they must pay a special tax [*jiziya*] and are forbidden to proselytize and hold public positions of authority over Muslims. Muslims who leave the faith are subject to the law of apostasy, which is punishable by death in some jurisdictions.)

Despite these challenges to cultivating equal rights for women in the context of Islamic law, it is important to note that the law can be interpreted in ways that affirm the dignity of all persons without regard to gender, race, nationality, or religion (Surah 49:13). The interpretation of *Shari'a* based on the early Mecca teachings of Mohammad, before the flight to Medina and the establishment of a Muslim state, refer to humanity as a whole or to all "children of Adam" (The Holy Quran 17:70). The conservative, Wahhabi sect of Sunni Islam dominant in Saudi Arabia and the literalist Hanbali school of jurisprudence associated with it invoke the interpretative doctrine of supercession (*naskh*) in arguing that the later writings of the Medina period accurately preserve the complete and final meaning of the earlier writings.[27] But Shiism and branches of Sufism (Islamic mysticism) view the revelation of divine meaning as a dynamic and progressive process. The Mevlevi Order founded in thirteenth-century Turkey and the Republican Brotherhood founded in the twentieth century by Mahmoud Mohamad Taha in Sudan (of which Abdullahi Ahmed An-Na'im is a follower) also encourage individual appropriation of divine texts through spiritual exercise and secular education.

Dallmayr himself devotes considerable attention to discussing the progressive, democratic strands of Islam as exemplified in the writings of such thinkers as Iranian philosopher Abdolkarim Soroush.[28] Although he does not address the problematic status of women in Islamic society, Dallmayr does remark that the divide between Western "secular" rationalism and Islamic holism presents a significant challenge that will have to be met before the question of liberalization and democratization can be fully resolved. In his forceful phrasing of the problem, "Islamic revivalism necessarily is at odds with the basic features of modern life—given that, in its core, 'modernity' (at least in its Western form) aims at the disaggregation and radical diffusion of the unified, holistic worldviews and political structures of an earlier age."[29]

To appreciate the depth of this divide one need only turn to the striking differences between Islamic and Western traditions of natural law.[30] Islamic traditions collapse natural law—or universal morality as revealed by reason—into divine law, whereas Western traditions (including Catholic Thomism) distinguish them. This difference has a deeper religious basis. Christian teaching since St. Augustine has emphasized the divided nature of humanity: the doctrine of original sin posits an infinite and unbridgeable gap between "rational" human nature and divinity, which is reflected in theological and human divisions (trinitarianism, the separation between ecclesiastical and secular powers, and the separation and dispersal of humanity from itself and from God). The logical trajectory of this movement was a Reformation whose pessimism regarding the capacity of human beings to redeem themselves and be one with God's knowledge (divine predestination) encouraged an epistemological and theological modesty conducive to the toleration of differences as well as skepticism regarding government amelioration of social inequality.

Islam, by contrast, does not recognize original sin and instead accepts the human capacity to achieve revelation of the unity (*tawhid*), harmony, and order of a creation that is in perfect oneness with Allah. Personalism, individualism, and pluralism—and therewith, separation of church and state—are less compatible with it. Although it allows the differential treatment of men and women, in principle it is opposed to distinctions based on race and class and enjoins the state to assist the poor (all Muslims are required to pay alms—the *zakat*, or about 2 percent of one's income). Unlike Western natural law traditions, Islamic teaching acknowledges the basic duty of state and community to provide for the economic subsistence and welfare of everyone. In addition to its stronger commitment to economic rights, Islamic tradition acknowledges the importance of social consensus (*ijima*) and consultation (*shura*) in collectively interpreting legal principles that are not clearly defined by the Qur'an and other holy traditions. In combination with the commitment to just community, these ideals provide a basis for popular, democratic participation in governance, however constrained by accepted religious authority.

In sum, however much some currents of Islamic legal interpretation recognize the equal rights of women in society, many others do not. Here we encounter trenchant differences in worldview that obstruct the full and equal realization of certain categories of human rights. Dialogue aimed at mutual understanding—among different strands of Islamic thought and between these strands and Western currents—can, however, lead to a loosening of dogmatic and literalist approaches to legal interpretation over time. Such an Islamic Reform would likely favor less authoritarian and more individual-centered appropriations of holy texts, thereby opening the way for a fuller appreciation of equal liberal and democratic rights for all. Conversely, dialogue between Western and Islamic legal traditions could lead the former to (re)acknowledge the fundamental community and interdependence of all "the children of Adam," thereby motivating it to take positive initiative in ameliorating economic inequalities between rich and poor countries.

Toward a Plural Cosmopolis

The three examples discussed above underscore the importance of resolving disagreements over the interpretation of human rights in accordance with the three-stage model outlined earlier. What these examples show is that it is futile to try to resolve trenchant disagreements in the definition of human rights using the model of dialogue conceived as argumentation. Argumentation already presupposes substantial agreement on the meanings attached to the language in use. Our examination of Buddhist, Chinese, and Islamic interpretations of human rights shows how little agreement there actually is between Western and Eastern notions of "right." In short, we cannot expect agreement on the concrete definition of rights without first reaching agreement on the deeper metaphysical relationships linking humanity, nature, and God, on one hand, and individual freedom and communal well-being, on the other. For it is within this nexus of relationships that "we" understand our most basic capabilities and, therefore, our most basic rights.

Argumentation, then, cannot mark the first stage in a civil dialogue on human rights, even if it might be a necessary final stage. Before that stage is reached, global dialogue must assume the form of an exploration of differences with the aim of reaching mutual understanding. Only by passing through this stage can interlocutors learn to trust one another enough for them to critically modify those aspects of their "being" in light of the authority and wisdom of the other.

None of what I have said diminishes the importance of preparatory stages of dialogue that might more appropriately be described as "exploratory negotiations." Before the real task of understanding gets underway, interlocutors must agree on the most general and superficial terms of discourse. The debate on human rights has already reached this level, where it is understood by all parties that certain general norms must be respected, even if each party interprets these norms in fundamentally different—and even opposed—ways. Prior to attaining this level of dialogue purely strategic negotiations involving minimal levels of trust and respect may be in order. Last but not least, in the complete absence of understanding—and in the presence of mutual fear—letting the other "live" so long as s/he "lets live" in return is at least a beginning when the only other option is war.

But "live and let live" cannot be a viable long-term option given the reality of today's global world. The problems of the world—ranging from water and resource depletion, climatic change, and environmental devastation to genocide and other systemic rights violations—demand solutions that will come about only through sustained dialogue involving us all. Indeed, only by "fusing" the Western secular tradition of liberal democracy with the Eastern spiritual tradition of holistic community—in effect, expanding the concept of dialogue to include nature and God—will these problems be properly understood in all of their secular and sacral significance. Such a mutual interpenetration and transformation of cultural standpoints would point the way toward redeeming the community of all living creatures from the narrow greed and wide destruction unleashed by global capitalism. At the same time, it would preserve the single most valuable contribution the capitalist economy has made to the modern world: the use of reason as a basis for individual freedom. Fusing West and East in this way would involve nothing less than fusing reason and faith—in Hegel's terms, articulating differences within the broader horizon of an ever-changing, ever-dissolving and expanding unity. As Dallmayr phrases it:

> In our globalizing age, the correlation of faith and reason carries into the relationship between historical faith traditions and the broader conversation of humankind, a conversation that includes as participants a variety of religious and non-religious voices. In this broader context, every particular faith tradition is compelled to look at itself both from the inside and the outside, that is, to shoulder the dual task of self-affirmation and self-assessment or self-critique. For a weak or shallow faith, this task is likely to be further debilitating and perhaps destructive. A living faith, however, will welcome the challenge of re-interpretation as the gateway to continuous self-renewal and reformation.[31]

NOTES

1. Fred Dallmayr, *Dialogue among Civilizations: Some Exemplary Voices* (New York: Palgrave Macmillan, 2002).

2. Samuel P. Huntington, *The Clash of Civilizations and the Remaking of World Order* (New York: Simon and Schuster, 1996).

3. John Rawls, *Political Liberalism* (New York: Columbia University Press, 1992), and *The Law of Peoples* (Cambridge: Harvard University Press, 1999).

4. Jürgen Habermas, "The Unity of Reason in the Diversity of Its Voices," in *Postmetaphysical Thinking: Philosophical Essays*, trans. William M. Hohengarten (Cambridge: MIT Press, 1992); Dallmayr, *Dialogue among Civilizations*, pp. 43–45.

5. Dallmayr, "Cosmopolitanism: Moral and Political," *Political Theory* 31 (June 2003): 421–42.

6. Ibid., p. 434.

7. Ibid., p. 429.

8. Dallmayr, *Dialogue among Civilizations*, chap. 4.

9. Rawls, *Law of Peoples*, pp. 125, 152, 171.

10. Ibid., p. 65.

11. Ibid., p. 80.

12. Donald Davidson, *Inquiries into Truth and Interpretation* (Oxford: Oxford University Press, 1984). Rawls refers to a "plurality of conflicting and incommensurable doctrines" in *Political Liberalism*, p. 135.

13. Jean-François Lyotard, *Le Différend* (Paris: Les Éditions de Minuit, 1983).

14. Charles Taylor, *The Sources of the Self: The Making of Modern Identity* (Cambridge: Harvard University Press, 1989), p. 510.

15. Dallmayr, *Dialogue among Civilizations*, p. 45.

16. Hans-Georg Gadamer, *Truth and Method* (New York: Seabury, 1975).

17. Cf. my essay "Jürgen Habermas and Hans-Georg Gadamer," in *Blackwell Guide to Continental Philosophy*, ed. R. Solomon and D. Sherman (New York: Blackwell, 2003).

18. For a more detailed discussion of the theory of rights proposed here, see my *Rights, Democracy, and Fulfillment in the Era of Identity Politics: Principled Compromises in a Compromised World* (Lanham, Md.: Rowen and Littlefield, 2004), chaps. 6–7.

19. Raimon Panikkar, *The Cosmotheandric Experience*, ed. Scott Eastham (Maryknoll, N.Y.: Orbis Books, 1993.

20. Dallmayr, *Dialogue among Civilizations*, p. 193.

21. Ibid., p. 199.

22. Ibid., p. 211. See D. P. Chattopadhyaya, *Knowledge, Freedom and Language: An Interwoven Fabric of Man, Time, and World* (Delhi: Motilal Banarsidass, 1989).

23. K. Inada, "A Buddhist Response to the Nature of Human Rights," in *Asian Perspectives on Human Rights*, ed. C. Welsh and V. Leary (Boulder: Westview, 1990); Charles Taylor, "Conditions of an Unforced Consensus on Human Rights," in *The East Asian Challenge for Human Rights*, ed. Joanne R. Bauer and Daniel A. Bell (Cambridge: Cambridge University Press, 1999), pp. 124–44.

24. Roger Ames, "Rights as Rites: The Confucian Alternative, in *Human Rights and the World's Religions*, ed. L. Rouner (Notre Dame, Ind.: University of Notre Dame Press, 1988).

25. Amartya Sen, "Population, Delusion, and Reality," in *New York Review of Books* 41, no. 15 (September 22, 1994): 62–71.

26. Ahmed An-Na'im, *Toward an Islamic Reformation: Civil Liberties, Human Rights, and International Law* (Syracuse: Syracuse University Press, 1990).

27. Ibid., p. 21.

28. Abdolkarim Soroush, *Reason, Freedom, and Democracy in Islam: Essential Writings of Abdolkarim Soroush* (New York: Oxford University Press, 2000).

29. Dallmayr, *Dialogue among Civilizations*, p. 170.

30. Russell Powell, "A Transcendental Framework for Christian–Muslim Dialogue Using Natural Law Tradition" (2002) (unpublished).

31. Dallmayr, *Dialogue among Civilizations*, pp. 183–84.

THIRTEEN

A Thought Experiment on Cross-Cultural Dialogue and Peacemaking

Calvin O. Schrag

The contributors to the festschrift honoring the person and works of Fred Dallmayr were charged with submitting brief essays in recognition of his outstanding scholarly contribution during his distinguished career in the field of political theory. I have chosen to offer a thought experiment involving two interrelated themes that have been an integral part of his research and teaching over the years and that have been given specific attention in two of his most recent books, *Dialogue among Civilizations* and *Peace Talks.*[1]

More specifically, I intend to carry out an experiment on the bearing of cross-cultural understanding and communication on strategies for achieving global peace within the international community. Given the limitations of space due to the interest on the parts of a great many scholars in contributing to this volume, my proposed experiment is limited to what is basically a sketch of a possible wider project, resembling something like a position paper. As an admirer from a philosophical perspective of Fred's writings in the area of political theory during recent decades, I wish to shape a trajectory that aims at a convergence of philosophical understanding and political organization. Such a trajectory, plainly enough, has been at the heart of much of Fred's research and teaching throughout his illustrious career—a career in which he has been advantageously situated as a philosophical voice and a political observer.

How does the discipline of philosophy as a voice in the conversation of humankind affect policies and procedures for sociopolitical organizations? This is a question that is often asked with an undertone of causticity. What possibly does philosophy have to do with politics anyway? Is not the semiotic construct "political philosophy" simply an oxymoron or an instance of semantic dissonance? What possible landscape is there on which philosophical and political interests converge? These are the general background questions that will guide our experiment as we think with Fred Dallmayr in exploring some possible avenues along life's philosophical and political ways.

It may be necessary to remind the reader that the issues at stake in our thought experiment on reconciling philosophical and political discourse are not issues of recent origin. They extend back to Plato's *Republic,* and very likely quite beyond that. The leading and undergirding question that Plato pursues in his age-resilient dialogue becomes transparent at the outset of Socrates' engagement with his interlocutors: "What is a good state and how does one go about in setting it up?" We note that this is a compound question, consisting of two parts. It projects an inquiry into the substantive-theoretical issue of the essence or "whatness" of a good state, and it calls for a procedural-practical analysis of how to install the essence of statehood in the rough and tumble of a concrete sociohistorical existence. This was an existentially urgent question for the inhabitants of Greece during the time of Plato. Greece was just emerging from the turbulence and upheaval occasioned by the Peloponnesian War, which led to a devastating defeat of the Athenian city-state by Sparta. The political state of affairs in Athens was in shambles. The city-state of Athens needed to be reconstituted. But how ought such a reconstitution proceed? This is the initial question in Plato's classic on philosophy and politics.

Socrates, the principal spokesperson in the dialogue and the mentor of Plato, taught his student well on the requirement to integrate "what" questions with "how" questions, to align the theoretical with the practical, and to conjoin thought and action. The philosophical task, as defined by Socrates, consists in knowing what the good life is and how to live it. We also note, and rather quickly along the way, that Socrates wants his interlocutors to understand that a search for the essence of a city-state works hand in glove with the determinant of ideality. Forms, in Plato's rather encompassing celestial citadel, have both a descriptive and a prescriptive denotation. They at once provide descriptions of what *is* the case and prescriptions for what *ought* to be the case, whether one deals with the lofty moral forms of wisdom, courage, temperance, and justice; the mathematical forms; or the forms of artifacts and natural kinds.

I have defined the task in my contribution as that of exploring the terrain of philosophy as politics and the terrain of politics as philosophy as we address the extensive scholarly contributions of Fred Dallmayr. I elected to begin with Plato's question regarding the ingredients of a good state and the measures required for its implementation. There are risks in doing this. Even though we may be quite ready to accord an intrinsic legitimacy and continuing relevance to the question itself as posed by Plato, there is no assurance that our answer to the question will be commensurate with his. Plainly enough, in addressing the question we are positioned at a different time and a different place.

In traversing the landscape from the ancient regime to that of the medievals, then to the moderns, and then later still to the postmoderns, it should come as a surprise to no one that the framework of questioning as regards the nature and role of political institutions undergoes significant modification. Clearly, the meaning of "state" does not attach to an abiding signifier. The city-state of the ancients is not the territorial feudal enclave of the medievals nor is it the nation-state of the moderns. An even more radical shift of reference occurs as one moves from the modern to the postmodern polis. Here one encounters not only problems in locating the proper referent in a semantics of "statehood," but also a profound uneasiness in regard to the semantic utility of "good." This complicates our experiment in seeking to achieve an understanding of "state" and "good" for the present age.

Samuel Huntington has been very much in the news for modulating the sense and reference in postmodern politics by proposing a vocabulary shift from a "clash of nation-states" to a "clash of civilizations." Admittedly, the concept of "civilization," which has been in the lexicon for some time, is not without its vagaries. Nonetheless, its usage has the advantage of calling one's attention to the political reality of an emerging world society that is no longer constituted by self-enclosed national enclaves, but rather one that is comprised of a configuration of cultural complexes that transcend the identities of modern nation-states.[2]

This complex landscape of contemporary politics intensifies the challenge to the projects that Fred Dallmayr has so masterfully pursued in his recent writings, *Dialogue among Civilizations* and *Peace Talks*. Given a clash of cultures overriding national identities, how does one achieve cross-cultural understanding and what are the available resources for implementing peace initiatives within a global body politic? What resources of communication are available for dealing with ideological conflicts, and how does one engage in peacemaking given the agonistic proclivities of postmodern politics with its preference for intervention over dialogue?

In the face of these apparent obstacles I propose a thought experiment consisting in transversal, cross-cultural understanding and communication. The operative term in this experiment is "transversal," which is proposed in the hope of avoiding some of the traditional glitches that travel with the uses of dialogue to ground claims for universality. To be sure, the concept of transversality has been in the vocabulary of academe for some time. It has done service in the disciplines of topology (as a generalization of orthogonality); physics (calculation of the ratio of accelerating force through the determination of transverse mass); anatomy (dynamics of the vertebrae); physiology (overlapping fibers); literary theory (structure of the novel); philosophy (unity of consciousness); and the social sciences (organizational communication). As we proceed in the effort of examining its applicability to the field of political science, we must keep in mind the root meaning of transversality that runs through its usage in the associated disciplines—convergence without coincidence, unity without identity, commonality without equivalence, assimilation without absorption, and cooperation without uniformity—setting forth a splitting of the difference between bedrock universality and unmanageable particularity.[3]

Let us suppose that the goal of dialogue in our efforts toward cross-cultural communication is not to achieve universal claims on knowledge and value, but rather to achieve an understanding and appreciation of divergent forms of discourse and action that extend across the boundaries of national identities. Let us further suppose that dialogue issues not from a fixation on sameness wherewith to establish a solidarity of unimpeachable consensus, but instead moves out from a transversal matrix in which the interlocutors remain respectful of the integrity of the proponents of differing perspectives, recognizing that otherness is constitutive of cultural understanding. Instead of an impediment to cross-cultural communication, otherness contributes a dialectical enrichment to the discourse on the requirements of the political. Communication across cultural divides moves about within the delicate balance of understanding *in spite of differences* and understanding *because of differences.* Comprehending dialogue within the political arena in this way would protect against the intrusions of "Orientalism"—a mindset that has wreaked havoc on the scene of international politics far too long. Orientalism is the doctrine that the "otherness" of the other culture constitutes a threat to one's national interests and must be contained if not indeed expunged. The first principle of Orientalism is that otherness needs to be reduced to sameness, opening the flood gates to conquest and colonialism, imperialism and genocide.[4]

It may well be that one of the most singularly important contributions of postmodern thought has been that of calling our attention to the vital significance of the vocabulary of difference and otherness. Clearly this vocabulary is not a recent invention. It was already given a prominent role to play in Plato's *Sophist,* where it became a marker for one of the ontological components in Plato's celebrated theory of "the greatest kinds of forms," along with the kindred components of identity or sameness and being itself. What one learns from Plato's intricate ontological schematization in the *Sophist* is that difference/otherness remains within the citadel of being as presence. To say that an entity is different or other than another entity, to say that it "is not," does not catapult us into an unintelligible chaos of nonbeing, as the followers of Parmenides had maintained. It is rather to articulate that the forms in question have not been properly combined. When I say that an entity illustrates the form of quadruped when in fact it is a biped, I am mistaken because "quadruped" does not properly combine or blend with "biped." A quadruped *is not* a biped. In the kingdom of forms, some combine and others do not. Assertions about not-being or difference/otherness are not assertions that have nothing at all before the mind but rather put into play the form of difference/otherness, which is itself constitutive of the entity in question. The not-being a quadruped remains constitutive of being a biped. Not-being as difference/otherness retains its liaison with being. Of everything that is one can offer a finite number of positive predicates that define what it is and an infinite number of negations that provide information of what it is not. Negative statements, within an ontology of difference/otherness, do not fall outside the landscape of being. They refer to a presence by virtue of their dialectical tie to identity or sameness.

As every schoolchild encountering the history of philosophy knows, the concept of difference/otherness unfolds as a serpentine development from the early Greeks to the medievals to the moderns and the postmoderns—

and it is the latter who have called the world's attention to the devalorization, if not indeed demonization, of the other in the history of Western metaphysics as a "white mythology," with its accompanying logocentrism, ethnocentrism, and phallocentrism.[5] That which is other than controlling and objectivating rationality, other than one's racial origins and ethnic beliefs, other than male-oriented perspectives is disparaged and despised. Otherness becomes a veritable coefficient of alienation, a threat to self understanding and social formation. The impact of such a disparaging read of otherness on cross-cultural communication is difficult to overestimate, and this is particularly the case when dialogues between West and East become inhibited by an insinuation of Eurocentrism. Fred Dallmayr, in his pointed discussion of "Western Culture and its 'Other,'" sums up matters rather nicely in the concluding paragraph of the chapter, by quoting Gadamer.

> So it may not be too bold to draw a final political consequence from our discussion, namely: that we may perhaps survive as humankind if—instead of simply exploiting our arsenals of power and control—we would stop and respect the Other as other, where the latter embraces nature as well as the grown cultures of peoples and nations, and if we thus could learn to experience otherness and the others as the "other" of ourselves in order to partake in one another.[6]

If the postmodern global political landscape indeed changes from that of a conflict of nation-states to a clash of civilizations, as Samuel Huntington would have us believe, then plainly enough our views of national identity, informed by a negativity of otherness, will need to undergo some revision. The identification of who we are will no longer find its decisive determinant in the shape, color, and number of our passports. A postnational culture requires new forms of self-understanding and societal formation, auguring in the direction of a transcultural consciousness and a postnational identity.

Addressing actual and potential clashes and conflicts on the global scene will require a transcendence of nation-state boundaries and lines of demarcation. Cross-cultural dialogue must take every opportunity to revitalize and implement the concept of a "world citizenship" that strives for respect of the multiple profiles of cultural forms (ethical, legal, economic, and religious) without seeking to reduce them to a common denominator—and, if this fails, without resorting to traditional strategies of conquest or indeed genocide. Admittedly, the task is a foreboding one, but unless it is under-taken we stand in peril of a continuing global terrorism of cultural imperial-ism and political subjugation.

It is at this juncture that the call for strategies of transversal communi-cation—strategies that inform a cross-cultural dialogue that is respectful of differences—converges with the implementation of peace initiatives, open-ing avenues for meliorating the clashes in the postmodern "clash of civiliza-tions." Peacemaking works hand in glove with persistent efforts to commu-nicate across divergent beliefs and practices. The power and resources of language, conferred on the human species as illustrative of a *homo narrans,* is a principal resource for the maintenance of a peaceful existence. Language opens a space for action. Discourse issues a call to social practices. Saying and doing, speech and action, conspire to produce entwined forms of communi-cative praxis. Plainly enough, the language and discourse that animates di-alogic interaction is more than the transmission of information and exchange of messages in cyberspace. It occasions openings to landscapes of creative human endeavor.

Implications for concrete political action follow directly from this amal-gam of discourse and action, linking communicative and peacemaking ven-tures, giving rise to the resources of a diplomacy that takes precedence over the technology for waging war. The task of a peace-oriented diplomacy, grounded in the transversality of cross-cultural understanding and commu-nication, is to decouple the nation-state apparatus from the war machine and to delimit the role of national identity in the shaping of political policy. This in turn would encourage a mindset of postnational identity and provide a bulwark against preemptive wars and unilateralism on the part of nation-states.

On the heels of a recognition of the need to move beyond national iden-tities to ground policies and procedures for a possible postnational politics, there is an emergent issue that will require careful consideration by both theo-rists and political activists across the board. The issue that comes to the fore calls for a critical examination of international politics based on the proto-cols of the United Nations. If the voice of nation-states, with their nation-making marks of identity, no longer provides the platform for political action, new forms of organization will be required. If not straightforwardly disman-tled as a vehicle for global peace, the United Nations will need to be robustly delimited as an agency for dealing with the clash of civilizations, even though the ideals that informed the U.N. charter can be salvaged. What is required is a new structure for mediating global conflict, shifting attention away from voices of national interests to the configuration of voices in a global society that speak across differing cultural beliefs and practices, ever striving for a convergence without coincidence.

In pursuit of global peace initiatives, the accentuated delimiting of the nation-state apparatus, with its accompanying technology of the war machine, has the radical consequence of placing into question the long-standing ontology of friend-versus-enemy polarization. Jacques Derrida, in his provocative little volume *The Politics of Friendship,* broaches a critique of that ontology by way of a radicalization of the meaning of friendship as it augurs in the direction of a democracy "always yet to come," with its aspirations for a global justice anchored in civic responsibility and public legitimation.[7] An even more radical deconstruction of the friend–enemy ontological matrix is offered by Søren Kierkegaard in his masterful *Works of Love,* in which he provides a hermeneutic on the imperative to love one's neighbor as oneself. The enemy too, avers Kierkegaard, is a neighbor, someone who is "near-by" in the space of a neighborhood that reaches beyond geometric coordinates. As such the friend and enemy share a common earth, and in their common bond as neighbors solicit from each other a transcending and unconditional love, beyond all economics of immanent exchange relations in which love remains conditioned by expectations of return.[8]

Like Derrida's democracy of friendship as promise of event always yet to unfold in an immemorial time, situated within a messianic horizon, so also Kierkegaard's kingdom of unconditional love is eschatologically defined, located in a dimension of hope. Derrida's envisioning of a politics of friendship with its justice and equality for all illustrates a "messianicity" without "messianism," a messianic call that functions as "the opening to the future or to the coming of the other as the advent of justice."[9] Kierkegaard's eschatology of an unconditional love of neighbor that overrides the distinction between friend and enemy opens toward a time of promise beyond the fragility and fractures of a vulnerable finite existence. Truth to tell, Derrida's democracy of friendship yet to come and Kierkegaard's kingdom of economic love in which friends and enemies acknowledge each other as neighbors illustrate the workings of what Derrida has named an "impossible possibility."

The envisioned democracy of friendship and kingdom of love are impossible as historically actualized states of affairs, given the frailty of terrestrial finitude; but they are possible as continuing preenactments of a vision for global peace and social harmony. Situated beyond the topos of historical existence, they remain *trans*historical, albeit not *a*historical. And it is at this juncture that we are able to discern a somewhat unexpected return to the introduction of our thought experiment with its recollection of Plato's *Republic*—unexpected because one might wonder what the premodern politics of Plato could possibly have to do with the postmodern politics of our present age. Often overlooked in Socrates' dialogic exchange with Glaucon on the nature and implementation of the ideal city-state is when Glaucon reaches the point where he is unable to contain his exuberance and presses Socrates to announce when this state will come to pass in the civil society of Athens. Socrates's response is measured and straightforward. The ideal state, designed in accord with the eternal forms of wisdom, courage, temperance, and justice is precisely an *ideal*, laid up in heaven as it were, capable of actualization only to the degree that such is possible for finite beings. So it is that from Plato, Kierkegaard, and Derrida we are able to learn that the impossible, in the affairs of both our personal and civic existence, retains its validity as a condition for the possible.

Notes

1. Fred Dallmayr, *Dialogue among Civilizations: Some Exemplary Voices* (New York: Palgrave Macmillan, 2002), and *Peace Talks—Who Will Listen?* (Notre Dame, Ind.: University of Notre Dame Press, 2004).

2. Samuel P. Huntington, *The Clash of Civilizations and the Remaking of World Order* (New York: Simon and Schuster, 1996).

3. For a discussion of the philosophical use of the concept of transversality, see my *The Resources of Rationality: A Response to the Postmodern Challenge* (Bloomington: Indiana University Press, 1992), particularly chapter 6, "Transversal Rationality," pp. 148–79.

4. One of the more penetrating and multifaceted discussions of the meaning and misfortunes of Orientalism can be found in Edward W. Said, *Orientalism* (New York: Vintage Books, 1979).

5. See Jacques Derrida, "White Mythology: Metaphor in the Text of Philosophy," in *Margins of Philosophy*, trans. Alan Bass (Chicago: University of Chicago Press, 1982), pp. 207–71.

6. Dallmayr, *Dialogue among Civilizations,* p. 65.

7. Jacques Derrida, *The Politics of Friendship,* trans. George Collins (New York: Verso Press, 1997).

8. Søren Kierkegaard, *Works of Love,* trans. Howard V. Hong and Edna H. Hong (Princeton: Princeton University Press, 1995).

9. Jacques Derrida, "Faith and Knowledge," in *Religion,* ed. Jacques Derrida and Gianni Vattimo (Stanford: Stanford University Press, 1998), p. 17.

Response

Fred Dallmayr

Getting old is no accomplishment, but it is an opportunity: it allows one to reflect calmly and in a more seasoned way on issues that have preoccupied and sometimes tormented one in earlier decades. It also permits one to reflect on the path—or rather the jumble of paths—that one has tended to pursue in preference over other paths or "roads not chosen." Actually, the direction of one's life and thought is only to a very small extent the result of free-standing choice; in large measure, the direction is the consequence of opaque cues or hunches, of recessed dispositions, and of the challenges and provocations that fortune or misfortune places on one's way. In my own case, intellectual initiatives—in terms of writings or arguments—have never been entirely self-generated or self-produced; they have always been a response to, or "responsive" to, certain quandaries or dilemmas that questions of friend or colleagues, or else historical circumstances, have imposed on me. With regard to friends and colleagues, intellectual engagements have by necessity the character of conversations—which means that responses can never be definitive or claim to "solve" questions once and for all. There is always room for new inquiries and rejoinders—just as there is ample space for misunderstandings, silent chiasms, and innuendoes.

The "response" that I am offering in the present context needs to be seen in this light. I am deeply grateful to the colleagues and friends who have contributed essays to this volume. I know their busy schedules and multiple commitments. Many of the contributors have been friends for several decades: they have accompanied me on my life's journey, and their presence—either near or more distant—has nurtured and stimulated my own thinking, even (or especially) when we were not always in full accord. Some contributors are junior colleagues whose own academic journey has intersected with mine more recently, in (I hope) a mutually beneficial and enriching manner.

Three of the contributors are former students whom I had the privilege of guiding through graduate degree programs toward their own academic careers. The editor of the present volume, Stephen Schneck, was my first doctoral student at the University of Notre Dame. To him I owe a special debt of thanks for undertaking the labor of assembling this volume. Schneck has arranged the different contributions under three main thematic rubrics—an arrangement that seems sensible to me (despite frequent overlaps between the rubrics). In the following I shall try to respond in sequence to some of the main points—by no means all the points—raised in the individual essays, and I shall try to do so in the engaged, conversational spirit I mentioned before.

The first rubric is "Political Theory and Modern Philosophy." The section is appropriately placed at the beginning because it indicates my intellectual background and the main area of my work. Basically, my training has been in modern Western philosophy and political theory, that is, in modes of theorizing and philosophizing dominant in the West roughly since the Renaissance. Philosophically, a main source of inspiration for me—next to Herder and Hegel—has been European phenomenology as inaugurated by Edmund Husserl and continued in the offshoots of hermeneutical and existential phenomenology. In my understanding, existential phenomenology means basically a focus on lived human experience, prior or in opposition to abstract propositions, or else a thinking that is nurtured by and in turn infuses lived experience. This kind of outlook strongly shaped my early professional life (and, in fact, was never really abandoned later). The first contribution, on "Seeing the Sovereign," directly refers to this background. Written by fellow political theorist Tracy Strong, the chapter takes its departure from one of my earliest essays titled "Hobbes and Existentialism: Some Affinities."[1] What interested me in Hobbes at that time was not the Hobbes still steeped in natural law theory, nor Hobbes the intrepid social engineer, nor Hobbes the advocate of arbitrary will-to-power, but the "experiential" Hobbes—that is, the thinker taking his beginning from the elementary human dilemma of life and death, surfacing in the pervasive "fear" of violent death. (In our contemporary period of "terror" and "terror wars," this kind of Hobbes may still gain a hearing.)

To show more clearly what concerned me at the time, I may be permitted to quote a few passages from that early essay. As I indicated at the outset, my interest was not "antiquarian" or historicist in a narrow sense; rather my hope was to derive lessons for myself and for my own time (citing in support the hermeneutical maxim that interpretation always proceeds from one's "prejudgments"—which, of course, are corrigible). My main hope was to derive lessons for contemporary political theory—which, in my view, was wedged between lofty perennial formulas, on the one hand, and a myopic power-political realism, on the other (resembling the Kantian noumenal/phenomenal split). Turning to an "experiential" Hobbes seemed to provide some guidance—as long as one assumed that human experience (fear of violent death) could induce a learning experience guiding humans from a brutal, war-like situation to a more peaceful, civic condition. I found a similar outlook at the time in some French phenomenologists who insisted on an initial brokenness or "alienation" in the human condition requiring a constant effort of renegotiation of human relations predicated on experiential learning. As I stated then: "Although implanted in man by nature, reason in Hobbes's view is a tender faculty requiring cultivation and industry. Especially in the state of nature where passions abound, rational awareness is liable to be a fragile gift" demanding steady nurturing (somewhat akin to the labors of *Sisyphus* portrayed by Albert Camus). Re-reading the concluding lines of the essay, I find them more pertinent today than at the time they were written:

> Hobbes's writings may still speak to us with the voice of a contemporary. Our generation, like his, has been nearly overwhelmed by violence. How can we fail to appreciate his serenity and quiet perseverance in an age in which the potential of destruction has reached global proportions and in which civil life reveals more than ever its extreme fragility?

To be sure, as Strong notes, I did not believe then (and do not believe now) that Hobbes pursued his own thought properly to the end. Basically, Hobbes concludes his argument with the erection of an all-powerful Leviathan-state ruled by sovereign will to which citizens have to submit unless they choose to rebel by marshaling their own arbitrary will-to-power. But this cannot be the end. In my view, with the establishment of a civil condition, learning does not stop but really only begins on an interactive level where citizens come to learn about each other and their own proper interests, and where even the "sovereign" comes to learn about the well-being of citizens and about the demands of a good and just civil order. Of course, in pursuing this line of thought, Hobbes would have faced a dilemma: he would finally have encountered anew the very Aristotle whom he had so unceremoniously dismissed at the beginning of his argument. By "Aristotle" I do not mean so much the "metaphysical" thinker wedded to a substantive ontology and teleology, but rather the "practical" Aristotle delineating the complex learning processes involved in the cultivation of personal and civic virtues. No doubt, with this practical turn the entire course of modern philosophy and political theory would have been altered: away from a narrow voluntarism, nominalism, and "logocentrism" in the direction of a more engaged and participatory mode of thinking and acting (as exemplified, for example, in existential phenomenology).

Tracy Strong pursues Hobbes's "shortcoming" or incomplete development of his thought in a different direction: involving the fuller elaboration of the "representative" character of sovereignty and its inherent "theatricality." His account is nuanced and erudite; it traces the transformations of sovereign representation from Hobbes to Rousseau and all the way to Nietzsche. I do not follow him, however, in this direction. This does not mean that symbolic representation of power is not important. In an instructive manner, Eric Voegelin (in his *The New Science of Politics*) has highlighted the significance of the symbolic representation of regimes—what he calls "representation of truth"—focusing his attention chiefly on ancient and medieval traditions.[2] Following up on his account, I myself have continued the story of representation from early modernity to the present time—noting, however, a basic break or rupture in its status and public role. Referring to the work of Claude Lefort, I indicated that—in contrast to traditional metaphysics that allowed power to be substantively represented by kings or emperors—modern democracy introduces a slippage or reversal: by pushing sovereign power from the limelight into latency or concealment. In Lefort's pointed language, modern democracy transforms sovereignty into an "empty [or hidden] place" that no one can definitively occupy or represent—thus eroding the traditional "markers of certainty." To be sure, efforts have not been lacking to re-occupy and monopolize the public space—mainly through resort to nationalism, racism, and the myth of the "People-as-One"; but all these efforts are in the end illusory. As regards "theatricality," much labor goes into retrieving the pomp and circumstances of the past; but in fact, the *arcana* of government have been reduced to "show business" (performed in off-off-Broadway theaters or *Schmierentheater*).[3]

Next to the role of phenomenology in its hermeneutical and existential variants, another perspective has had a major influence on my intellectual development: that of "critical theory" as formulated by the Frankfurt School of Social Research. For many years, the two perspectives held a nearly equal attractiveness for my thinking—alternating in their appeal slightly from occasion to occasion. Stated in a simplified manner, phenomenology appealed to me mainly for philosophical reasons, critical theory more for its political (and social-scientific) implications. The combined influence of the two perspectives was for me a challenge and an agony: although perhaps not incompatible, they were also not obviously in accord (as reflected in the quarrels between representatives of the two schools). Over the years, I managed to establish in my mind a tenuous truce or symbiosis of the respective influences—a truce reflected in the title of one of my books, *Between Freiburg and Frankfurt,* and in the use of such labels as "critical phenomenology" or "critical ontology."[4] To a significant degree, the truce was facilitated by certain features of the "early" Frankfurt school that seemed to me then (and still seem to me today) to show affinities with the works of "Freiburg" thinkers. Among early Frankfurt theorists, the writings of Adorno, Horkheimer, and Benjamin have from early on held great fascination for me. My second book, titled *Twilight of Subjectivity* (1981), contained extensive references to these writers, and above all to Theodor Adorno's *Negative Dialectics* and his views on natural history. As I stated then, echoing Adorno: the traditional *reductio ad hominem* inaugurated by Descartes and Enlightenment philosophy "has to be replaced by or at least coupled with a 'reductio hominis'—the debunking of anthropocentric pretensions (which is not synonymous with the elimination of reflection in favor of objectivism)."[5]

My fascination for Adorno never ceased, as is reflected in several of my subsequent writings. The second contribution to this volume, written by political theorist Morton Schoolman, appropriately stresses the impact of Adorno's work on contemporary thought, especially in the field of aesthetics. As he shows, Adorno's initiatives in this field have been controversial—but often for the wrong reasons: analytical and neo-Kantian thinkers (some of them younger members of the Frankfurt school) have denounced Adorno's thought as "irrational" because not in conformity with the standards of apodictic reasoning. Schoolman bravely rebuts this charge by arguing that "reason" is not the monopoly of apodictic rationalists and that it makes sense to speak of a distinctive "aesthetic reason" in Adorno's vein. On this issue, I wholeheartedly applaud his contribution. For too long, it seems to me, "rationality" and "irrationality" have served as weapons of abuse—with the latter being chiefly directed against artists and literary humanists. I also applaud his recuperation of the notion of "mimesis" as an ingredient of aesthetics—regardless of whether mimesis is seen as part of aesthetic reason or as a preform of rationality (Günter Figal) or an inherent potentiality for reason (Ulrich Müller). Schoolman seems to me on target when he writes that "aesthetic reason becomes the praxis of thinking that establishes the primacy of aesthetic rationality not only over instrumental reason, but over every form of thought resting on the principle that thinking can [fully] overcome the difference between an object and its concept" or between sensibility and cognition. As he adds: "Aesthetic reason's relentless assault on [abstract] rationality is hardly a retreat from rationality, but supposes reason's capacity to make rationality its own achievement."

Among Adorno's arsenal of aesthetic categories, none has been more severely castigated than his notion of "mimesis." While Jürgen Habermas denounced it as a relapse into primitive "impulses," Seyla Benhabib rebuked it as "fuzzy precisely because it cannot suggest a real alternative to relations of domination."[6] Schoolman credits me with having moved some distance beyond these reductive criticisms. Referring to my *Between Freiburg and Frankfurt*, he finds there a "perceptive reading" that locates mimesis on a "quasi-sensual" level, approximating it to an "anti-instrumental, reflective form of play." By virtue of its playful character, he notes, mimesis in my account serves as a bridge "between the cognitive and noncognitive," between sensibility and intelligibility, thus resisting its reduction to a primitive or unreflective naturalism. I appreciate Schoolman's attentiveness to my comments in the cited text—comments I have tried to elaborate and deepen in some subsequent writings. In an essay penned at the time of Hans-Georg Gadamer's hundredth anniversary, I argued that Adorno's notion of mimesis was meant as an antidote both to the instrumental mastery of nature (inaugurated by Bacon and Descartes) and the lapse into mere naturalism (along Darwinian lines). By contrast to these alternatives, I stated, "Adorno recommends not a naturalistic mimicry, but rather a new form of 'mimesis' involving a reflective 'opening up' of reason"—an opening up to the resources beyond reason's cognitive control. In light of this liberating potential, Adorno's entire *Aesthetic Theory* can be read as a document counseling not nostalgia but "resistance in the midst of industrial and commercialized society."[7]

The third contribution, by philosopher Thomas McCarthy, pinpoints clearly some important crossroads and partings of the ways along my intellectual journey. Together with McCarthy I published one of my first edited volumes, dealing with *Understanding and Social Inquiry* (1977). We were linked by both a shared interest in social science methodology and a joint attachment to the Frankfurt school, including the early writings of Habermas. As it seemed to me, these early writings—including *Theory and Praxis* and *Knowledge and Human Interests*—showed a close affinity with accents manifest in existential phenomenology. As in the case of the latter, the emphasis seemed to rest on correlation rather than separation, on bridging rather than dividing—as was evident, for example, in the linkage between theory and praxis and between knowledge or cognition and interested motivation. It was only subsequently, in the aftermath of *Knowledge and Human Interests,* that Habermas introduced sharp "cuts" or chiasms into his work: cuts between rationality and interested praxis, between knowledge and existential motivation. It was at this point that he launched a critique of hermeneutics in favor of an "emancipatory" social-science methodology, and more generally a broad-scale attack on "Nietzscheans" and other presumed "irrationalists" (including members of the early Frankfurt school). From my angle, this move appeared, and could only appear, as a return to a very traditional kind of rationalism—a rationalism hovering in midair adrift from concrete engagements. This impression persisted despite a much-vaunted "linguistic turn" accompanying the move: that is, the turn beyond Kantian, egological reflection to language and communication. While appreciating this concern with language, I felt then (and still feel today) that the program of "communicative rationality" exhibited an excess of cognitive rationality and a shortfall of engaged communication. Aggravated by some additional features— including (what seems to me) a dogmatic or visceral anti-Heideggerianism— the sketched developments were bound to lead over time to a certain intellectual (though not necessarily a personal) parting of the ways.

To return to the third contribution: as the sketched developments occurred, McCarthy preferred to stay closer to Habermas and his circle. As a result, the emerging difference between Habermas and me translated into a distinct divergence (again intellectual not personal) between McCarthy and myself. His essay pinpoints sharply the nature of our divergence. "Our disagreements," he writes, "are not haphazard but consistent; they might be characterized roughly as stemming from the differences between his brand of hermeneutics and my brand of critical theory, or between his sources of inspiration in Hegel and Heidegger and my own in Kant and Habermas." I fully concur with this characterization (although I would like to add Aristotle to my sources of inspiration—I mean again the "practical" rather than metaphysical Aristotle). I also agree that these are "reasonable disagreements" allowing for considerable "overlapping consensus," including an overlap on the idea and prospect of a "multicultural cosmopolitanism." But, of course, the roads we travel toward this goal are different and need to be respected in their difference. Obviously, I would not have followed my path (inspired by Aristotle-Hegel-Heidegger), if I had found the alternative route equally persuasive and cogent. As it happens, I find the latter route not only not fully persuasive but also in many ways both ethically and politically deficient. In McCarthy's essay, the difference is somewhat submerged in a welter of details. I shall first attend to some of these details before returning to the divergent roads.

I have little or no quarrel with his account of the idea of "universal history," as inaugurated by Kant, and its subsequent revisions or transformations. Actually, he moves a considerable length in my direction in his portrayal of central features of Kant's "subjectivistic critique of reason," which recent philosophy has renounced on good grounds: "The monological character of his conception of reason and rationality; the monocultural character of his idea of humanity; the repression of nature and subordination of happiness built into his concept of moral autonomy; connected with that, his insufficiently relational—social, historical, cultural, embodied—conception of subjectivity; and, of course, the residually metaphysical aspects of his distinction between noumenal and phenomenal."

I also concur with his critique of the metaphysical-idealist ingredients in Hegel's thought, and with the still monological and "totalizing" bent in both Marxist and liberal-evolutionary notions of progress. The difference of roads begins to surface in the discussion of Habermas's quasi-Kantian and "quasi-transcendental" developmentalism. Still, Habermas's turn to language—McCarthy correctly notes—could be endorsed by "theorists in the hermeneutic tradition" (provided the meaning of language and communication is radicalized). I agree again with his statement that "posttraditional" does not mean "floating free of tradition altogether"—although our emphases might vary. For instance, when for Habermas modernization—seen as "rationalization"—"exposes the authority of tradition to discursive questioning" and "displaces particularistic norms and values by more general and abstract ones," I might interject that tradition may also expose modernity to questioning and that abstract norms require particular instantiation (I shall return to this point). McCarthy again narrows our divergence by admitting that "not only claims to universal validity have to stand up to transcultural scrutiny but developmental claims as well, for *they implicate claims to superiority*" (my italics). Our concordance deepens still further when he states that the role of cultural or societal innovation "cannot be decided simply by arguing that a certain transformation represents a developmental advance, either of 'rational capacity' or of 'adaptive capacity'"; in our post-metaphysical age, such advances no longer carry the "imprimatur of divine providence, ends of nature, or even the cunning of reason."

As can be seen, McCarthy's account presents a highly attenuated version of the Kant-Habermas trajectory mentioned at the beginning of his essay—perhaps too attenuated from Habermas's own perspective. To bring out the difference, it may be advisable to sharpen the contours—something Habermas has never been loathe to do. As it seems to me, the difference is most pronounced in the ethical field (although it radiates from there into other domains). McCarthy is thoughtful enough not to call me an anti-Kantian (or else a relativist or emotivist). In point of fact, I consider Kant's formulations of the categorical imperative impeccable—but also insufficient in ethical terms. Mere knowledge of moral principles does not make one an ethical person (Adolf Eichmann is said to have "known" several versions of Kant's imperative); sustained practice is needed involving the cultivation of talents and dispositions. As everyone knows, mere knowledge of rules does not make one a good chess player without continuous practice; the same is true of playing the flute or the piano—and also of ethical conduct. It is here that we find the real significance of Aristotelian ethics and Hegelian *Sittlichkeit,* with their accent on practice in concrete settings. In several of his writings, Habermas has commented on Hegelian ethics—invariably distorting entirely Hegel's views. Typically, he has presented Hegelian *Sittlichkeit* as a localized or ethnocentric mode of conduct empirically prevailing at a given time and place, while Kant is said to ascend to the higher level of universally valid norms.[8] In doing so, he has injected into Hegel's thought the very dichotomy between "facts" and "norms," between "is" and "ought," that Hegel was at such great pains to overcome or mediate. Like Aristotelian ethics, Hegelian *Sittlichkeit* was not merely a factual occurrence to be transcended by higher norms. Rather, the point was that whatever norms or principles may be theoretically or cognitively postulated become properly ethical only by being practiced—which requires the molding of motivations and can only happen in concrete situations.

From ethics, these considerations radiate into other domains (to which I can only gesture here). Take the example of democratic theory where Habermas has for long been a defender of "procedural democracy."[9] As it seems to me, mere knowledge of constitutional procedures, including procedures of deliberation, does not make for a vibrant democracy in the absence of engaged practice (a fact shown by widespread voter apathy in Western democracies and also, in the United States, by recurrent episodes of McCarthyism and xenophobia). Closely connected with the preference for proceduralism is the often-claimed "primacy of right over good"—when clearly right(s) cannot function or be respected unless perceived as corollaries of something good (or of goodness). Equally and even more dubious is the accent on "rationalization" as the yardstick of social and cultural development. Apart from the ambivalence of the notion of rationality itself, the priority assigned to reason diminishes or impoverishes the other dimensions of human life and experience. Instead of "rationalization," I would prefer to place the emphasis on human seasoning and maturation, on "humanization" (in the sense of Herder's "cultivation to *Humanität*"), or on a deepening of the faculties of solicitude and "care" (in Heidegger's sense).[10] Finally, these considerations spill over into the prospect of a "multicultural cosmopolitanism" that McCarthy associates both with critical theory and my own work. Here it may be a matter of nuance—but a nuance that is significant. As it appears to me: from the vantage of critical universalists, concrete cultural contexts are basically a (regrettable) limitation of universal rules, something one accepts mainly for pragmatic reasons; from a hermeneutical vantage, by contrast, concrete particularity is a condition of possibility of universal norms (which remain contestable). This seems to be acknowledged by McCarthy when he writes: "Habermas's cosmopolitan ideal does not allow for as broad a scope of variations among political cultures; it makes cosmopolitan justice turn on institutionalizing at a global level a generalized version of the same rights and principles already variously institutionalized in [Western?] national constitutional traditions."

The discussion so far has highlighted the significance of Aristotle and Hegel in my thought, but perhaps not sufficiently Heidegger's role. The contributed essay by Krzysztof Ziarek on "The Other Politics" appropriately moves this role into the foreground. As he correctly points out, the starting point of my work is indeed human finitude as expressed in the Heideggerian notions of *Dasein* (being-there) and "being-in-the-world"—a finitude that operates not as lamentable restraint but rather as the precondition for philosophical inquiry and practical conduct. It is in Heidegger's work that the "overcoming of metaphysics" really bears fruit (requiring a rethinking of the entire course of Western philosophy, including Aristotle and Hegel). Ziarek also notes correctly that it was mainly Heidegger's thought that served for me as a gateway to "Eastern" or Asian culture, and especially to such key terms of Buddhist thinking as "nothingness" and "emptiness" (*sunyata*). Akin to Heidegger's discussion of the "nihilating" character of nothingness, these terms point in the direction of an (in Western terms) "unprecedented de-anthropocentrization, even de-anthropization, of thinking and of the 'event'" (*Ereignis*). To be sure, care must be taken not to confuse "nihilation" with simple negation or to construe Heidegger's notion of *Entmenschung* as equivalent to antihumanism or dehumanization; rather, what the notion entails is a debunking of human self-centeredness and will-to-power in favor of a thoroughgoing rethinking of human *Dasein* as a creature of care whose main concern is neither pure knowledge nor will power but care for "being" in all its forms. Contrary to widespread misreadings (favored, among others, by Habermas), this rethinking of *Dasein* does not lead to apathy or political quietism, but rather to a generous kind of "letting-be"—a mode of conduct that, far removed from domination or fabrication, allows the "otherness" of "being" and fellow beings to come into its own.

From this perspective, the phrase "Letting Be" was properly chosen as title of the present volume because it denotes both a philosophical and a practical orientation that I consider worth fostering and contemplating. As it seems to me, letting be escapes the bifurcation between autonomy and heteronomy; it is equivalent neither to a voluntaristic agency nor to a purely submissive passivity. As Ziarek observes, letting be—as *Dasein's* participation in being/nihilation—always happens "in the middle voice." This means that *Dasein's* participation is not "active" or productive in the sense that it "does not make nihilation happen"; but nor is it purely passive or reactive. Instead, it lets being/nihilation "unfold its enabling momentum of emptiness." Differently (and perceptively) phrased: "Enabling without positivity or empowerment, nihilation without negativity or inaction: those are the vectors of *Da-sein*'s 'acting' in the middle voice." Ziarek also clearly pinpoints the implications of this perspective for modern power politics. As he notes, modern politics is largely wedded to the unlimited unleashing of power, to the reduction of everything on earth to resources of techno-power (*Gestell*). Without lapsing into the negativity of sheer powerlessness, Heidegger's thought guides us into a dimension he calls "power-free" (*machtfrei*), a dimension beyond will-to-power and powerlessness in which relations can unfold without domination or submission. To open up this dimension is clearly crucial for the prospect of a multicultural cosmopolitanism in our time. As Ziarek concludes his essay: "In the age of globalization, with the intensifying planetary powers in play and the issue of planetary (in)justice increasingly salient, this question of the enabling 'politics' of nihilation [*sunyata*] both remains unheard and rises up with a particular, 'otherwise human,' poignancy and urgency."

The second thematic rubric of the volume is "Multiculturalism and Comparative Political Theory." The title is indicative of a path that I have in fact pursued. About two decades ago I was invited to attend a conference in India—a country of whose culture and traditions I was largely ignorant.[11] The visit was for me deeply troubling, even traumatic: in many ways I came away transformed or "altered." Many of my cherished intellectual habits or assumptions—including premises of modern Western philosophy—became questionable to me as I looked for the first time at my Western upbringing with new and somewhat estranged eyes. What chagrined me particularly was the fact that I could not converse with Indian colleagues on their own terms— while most Indian intellectuals (I discovered) were quite familiar with Western traditions of thought. It was then and there that I resolved to try to move "beyond Orientalism" by immersing myself more thoroughly in non-Western cultures and ways of life. During subsequent decades I returned to India repeatedly, visiting many corners of this vast and intriguing subcontinent— though keeping my headquarters usually in Baroda, the site of my first visit and a city in the home state of Gandhi to whose philosophy and way of doing politics I became increasingly attracted over the years. To be sure, moving "beyond Orientalism" could not mean a simple exit from my past. As a student of hermeneutics, I knew fully that one's life is historically sedimented such that past and future remain mutually embroiled. In this respect, Gandhi was for me also exemplary: by showing that a forward movement—no matter how radical—does not have to cancel the past and that actually the best way to proceed is to imagine the future by reappropriating and reinterpreting tradition in enabling or liberating ways.[12]

In his essay "Encounters with Modernity and Tradition," Ronald Terchek places himself in the context of India's liberation struggle, a context populated by figures like Gandhi, Tagore, Sri Aurobindo, and many others. In its opening section, Terchek refers to my (hermeneutically informed) views on the relation of tradition and modernity, and especially to my critique of an overbearing or "self-confident modernity" in favor of an admission of the possibility of "multiple modernities" and different mediations between past and future. As he writes: "Dallmayr invites us to search for a generous reading of modernity, one that recognizes important parts of its legacy, such as its ideals of critical reason, freedom, equality, and autonomy, while simultaneously leaving behind its dangerous parts, or at least challenging them." He notes correctly that I refuse to proceed in a "binary fashion" and that tradition for me can be a "a vehicle to interrogate modernity," for the simple reason that it "makes room for much that is lost" in modern times. In fact, tradition—or a certain kind of tradition—can serve as an effective counterweight or "antidote to the ongoing process of global standardization and Westernization, a source of *resistance* for non-Western societies in the grip of Western hegemony"—provided the counterweight does not slip into reactionary parochialism. Terchek cites a passage from my book *Dialogue among Civilizations* to the effect that we "need to find a path between (Habermasian) modernity and its radical opponents (or antimodernists), a path that acknowledges the beneficial or emancipating dimensions of modernity while refusing to canonize is defects." A similar outlook, in his view, can be found in the Indian pre-independence thinker Sri Aurobindo, whose intellectual development is traced in the chapter with sensitivity and insight. For Aurobindo, Terchek writes, "the supreme challenge is how India can be vitally connected to the core of its tradition, which he believes to be life-affirming and spiritual, while at the same time removing the disabilities that have accumulated over the centuries." Gandhi's entire life, it seems to me, was animated precisely by this kind of outlook or conviction.

In her contribution, "Between Athens and Jerusalem (or Mecca)," Michaelle Browers shifts the accent to the Islamic world. This move again corresponds to a certain shift in my own interests during recent years. To be sure, Islamic thought and traditions were familiar to me from earlier times, and especially from my travels in India. However, recent events have thrust the status of Islamic civilization into the limelight of international attention. Partly in response to these events, I have explored facets of that important world (within the limits of my linguistic competence). A main challenge for me in this respect was to navigate the straits between tradition and modernity, between West and East, and also between philosophical reason and faith. With regard to the first divide, I examined some classical Islamic thinkers and poets (like Ibn Rushd and Rumi) as well as some contemporary philosophers (like the Iranian Abdolkarim Soroush and the Moroccan al-Jabiri). Regarding the second divide, I revisited Goethe's "West-Eastern Divan," containing his famous dialogue with the Persian poet Hafiz. Most important for me, however, was the third issue: the relation between reason and faith, or else between Athens and Jerusalem (or Mecca). On this issue I returned to a classical text by Ibn Rushd devoted precisely to this question. As I tried to show, Ibn Rushd did not pit reason against faith or elevate one above the other; bypassing the options both of facile synthesis or radical opposition, he rather stressed their nondichotomous "difference" (in the sense of the Heideggerian *Unterschied*, which respects difference in complementarity).[13] Michaelle Browers sensitively notes this point and credits me with the effort "to reconstruct conflictual dualisms as creative tensions."

As Browers observes, Islamic thought has for some time been the target of Western inquiries—but often with Orientalizing connotations. Her essay singles out the work of Leo Strauss and his followers whose interpretations have tended to erect a (quasi-Platonic) gulf between "esoteric" knowledge and mere opinion, between elect thinkers and the masses, and above all between Athens and Jerusalem. She quotes Strauss to the effect that (Western) tradition consists "of two heterogeneous elements, of two elements which are ultimately incompatible with each other: the Hebrew element and the Greek element"—a dichotomy allowing one to speak of "the antagonism between Jerusalem and Athens, between faith and philosophy." A close student of Arab and Islamic thought herself, Browers has been troubled by the predominance of this "esoteric" approach to Islamic tradition, and especially by the doctrinaire insistence on the radical gulf between reason and faith (or else the radical privileging of one over the other). Pointing to some of my writings, she finds there "a hermeneutic, or perhaps more accurately, an 'ethic'" to guide cross-cultural inquiries in a direction that moves "beyond that of strife, competition, and contention of unbridgeable gulfs" (postulated by neo-Kantian and Straussian perspectives). The goal of such a hermeneutics (to repeat the point) is not to produce a bland synthesis, but rather to foster a "differential" complementarity—something that becomes more feasible when one considers the "third dimension" of a political community in which participants have to "live that conflict" (between reason and faith) by negotiating the tension in daily living. Browers at this point proceeds to a detailed reading of Ibn Rushd's classical text, emphasizing the role of a "political praxis of companionship" (or Aristotelian political friendship). By way of conclusion she turns to the Moroccan philosopher al-Jabiri in an effort to shield him against charges of both fideism and secular agnosticism and to vindicate his own journey "beyond the secular-religious divide."

In the next essay, Neve Gordon (a former student of mine who now teaches in Israel) delves resolutely into the arena of the "political praxis of companionship" in one of the most difficult imaginable settings: the lived relation between Jews and Palestinians in contemporary Israel. As a university teacher, he localizes and concretizes the salient issues even more by focusing on very personal encounters in the context of his own university. It is on this level that the teachings of "high theory" are either disconfirmed or show their mettle. A case in point is the (Hegelian) maxim of civic "recognition"— of which Palestinians and Bedouins are largely deprived. "Insofar as our identity is formed by recognition," Gordon correctly asserts, "nonrecognition, in and of itself, should be considered a form of abuse." Another example of possibly high theory is Heidegger's philosophy, which for some time I have tried to translate into "vernacular" praxis—and which (I am happy to see) Gordon concretizes even further. With regard to Heidegger's notion of letting be, he (like Ziarek) focuses properly on the "middle voice" between passivity and activity, stating: "In order to let Being *be* one must be passive, while in order to *let* Being be one must be active." In his concrete encounter with his Bedouin student Amal, he allows her to tell her own story in her own way, thus letting her "be," while simultaneously practicing a supportive "letting" that needs to be carried out with sensitivity and care. Beyond his immediate university setting, Gordon has cultivated the "praxis of companionship" in a wider context—to which he refers when speaking of "my day-to-day endeavors in Israel/Palestine, particularly as a member of a group called *Ta'ayush*, Arab-Jewish partnership." Basically, this notion of partnership or companionship reflects one of my deepest convictions about both ethics and religion: namely, that what matters most is not "orthodoxy" (correctness of theories or beliefs) but rather "orthopraxis" revealed in one's conduct toward others.[14]

The praxis of companionship cultivated by Gordon is tailored to concrete Jewish–Palestinian relations in contemporary Israel; but a similar cultivation (he would agree) is needed today in numerous other settings where cross-cultural or interethnic relations are fraught with enormous burdens of resentment and ill-will. The contexts of Northern Ireland, Kashmir, and Chechnya readily come to mind. However, given the worldwide prominence of multiculturalism, situations of interethnic and interreligious conflict— perhaps on a less grievous scale—can also be found inside Western "liberal" societies otherwise proud of their legacy of civic harmony and homogeneity. A case in point is the powerful upsurge of Latino culture in the United States today. John Francis Burke (a former doctoral student of mine who now teaches in Houston) examines this upsurge by focusing on the spreading of *mestizaje*, that is, the rapidly accelerating intermingling of Hispanic and Anglo cultures in the American Southwest. Some observers, including Samuel Huntington, portray this growing Latino presence in North America as a threat to traditional (Protestant) American ways of life, as a localized incident of the ominously predicted "clash of civilizations" worldwide. Burke vigorously contests and debunks this imagined peril (what some have called the looming specter of "Mexifornia"). Relying on the teachings of Edward Said, José Vasconcelos, and a number of Latin American liberation theologians, his essay upholds the "ethos of crossing borders" or cross-cultural companionship, stressing its importance not just for Latinos but for North American culture in general. As he writes: "Aimed at more than just transforming liberation theology in a cultural hermeneutical fashion, *mestizo* spirituality moves beyond the Reformation–Counter Reformulation [or modernity–antimodernity] debate to engender inclusive and hospitable intersections of spiritual traditions." In terms of social and political implications, *mestizo* democracy—far from being a passing fashion—plays an equally crucial mediating role by combating "the growing gaps between the rich and the poor, both in the United States and between the developed and the developing world."

Prior to entering the doctoral program at Notre Dame, Burke also studied with my Korean American friend Hwa Yol Jung, whose own work eloquently testifies to the "ethos of crossing borders" and the praxis of companionship. This intersection of our lives no doubt accounts for certain intellectual commitments shared by the three of us, including the influence of Merleau-Ponty's existential phenomenology. In his contribution to the present volume, Jung allows his own East Asian experiences only occasionally to enter the discussion—for instance, by alluding to Akira Kurosawa's *Rashomon* (with its accent on plural hermeneutics) and to the story of Hu Ruowang, the first Chinese traveler to Europe and more particularly to Paris (a story underscoring the hazards of cross-cultural encounters). Jung's essay draws attention mainly to a number of thinkers who—in addition to Heidegger and Gadamer—have paved the way for cross-cultural or comparative studies in our time. An important guidepost in this respect is the work of Calvin Schrag whose notion of "transversality" is said to clear a path between abstract or "top-down" universalism and a retreat into local fragmentation. In Jung's words, transversality navigates "the stormy space between the two dichotomous poles of the modernist obsession with identity and universalism and the postmodernist drive for difference and pluralism. Transversality actively seeks a transformation"—especially the transformation of bipolarity itself. By proceeding in the middle voice, he adds (echoing Ziarek), transversality "touches the soul and heart of Buddhism" by intimating "the arrival of Maitreya" (or impending enlightenment). Jung also refers to the French Sinologist François Jullien who relied on the tradition of Chinese thought in order "to interrogate Western philosophy and to liberate it from its own 'mental cage.'" Sustained attention in his chapter, however, is given to Maurice Merleau-Ponty, whose work is too often ignored by contemporary comparativists. Through his notion of the "lateral universal," Jung states (supporting a point made by Burke), Merleau-Ponty placed the accent on a grassroots approach: "the ethnography of sociocultural life-worlds without which philosophy is a vacuous if not fatal abstraction." As a concrete instance of such an approach, the essay alerts readers to the work of the Caribbean Éduard Glissant with his focus on "diversality" and "créolité."

In its concluding comments, Jung's essay points to the linkage between transversality and "cosmopolitanism"—the latter seen not as a uniform globalism but as a differentiated and "heterocentric" network of lived spaces. In doing so, it guides the discussion directly into the third thematic rubric: "Globalization and Cosmopolitics." In her contribution to this section, international-relations theorist Franke Wilmer emphasizes the growing interpenetration between traditional academic fields and subfields—despite an opposing tendency to ossify them further. A case in point is the relation between political theory and international politics. While political theorists in the past often preferred to theorize about other theorists, the pressures of globalization and global politics confront theorists with formidable new challenges. Wilmer observes how my own work has moved from traditional political theory concerns in the direction of multiculturalism and cosmopolitics. Along the way, and partly under "postmodern" influence, the centrality of the Cartesian *cogito* or modern subjectivity has tended to be displaced or called into question. Transferring this trajectory to the international arena, Wilmer distinguishes between two global scenarios. The first—corresponding largely to the so-called Westphalian system—she sees as "populated by billiard ball 'selves'" who are "solid, impenetrable, and unconnected" and who go about "bumping into each other" in a "bump or be bumped" world. The second scenario, of more recent vintage, is that of an interconnected "human chain" with all participants "holding hands and unable to let go" and where "[a]nytime one person tugs, others are moved, creating a 'chain' reaction." As she states: "I think of the world in which the Cartesian self developed as a billiard-ball world, and the world today as made up of one tremendous human chain"—an observation I heartily endorse.[15]

With regard to the possibility of a global ethics, Wilmer points to the important book *Moral Spaces: Rethinking Ethics and World Politics,* whose editors (David Campbell and Michael Shapiro) forcefully state that "rather than being concerned with a *theory of ethics,* the contributors . . . are motivated by the *ethical relation* in which our responsibility to the other is the basis for reflection." Her chapter also alludes to the role of political psychology as a possible link between ethics and world politics, and especially to the interactive approach of Melanie Klein. From a Kleinian vantage, and in opposition to top-down theorizing, she writes, "our relations with Others are shaped by the emotional potentialities that emerge with selfhood—attachment, rejection, love, hate, and guilt, . . . for example" (a point again deeply congenial to me).[16] Partly in a Kleinian spirit, Wilmer goes on to construct a typology of self–other relations, all revolving around the identity/difference syndrome.

She credits me with articulating a "dialectical self" (I would prefer calling it "dialogical")—one which is "born into a nexus of transactions and relationships" and whose existence is "inextricably linked to Others in a world of complex, overlapping, intersecting, and interdependent agents and identities." Moving into a concretely lived terrain, she compares this notion with the Native American experience of identity, particularly with the Ojibway experience of being both the victims and the accomplices of North American policies. An even more telling comparison is with the South African concept of *ubuntu,* which means that "my humanity depends on and can only be realized through my relationship with others." Examples like these could be multiplied and might serve—in her view and mine—as building blocks for a global ethical community.

To be sure, an ethical community cannot simply be a substitute for global politics. Operating mainly on a "civil society" level, global ethics by itself does not ensure the legitimate aspirations of peoples for democratic self-government—a point forcefully articulated by Chantal Mouffe in her contribution. Relying in part on one of my essays ("Cosmopolitanism: Moral and Political") she stresses the likely divergence between ethics and politics, between good dispositions and real-life circumstances. The danger is particularly great when global norms—operating in a "top-down" fashion—are utilized by hegemonic political powers for purposes of global domination. Treated as an abstract standard, even democracy can be utilized in this manner and be reduced to a missionary slogan. Mouffe critiques especially the notion of "cosmopolitan democracy" (put forward by David Held, Daniele Archibugi, and others) for privileging high-level theorizing while neglecting pressing political issues—such as continuing neocolonial domination and inequality on the ground. As she notes, what is missing in ideas of this kind is "the political dimension" and there are ample reasons to be "more than skeptical about the democratizing impact" of this approach. More sharply stated: the implementation of a cosmopolitan order (along Held's lines) might "in fact result in the imposition of the liberal democratic [read: neoliberal] model on the whole world, thus bringing more people directly under the control of the West." In light of the ongoing invasion of non-Western societies by neoliberal policies of economic restructuring, no one can gainsay the gravity of these dangers. Pointedly, Mouffe finds fault with prominent Western conceptions of democracy—including procedural and "deliberative" models—charging them with pursuing merely the aim to reach a compromise but "not to challenge the prevailing hegemony" in world politics.

In an effort to overcome these shortcomings, Mouffe's essay turns to the work of Carl Schmitt, who challenged liberal high-mindedness by insisting that "mere deliberation without the moment of decision and the mechanism to enforce these decisions means very little" (echoing Hobbes's comments on "words without the sword"). In her reading, Schmitt's work teaches that "power relations are constitutive of the social" and that "every order is *by necessity* an hegemonic order." Seen from this vantage, cosmopolitan democracy—by sidelining politics—constitutes a "dangerous illusion" and even a repressive nightmare. The danger in recent times has surfaced in the form of terrorism that—for Mouffe—results (at least partly) from the lack of legitimate channels of dissent in our world. As she writes provocatively: "[W]e can see terrorism as the product of a new configuration of the political that is characteristic of the type of world order being implemented around the hegemony of a single hyperpower." As an antidote to global domination, Schmitt in his later years (especially in *The Nomos of the Earth*) articulated the vision of a "multipolar" world order predicated on the competition among several autonomous regional blocs. This is not the place to enter in detail into my agreements and disagreements with Mouffe about Schmitt.[17] Briefly, I fully support the formation of viable regional blocs (like the European Union, the African Union, and the like) to compete politically on the global scene—as I have stated in some of my recent writings. For this reason, I find the term "cosmopolitics" preferable to the somewhat bland label of "cosmopolitanism."[18] I also concur with Schmitt regarding the inescapability of "politics"—provided the meaning of that term is changed. I do not accept Schmitt's definition of politics as the distinction between "friend and enemy" because, by likening politics to warfare, it tends to support the ongoing militarization of the globe. This does not mean that I deny the reality of conflict (Burke's essay stresses this point). But conflict cannot just be about power, or about the replacement of one hegemonic power with another. To make sense, conflict involves a struggle against oppression and injustice and an endeavor to bring about more just and equitable conditions. Thus, while not collapsing politics and ethics, I maintain also (in the spirit of *Unterschied*) that their linkage must not be sundered.

In part, my opposition to the "friend/enemy" formula derives from prominent developments in the global arena, especially from the Manichean tendency to divide the world into "the West" versus "the rest" and to demonize a good part of the non-Western world as an "axil of evil." Given this tendency, as David Ingram argues in his contribution, the much-discussed "clash of civilizations" becomes a self-fulfilling prophesy, all the more so since Manicheism is buttressed in the West by other forms of oppositional thinking (such as the dichotomies between theory and praxis, reason and religion, culture and nature). In contrast to these bifurcations, Ingram favors something like a "dialogue among civilizations"—provided dialogue is properly understood. To have its transformative effect, dialogue for him (and me) has to move beyond a mere sharing of procedures or an exchange of (Habermasian) validity claims and to penetrate to the level of existential engagements. Operating on this level, dialogue necessarily has overtones of that agonistic tension stressed by followers of Schmitt and Nietzsche—although conflict does not need to have a veto power over friendship and mutual respect. Ingram is primarily concerned with the global contest over human rights—a crucial issue today. He passes in review several models of dialogue or communication, moving from John Rawls's procedural model to Habermas's formal communication model—remonstrating against the latter that interlocutors cannot "assign univocal meanings" to their words (without stifling the exchange). Although willing to make room for various elements of these models, he opts in the end for what I have called a "thick conversation" or a "thick dialogue," meaning "a communicative interchange willing to delve into the rich fabric of different life-worlds and cultures."[19] Turning to global human rights, he features three areas of needed dialogical engagement: the tension between Eastern religion and Western rationalism; the dispute between Western individualism and Chinese holism; and the debate over women's rights in Islam. We cannot expect agreement in these domains, he concludes, "without first reaching agreement on the deeper metaphysical relationships linking humanity, nature, and God, on the one hand, and individual freedom and communal well-being, on the other."

Cross-cultural dialogue is also at the heart of the concluding contribution by Calvin Schrag, who pursues the potential of such engagement for global peacemaking. In accord with Jung's account, Schrag accentuates the "transversal" character of cross-cultural interactions, placing it in opposition to an abstract universalism. As he indicates, the term is chosen "in the hope of avoiding some of the traditional glitches that travel with the uses of dialogue to ground claims for universality." In line with Heideggerian and related postmodern formulations of the identity/difference syndrome, Schrag locates the "root meaning of transversality" in a set of hybrid expressions: "convergence without coincidence, unity without identity, commonality without equivalence, assimilation without absorption, and cooperation without uniformity."[20] Disregard of this hybridity, he adds, undergirds all kinds of bipolar constructions, such as those between Occident and Orient, between "the West" and "the rest." By contrast, transversality and peacemaking are closely related. Proceeding along transversal lines of communication, the goal of peacemaking for Schrag is "to decouple the nation-state apparatus from the war machine and to delimit the role of national identity in the shaping of political policy." This approach, and it alone, can "provide a bulwark against preemptive wars and unilateralism on the part of nation-states." In the end, Schrag also debunks the "friend–enemy" formula by appealing to the transgressive (and quasi-eschatological) writings of Derrida and Kierkegaard on friendship and love. Both friend and enemy, we read, "share a common earth" and in their mutual bondedness "solicit from each other a transcending and unconditional love, beyond all economics of immanent exchange relations" (where love remains tied to "expectations of return").

The volume could not end on a better note. Surely, love and friendship is what holds the world together and what affirms again and again, in the midst of chaos and despair, the continuing possibility—or perhaps the "impossible possibility"—of goodness and of a just and humane way of life on earth. It is such a friendship, or at least a friendly sympathy, that links me with all the contributors to this volume—no matter how different their perspectives may be from my own and how long-term or recent our relationship. In every instance, I am deeply grateful to the contributors for their comments. Part of this gratitude is prompted by the sheer joy of seeing the fruit of their labors. On a deeper level, however, the gratitude is due to the intellectual and personal benefit derived from their work: all the contributions have helped me to reflect more clearly on the paths I have traveled and to ponder more seriously their implications. To this extent, the contributions have induced in me a further seasoning or maturation—which is high time at the age I have now reached. As previously indicated, my response to the various essays cannot be—and is not meant to be—a concluding point in our relationships but only another gambit in our ongoing conversation. It seems appropriate that I finish my comments with some lines that Hans-Georg Gadamer placed at the end of his *Truth and Method:* "I will stop here. The ongoing debate permits no final conclusion. It would be a poor hermeneuticist who thought he could have, or had to have, the last word."[21]

NOTES

1. See Fred Dallmayr, "Hobbes and Existentialism: Some Affinities," *Journal of Politics* 31 (1969): 615–40. A revised version of the essay was included in my first (single-authored) book, *Beyond Dogma and Despair: Toward a Critical Phenomenology of Politics* (Notre Dame, Ind.: University of Notre Dame Press, 1981), pp. 120–38 (I cite from that version). The chosen title *Beyond Dogma and Despair* was meant to signal an overall direction: that is, an effort to steer a path between abstractly rational propositions, on the one hand, and an immersion in wholly opaque, random experiences, on the other. In my introduction to that volume (p. 3), I referred to Merleau-Ponty's statement, in his *In Praise of Philosophy,* that philosophy is not a set of ready-made doctrines but an endeavor that links "inseparably the taste for evidence and the feeling for ambiguity."

2. See Eric Voegelin, *The New Science of Politics: An Introduction* (Chicago: University of Chicago Press, 1952), pp. 47–98.

3. See Fred Dallmayr, "Post-metaphysics and Democracy," *Political Theory* 21 (1993): 101–27; a revised version under the title "Post-metaphysical Politics: Heidegger and Democracy," appears as chapter 3 in my *The Other Heidegger* (Ithaca: Cornell University Press, 1993), pp. 77–105 (I am citing from this chapter). See also Claude Lefort, *Democracy and Political Theory,* trans. David Macey (Minneapolis: University of Minnesota Press, 1988), esp. pp. 17–19, 223–26.

4. See Fred Dallmayr, *Between Freiburg and Frankfurt: Toward a Critical Ontology* (Amherst: University of Massachusetts Press, 1991). The label "critical phenomenology" was used as subtitle in my earlier book *Beyond Dogma and Despair.* (The change of labels reflects a certain ascendancy of Heidegger's influence during the intervening years.)

5. See Fred Dallmayr, *Twilight of Subjectivity: Contributions to a Post-Individualist Theory of Politics* (Amherst: University of Massachusetts Press, 1981), p. 57. In the opening chapter of that volume, "Beyond Possessive Individualism," I drew a parallel between Adorno's antisubjectivism and Heidegger's arguments in his "Letter on Humanism" (as well as with Foucault's and Derrida's critiques of "egology").

6. See Jürgen Habermas, *The Theory of Communicative Action,* vol. 1, *Reason and the Rationalization of Society* (Boston: Beacon Press, 1984), p. 390; Seyla Benhabib, *Critique, Norm, and Utopia* (New York: Columbia University Press, 1986), p. 219.

7. See Fred Dallmayr, "The Enigma of Health: Gadamer at Century's End," in *Language and Linguisticality in Gadamer's Hermeneutics,* ed. Lawrence K. Schmidt (Lanham, Md.: Lexington Books, 2000), p. 166. I referred there especially to Adorno, *Negative Dialectics,* trans. E. B. Ashton (New York: Seaburg Press, 1973), pp. 14–15, 179–80; and *Aesthetic Theory,* ed. Gretel Adorno and Rolf Tiedemann, trans. C. Lenhardt (London: Routledge and Kegan Paul, 1984), esp. pp. 453–55. See also Dallmayr, *Between Freiburg and Frankfurt,* p. 93.

8. See, e.g., Jürgen Habermas, "On the Pragmatic, the Ethical, and the Moral Employments of Practical Reason," in his *Justification and Application: Remarks on Discourse Ethics,* trans. Ciaran P. Cronin (Cambridge: MIT Press, 1994), pp. 1–17. With regard to Hegelian *Sittlichkeit* (termed here "ethical-existential discourses"), the essay states (p. 12) that participants "cannot distance themselves from the life histories and forms of life in which they actually find themselves. Moral-practical discourses [along Kantian lines], by contrast, require a break with all the unquestioned truths of an established, concrete ethical life." Habermas does admit, however, that "moral insights do not of themselves lead to autonomous [ethical] actions" (p. 14).

9. See, e.g., Jürgen Habermas, "Three Normative Models of Democracy," in *Democracy and Difference: Contesting the Boundaries of the Political,* ed. Seyla Benhabib (Princeton: Princeton University Press, 1996), pp. 21–30. The "procedural" in this essay is distinguished from both the "liberal"(or Lockean) and "republican" (or communitarian) paradigms.

10. I am inspired here also by Goethe's statement: "To become a nation, you Germans attempt it in vain. Develop yourselves instead into human beings." Regarding the role of ethics in Heidegger's work, compare Lawrence J. Hatab, *Ethics and Finitude: Heideggerian Contributions to Moral Philosophy* (Lanham, Md.: Rowman and Littlefield, 2000); also my chapter "Heidegger on Ethics and Justice," in *The Other Heidegger,* pp. 106–31.

11. The conference was organized by political theorist Bhikhu Parekh (now Lord Parekh), who at the time was vice chancellor of the M.S. University of Baroda in Gujarat. At the conference I was fortunate enough to meet a large number of Indian colleagues, several of whom subsequently became dear friends, among them Thomas Pantham of the University of Baroda; Vrajendra Raj Mehta, then at the University of Jaipur (and later vice chancellor of the University of Delhi); Ashis Nandy, a senior fellow at the Center for the Study of Developing Societies (CSDS) in Delhi; and Partha Chatterjee of the Center for Social Studies in Calcutta. At the conference I also met Prafulla Kar, professor of English at the University of Baroda, in whose annual nationwide conferences on "contemporary thought" I came to participate on a (more or less) regular basis.

12. For some of my writings on Gandhi, see, e.g., "Gandhi as Mediator between East and West," in *Margins of Political Discourse* (Albany: SUNY Press, 1989), pp. 22–38; "What is Self-Rule? Lessons from Gandhi," in *Dialogue among Civilizations: Some Exemplary Voices* (New York: Palgrave Macmillan, 2002), pp. 213–28; and

"Gandhi and Islam: A Heart-and-Mind Unity?" in *Peace Talks—Who Will Listen?* (Notre Dame, Ind.: University of Notre Dame Press, 2004), pp. 132–51. On the relation between freedom and tradition, compare Jeffrey Stout, *Democracy and Tradition* (Princeton: Princeton University Press, 2004).

13. For the above, see especially the chapters "Reason, Faith, and Politics: A Journey to Muslim Andalusia," "West-Eastern Divan: Goethe and Hafiz in Dialogue," and "Islam and Democracy: Reflections on Abdolkarim Soroush," in my *Dialogue among Civilizations*, pp. 121–46, 147–66, 167–84. Compare also Martin Heidegger, *Identität und Differenz* (Pfullingen: Neske Verlag, 1957).

14. In my view, such partnership was at the core of Gandhi's endeavor to foster "heart-unity" with his Muslim compatriots (see the reference in note 12 above). In America, partnership is promoted by various interfaith encounters and most specifically by the so-called *Tikkun* community inaugurated by Rabbi Michael Lerner and devoted to the reconciliation and healing of wounds between ethnic and religious groups, including Israelis and Palestinians.

15. My friend Benjamin Barber has actively sponsored a global politics of "interdependence" and has been involved in formulating a "Declaration of Interdependence" as part of the "CivWorld" Global Citizens Campaign. See, e.g., Barber, *Fear's Empire: War, Terrorism, and Democracy* (New York: Norton, 2003), pp. 209–11. As an aside, I might add that, for a long time, I have been supportive of Barber's notion of democracy as practical citizens' engagement. See, e.g., the conclusion of my book *G. W. F. Hegel: Modernity and Politics*, rev. ed. (Lanham, Md.: Rowman and Littlefield, 2002), pp. 258–59.

16. As it happens, I have for some time been involved in a political psychology network. For a number of years, I participated at meetings of the American Political Science Association on panels together with such noted political psychologists as C. Fred Alford, James Glass, and Victor Wolfenstein. Alford especially has been a close student of Klein's work; see, e.g., his *Melanie Klein and Critical Social Theory* (New Haven: Yale University Press, 1989). Compare also my "Heidegger and Freud," *Political Psychology* 14 (1993): 235–53; and "Political Evil: A Response to Alford," *Political Psychology* 11 (1990): 29–35.

17. See, e.g., my review essay "The Return of the Political: On Chantal Mouffe," *Constellations* 3 (1996): 115–20; see also "Die Heimkehr des Politischen," *Deutsche Zeitschrift für Philosophie* 44 (1996): 517–26.

18. Compare on these points my "Lessons of September 11," in *Peace Talks—Who Will Listen?* pp. 205–16, previously published in *Theory, Culture, and Society* 19 (2002): 173–89. Regarding the notion of cosmopolitics, see especially Pheng Cheah and Bruce Robbins, eds., *Cosmopolitics: Thinking and Feeling beyond the Nation* (Minneapolis: University of Minnesota Press, 1998). As Bruce Robbins remarks in his introduction (p. 12), the title of the book "points to a domain of contested politics. . . . Thinking of cosmopolitics not as universal reason in disguise, but as one on a series of scales, as an area both within and beyond the nation (and yet falling short of 'humanity') that is inhabited by a variety of cosmopolitanisms, we will not perhaps be tempted to offer

the final word" on the dilemmas discussed in the book. For Pheng Cheah, in turn, cosmopolitics raises "the most difficult question: In an uneven neocolonial world, how can struggles for multicultural recognition in constitutional-democratic states in the North be brought into a global alliance with postcolonial activism in the periphery?" (p. 37).

19. More recently I have come to think that, as a precondition of cross-cultural dialogue, there needs to be a mutual airing of grievances and sufferings resulting from unjust or oppressive actions (in the past or present). Hence, the idea came to me of a global "Truth and Justice Commission" or "Truth and Reconciliation Commission" patterned on the commissions established in South Africa and parts of Latin America. Great was my surprise when I learned that a research institute in Finland had actually formulated such a proposal. See Tuomas Forsberg and Teivo Teivainen, *Past Injustice in World Politics: Prospects of Truth-Commission-Like Global Institutions* (Helsinki: Crisis Management Initiative, 2004).

20. It was in line with such hybrid formulas that I tried to transfer Jean-Luc Nancy's idea of an "imperative community" (*communauté désoeuvrée*) to the global arena; see my "An 'Inoperative' Global Community? Reflections on Nancy," in *Alternative Visions: Paths in the Global Village* (Lanham, Md.: Rowman and Littlefield, 1998), pp. 277–97. Compare also Nancy, *The Inoperative Community*, ed. Peter Connor, trans. Peter Connor et al. (Minneapolis: University of Minnesota Press, 1991).

21. Hans-Georg Gadamer, *Truth and Method*, 2d rev. ed., trans. Joel Weinsheimer and Donald G. Marshall (New York: Crossroad, 1989), p. 579.

Dallmayr Bibliography

BOOKS

With Robert S. Rankin. *Freedom and Emergency Power.* New York: Appleton-Century-Crofts, 1964.

Beyond Dogma and Despair: Toward a Critical Phenomenology of Politics. Notre Dame, Ind.: University of Notre Dame Press, 1981.

Twilight of Subjectivity: Contributions to a Post-Individualist Theory of Politics. Amherst: University of Massachusetts Press, 1981. Chinese translation, Shanghai: Shanghai's People's Publisher, 1992.

Language and Politics: Why Does Language Matter to Political Philosophy? Notre Dame, Ind.: University of Notre Dame Press, 1984.

Polis and Praxis: Exercises in Contemporary Political Theory. Cambridge: MIT Press, 1984. Persian translation, Tehran: Porsegh Publications, 2003.

Critical Encounters: Between Philosophy and Politics. Notre Dame, Ind.: University of Notre Dame Press, 1987.

Margins of Political Discourse. Albany: SUNY Press, 1989.

Life-World, Modernity and Critique: Paths between Heidegger and the Frankfurt School. Cambridge, UK: Polity Press, 1991. American edition: *Between Freiburg and Frankfurt: Toward a Critical Ontology.* Amherst: University of Massachusetts Press, 1991.

G. W. F. Hegel: Modernity and Politics. Newbury Park, Calif.: Sage Publications, 1993. Paperback edition, 1995.

The Other Heidegger. Ithaca: Cornell University Press, 1993.

Beyond Orientalism: Essays on Cross-Cultural Encounter. Albany: SUNY Press, 1996. Indian edition, New Delhi: Rawat Publishers, 2001. Japanese translation, Tokyo: Shinhyoron, 2001.

Alternative Visions: Paths in the Global Village. Lanham, Md.: Rowman and Littlefield, 1998. Persian translation, Tehran: Porsegh Publications, 2004.

Achieving Our World: Toward a Global and Plural Democracy. Lanham, Md.: Rowman and Littlefield, 2001.

Dialogue among Civilizations: Some Exemplary Voices. New York: Palgrave Macmillan, 2002. Italian translation, Rome: Reset Publishers, 2006.

G. W. F. Hegel: Modernity and Politics. New ed. Lanham, Md.: Rowman and Littlefield, 2002.

Peace Talks—Who Will Listen? Notre Dame, Ind.: University of Notre Dame Press, 2004.

Small Wonder: Global Power and Its Discontents. Lanham, Md.: Rowman and Littlefield, 2005.

In Search of the Good Life: A Pedagogy for Troubled Times. Forthcoming.

EDITED BOOKS AND VOLUMES

Materialienband zu Habermas' Erkenntnis und Interesse. Frankfurt: Suhrkamp Verlag, 1974.

With Thomas A. McCarthy. *Understanding and Social Inquiry.* Notre Dame, Ind.: University of Notre Dame Press, 1977.

From Contract to Community: Political Theory at the Crossroads. New York: Dekker Publishing, 1978.

With Gisela J. Hinkle. "Foucault Memorial Issue." *Human Studies* 10, no. 1 (1987): 3–170.

With Seyla Benhabib. *The Communicative Ethics Controversy.* Cambridge: MIT Press, 1990.

With Peter R. Moody. "Non-Western Political Thought." Special issue of *Review of Politics* 59, no. 3 (1997): 421–647.

With Ganesh Devi. *Between Tradition and Modernity: India's Search for Identity.* New Delhi: Sage Publications India, 1998.

Border Crossings: Toward a Comparative Political Theory. Lanham, Md.: Rowman and Littlefield, 1999.

With Philip Pettit and B. N. Ray. *Republicanism and Political Theory.* New Delhi: Kanishka Publishers, 2000.

With José M. Rosales. *Beyond Nationalism? Sovereignty and Citizenship.* Lanham, Md.: Lexington Books, 2001.

With José M. Rosales. *Mas allá del Nacionalismo: Sovereignidad y ciudadanía.* Valencia, Spain: Tirant lo Blanch, 2004.

With Roxanne Euben and Anthony Parel. *Introduction to Non-Western Political Thought.* Forthcoming.

BOOK CHAPTERS

"Hobbes and Existentialism: Some Affinities." In Reinhart Koselleck and Roman Schnur, eds., *Hobbes-Forschungen.* Berlin: Duncker and Humblot, 1969. Pp. 259–85.

"Equality and Social Change." In Carl Beck, ed., *Law and Justice. Festschrift for Robert S. Rankin.* Durham: Duke University Press, 1970. Pp. 181–206.

"Empirical Political Theory and the Image of Man." In Glen Gordon and William E. Connolly, eds., *Social Structure and Political Life*. Lexington, Mass.: D. C. Heath, 1973. Pp. 168–91.

"Phenomenology and Marxism: A Salute to Enzo Paci." In George Psathas, ed., *Phenomenological Sociology*. New York: Wiley Press, 1973. Pp. 305–56.

"Phenomenology and Social Science: An Overview and Appraisal." In Edward S. Casey and David Carr, eds., *Explorations in Phenomenology*. The Hague: Nijhoff, 1975. Pp. 13–66.

"Phänomenologie und Marxismus in geschichtlicher Perspektive." In Bernhard Waldenfels, ed., *Phänomenologie und Marxismus: I. Konzepte und Methoden*. Frankfurt: Suhrkamp, 1977. Pp. 13–44.

"Genesis and Validation of Social Knowledge: Lessons from Merleau-Ponty." In Joseph Bien, ed., *Phenomenology and Social Science*. The Hague: Nijhoff, 1978. Pp. 74–106.

"Fragen an Habermas und Apel." In W. Oelmüller, ed., *Transzendentalphilosophische Normenbegründungen*. Paderborn: Schöningh, 1978. Pp. 27–37.

"Response" (to MacIntyre and Braybrooke). In Maria J. Falco, ed., *Through the Looking-Glass: Epistemology and the Conduct of Inquiry*. Washington, D.C.: University Press of America, 1979. Pp. 83–90.

"Critical Theory and Public Policy." In Ernest R. House, ed., *Evaluation Studies. Review Annual*, vol. 7. Beverly Hills: Sage Publications, 1982. Pp. 740–52.

"Kommunikation und Gemeinschaft." In W. Kuhlmann and D. Boehler, eds., *Kommunikation und Reflexion: Festschrift für Karl-Otto Apel*. Frankfurt: Suhrkamp, 1982. Pp. 191–220.

"The Theory of Structuration: A Critique." In Anthony Giddens, ed., *Profiles and Critiques in Social Theory*. New York: Macmillan, 1982. Pp. 18–27.

"Introduction." To Michael Theunissen, *The Other: Studies in the Social Ontology of Husserl, Heidegger, Sartre, and Buber*. Cambridge, Mass.: MIT Press, 1984. Pp. ix–xxv.

"Comments on Giddens." In Gary Shapiro and Alan Sica, eds., *Hermeneutics: Questions and Prospects*. Amherst: University of Massachusetts Press, 1984. Pp. 231–38.

"Phenomenology and Marxism in Historical Perspective." In Bernard Waldenfels, J. M. Broekman, and Ante Pazanin, eds., *Phenomenology and Marxism*. London: Routledge and Kegan Paul, 1984. Pp. 3–30.

"Critical Theory and Public Policy" (expanded version). In William N. Dunn, *Policy Analysis: Perspectives, Concepts and Methods*. Greenwich, Conn.: JAI Press, 1986. Pp. 41–67.

"Life-World and Communicative Action." In Bhikhu Parekh and Thomas Pantham, eds., *Political Discourse: Explorations in Indian and Western Political Thought*. Newbury Park, Calif.: Sage Publications, 1987. Pp. 152–78.

"Political Inquiry: Beyond Empiricism and Hermeneutics." In Terence Ball, ed., *Idioms of Inquiry*. Albany: SUNY Press, 1987. Pp. 169–85.

"Heidegger, Hölderlin and Politics." In Joseph Buttigieg, ed., *Criticism without Boundaries*. Notre Dame, Ind.: University of Notre Dame Press, 1987. Pp. 111–28.

"Praxis and Reflection." In Alan Blum, Michael Brown, Fred Dallmayr, Maurice Roche, and Kurt Wolff, eds., *Self-Reflection in the Human Sciences*. Edmonton, Alberta: University of Edmonton Press, 1987. Pp. 1–15.

"Life-World: Variations on a Theme." In Stephen K. White, ed., *Lifeworld and Politics: Essays in Honor of Fred Dallmayr*. Notre Dame, Ind.: University of Notre Dame Press, 1989. Pp. 25–65.

"Hermeneutics and Deconstruction: Gadamer and Derrida in Dialogue." In Diane P. Michelfelder and Richard E. Palmer, eds., *Dialogue and Deconstruction: The Gadamer–Derrida Encounter*. Albany: SUNY Press, 1989. Pp. 75–92.

"On Being and Existence: A Western View." In G. Parthasarathi and D. P. Chattopadhyaya, eds., *Radhakrishnan: Centenary Volume*. Delhi: Oxford University Press, 1989. Pp. 217–45.

"Hermeneutics and Justice." In Kathleen Wright, ed., *Festivals of Interpretation: Essays on Hans-Georg Gadamer's Work*. Albany: SUNY Press, 1990. Pp. 90–110.

"Kant and Critical Theory." In Martyn P. Thompson, ed., *John Locke und/and Immanuel Kant*. Berlin: Duncker and Humblot, 1991. Pp. 288–312.

"Rethinking the Hegelian State." In Drucilla Cornell, Michael Rosenfeld, and David G. Carlson, eds., *Hegel and Legal Theory*. New York: Routledge, 1991. Pp. 321–46.

"Hermeneutics and the Rule of Law." In Gregory Leyh, ed., *Legal Hermeneutics: History, Theory, and Practice*. Berkeley: University of California Press, 1992. Pp. 3–22.

"Heidegger and Politics: Some Lessons." In Tom Rockmore and Joseph Margolis, eds., *The Heidegger Case: On Philosophy and Politics*. Philadelphia: Temple University Press, 1992. Pp. 282–312.

"Critical Theory and Reconciliation." In Don Browning and Francis Schüssler Fiorenza, eds., *Habermas, Modernity, and Public Theology*. New York: Crossroad/Continuum, 1992. Pp. 118–50.

"Modernity in the Crossfire: Comments on the Postmodern Turn." In John Paul Jones III, Wolfgang Natter, and Theodore R. Schatzki, eds., *Postmodern Contentions: Epochs, Politics, Space*. New York: Guilford Press, 1993. Pp. 17–38.

"Politics and Power: Ricoeur's Political Paradox Revisited." In David Klemm and William Schweiker, eds., *Meanings in Texts and Actions: Questioning Paul Ricoeur*. Charlottesville: University of Virginia Press, 1993. Pp. 176–94.

"Modernity and Postmodernity." In Thomas Flynn and Dalia Judovitz, eds., *Dialectic and Narrative*. Albany: SUNY Press, 1993. Pp. 105–20.

"Introduction." In Keith Hanley and Greg Kucich, eds., *Colonialisms*, special issue of *Nineteenth-Century Contexts* 18 (1994). Pp. 1–8.

"Max Weber and the Modern State." In Asher Horowitz and Terry Maley, eds., *The Barbarism of Reason: Max Weber and the Twilight of Enlightenment*. Toronto: University of Toronto Press, 1994. Pp. 44–63.

"Foreword." In David Dickens and Andrea Fontana, eds., *Postmodernism and Social Inquiry.* New York: Guilford Publications, 1994. Pp. ix–x.

"Heidegger on Ethics and Justice." In Arleen B. Dallery and Stephen H. Watson, eds., *Transitions in Continental Philosophy.* Albany: SUNY Press, 1994. Pp. 189–210.

"Heidegger and Freud." In Babette E. Babich, ed., *From Phenomenology to Thought, Errancy, and Desire: Topical Essays on the Work of William J. Richardson.* Amsterdam: Kluwer, 1995. Pp. 549–67.

"Beyond Ideology: Gandhi's Truth Revisited." In Manmohan Choudhuri and Ramjee Singh, eds., *Mahatma Gandhi: 125 Years.* Varanasi: Gandhian Institute of Studies, 1995. Pp. 35–51.

"Democracy and Multiculturalism." In Seyla Benhabib, ed., *Democracy and Difference: Contesting the Boundaries of the Political.* Princeton: Princeton University Press, 1996. Pp. 278–94.

"The Discourse of Modernity." In Maurizio Passerin d'Entrèves and Seyla Benhabib, eds., *Habermas and the Unfinished Project of Modernity.* Cambridge, UK: Polity Press, 1996. Pp. 59–95.

"Postmodernism and Democracy." In D. L. Sheth and Ashis Nandy, eds., *The Multiverse of Democracy: Essays in Honor of Rajni Kothari.* Newbury Park, Calif.: Sage Publications, 1996. Pp. 183–99.

"Modes of Cross-Cultural Encounter." In Anindita Balslev, ed., *Cross-Cultural Conversations.* Atlanta: Scholars Press, 1996. Pp. 211–36.

"Culture and Global Development." In Ninian Smart and B. Srinivasa Murthy, eds., *East–West Encounters in Philosophy and Religion.* Long Beach, Calif.: Long Beach Publications, 1996. Pp. 321–32.

"Foreword." In Bernhard Waldenfels, *Order in the Twilight.* Trans. David J. Parent. Athens: Ohio University Press, 1996. Pp. xi–xv.

"Agency and Structure." In Christopher G. A. Bryant and David Jary, eds., *Anthony Giddens: Critical Assessments,* vol. 2. London: Routledge, 1997. Pp. 53–67.

"'Inoperative' Global Community? Reflections on Nancy." In D. Sheppard, S. Sparks, and Colin Thomas, eds., *On Jean-Luc Nancy: The Sense of Philosophy.* London: Routledge, 1997. Pp. 174–96.

"Exit from Orientalism: Comments on Wilhelm Halbfass." In Eli Franco and Karin Preisendanz, eds., *Beyond Orientalism: The Work of Wilhelm Halbfass and Its Impact on Indian and Cross-Cultural Studies.* Amsterdam: Rodopi, 1997. Pp. 49–69.

"Global Development: Alternative Voices from Delhi." In Chanda Gupta and D. P. Chattopadhyaya, eds., *Cultural Otherness and Beyond.* Leiden: Brill, 1998. Pp. 143–67.

"Ethics and the Limits of Politics: Comments on Elshtain." In Jean Bethke Elshtain, *New Wine in Old Bottles: International Politics and Ethical Discourse.* Notre Dame, Ind.: University of Notre Dame Press, 1998. Pp. 53–71.

"Introduction." In F. Dallmayr and G. N. Devy, eds., *Between Tradition and Modernity: India's Search for Identity.* New Delhi: Sage Publications, 1998. Pp. 15–52.

"Freedom—East and West: A Tribute to D. P. Chattopadhyaya." In Daya Krishna and K. Satchidananda Murty, eds., *History, Custom and Truth: Essays Presented to D. P. Chattopadhyaya.* New Delhi: Kalki Prakash, 1999. Pp. 46–57.

"The Enigma of Health: Gadamer at Century's End." In Lawrence K. Schmidt, ed., *Language and Linguisticality in Gadamer's Hermeneutics.* Lanham, Md.: Lexington Books, 2000. Pp. 155–69.

"What is *Swaraj?* Lessons from Gandhi." In Anthony J. Parel, ed., *Gandhi: Freedom and Self-Rule.* Lanham, Md.: Lexington Books, 2000. Pp. 103–18.

"Derrida and Friendship." In Preston King and Heather Devere, eds., *The Challenge to Friendship in Modernity.* London: Frank Cass, 2000. Pp. 105–30.

"Dezentrierter Dialog: Waldenfels an vielfachen Diskursüberkreuzungen." In Matthias Fischer, Hans-Dieter Gondek, and Burkhard Liebsch, eds., *Vernunft im Zeichen des Fremden: Zur Philosophie von Bernhard Waldenfels.* Frankfurt: Suhrkamp Verlag, 2001. Pp. 130–56.

"Beyond Fugitive Democracy? Some Modern and Postmodern Reflections." In Aryeh Botwinick and William E. Connolly, eds., *Democracy and Vision: Sheldon Wolin and the Vicissitudes of the Political.* Princeton: Princeton University Press, 2001. Pp. 58–78.

"Mas allá de la democracia fugitivia." In Isidoro Cheresky and Inés Pousadela, eds., *Política e instituciones en las nuevas democracias latinoamericanas.* Buenos Aires: Editorial Paidós, 2001. Pp. 407–30.

"Liberation beyond Liberalism: Lessons from Buddhism and Islam." In Ananta K. Giri, ed., *Rethinking Social Transformation.* New Delhi: Rawat Publishing, 2001. Pp. 109–33.

"Democracy: Modern and Postmodern." In Sudha P. Pandya and Prafulla C. Kar, eds., *Interdisciplinary Perspectives on Modernity.* Delhi: Pencraft International, 2001. Pp. 23–46.

"Para além da democracia fugidia: Algumas reflexóes modernas e pós-modernas." In Jessé Souza, ed., *Democracia hoje: Novas desafios para a teoria democratica contemporânea.* Brasilia, DF: Editora Universidade de Brasilia, 2001. Pp. 11–38.

"Memory and Social Imagination: Latin-American Reflections." In Enrique R. Larreta and Candido Mendes, eds., *Collective Imagination: Limits and Beyond.* Rio de Janeiro: UNESCO, 2001. Pp. 159–84.

"Christianity and Civilization." In Majid Tehranian and David W. Chappell, eds., *Dialogue of Civilizations: A New Peace Agenda for the New Millennium.* New York: Tauris, 2002. Pp. 125–37.

"Polis and Cosmopolis." In Hwa Yol Jung, ed., *Comparative Political Culture in the Age of Globalization.* Lanham, Md.: Lexington Books, 2002. Pp. 419–42.

"Introduction." In Ananta K. Giri, *Conversations and Transformations: Towards a New Ethics of Self and Society.* Lanham, Md.: Lexington Books, 2002. Pp. xix–xxv.

"Transversal Liaisons: Calvin Schrag on Selfhood." In Martin J. Matustik and William L. McBride, eds., *Calvin O. Schrag and the Task of Philosophy after Postmodernity.* Evanston, Ill.: Northwestern University Press, 2002. Pp. 129–51.

"Ethics and Public Life: A Critical Tribute to Paul Ricoeur." In John Wall, William Schweiker, and W. David Hall, eds., *Paul Ricoeur and Contemporary Moral Thought*. New York: Routledge, 2002. Pp. 213–32.

"What Is *Swaraj?* Lessons from Gandhi." In Anthony J. Parel, ed., *Gandhi, Freedom and Self-Rule*. New Delhi: Vistaar Publications, 2002. Pp. 103–18.

"The Ambivalence of Europe: European Culture and Its 'Other.'" In Ralf Elm, ed., *Europäische Identität: Paradigmen und Methodenfragen*. Baden-Baden: Nomos Verlag, 2002. Pp. 75–91.

"Sacred Nonsovereignty." In John D. Carlson and Erik C. Owens, eds., *The Sacred and the Sovereign: Religion and International Politics*. Washington, D.C.: Georgetown University Press, 2003. Pp. 256–64.

"Modernity and Postmodernity." In Prafulla C. Kar, Kailash C. Baral, and Sura P. Rath, eds., *Theory and Praxis: Curriculum, Culture and English Studies*. Delhi: Pencraft International, 2003. Pp. 23–33.

"Derrida and Friendship." In Eduardo A. Velásquez, ed., *Love and Friendship: Rethinking Politics and Affection in Modern Times*. Lanham, Md.: Lexington Books, 2003. Pp. 549–74.

"Global Spiritual Resurgence? On Christian and Islamic Spiritualities." In Fabio Petito and Pavlos Hatzopoulos, eds., *Religion in International Relations: The Return from Exile*. New York: Palgrave Macmillan, 2003. Pp. 209–36.

"Social Identity and Creative Praxis." In Kailash C. Baral and Prafulla C. Kar, eds., *Identities: Local and Global*. Delhi: Pencraft International, 2003. Pp. 13–30.

"But on a Quiet Day. . . . A Tribute to Arundhati Roy." In Sura P. Rath, Kailash C. Baral, and D. Venkat Rao, eds., *Reflections on Literature, Criticism and Theory: Essays in Honour of Professor Prafulla C. Kar*. Delhi: Pencraft International, 2004. Pp. 231–47.

"Confucianism and the Public Sphere: Five Relationships Plus One?" In Chaihark Hahm and Daniel Bell, eds., *The Politics of Affective Relations: East Asia and Beyond*. Lanham, Md.: Lexington Books, 2004. Pp. 41–59.

"An Islamic Reformation? Some Afterthoughts." In Michaelle Browers and Charles Kurzman, eds., *An Islamic Reformation?* Lanham, Md.: Lexington Books, 2004. Pp. 178–84.

"Habermas and the Discourse of Modernity: Nietzsche as *Turnwheel*." In Babette E. Babich, ed., *Habermas, Nietzsche, and Critical Theory*. Amherst, N.Y.: Humanity Books, 2004. Pp. 81–104.

"Laclau and Hegemony: Some (Post) Hegelian Caveats." In Simon Critchley and Oliver Marchart, eds., *Laclau: A Critical Reader*. New York: Routledge, 2004. Pp. 35–53.

"Global Ethics: Beyond the Dichotomy of Universalism and Particularism" (Russian). In Marietta Stepaniants, ed., *Cravnitelnaya Philosophiya*. Moscow: Russian Academy, 2004. Pp. 274–97.

"Dialogue among Civilizations: A Hermeneutical Perspective." In Hermann-Josef Scheidgen, Norbert Hintersteiner, and Yoshiro Nakamura, eds., *Philosophie, Ge-*

sellschaft und Bildung in Zeiten der Globalisierung. Amsterdam–New York: Rodopi, 2005. Pp. 67–84.

"The Underside of Modernity: Adorno, Heidegger, and Dussel." In Santosh Gupta, Prafulla C. Kar, and Parul D. Mukherji, eds., *Rethinking Modernity.* Delhi: Pencraft International, 2005. Pp. 22–41.

"Empire and Cosmopolis: Civilization at the Crossroads." In Raúl Fornet-Betancour, ed., *New Colonialisms in North-South Relations.* Frankfurt-London: IKO Verlag für Interkulturelle Kommunikation, 2005. Pp. 45–70.

"Gandhi and Islam: A Heart-and-Mind Unity?" In V. R. Mehta and Thomas Pantham, eds., *Political Ideas in Modern India: Thematic Explorations.* New Delhi: Sage Publications, 2006. Pp. 206–20.

"Encounters between European and Asian Social Theory." In Gerard Delanty, ed., *Handbook of Contemporary European Social Theory.* London–New York: Routledge, 2006. Pp. 372–80.

ARTICLES

"Initiation a l'idée du 'supranational.'" *Chronique de politique étrangère* 8 (1955): 1–9.

"Proudhon et la coexistence." *Revue international d'histoire politique et constitutionnelle* 5 (1956): 205–17.

"Studie über Norberto Bobbio." *Archiv für Rechts- und Sozialphilosophie* 42 (1956): 403–28.

"Integrierung und Differenzierung in der nord- und südamerikanischen Rechtslehre." *Archiv für Rechts- und Sozialphilosophie* 43 (1957): 399–417.

"Epimeteo Cristiano o Prometeo Pagano?" *Revista Internazionale di Filosofia del Diritto* 35 (1958): 657–79. (On Carl Schmitt.)

"Thomas Hobbes." *Staatslexikon,* vol. 6. 6th ed. Freiburg, Görres-Gesellschaft, 1960. Pp. 108–12.

"Public and Semi-Public Corporations in France." *Law and Contemporary Problems* (Fall 1961): 755–93.

With Robert S. Rankin. "Rights of Patients in Mental Hospitals." In U.S. Senate, Hearings before the Subcommittee on Constitutional Rights of the Committee on the Judiciary, *Constitutional Rights of the Mentally Ill,* 87th Cong., 1st Sess. (March 1961). Pp. 329–70.

"Background and Development of the Austrian Constitutional Court." *Journal of Central European Affairs* 21 (January 1962): 403–33.

"Heinrich Rickert und die amerikanische Sozialwissenschaft." *Der Staat* 5 (Spring 1966): 17–46.

"Strauss and the 'Moral Basis' of Thomas Hobbes." *Archiv für Rechts- und Sozialphilosophie* 52 (Spring 1966): 25–66.

"Functionalism, Justice and Equality." *Ethics* 78 (October 1967): 1–16.

"Political Science and the Two Cultures." *Journal of General Education* 19 (January 1968): 269–95.

"Wissenschaft und Gesellschaft in den USA: Das Triumvirat von Wissenschaft, Staat und Wirtschaft." *Verein Deutscher Ingenieure-Zeitschrift* (VDI-Z) 111 (April 1969): 413–21.

"Bilanz der amerikanischen Politikwissenschaft." *Politische Vierteljahresschrift* 10 (Spring 1969): 149–53. (Review article.)

"Hobbes and Existentialism: Some Affinities." *Journal of Politics* 31 (August 1969): 615–40. (Revised and condensed version.)

"Empirical Political Theory and the Image of Man." *Polity* 2 (1970): 443–78.

"History and Class Consciousness: George Lukács' Theory of Social Change." *Politics and Society* 1 (1970): 113–31.

"Reason and Emancipation: Notes on Habermas." *Man and World* 5 (1972): 79–109.

"Critical Theory Criticized: Habermas' *Knowledge and Human Interests* and Its Aftermath." *Philosophy of the Social Sciences* 2 (1972): 211–29.

"Ingens Sylva: Begegnung mit Vico." *Philosophische Rundschau* 19 (Fall 1972): 74–82.

"Plessner's Philosophical Anthropology: Implications for Role Theory and Politics." *Inquiry* 17 (1974): 49–77.

"Toward a Critical Reconstruction of Ethics and Politics." *Journal of Politics* 36 (1974): 926–57.

"Beyond Dogma and Despair: Toward a Critical Theory of Politics." *American Political Science Review* 70 (1976): 64–79.

"Marxism and Truth." *Telos* 29 (Fall 1976): 130–59.

"Expérience du sens et reflexion sur la validité: K. O. Apel et la transformation de la philosophie." *Archives de philosophie* 39 (1976): 367–405.

"Natural History and Social Evolution: Reflections on Vico's 'Corsi e Ricorsi.'" *Social Research* 43 (Winter 1976): 857–73.

"Phenomenology and Critical Theory: Adorno." *Cultural Hermeneutics* 3 (1976): 367–405.

"Hermeneutics and Historicism: Reflections on Winch, Apel and Vico." *Review of Politics* 39 (January 1977): 60–81.

"Sinnerlebnis und Geltungsreflexion: K. O. Apels Transformation der Philosophie." *Philosophische Rundschau* 25 (1978): 1–42.

"Vico and Herder." *Review of Politics* 40 (1978): 140–45. (Review essay.)

"Knowledge and Commitment: Variations on a Familiar Theme." *Polity* 12 (1979): 291–302.

"On Critical Theory." *Philosophy of the Social Sciences* 10 (1980): 93–109. (Review essay.)

"Between Theory and Practice." *Human Studies* 3 (1980): 175–84. (Review essay.)

"Heidegger on Intersubjectivity." *Human Studies* 3 (1980): 221–46.

"Critical Theory and Public Policy." *Policy Studies Journal* 9 (1981): 522–34.

"Frankfurt School: An Essay." *Review of Politics* 43 (1981): 141–46.

Life-World and Politics." *Research in Phenomenology* 11 (1981): 256–63.

"Conversation, Discourse, and Politics." *Phenomenology and the Human Sciences* 1 (1982): 49–88.

"Agency and Structure." *Philosophy of the Social Sciences* 12 (1982): 427–38. (Review Essay.)

"Language and Praxis." *Human Studies* 5 (1982): 249–59.

"The Relevance of Relevance: Comments on McBride." *Philosophy in Context* 13 (1983): 71–75.

"Response" (to Rasmussen and McCarthy), *Philosophy and Social Criticism* 10 (Fall 1984): 121–29.

"Is Critical Theory a Humanism?" *Boundary 2* 12–13 (1984): 463–93.

"Continental Perspectives and the Study of Politics." *News for Teachers of Political Science* 44 (Winter 1985): 15–17.

"Pragmatism and Hermeneutics." *Review of Politics* 47 (1985): 411–30. (Review essay.)

"Heidegger, Hölderlin and Politics." *Heidegger Studies* 2 (1986): 81–95.

"Tradition and Modernization in India." *Review of Politics* 48 (1986): 621–26. (Review essay.)

With Gisela Hinkle. "Foucault *in memoriam* (1926–84)." *Human Studies* 10 (1987): 2–9.

"Democracy and Post-Modernism." *Human Studies* 10 (1987): 143–70.

"Praxis and Reflection." *Phenomenology and Social Science* 12 (1987): 2–9. (Review essay.)

"Politics of the Kingdom: Pannenberg's *Anthropology*." *Review of Politics* 49 (1987): 85–111.

"Politics against Philosophy: Strauss and Drury." *Political Theory* 15 (1987): 326–37.

"Introduction: Reading Horkheimer Reading Vico." *New Vico Studies* 5 (1987): 57–62.

Translation of Horkheimer, "Vico and Mythology." *New Vico Studies* 5 (1987): 63–76.

"Public or Private Freedom? Response to Kateb." *Social Research* 45 (1987): 617–28.

"Politics and Conceptual Analysis: Comments on Vollrath." *Philosophy and Social Criticism* 13 (1987): 31–37.

"The Discourse of Modernity: Hegel and Habermas." *Journal of Philosophy* 84 (1987): 682–92.

"Heidegger and Marxism." *Praxis International* 7 (1987–88): 207–24.

"Hegemony and Democracy: A Review of Laclau and Mouffe." *Philosophy and Social Criticism* 13 (1987): 283–96.

"Habermas and Rationality." *Political Theory* 16 (1988): 553–79.

"Between Kant and Aristotle: Beiner's *Political Judgment*." *New Vico Studies* 6 (1988): 147–54. (Review essay.)

"Understanding Nietzsche's Anti-Politics." *Review of Politics* 50 (1988): 133–39. (Review essay.)

"Rethinking the Hegelian State." *Cardozo Law Review* 10 (1988): 1337–61.

"Nature and Community: Comments on Michael Perry." *Tulane Law Review* 63 (1989): 1405–21.

"The Discourse of Modernity: Hegel, Nietzsche, Heidegger (and Habermas)." *Praxis International* 8 (1989): 377–406.

"Freud, Nietzsche, Lacan: A Discourse on Critical Theory." *Politics, Culture and Society* 2 (1989): 467–92.

"Marxism and Eschatology: Bloch's *Principle of Hope.*" *Religious Studies Review* 15 (1989): 112–16.

"On Bernhard Waldenfels." *Social Research* 56 (1989): 681–712.

"Voegelin's Search for Order." *Journal of Politics* 51 (1989): 411–30.

"Adorno and Heidegger." *Diacritics* 19 (1989): 82–100.

"Political Evil: A Response to Alford." *Political Psychology* 11 (1990): 29–35.

"Hermeneutics and the Rule of Law." *Cardozo Law Review* 11 (1990): 1449–69.

"Rethinking the Political: Some Heideggerian Contributions." *Review of Politics* 52 (1990): 524–52.

"A Response to My Critics." *Human Studies* 14 (1991): 23–31.

"Modernity and Postmodernity." *Journal of Contemporary Thought* (India) 1 (1991): 25–35.

"Connolly's Deconstruction of Modern Political Theory." *Strategies* 4/5 (1991): 45–58.

"Justice and Violence: A Response to Jacques Derrida." *Cardozo Law Review* 13 (1991): 1237–43.

"Nothingness and Sunyata: A Comparison of Heidegger and Nishitani." *Philosophy East and West* 42 (1992): 37–48.

"Modernization and Postmodernization: Whither India?" *Alternatives* 17 (1992): 421–52.

"Heidegger and Freud." *Political Psychology* 14 (1993): 235–53.

"Postmetaphysics and Democracy." *Political Theory* 21 (1993): 101–27.

"Tradition, Modernity, and Confucianism." *Human Studies* 16 (1993), pp. 203–11.

"Heidegger and Psychotherapy." *Review of Existential Psychology and Psychiatry* 21 (1993): 9–34.

"Self and Other: Gadamer and the Hermeneutics of Difference." *Yale Journal of Law and the Humanities* 5 (1993): 101–24.

"Heidegger and Zen Buddhism: A Salute to Keji Nishitani." *Chinese and Western Philosophy and Culture* 12 (1993): 25–67.

"Western Thought and Indian Thought: Comments on Ramanujan." *Philosophy East and West* 44 (1994): 527–42.

"Modernity Rescued from Knockers and Boosters." *Review of Politics* 56 (1994): 153–57.

"Culture and Global Development." *Journal of Contemporary Thought* (India) 4 (1994): 99–111.

"Leo Strauss Peregrinus." *Social Research* 61 (1994): 877–906.

"Political Thought beyond Metaphysics." *Review of Politics* 57 (1995): 138–43.

"Thinking Politically beyond Metaphysics." *Research in Phenomenology* 25 (1995): 282–88.

"Rights versus Rites: Justice and Cultural Transformation." *Social Science and Policy Research* (Seoul National University) 17 (1995): 3–30.

"The Return of the Political: On Chantal Mouffe." *Constellations* 3 (1996): 115–20. (Review essay.)

"Die Heimkehr des Politischen." *Deutsche Zeitschrift für Philosophie* 44 (1996): 517–26.

"Global Development: Alternative Voices from Delhi." *Alternatives* 21 (1996): 259–82.

"Splitting the Difference: Comments on Calvin Schrag." *Human Studies* 19 (1996): 229–38. (Review essay.)

"Heidegger, Bhakti, and Vedanta: A Tribute to J. L. Mehta." *Journal of Indian Council for Philosophical Research* 13 (1996): 117–44.

"Return to the Source: African Identity (after Cabral)." *Theoria* 88 (1996): 1–23.

"Cultura y Desarrollo Global." *Topicos* 10 (1996): 9–24.

"Truth and Diversity: Some Lessons from Herder." *Journal of Speculative Philosophy* 11 (1997): 101–24.

"The Politics of Nonidentity: Adorno, Postmodernism—and Edward Said." *Political Theory* 25 (1997): 33–56.

"International Vedanta Congress in Madras: A Report." *Philosophy East and West* 47 (April 1997): 255–58.

"Introduction: Toward a Comparative Political Theory." *Review of Politics* 59 (1997): 421–27.

"A Response to Friends." *Human Studies* 21 (1998): 295–308.

"Some Rays of Hope?" *Commentary* (International Movement for a Just World) 18 (November 1998): 13–14.

"Rethinking Secularism (with Raimon Panikkar)." *Review of Politics* 61 (Fall 1999): 715–35.

"Globalization from Below." *International Politics* 36 (September 1999): 321–34.

"Derrida and Friendship." *Critical Review of International Social and Political Philosophy* 2 (Winter 1999): 105–30.

"Achieving Multiple Countries: Millennial Reflections." *Journal of Contemporary Thought* (*India*) 10 (Winter 1999): 5–26.

"The Enigma of Health: Hans-Georg Gadamer at 100." *Review of Politics* 62 (Spring 2000): 327–50.

"A Final Postmortem?" *Review of Politics* 62 (Summer 2000): 616–20. (Review essay.)

"Decentered Dialogue: Bernhard Waldenfels and Multiple Selves." *Review of Existential Psychology and Psychiatry* 25 (2000): 55–71.

"The Future of the Past." *Journal of Contemporary Thought* 12 (Winter 2000): 5–16.

"Governo global e diversidade cultural." *Sociedade e Estado* 15 (2000): 11–32.

"Reason, Faith, and Politics: A Journey to Muslim Andalusia." *Maghreb Review* 25 (2000): 194–16.

"Dogu-Bati Divani: Goethe ve Hafiz digalogue." *Divan* 5, no. 9 (2000), pp. 113–31. (Turkish.)

"The Highest Purpose." *CSD Bulletin* 8 (Winter 2000–1): 11–13.

"Borders or Horizons? Gadamer and Habermas Revisited." *Chicago-Kent Law Review* 76 (Spring 2001): 101–27.

"Heidegger on *Macht* and *Machenschaft*." *Continental Philosophy Review* 34 (2001): 247–67.

"Achieving Our World Democratically: A Response to Richard Rorty." *Theoria* 97 (2001): 23–40.

"Memory and Social Imagination: Latin American Reflections." *Critical Horizons* 2 (2001): 153–71.

"Islam: Friend or Enemy?" *International Studies Review* 3 (2001): 171–74. (Review essay.)

"Walking Humbly with Your God: Jñaneshwar and the Warkaris." *Journal of Contemporary Thought* 13 (2001): 33–53.

"Dialogue of Civilizations: A Gadamerian Perspective." *Global Dialogue* 3 (2001): 64–75.

"Conversation across Boundaries." *Millennium: Journal of International Studies* 30 (Fall 2001): 331–47.

"Beyond the Clash of Civilizations." *Sandhan-Journal of Centre for Studies in Civilizations* (New Delhi) 1 (January–June 2001): 71–79.

"Gandhi on Self-Rule." *Re-Vision* 24 (Summer 2001): 9–18.

"Clock-Time or Lived Time? Twenty-five Years of *Human Studies*." *Human Studies* 25 (2002): 473–75.

"Globalization and Inequality: A Plea for Global Justice." *International Studies Review* 4 (Summer 2002): 137–56.

"'Asian Values' and Global Human Rights," *Philosophy East and West* 52 (2002): 173–89.

"Lessons of September 11." *Theory, Culture and Society* 19 (2002): 137–45.

"Social Identity and Creative Praxis." *Journal of Contemporary Thought* 16 (2002): 5–24.

"Cosmopolitanism: Moral and Political." *Political Theory* 31 (June 2003): 421–42.

"Multiculturalism and the Good Life: Comments on Bhikhu Parekh." *Good Society* 12, no. 2 (2003): 40–44. (Review essay.)

"Confucianism and the Public Sphere: Five Relationships Plus One?" *Dao: A Journal of Comparative Philosophy* 2 (2003): 193–212.

"On Human Rights-in-the-World: A Response to Jamie Morgan." *Philosophy East and West* 53 (October 2003): 587–90.

"Global Ethics: Between Universalism and Particularism." *Voprosi Philosophii* (2003): 13–29. (Russian.)

"Gandhi and Islam." *Radical Philosophy Review* 6, no. 1 (2003): 29–48.

"The Underside of Modernity: Adorno, Heidegger, and Dussel." *Constellations* 11, no. 1 (2004): 102–20.

"Religion and Rationality: Habermas and the Early Frankfurt School." *Constellations* 11, no. 2 (2004): 300–4. (Review essay.)

"Beyond Monologue: For a Comparative Political Theory." *Perspectives on Politics* 2, no. 2 (2004): 249–57.

"The *Law of Peoples* and the Laws of War." *Peace Review* 16 (September 2004): 269–77.

"The Dignity of Difference: A Tribute to Jonathan Sacks." *Millennium* 33 (2004): 397–405. (Review essay.)

"Vista on European Philosophy." *Review of Politics* 67 (2005): 687–90.

"Empire or Cosmopolis? Civilization at the Crossroads." *Globalizations* 2, no. 1 (2005): 14–30.

"Imparatorluk mu Kozmopolis mi? Medeniyet yol Ayriminda." *Notlar* 2 (2005): 3–31. (Turkish.)

"On the Natural Theology of the Chinese: A Tribute to Henry Rosemont, Jr." *Ex/Change* (Centre for Cross-Cultural Studies, City University of Hong Kong) 13 (June 2005): 16–22.

"Ricoeur's Negotiated Settlements." *Philosophy Now* 52 (August/September 2005): 32–33.

"Globalization and Inequality: A Plea for Cosmopolitan Justice." *Comparative Studies of South Asia, Africa and the Middle East* 26 (2006): 63–74.

Contributors

Michaelle Browers is assistant professor of political science at Wake Forest University. She teaches and writes in the field of political theory and is the author of *Democracy and Civil Society in Arab Political Thought: Transcultural Possibilities.*

John Francis Burke is professor of political science at the University of St. Thomas in Houston. His research is in political theory. He is the author of *Mestizo Democracy: The Politics of Crossing Borders* (2002), and his writings have appeared in numerous journals, including *The Review of Politics, Presidential Studies Quarterly, Concilium,* and *Commonweal.* He also advises community groups wrestling with the challenges of political mobilization, social justice, and multiculturalism at the grassroots level in Houston.

Neve Gordon is a senior lecturer in the Department of Politics and Government at Ben-Gurion University, where he specializes in the field of political theory and human rights. He is editor of *Torture: Human Rights, Medical Ethics, and the Case of Israel* and *On the Margins of Globalization: Critical Perspectives on Human Rights.* He is author of *Israel's Occupation: Tracing the Technologies of Control* (forthcoming).

David Ingram is professor of philosophy at Loyola University, Chicago. His research focuses on philosophy of law, democratic theory, human rights, and philosophy of social science. He has written extensively on German, French, and Anglo-American social thought and his research has appeared in many journals, including *The Review of Metaphysics, Political Theory, Kant-Studien, Constellations, The Philosophical Forum,* and *Philosophy and Social Criticism.* He is the author of six books: *Habermas and the Dialectic of Reason; Critical*

Theory and Philosophy; Reason, History, and Politics; Group Rights; Rights, Democracy, and Fulfillment in the Era of Identity Politics; The Complete Idiot's Guide to Understanding Ethics; and *Law: Key Concepts.*

Hwa Yol Jung is professor emeritus of political science at Moravian College, Bethlehem, Pennsylvania. He was trained in international relations, Western comparative politics, and Western political theory. In addition to political theory, he has further developed an interest in comparative philosophy, comparative literature, communication theory, environmental philosophy, and cultural studies. His major works include *Existential Phenomenology and Political Theory: A Reader; The Crisis of Political Understanding: A Phenomenological Perspective in the Conduct of Political Inquiry; The Question of Rationality and the Basic Grammar of Intercultural Texts; Rethinking Political Theory;* and *Comparative Political Culture in the Age of Globalization: An Introductory Anthology.*

Thomas McCarthy is professor of philosophy and John Shaffer Professor in the Humanities at Northwestern University. He has published extensively in social and political theory, especially on critical theory, and is currently working on the roles of "race" and "development" in modern and contemporary thought. His published works include *The Critical Theory of Jürgen Habermas, Ideals and Illusions,* and (with David Hoy) *Critical Theory.* He is the general editor of the MIT Press series titled *Studies in Contemporary German Social Thought,* in which some one hundred translations and monographs have appeared.

Chantal Mouffe is professor of political theory at the Centre for the Study of Democracy at the University of Westminster in London. She has taught and researched in many universities in Europe, North America and South America, and is a member of the Collège International de Philosophie in Paris. She is the author of *The Return of the Political; The Democratic Paradox; On the Political;* and (with Ernesto Laclau) of *Hegemony and Socialist Strategy: Towards a Radical Democratic Politics.* She is the editor of *Gramsci and Marxist Theory; Dimensions of Radical Democracy: Pluralism, Citizenship, Community; Deconstruction and Pragmatism;* and *The Challenge of Carl Schmitt.*

Stephen F. Schneck is associate professor in the Politics Department at The Catholic University of America. He teaches and writes in the field of political theory. His works have appeared in the journals *Polity, Review of Politics, International Journal of Philosophy, Political Theory,* and *Human Studies.* He is the author of *Person and Polis.*

Morton Schoolman is professor in the Department of Political Science, State University of New York at Albany, where he teaches modern political thought. His most recent book is *Reason and Horror: Critical Theory, Democracy, and Aesthetic Individuality,* and he is editor of the Rowman and Littlefield series titled Modernity and Political Thought. He is currently working on a new book—*The Next Enlightenment: Aesthetic Reason in Mass Culture and Modern Democracy*—of which the essay included here is a part.

Calvin O. Schrag is George Ade Distinguished Professor of Philosophy Emeritus at Purdue University, where he has been for the majority of his career. He is the author of many books including *Radical Reflection and the Origin of the Human Sciences; Existence and Freedom; Communicative Praxis and the Space of Subjectivity; Experience and Being; Resources of Rationality; The Self after Postmodernity;* and *God as Otherwise than Being.* He is the recipient of Fulbright and Guggenheim Fellowships and is founding editor of the international philosophical quarterly *Continental Philosophy Review.*

Tracy B. Strong is professor of political science at the University of California, San Diego. He is the author of several books, among them *Friedrich Nietzsche and the Politics of Transfiguration; Jean Jacques Rousseau and the Politics of the Ordinary; The Idea of Political Theory,* and many articles. He is presently working on a book on the relation of aesthetics and politics in early twentieth-century thought. From 1990 until 2000 he was editor of *Political Theory.* He is the recipient of fellowships from the National Endowment for the Humanities, the Rockefeller Foundation, the Juan March Institute, and Princeton University.

Ronald J. Terchek is professor emeritus in Government and Politics at the University of Maryland at College Park. His recent works include *Gandhi: Struggling for Autonomy; Republican Paradoxes and Liberal Anxieties: Retrieving Neglected Fragments in Political Theory;* and (with Thomas Conte) co-editor of *Democratic Political Theory: A Reader.* He has contributed to numerous edited works as well as journals including *The American Political Science Review; Gandhi Marg, Journal of Gandhian Studies;* and *Ethics.* His principle areas of teaching and research have been liberal democratic theory, twentieth-century Indian political thought with particular emphasis on Gandhi, and American political theory. He is currently completing a book on democratic theory and is also writing another book on Gandhi.

Franke Wilmer is professor of political science at Montana State University. She is author of *The Indigenous Voice in World Politics: Since Time Immemorial,* which evaluates the global political activism of indigenous peoples as a social movement, and *The Social Construction of Man, the State, and War: Identity, Conflict, and Violence in Former Yugoslavia,* which examines the deep origins and modes of the Yugoslav wars of the 1990s. She is currently researching the development of international norms regulating the use of force in international relations.

Krzysztof Ziarek is professor of comparative literature at the State University of New York at Buffalo. He is the author of *Inflected Language: Toward a Hermeneutics of Nearness; The Historicity of Experience: Modernity, the Avant-Garde, and the Event;* and *The Force of Art.* He has also published numerous essays on Coolidge, Stein, Stevens, Heidegger, Benjamin, Irigaray, Levinas, and coedited a collection of essays titled *Future Crossings: Literature between Philosophy and Cultural Studies.* He has published two volumes of poetry in Polish, *Zaimejlowane z Polski,* and *Sad dostateczny.* He is currently working on aesthetics and globalization.

Index

academia, 4
actor, 35–37, 42, 45, 48
accommodation, 273
Adorno, Theodor, 11, 16–17, 21, 56, 57–76, 93, 136n4, 324–25, 342n5, 343n7
Aeschylus, 49
Aesop, 207
aesthetic (aesthetics, aesthetic theory), 48, 59, 61–62, 64, 83, 85, 325
aesthetic form, 68–69, 75, 82–83
aesthetic reason, 55–62, 66–68, 75–77, 83–85, 324–25
Africa/African, 206, 214, 217–18, 231, 287
African Americans, 50, 211. *See also* blacks
African thought, 268
African Union, 339
agency, 6, 16
agonism, 10, 19, 207, 212, 216, 219, 223, 225, 278, 339
agora, 39, 45
Alford, C. Fred, 271n12, 344n16
alienation/world-alienation, 23, 47, 298, 315, 322
Almond, Gabriel, 233
alterity, 253, 260. *See also* otherness
ambiguity, 13–14, 179, 266
American culture (United States' culture), 210–11
American society, 184, 186, 299
Americas, 214, 216, 218
Ames, Roger, 302, 308n24
anarchism, 14, 206
Anaximander, 195
Anderson, Benedict, 201, 204n35
Anglo-Protestant values/culture, 209–11

Anglo-Saxon Protestant, 211–12
An-Na'im, Abdullah Ahmed, 303–4, 309n26
anomie, 23
anthropocentrism, 114, 118–19, 122, 124, 130, 132, 135, 136n4, 137n10, 177, 324. *See also Vermenschung*
antihumanism, 11, 122, 330. *See also* post-humanism
antimodernism, 96, 145, 162, 332
antinomy, 169, 180n16, 225
Anzaldúa, Gloria, 207, 216–18, 227n41
Apel, Karl-Otto, 5, 7–8, 272
apriorism, 5
Aquinas, Thomas, 221–22, 228n58, 291
Arab modernity, 177
Arab/Arabian thought, 168–69, 176–77, 333
Arab world, 175–76, 200
Arab-Islamic heritage, 176–78, 181n37
Arab-Jewish relations, 200, 334–35
Archibugi, Daniele, 273–74, 338
Arendt, Hannah, 7, 10–11, 26, 241–42, 253
Aristotle, 7, 11, 22, 26, 29n58, 49–50, 169, 180n4, 230, 323, 327, 329–30, 334
Arslan, Amir Shakib, 176, 181n36
art (artwork, work of art), 48, 55–56, 59–85, 325. *See also* modern art
artificial/articifiality, 43
Asensi, Manuel, 249n40
Asia, 206, 287
Asiatic mode of production, 233
assimilation, 170, 205, 207, 210–14, 215, 216, 220, 225

Athens, 167, 169, 171–72, 174, 311, 318, 332–33
audience, 45, 48–49
Augustine of Hippo/Augustinian, 23, 207, 220–23, 225–26, 228n59, 304
Auribindo, Sri, 141–61, 163n1, 163nn13–14, 164n16, 164n20, 164n25, 164n29, 164n31, 165n34, 165n37, 165nn39–40, 165nn44–45, 165n49, 165n52, 166n53, 332
authenticity, 21, 25
author (*auctor*), 43, 51
authority, 41, 43, 156
autonomy, 143–44, 301. *See also* independence
Averroës/Averroism, 168–69, 174, 180n4. *See also* Ibn Rushd
axis of evil, 340
Azande, 4

Bacik, James, 222, 228n57
Bacon, Francis, 52n25, 242, 325
Bakhtin, Mikhail, 240–41, 248n38
Balibar, Etienne, 53n43
Bañuelas, Arturo, 218, 227nn36–37, 228n51
Barber, Benjamin, 8, 205, 344n15
Barish, Jonas, 53n38
Battle, M. J., 271n18
Bauman, Zygmunt, 232, 245n4, 245n11
Bavaria, Germany, 3
beauty, 80, 81, 160
Beck, Ulrich, 243, 249n47, 249n49
Becoming, 123, 240
Bedouin, 183–90, 202n2, 202nn6–7, 334
behavioralism, 4
Being, 7, 10, 16, 114, 116, 118, 120–22, 126–27, 130–31, 135n2, 195–97, 199, 242
being-in-the-world, 114, 127, 131, 197, 228n58, 330
being selves in the world, 253, 255, 258
beings, 127–28
belief (beliefs, customary beliefs), 96–98, 100–102, 300
Bellah, Robert, 212, 227n24

Bengal, 146–48
Ben-Gurion, David, 184
Benhabib, Seyla, 62, 69, 83, 86n8, 86n22, 87n39, 247n23, 325, 342n6, 343n9
Benjamin, Walter, 324
Bennett, Jane, 62, 86n20
Bernabé, Jean, 248n35
Bernauer, James, 54n49
between (in-between), 170, 213, 235
Bhakti, 190
Bhengu, M. J., 271n18
Bible, 171
Biemel, Walter, 28n49
Bildung, 9, 11, 13, 22–23, 26, 27n28, 329
blacks, 184, 186–87, 202n2, 299. *See also* African Americans
Blecher, Robert, 203n12
Bloom, Allan, 175
Bluhm, William T., 228n53
Bobbio, Noberto, 25
body, 67, 70–74, 159, 179, 232
Bonss, Wolfgang, 86n8
Boulding, Elise, 22
Bourdieu, Pierre, 203n17
Bramhall, John (bishop), 34, 36
Breecher, Jeremy, 205, 226n1
Bremer, Paul, 291
Brimelow, Peter, 226n8
Browers, Michaelle, ix, 167, 332–34
Brown, Norman O., 230
Buber, Martin, 204n26
Buchanan, Patrick, 226n8
Buddha, 235
Buddhism, 115, 119, 206, 208, 219, 224, 235, 301–2, 306, 330, 336
building, 19
bureaucracy/bureaucratic state, 101–4, 162
Burke, John Francis, ix, 205, 228n56, 335–36, 339
Bush, George W., 286, 291
Butler, Judith, 109
Butterworth, Charles, 169

Cacciari, Massimo, 284, 285n26
California, 210–11
Calvino, Italo, 248n39
Campbell, David, 260, 271n9, 337
Camus, Albert, 33, 322
Canton, China, 234
capitalism, 55, 89, 93, 111, 281, 291, 296, 307
care, 11, 16, 131–32, 134, 329
Caribbean, 238, 247n25
Cartesian, 5, 337
caste, 156
Catholics, 212, 217, 222, 299, 304
Cavell, Stanley, 54n59
Celan, Paul, 191
Chamoiseau, Patrick, 248n35
Chandler, David, 276–77, 285n10
Chantal, Jane de, 25
charity, 150
Chatterjee, Partha, 343n11
Chattopadhyaya, Debiprasad P., 301
Cheah, Pheng, 344n18
Chechnya, 335
Chicanos, 210, 211, 212, 215
Children of Light/Children of Darkness, 161
China/Chinese, 234, 236–37, 240, 302, 306, 336
La Chingada/Malinche, 217
Chomsky, Noam, 7
Chow, Rey, 234, 245n9
Christian democracy, 222
Christian/Christianity, 13, 36, 178, 209, 216, 217–18, 222
Chuang-tse, 114
Cicero, 35, 36
citizen/citizenship, 24, 43–47, 51, 107, 217, 230, 253–54, 274, 277–79, 315, 322
city, 14, 23, 26, 42, 253–54. See also city-state; civitas; polis
city-state, 318
civic virtue, 12, 323
Civil Rights Act of 1964, 224
civil society, 12, 22, 255, 269, 276, 279, 283, 338

civility, 254, 269, 286, 292–295
civilization/civilizing, 11–13, 16, 22–26, 205–6, 208–9, 212–13, 244, 268, 280, 287, 312, 333
civitas, 23–24, 26
clash of civilizations, 168, 207, 209–10, 220, 221, 244, 284, 287, 312, 316, 335, 340
class, 156, 240
Cold War, 208, 280, 282
Coles, Romand, 60, 86n12
colonialism/colonization, 143, 160, 212
commerce, 141
common good, 219, 223
Commonweal, 212, 219
commonwealth, 33–35, 41, 106
communications theory, 231
communicative action, 10, 84, 95, 110, 225
communism, 273, 281–82
community, 7, 22–23, 47, 121, 152, 160, 213, 215, 220, 221–22, 223, 269, 291, 298, 307
comparative literature, 234
comparative political theory, 1–2, 19, 142, 162, 167, 205–7, 230–33, 244, 248n37, 331
comparative politics, 3
comparison, 233
competition, 159–60
Confiant, Raphaël, 239, 248n35
conformity, 152, 155, 158, 161
Confucius/Confucianism, 2, 206, 302
Connolly, William, 56, 178–79, 182n45, 182n49, 228n59
consciousness, 5, 13, 15, 64, 88, 108–9
consensus, 19, 286, 288, 293–94, 305
consent, 48
conservatism, 10, 21, 174
constitution, 51n13, 107. See also fundamental law
consumption, 143
contract, 40, 42, 46–47. See also covenant; social contract

Cook, Jonathan, 202n4
Coole, Diana, 60, 86n15
Copernicus, Nicolaus, 236, 241
Corbin, Henry, 169
cosmopolitanism (cosmopolis,
    cosmopolitical), 2–3, 9, 11–12, 14–15,
    19–22, 24–25, 88, 106–7, 108, 112, 144,
    168, 230, 241–44, 249n47, 272–83,
    286, 288, 290, 329, 331, 336–39, 344n18
cosmotheandric, 301
Council of Trent, 217
Counter-Reformation, 219
covenant, 41. See also contract
Creoles, 238–39
Créolité, 238–39, 336
crisis of democracy, 176
crisis of modernity, 171, 176–77
critical ontology, 16, 324
critical phenomenology, 5–6, 15, 19, 324
critical reason, 143, 145, 149, 150, 153, 155,
    157, 159–61, 178
critical theory, 1, 4–7, 10–11, 15–17, 88, 324,
    327. See also Frankfurt School of
    Social Research
critique, 4–5, 7, 9–11, 15, 20, 84, 91, 95, 131,
    149, 192
cross-cultural, 22, 108, 111, 112, 170, 184,
    189, 199–201, 237, 240, 256, 310, 313,
    315, 333, 335, 340
crossing borders, 2, 19, 214–217, 218–219,
    223, 225, 237, 244, 256, 335–36
Culler, Jonathan, 234, 245n8
cultural disorder, 176
culture, 11–12, 22, 49, 55, 58, 68, 88, 93, 95,
    97, 99–100, 107, 118, 146, 153, 190,
    205–6, 210–14, 214–18, 218–20, 242,
    262–63, 270, 287, 313. See also mass
    culture
Cynics, 253

Dahl, Robert, 278–79, 285n16
Dallmayr, Fred, ix–x, 1–26, 26nn4–5,
    27n16, 27n22, 27n28, 43, 45, 50, 53n43,
    55–56, 62–63, 88, 95, 101, 106, 108,
    110, 112, 113n11, 114–15, 119, 135n1,
    141–45, 162, 163n5, 167–73, 178–179,
    180n16, 190, 192, 195–97, 199–202,
    203n23, 206–7, 213–14, 225, 229n62,
    229n76, 230, 241–44, 245n1, 246n15,
    253–57, 266–69, 272–73, 276, 284,
    286–93, 297, 300–301, 304, 307,
    310–12, 315, 320, 332, 342n1, 342nn3–5,
    343n7, 343nn10–12, 344nn14–18,
    345nn19–20
Dalton, Dennis, 163n1, 165n34
Danube, 18–19
Darwin, Charles, 92, 98, 325
Dasein (spelled variously), 10, 116–19,
    122–127, 130–33, 135, 135n2, 190–91,
    197, 330–31
Davidson, Donald, 294, 308n12
Davos, 283
decentered subjectivity, 6–7, 10, 15,
    116–117, 192, 256, 266. See also
    Entmenschung;
    nonanthropocentrism
decisionism, 9
deconstruction, 1, 7, 9, 11–13, 16, 20, 88–89,
    170, 235, 257
Degas, Edgar, 79
Deleuze, Gilles, 117, 178, 232, 241–42
democracy, 2, 20, 22, 24, 42–43, 88, 104,
    107, 142, 148, 175, 201, 205–6, 209, 211,
    219–20, 223, 225, 273–79, 292, 302,
    307, 317–18, 323, 328, 338
    —cosmopolitical democracy, 273–75,
    279–80, 338
    —democracy of friendship, 318
    —global democracy, 292
    —liberal democracy, 222, 273, 276, 294,
    307, 338
    —Mestizo democracy, 211, 219–20, 223,
    225, 335
    —procedural democracy, 329,
    338–39
democratic ethos, 179

democratic theory, 218
Derrida, Jacques, 1, 7, 9, 11, 13, 15, 20, 22,
    117, 135n2, 191, 232, 254, 257, 260, 264,
    317–18, 341, 342n5
Descartes, René (and Cartesian), 67, 70,
    242, 257, 259–260, 266–268, 270,
    324–325
desire, 157
destiny, 148
detachment, 157
Deutsch, Kenneth, 163n1
development/historical development, 91,
    92, 93, 104, 108. *See also* progress;
    historical change
Devi, G. N., 270n2
Dharma, 165n37
dialectic, 6, 16, 74–75, 81, 109, 121, 125–26,
    240–41, 268, 270, 300
dialectical (or dialogical) self, 266–68,
    338
dialogical civility, 295. *See also* civility
dialogue, 23–24, 48, 241, 295–298,
    298–300, 301–2, 305, 306, 310–313,
    315, 340
Diderot, Denis, 89
Diego, Juan, 216
Dietz, Mary, 224, 229n61
difference, 2–3, 13–14, 19–21, 88, 121,
    163, 179, 197, 201, 205, 218–20, 221,
    223, 225, 235, 238, 240, 244, 247n24,
    260, 263, 313–314, 333, 337, 341
differends, 296
Diggers, 39
dignity, 98, 154
Dilthey, Wilhelm, 4
Diogenes of Sinope, 230
Dionysius the Areopagite, 228n55
Dionysus (and Dionysian), 49
discourse, 8, 23–24, 26
discrimination, 257
disenchantment, 62, 151, 235. *See also*
    enchantment
disorder, 13–14, 221, 222

disruption, 13
diversity, 99, 144, 154–155, 160, 220, 222,
    238, 240, 297
divine law, 172
dogma, 154, 158–161
domination/relations of domination, 69,
    155, 158–160
drives/biological drives, 157
dualism, 91, 169, 260
Duffy, Diane, 271n16
Dugan, C. N., 54n54
Duke University, 3
Dumouchel, Paul, 42, 52n26, 53n36
Durkheim, Émile, 92, 93, 96
Dussel, Enrique, 223, 228n60
duty, 150, 152, 160
dwelling, 19, 26

Eagleton, Terry, 62, 86n23
Earle, Duncan, 227n39
East (and Eastern thought, Eastern
    civilization), 2, 18–20, 39, 115, 119,
    236, 301–2, 306–7, 315, 333
eclipse of reason, 83
ecology, 24, 242–43, 249n45, 302. *See also*
    environmental movement
economics/economic conditions, 142,
    159, 161, 178
education, 156. *See also* Bildung
egoism, 160
Egypt, 184
Eichmann, Adolf, 241, 328
Eitam, Efraim, 187
elites, 184
Elizabeth I, 41
Elizondo, Virgilio, 216, 217, 225, 227n35,
    227n40, 229n70
Elshtain, Jean Bethke, 221, 228n52
emancipation/emancipatory, 4–7, 108,
    110, 142–143, 145, 231–232, 326
emotion, 42, 67
empire, 254
emptiness, 115

enchantment, 61. *See also* disenchantment

end of history, 90, 111, 231–232, 244

enemy, 280, 317, 339

engagement, 17–18, 170–171, 179

England, 24, 34, 39, 141. *See also* Great Britain

English language, 183, 187, 189–190, 209

English Revolution, 39

Enlightenment, 5, 15–16, 21, 43, 55, 57–59, 64, 66, 68–69, 75–76, 83–84, 88–89, 99, 143–45, 162, 177, 231–32, 249n47, 259, 287, 324

Entmenschung, 115, 116, 119, 127, 135, 136n9, 330. *See also* nonanthropocentrism

environmental movement, 213, 301

epistemology, 6, 15, 74, 75, 260

equality, 47, 143, 148, 156, 266

equality of opportunity, 156

Erasmus, Desiderius, 25

Ereignis, 116, 120, 136n2, 197, 330. *See also* event

error, 156

escapism, 11

eschatology, 317

esotericism, 168, 180n2, 333

Espín, Orlando, 217, 228n48

ethic of compassion, 255, 267

ethic of reciprocity, 255

ethics, 2–3, 11–13, 16, 98, 110, 116, 118–19, 122, 132–33, 135, 195, 241, 253, 255, 260, 266, 272, 280, 302, 335, 337, 339

ethnic cleansing, 257

ethnic conflict, 270

ethnicity, 90

ethnography, 237

ethnomethodology, 4

Euben, Peter, 273, 284n3

Euripides, 49

Euro-arrogance/Euro-denial, 163n5

Eurocentrism, 174, 218, 232–33, 235–36, 238, 246n16, 248n37, 284, 315

Europe/Europeans, 19, 143–144, 153, 179, 205, 232, 237, 287

European philosophy, 115

European Union, 339

evangelicals, 288

Evans-Pritchard, E, E, 4

event, 115, 126, 330

evil, 128, 159–161, 241, 261

exegesis/critical exegesis, 8–9

existence, 197

existentialism, 3, 33, 45, 50, 133

face, 37

fairness, 98

faith, 21, 144, 169–172, 179, 307, 333–334

Falah, Ghazi, 202n7

Falasifa, 169, 180n4. *See also* medieval Muslim philosophers

Falk, Richard, 22, 205, 226n1, 282–83, 285nn24–25

family, 209

fanaticism, 175

Farias, Victor, 15, 17

fascism, 17, 195

fatalism, 158, 160, 162, 211

Faulkner, William, 241

Felski, Rita, 248n32

Feuerbach, Ludwig Andreas von, 241

Figal, Günter, 58, 65, 74, 86n11, 325

film/motion pictures, 76–82, 85

Flathman, Richard, 53n40

form, 68, 75

Forsberg, Tuomas, 345n19

Foucault, Michel, 1, 9–10, 21, 53n29, 53n32, 54n49, 118, 232, 234, 236, 247n19, 253, 259, 264, 342n5

France, 101, 234

Frankfurt School of Social Research, 255, 324, 326. *See also* critical theory

freedom, 10, 12, 17, 24, 105–6, 125–28, 130, 143, 145, 148, 154–61, 164n16, 165n37, 165nn45–45, 255, 268, 300, 302, 306, 340. *See also* liberty

freedom of conscience, 292

Frege, Friedrich Ludwig Gottlob, 8

Freud, Sigmund, 263, 344n16

friend/friendship, x, 10–11, 14, 22–23, 25, 179, 209, 223, 229n62, 231, 286, 298, 300, 317, 334, 339, 341
Fukuyama, Francis, 244
fundamental law, 48
fundamental ontology, 16
fundamentalism, 143, 287, 294
future, 108

Gabilondo, Joseba, 227n34
Gadamer, Hans-Georg, 3–4, 11–13, 19–21, 23, 191–92, 203n23, 241, 248n37, 290, 294, 299–300, 308n17, 325, 336, 342
Galileo (Galileo Galilei), 98
Galston, Miriam, 169
game theory, 259
Gandhi, Mohandas Karamchand (Mahatma), 2, 15, 24–26, 141, 146, 149, 163n2, 164n22, 165n52, 166n53, 188, 331–32, 343n12, 344n14
Gaonkar, D. P., 113n9
Garrow, David, 229n69
gender, 156, 216–18
genealogy, 9, 88
genetic engineering, 134
genocide, 257
geophilosophy, 242–43, 249n44, 249n49
Gestell, 124, 128, 331
Geyer, Georgie Anne, 226n8
Giddens, Anthony, 22
Gilroy, Paul, 239, 248n31
Giri, Ananta Kumar, 270
Glass, James, 344n16
Glissant, Édouard, 238–39, 247n25, 248n27, 336
global civil society, 269, 283, 317
global federalism, 284
globalization (global, globalism), 2, 14, 20–21, 23, 88–89, 99, 104–7, 115, 134, 143, 162, 170, 200, 205–7, 213–14, 231, 242–44, 254, 256, 270, 272–73, 279, 282, 302, 303, 306–7, 315, 331–32, 337
Global Parliamentary Assembly, 283

God (Providence, divinity, the divine, Allah), 35–37, 77, 90, 99, 104, 179, 214, 218, 221, 223, 240, 269, 287–88, 292–93, 298, 304–7, 340
Goethe, Johann Wolfgang von, 244, 333, 343n10, 344n13
González, Justo, 215, 227n38
good, 159–61, 261
Gordon, Neve, ix, 183, 203n13, 334–35
governance, 39
government, 14, 23, 107, 183, 277
Great Britain, 141, 146–48, 158, 160. See also England
Greece (Greeks, Greek), 24, 35, 45, 48, 132, 169, 171, 180n4, 231, 233, 253, 311, 333
Greek philosophy, 171, 310–14
Greeley, Andrew, 228n54
Greenblatt, Stephen, 53n33
Guattari, Félix, 242, 249n44
Gusdorf, Georges, 7
Gutenberg, Johannes Gensfleisch zur Laden zum, 231
Gutman, Amy, 203n8

Habermas, Jürgen, 1, 4–5, 8, 10–11, 57, 62, 63–64, 66, 69, 83–84, 88, 91–96, 99, 100, 103, 105–7, 108, 110–11, 113n11, 136n4, 145, 164n22, 272, 289–90, 292, 294–96, 298, 300, 308n17, 325–29, 332, 340, 343nn8–9
Hafiz-i Shirazi, Khwaja Shams ud-Din, 333, 344n13
Hajime, Tanabe, 246n15
Halbfass, Wilhelm, 20
Hamarnehi, Walid, 182n44
Hanafi, Hasan, 181n31, 182n38
Hanbali school of jurisprudence, 304
Hanh, Thich Nhat, 224, 225, 229n68
Hansen, Victor Davis, 207–8, 210–12, 213, 220, 222, 223, 225–26, 226n9
happiness, 298
harmony, 157, 159, 212, 222, 223, 224, 305
Hartshorne, Charles, 250n51
Hassan, Manar, 203n16

Hatab, Lawrence J., 343n10
Havel, Vaclav, 25
Hawthorne, Nathaniel, 53n32
heart, 38, 39
Hebrew, 169, 187, 189, 193, 202, 333
Hegel, Georg Wilhelm Friedrich
    (Hegelian), 28n50, 63, 88, 91, 92,
    94–95, 105, 143, 218, 233, 236–38, 240,
    246n16, 247n22, 255, 279, 291, 300,
    307, 321, 327–34, 343n8, 344n15
hegemonic, 170
Heidegger, Martin, 1, 3, 9–10, 15–19, 26,
    27n16, 27n25, 27n28, 88, 114–33,
    135n2, 136n4, 136n9, 190–91, 195–96,
    199–201, 228n58, 232, 245n12, 246n15,
    247n21, 253, 255, 326–27, 329–30,
    333–34, 336, 341, 342nn4–5, 343n10,
    344n13, 344n16
Held, David, 22, 226n1, 273–75, 277,
    338
Hénaff, Marcel, 52n
Heraclitus (of Ephesus), 26
Herder, Johann Gottfried von, 21, 143,
    236, 246n17, 321, 329
hermeneutics of difference, 20, 191.
    See also hermeneutics
hermeneutics, 1, 3, 5, 7–9, 11–12, 19–20,
    21, 23, 88, 110, 170, 173, 218, 219, 223,
    248n37, 321–22, 326–27, 329, 331–35,
    342
Herodotus, 39, 233
heteronomy, 301
Hinduism, 141, 146, 149, 155, 160, 165n37,
    165n45, 165n49, 206, 219, 267
Hindu-Moslem relations, 141
historical change, 96
historical consciousness, 88
historical science, 4
historicism, 6, 7
historicity, 117, 121
history/theory of history, 5, 7, 13, 90–94,
    109, 112, 116–21, 123, 127, 129, 131–32,
    148, 149, 172, 231–32, 238. See also end
    of history; universal history

Hobbes, Thomas, 3, 33–51, 51n5, 51n10,
    52nn20–21, 52nn25–28, 53n35, 53n40,
    53n43, 150, 253, 299, 321–23, 339
Hölderlin, Johann Christian Friedrich,
    17–18, 23, 26
holism, 297, 299–300, 302, 304, 307, 340
Holocaust, 76, 203n23
home (and Heimat), 2, 24
homecoming, 19
Homer, 231
Horkheimer, Max, 56–66, 75–76, 83–84,
    86n8, 86n14, 93, 324
Hoy, David, 113n17
Hu, John (Hu Ruowang), 234, 336
human sciences, 5, 110. See also social
    science
humanism, 11, 122, 133, 224, 269, 302
Hume, David, 51n13, 150
humility, 4
Huntington, Samuel P., 23, 206–8, 210–12,
    213, 218–23, 225–26, 244, 284, 287, 312,
    315, 335
Husserl, Edmund, 6, 7, 321
hybridity, 207, 212–14, 220, 223, 231, 239,
    240, 244, 246n15, 246n25, 248n30,
    248n37, 267, 340
hyperdialectic, 240–41

Ibn Rushd, Abu'l-Walid Muhammad, 2,
    167–69, 172–74, 177–79, 181nn25–26,
    333–34. See also Averroës
ideal speech situation, 7
idealism, 153
identity, 2–3, 9, 11, 18, 20–22, 61, 64, 76,
    121, 133, 135, 175, 210, 220, 225, 233–34,
    237, 255, 263, 266–69, 313, 337, 341
ideology, 2, 75, 177, 289, 302
illusion, 79, 80, 81, 82
Illych, Ivan, 52n23
immigrants/immigration, 208–11
imperialism, 89–90, 147, 212, 236, 280
impulse, 62, 63. See also drives; passion
Inada, Kenneth K., 308n23
independence, 24, 148, 212

India/Indian, 20, 24, 115, 141–49, 152, 154, 156, 158, 160, 206, 237, 301, 303, 331, 332–33
Indian National Congress, 146, 147, 163n14
Indian Rebellion (Indian Mutiny), 141
indifference, 12, 18, 130, 136n4, 137n10, 163
individualism/individual autonomy, 9, 15, 47, 96, 142, 154, 192, 209, 283, 291, 302, 305, 340
Indology, 20
inequality, 47, 144, 219, 222
information management, 134,
Ingram, David, ix, 286, 308nn17–18, 340
instrumental freedom, 154
instrumental reason/instrumental rationality, 56, 59–60, 63–67, 73, 76, 84, 92–93, 150
Interbeing, 224, 242
international civil war, 280–81,
international courts, 274–75
international relations, 208, 221, 253, 263, 286
international relations theory, 208, 253
interpretation, 8, 88, 322
intersubjectivity, 6
Intifada, 194
Iraq, 25, 291
irrationalism/irrationality, 21, 63, 65, 325
"iron cage," 93
Isasi-Díaz, Ada María, 228n50
Islam, 173, 175, 178, 206, 208, 213, 219, 294, 304–6, 332–33, 340, 343n12
Islamic law, 169, 173, 303. *See also Shari'a*
Islamic philosophy/Islamic thought, 168, 170, 173, 305, 333
Islamic political thought, 168, 174, 177
Islamic society, 303–4
Israel/Israelis, 183–88, 193–94, 200–201, 202n2, 202nn6–7, 299, 334
Italy, 101

Jabiri, Muhammad 'Abid al- (al-Jabiri), 167, 174–79, 181n31, 181n37, 333–34

James, William, 230
Japan, 236, 246n15, 250n51
Jay, Martin, 57, 86n4
Jefferson, Thomas, 184–85, 187–88, 197, 202, 202n2
Jerusalem, 167, 169, 171–72, 332
Jervis, John, 248n33
Jewish philosophers, 169
Jewish state, 189
Jews, 76, 184, 186, 189, 201, 222, 334
Johnston, Rosemary, 227n40
Jordan, 184
Judeo-Christian tradition, 219, 222
judgment, 5
Jullien, François, 236, 246n18, 336
Jung, Hwa Yol, ix, 228n60, 229n67, 230, 247n38, 249nn42, 44, 336, 340
Jus Publicum Europaeum, 281
justice/social justice, 2, 22–23, 25, 95, 132, 145, 195, 280

Kaldor, Mary, 279, 285n18
Kant, Immanuel/Kantian, 11, 16, 22, 88–91, 93–94, 104–6, 108–9, 112, 113n10, 231, 233, 236, 249n47, 272–73, 322, 324, 326–28, 333–34, 343n8
Kar, Prafulla, 343n11
Kashmir, 335
Kearney, Richard, 270
Kehre (turning), 122, 128
Keiji, Nishitani, 246n15
Kervégan, Jean-François, 282, 285n23
Khatami, Mohammad, 23
Kierkegaard, Søren, 317–18, 341
Kimmerling, Baruch, 203n9
King, Martin Luther, 25, 224–25
Kipling, Joseph Rudyard, 244
Kitaro, Nishida, 246n15
Kitayama, Shinobu, 262, 270, 271n11
Klein, Melanie/Kleinian psychoanalysis, 262, 337, 344n16
knowledge, 74, 75
Koran. *See Qur'an*
Krell, David Farrell, 245n12

Krishna, 165n52
Kügelgen, Anke von, 181n30
Kuhn, Thomas, 4
Küng, Hans, 272
Kurosawa, Akira, 336
Kyoto school, 119, 246n15

labor, 296
Lacan, Jacques-Marie-Émile, 263
Laclau, Ernesto, 14, 28n36, 225,
    229n76
laicité, 178–179
land rights, 185, 188
Land, Philip, 228n58
language/theory of language, 7–9, 23–24,
    296, 316, 326
lateral universality, 205–6, 213, 220, 223,
    236–38, 336
Latin America, 206, 208, 209, 214, 215,
    217, 219, 222
Latin Averroism, 174
Latin, 24, 36
Latino values, 209
Latinos, 206–7, 210–11, 213–17, 218–20, 223,
    335. See also Chicanos
law/rule of law, 2, 14, 24, 38, 39, 46, 48,
    51n13, 100, 106–7, 110, 144, 169, 172,
    173, 274–75
Lawrence, T. E., 248
Leaman, Oliver, 180nn3–4
Lebenswelt, 2. See also lifeworld
Lefort, Claude, 323, 342n3
legitimacy, 105
Lerner, Michael, 344
Lerner, Ralph, 169
letting be/letting Being be, 3, 9–10, 14–20,
    24–26, 116, 134, 183, 195–96, 199,
    201–2, 330, 334
Levelers, 39
Leviathan, 33, 322
Levinas, Emmanuel, 136n4, 232, 241,
    249n41, 270n3
Lévy-Strauss, Claude, 8, 237
liberal society, 156, 335

liberalism/liberals, 89, 155, 156, 170, 177,
    280, 282–84, 293–94, 307
liberality, 8
liberation theology, 218–19, 301, 335
liberty/liberties, 41–42, 100, 148, 160.
    See also freedom
liberty of thought, 156
Lichtung, 197
Lieberman, Avigdor, 187
lifeworld/life world, 2, 4, 6, 9, 15, 21–22,
    94, 190, 237, 247n23, 336. See also
    Lebenswelt
Lifton, Robert Jay, 267
Lingis, Alphonso, 27n14
listening, 25–26
"little virtues," 25–26
La Llorona, 217
local (locality, localism), 21, 270
local knowledge, 238
Locke, John, 155, 343n9
logocentrism, 163, 323. See also
    rationalism
love, 150, 160, 166n53, 286, 300, 317–18, 341
Loyola University, Chicago, 7
Lyotard, Jean-François, 117, 232, 246n16,
    296, 308n13

Machiavelli, Niccolò, 39, 41, 42, 224,
    225, 253
MacIntyre, Alasdair, 13, 28n32, 56, 97
Macmurray, John, 249n42
Malia, Martin, 233, 245n5
Mandela, Nelson, 25
Maritain, Jacques, 222
market, 100–104, 142, 156
Markus, Hazel Rose, 262, 270, 271n15
Martinez, Bettia, 212, 227n25
Marx, Karl, 91, 92, 94, 108–9, 111, 113n5,
    233, 240, 253, 327
Marxism/Marxist, 133, 177, 218
Masao, Abe, 246n15
mass culture, 55–59, 76, 83, 85
mass society, 161
material/quasi-material, 62, 152

materialism, 92, 150, 158, 160, 291
maturity, 11, 24, 154, 329
Mauss, Marcel, 237
McBride, William L., 249n44
McCarthy, Thomas, ix, 4, 22, 27n7, 88,
    113n17, 326–28
McCarthyism, 329
McCole, John, 86n8
McLuhan, Herbert Marshall, 231
Mecca, 167, 174, 304, 332–33
medieval Europe, 180n4, 222, 314
medieval Muslim philosophers, 169
medieval Spain, 217
Medina, 304
Mehta, Vrajendra Raj, 163n1, 343n11
melting pot, 215
Menke, Christoph, 67
Merleau-Ponty, Maurice, 6, 7, 27n14, 33,
    206, 213, 223–24, 236–38, 240, 247n21,
    248n30, 336, 342n1
mestizo (mestizaje), 205, 207, 214–17,
    218–21, 223, 225, 335
metaphysics/metaphysical, 13, 97, 115,
    119–20, 124–125, 127–29, 135, 199,
    315, 323
Methodenstreit (methodology conflict),
    4, 55
methodology, 4, 326
Mevlevi Order, 304
Mexican American, 216–17
Mexico, 207, 209–11, 214–17
"Mexifornia," 210–11, 335
Middle Ages, 144
Middle East, 20, 179, 286–87, 299
Middle Way (maitreya), 235
military, 141, 146, 148, 178
Mill, John Stuart, 74, 84–85, 192, 233, 253
Miller, J. Hillis, 249n40
mimesis (and mimetic), 61–69, 73–75,
    83, 325
mind, 67, 70–73, 159. See also spirit;
    consciousness
minority, 184, 188, 201
Miro, Joan, 77

modern art, 55, 58–59, 69, 73, 76–77, 83, 85
modern society/modern societies, 99, 100
modernism, 154
modernity, ix, 9, 19, 45, 57, 75–76, 84, 90,
    96, 99, 101, 103, 108, 123, 129, 141–45,
    149–50, 153, 158, 160, 162, 164n22, 171,
    177, 213, 215, 231–32, 235–36, 242–43,
    249n49, 255, 287, 304, 307, 314, 328,
    332–33
modernization, 89, 91, 93–94, 104, 110,
    176, 232
Molodet, 187
Monet, Claude, 59–61
Montesquieu, Charles de Secondat,
    Baron de, 233
moral education, 272
morals (moral relations, morality), 95,
    97–98. See also ethics
Mörchen, Hermann, 16, 28n43
Mordecai (of Persia), 37
Morgenthau, Hans, 221
Morocco, 174–75, 333–34
Morris, Desmond, 250n51
Morris, Martin, 65, 66, 87n30
Mouffe, Chantal, ix, 14, 28n36, 225,
    229n76, 272, 338–39, 344n17
Mounier, Emmanuel, 225, 229n72
Muhammad (Prophet), 175
Müller, Ulrich, 65, 87n34, 325
multiculturalism/multicultural, 22, 24,
    88, 94, 99, 102, 207, 215, 219–20, 223,
    225, 235, 238, 244, 295, 329, 331,
    335, 337
multipolarity, 272–73, 281
Murray, John Courtney, 222
music, 54n54, 56
Musil, Robert, 248n39
Muslim philosophers, 169
Muslim state, 304
Muslim world, 168
Muslims, 188–89, 287–88, 293, 303,
    305
Muthu, Sankar, 112n3
mysticism, 20

Naess, Arne, 242, 149n
Nahda, 176
Nahuatl, 216
Nancy, Jean-Luc, 345n20
Nandy, Ashis, 164n22, 343n11
Nasr, Khalid al- (al-Nasr), 182n40
Nasr, Seyyed Hossein, 169
Nasr, Vali, 181n35
nation (nationality, nation-state), 22–23, 90, 146, 201, 254, 275, 312, 315, 341
National Socialism (and Nazism), 15, 17, 191, 195
nationalism, 146, 148, 270
Native Americans, 202n2, 206, 211, 214, 267, 338
natural attitutde, 6
natural law, 38, 291, 293, 302, 304–5
nature/natural, 7, 34, 62–63, 74, 90, 98–99, 104, 148, 213, 242, 287, 290, 292–93, 298, 300–301, 302, 304–5, 306–7, 322, 340
naturalism, 325
Negev, 184–185
negotiations, 288, 290, 298
Nehru, Jawaharlal, 146, 163n12
neighbor, 269, 317
neoconservatives, 286–87
neoliberal, 338
neo-Kantian, 324, 333–34
neo-Scholasticism, 222, 228n58.
    See also Thomism
Niebuhr, Reinhold, 166n56, 221
Nietzsche, Friedrich, 1–2, 17, 26, 46–49, 93, 123, 132, 171, 231, 244, 323, 340
Nietzscheans, 326
nihilation/negation, 114, 116, 118, 120–25, 127, 129–35, 330–31
nihilism/nihilistic, 120, 131, 247n21
nominalism, 323
nonanthropocentrism, 115, 116, 119–20, 122, 125–27, 130–33. See also *Entmenschung*
nonidentity, 21, 64, 65. *See also* difference
nonmetaphysical, 115, 116

nonviolence, 25–26, 224–25
non-Western, ix, 2, 19, 21, 116, 141, 145, 162, 170, 208, 219, 232, 256, 287, 331–32, 338, 340
non-Western studies, 167, 233
norms, 92, 96, 99
North American Free Trade Agreement, 207
Northern Ireland, 335
nothingness, 14, 115, 121, 129, 130
noumenon, 322
Nussbaum, Martha, 272–73

Oakeshott, Michael, 8, 27n18
object/objectivity, 7, 64, 72–73, 109, 190, 256
objectivism, 6
Ojibway, 267, 270, 338
Occidental, 153, 200, 232, 244, 341.
    See also West
Odysseus, 18, 61, 62
ontology, 2, 6–8, 10, 14–17, 21, 42, 74–75, 221, 260, 314, 317, 323. *See also* critical ontology; fundamental ontology; practical ontology
openness/openness to being, 4–5, 16, 23, 121, 124, 190–191
oppositional, 199. *See also* rupture
order, 13–14, 212, 221–222
ordinary language philosophy, 7
Orient/oriental, 141, 200, 232, 244, 341.
    See also East
Orientalism, 20–21, 115, 119, 163n2, 190, 200, 233, 256, 314, 318n4, 331, 333
original sin, 304–5
orthodoxy, 335
orthopraxis, 335
otherness (other), 11–12, 19, 22–23, 63, 117, 119–21, 132–34, 190, 197, 215, 219, 221, 232, 253–56, 260, 262–70, 287, 313–15, 337–38
Ott, Hugo, 15, 17, 28n39
Our Lady of Guadalupe, 216–18

Paci, Enzo, 6
Palestine/Palestinians, 186–87, 193, 194,
    200–201, 202n2, 202n7, 299, 334
Panikkar, Raimon, 301, 308n19
Pantham, Thomas, 163n1, 164n22, 343n11
Parekh, Bhikhu (Lord Parekh), 343n11
Parkin, David, 270, 271n10
Parliament, 41
participation, 11–12, 100, 105
particularism, 205–6, 207
passion, 38
past, 108, 152
patriotism, 267, 270
peace/peacemaking, 2, 20, 22, 25–26, 221,
    224, 266, 280, 310, 313, 316
Peace of Westphalia, 299, 337
Peloponnesian War, 311
people, 36. *See also* nation
Persia, 37, 233, 333. *See also* Iran
person, 7, 33–37, 39, 50, 98, 123, 125,
    137n10, 156–58, 270, 305
Pettit, Philip, 165n41
phenomenology/existential
    phenomenology, 1, 4–7, 11, 15, 234,
    237, 321–24, 326, 336
phenomenon, 322
Philia politike, 11. *See also* friendship
philosophers, 145, 167, 174, 272
philosophy, 1, 7, 24, 115, 151, 168–71, 173–74,
    179, 191, 200, 241–42, 255, 310–12, 321
    —continental, 167
    —European, 115
    —geophilosophy, 242, 249n44
    —of history, 92
    —Islamic, 168
    —of language, 1, 241
    —of social sciences, 4
    —Western, 200, 236, 321, 331
phronesis, 24
Physicians for Human Rights, 194
Pitkin, Hanna F., 52n16, 53n37
Plato, 13, 169, 230, 253, 311, 313, 318
play, 62, 63, 132, 325

pleasure, 67
pluralism (pluralistic, deep pluralism),
    14, 24, 97, 152, 179, 197, 212, 219–20,
    220–23, 235, 253–54, 256–57, 267, 273,
    281–82, 292–93, 305
puriverse, 280
poet, 153, 216–17
poetry, 17–18, 23, 25–26, 206, 218, 333
polis, 10–11, 14, 24, 26, 213, 230. *See also*
    city; city-state; *civitas*
polity, 269
political science, 3, 55
political theory/political philosophy, 1, 3,
    12, 14, 17, 19, 25, 37, 39, 43, 55, 84, 88,
    114, 167–68, 193, 200, 220–21, 233,
    253–55, 263, 286, 310–11, 321–23, 337
politics (political action, political
    practice), 2, 10–12, 14, 16, 24–25, 48,
    49, 94, 110, 114–19, 122, 124–25,
    130–35, 144, 148, 166n53, 172, 176, 199,
    206–7, 220–22, 223–26, 253, 255, 276,
    278, 281, 284, 310, 312, 316, 331, 339
politics of nihilation, 130
polyphony, radical, 8
Pondicherry (India), 148
poor, 158, 218, 219
positivism, 10, 11, 74, 213
post-Cartesian, 267–68
postcolonialism, 222–23, 239, 247n25,
    248n30
post-humanism, 117
postmetaphysics/postmetaphysical, 90,
    91
postmodernism, 13, 96, 117, 213, 218,
    222–23, 228n59, 232, 234, 243–44,
    246n16, 247n25, 255–56, 258, 266,
    268, 312, 314–15, 337, 341
(post)modernity, 95, 96, 97, 98, 103,
    111
postnational, 88, 315–16
poststructuralism, 9, 10, 11, 14, 247n25
posttraditional, 96, 97, 327
poverty, 158, 209

Powell, Russell, 309n30
power, 33, 34, 38, 41, 43, 50, 114, 123–35, 149, 258–60, 323
powerlessness (*Machtlose, Ohnmacht,* power-free), 125, 126, 127, 128, 130, 132, 134, 331
practical ontology, 2, 6–9, 12, 15. *See also* ontology
practical reason, 106
pragmatism 8, 11
—neopragmatism, 11
praxis, 7, 14, 16, 22, 61, 62, 172–173, 179, 316, 325–26, 334
predestination, 305
premodern, 97
pre-reflective, 5
prince, 41, 42
production, 124, 133, 134–35, 143
progress, 93, 231–32, 280
proletariat, 233, 240
Protestants, 211–12, 222, 299, 335
prudence, 24. *See also phronesis*
psychoanalysis, 261
Ptolemy, 241
public, 50

quasi-transcendental, 94, 327
Quine, Willard van Ormen, 7
Qu'ran (Quran, Koran), 173, 175, 304–5

race, 78–79, 90, 98, 156, 187, 213, 214, 219
Rahner, Karl, 228n58
Rajchman, John, 248n39
Rasmussen, David M., 26n5, 54n49, 169, 180n10
rational society, 151
rationalism/rationalization, 6, 8–9, 15, 21, 92, 94, 108, 175, 304, 324, 326, 340
Rawls, John, 54n51, 54n59, 108, 112n1, 113n15, 272, 289–90, 292–95, 299, 308n12, 340
raza nueva (*la raza* cósmica), 214, 218
reactionism/reactionary, 145, 152, 162
realism, 208, 223, 286

Realpolitik, 25
reason (rational, rationality), 6, 61–69, 73–75, 83–84, 91, 104, 141–45, 149–51, 153–55, 157, 159–61, 164n25, 164n29, 168, 170, 172–174, 177, 231, 246n16, 272, 287, 292, 301, 307, 322, 325, 333–34. *See also* aesthetic reason; critical reason; instrumental reason
recognition, 186
reconciliation, 269
reflection, 5, 67, 96. *See also* critique
Reformation, 144, 219, 305, 335
Reid, T. R., 250n51
relativism, 162, 211, 220, 257
religion, 12, 24, 97, 141, 143, 144, 155–56, 159, 161, 174–77, 209, 217, 287, 289, 292, 300–301, 304, 334–35, 340
religious war, 292
Renaissance, 144, 321
representation, 37, 40–44, 47–48, 60, 74, 82–83, 124
Republican Brotherhood, 304
respect, 14
responsibility, 118, 131, 134, 241
revaluation of values, 123
revealed law, 172–73
Revelation, 13, 97, 168, 173–74, 179
revolution/revolt, 41
rich, 158
Ricoeur, Paul, 6, 8–9, 12–13, 23
rights (human rights, natural rights, political rights), 2, 44, 99, 100, 105, 107–8, 111, 113n11, 125, 142–43, 155, 175, 184, 209, 213, 257, 268–69, 273–74, 276–78, 283, 288–90, 292–95, 297–99, 300–303, 305, 306–7, 308n18, 340
Riley, Patrick, 54n54
risk, 243
ritual, 154, 159
Robbins, Bruce, 344n18
Rodin, Auguste, 70–73
romanticism, 21, 68
Rorty, Richard, 8, 27n17
Rosales, José, 270

Rosenthal, Erwin, 169, 180n5
Rousseau, Jean-Jacques, 45–49, 53n44, 54n51, 54n54, 233, 253, 323
Rūmī, Mawlānā Jālāl ad-Dīn Muhammad, 333
rupture (of thought), 168, 177, 180n16
Ryle, Gilbert, 8

Sache. See thing(s)
Said, Edward W., 20–21, 163n2, 212–13, 247n22, 248n30, 318n4, 335
Salvatore, Amondo, 176–77, 182n38, 182n43
Sartre, Jean-Paul, 33
Saudi Arabia, 304
Saussure, Ferdinand de, 7
Schelling, Friedrich Wilhelm Joseph von, 10, 17
Schmitt, Carl, 53n43, 273, 280–82, 339–40
Schneck, Stephen F., ix, x, 1, 321
Schoenberg, Arnold, 56
Schoolman, Morton, ix, 55, 85n2, 86n7, 324–25
Schrag, Calvin O., ix, 22, 223, 228n60, 230, 234–35, 246n13, 248n37, 249n44, 310, 318n3, 336, 340–41
Schütz, Alfred, 4, 6
Schwartz, Ulrich, 74, 87n44
science/natural sciences, 4, 98, 101, 103, 110–11, 141–42, 149–51, 154, 160, 177
scientific method, 153, 298
Scientism, 109
sculpture, 69–73
Searle, John R., 7
secularism/secularization, 171, 174–78, 219, 294, 301, 304, 307, 334
seeing/sight, 33–37
Segovia, Fernando, 215, 227n36
segregation, 50
self, 21–23, 38, 197, 257–60, 262–70, 337
self-critique, 192, 307
self-determination/self-governance, 24, 156

self-knowledge/self-understanding, 38, 44, 56, 268
self-reliance, 24
semiotics, 7
Sen, Amartya, 303, 308n25
sensual (sense, quasi-sensual, sensuousness), 62, 67–69, 72–75
separation of church and state, 305
separatism, 207
September 11, 2001, 206, 210, 258
sex (sexuality, homosexuality, heterosexuality), 77–78, 98, 216, 265
Shapiro, Ian, 285n8
Shapiro, Michael, 260, 268, 271n17, 337
Shari'a, 169, 173, 303–4
Shiites/Shiism, 291, 304
sin, 304
Singh, Karan, 163n12
Sittlichkeit, 328–29, 343n8
slavery, 184, 188, 202n2, 292
social contract, 46, 48, 254, 266, 302. See also contract
Social Darwinism, 159
social psychology, 264
social science, 4–5, 20, 90, 255, 326
Socialism, 14, 174–75
sociality, 2, 5
society, 12, 104, 149
sociology, 96, 243, 293
Socrates, 49, 153, 230, 253, 260, 297, 311, 318
solipsism, 11
Sophists, 253
Soroush, Abdolkarim, 1, 304, 309n28, 333, 344n13
South Africa, 269, 338
Southern Christian Leadership Conference, 224–25
Southwestern United States, 207, 209, 214–16, 218, 335
sovereign/sovereignty, 33–51, 254, 276, 322–23

space/spacing, 23, 39, 43, 50, 114, 119, 120, 121, 129, 131, 132, 170–71, 199, 231, 253–54, 260–61, 267, 316, 323, 336–37

spacio-temporal condition, 116–17, 118, 120–21, 123, 126–27, 129, 131, 134–35. *See also* space; time

Spain, 223

Spaniards, 214, 216

Spanish language, 211

Sparta, 311

spectatorship, 48–51

Spence, Jonathan D., 245n10

Spencer, Herbert, 159

spirit, 63, 92, 159, 175, 290. *See also* mind

spirituality/spiritual, 145, 148–49, 152, 156–61, 163n1, 165n37, 165n45, 165n49, 213–14, 216, 217–18, 219, 223, 224, 225, 291, 298, 304, 307, 332, 335

stage, 35–39, 42, 45, 48–49, 52n

state, 14, 22, 93, 100–101, 104, 149, 155, 174–76, 201, 240, 254, 268, 283, 311–12, 315, 318, 322

state of nature, 106

Stoicism, 14, 272–73

Strauss, Andrew, 282–83, 285nn24–25

Strauss, Leo, 4, 53n43, 167–72, 177–79, 180n2, 180n4, 333–34

Straussian, 168–72

Strong, Tracy B., ix, 33, 52n27, 54n54, 321–23

structuralism, 7

students, 183–86, 189, 193

subjectivism, 91

subjectivity/subject, 2, 5–7, 9–10, 15–16, 21, 64, 117, 123, 125–27, 133, 135, 190, 256–58, 260, 266

Sudan, 304

Sufis (and Sufism), 304

Sunnis, 291, 304

Swabia (Germany), 18

swaraj, 24–26, 163n2

Sweden, 101

system, 2

Tagore, Rabindranath, 141, 332

Taha, Mahmoud Mohamad, 304

Tarnas, Richard, 270

Taylor, Charles, 1, 25, 55, 101, 203n8, 233, 247n21, 264, 297, 308n23

Taylor, Harriet, 192

technicity, 133, 134, 135

technology, 101, 102, 103, 118, 123, 133, 135, 141, 208

Teitaro, Suzuki Daisets, 246n15

Teivainen, Teivo, 345n19

Tel Aviv, 194

teleology, 6, 13, 90, 91, 104, 297

Terchek, Ronald, ix, 141, 164n22, 332

terrorism, 282, 286, 316, 321, 339

theandric, 301

theater, 39, 42, 50, 52n

theatricality, 33, 37, 42–43, 45, 50, 323

theocracy, 294

theodicy, 90, 104

theologians, 174, 207, 214, 215, 218, 219, 221, 223, 272

theology, 168, 174, 179, 216, 218, 219, 305. *See also* liberation theology

thing(s), 7, 98, 191

Third World, 233

Thomism, 221, 222, 223, 228n58, 304. *See also* Aquinas

time/temporalizing, 48, 108, 119–20, 122, 132, 261, 267

tolerance/toleration, 4, 8, 13–14, 20, 98, 212, 287, 293, 298

Tonantzin, 216, 217

totalitarianism, 45

Toulmin, Stephen, 22

tradition, 21, 96, 97, 100, 141–46, 152–53, 155, 157, 160–62, 327, 332–33

tragedy, 48, 49

transcendental/transcendence, 6, 8–9, 14, 21, 149–50, 152, 154, 157–58, 213–14, 218–19, 223, 228n59, 235, 260, 287, 294, 298–99, 301

transnational, 206–7, 209, 213, 215, 220, 221, 223, 225, 243, 275, 282

transversality, 230, 233–36, 239–40, 242, 246n13, 246nn15–16, 247n25, 248n37, 249n44, 313, 316, 318n3, 336, 340–41
Turkey, 304
truth, 74, 84, 95, 216, 219, 222–23, 235–37
Tutu, Desmond, 268–69, 271n18

ubuntu, 268–70, 338
umma, 169
understanding, 4–6, 12, 15, 19–21, 88, 108, 154, 190–191, 290, 294, 298–99, 305–6, 313. See also Verstehen
udocumented immigrants (illegal immigrants), 210
Union of the Soviet Socialist Republics (USSR, Soviet Union), 186, 280
United Nations, 274, 292, 316–17
United Nations General Assembly Resolution 53/22, 23, 29n62
United States of America, 4, 25, 101, 141, 144, 156, 184, 205, 207, 209, 212, 214, 214–15, 218–19, 222–24, 280–82, 287, 328, 335
unity-n-diversity, 206–7, 218, 220, 223, 225
universal class, 279
Universal Declaration of Human Rights, 283, 302
universal history, 88, 89, 112, 232, 327
universal pragmatics, 8
universalism, 95, 99, 102, 106, 109, 111–12, 143, 205–8, 213–14, 218, 234, 238, 244, 257, 280, 282, 290–92, 329, 336
university, 183–90, 192–95, 200–201, 334
University of Notre Dame, 27n28, 114, 191, 321, 336
unordered, 13, 14
untouchables, 149, 156, 158
Urbinati, Nadia, 277, 285n15
utopia/utopianism, 6, 66, 108

values/value, 92, 96, 99, 100, 107, 123, 131, 133, 135, 150
Varma, V. P., 163n1
Vasconcelos, José, 214–15, 218, 227n33, 335

Vattimo, Gianni, 319n9
Vedanta, 190
Vermenschung, 119, 123, 135
Verstehen, 4. See also understanding
Vienna Circle, 7
Vietnam War, 55, 224
village, 21
violence, 265
Virgin Mary, 216, 217
Virginia (U.S. state), 184, 186
virtue, 13, 24–25. See also "little virtues"
Vivekananda [Swami] (Narendranath Dutta), 155, 165n39
Voegelin, Eric, 13, 323, 342n2
voluntarism, 323
Voting Rights Act of 1965, 224

Wahhabism, 304
Waldenfels, Bernhard, 13, 28n35
Walesa, Lech, 25
Walker, R. B. J., 270n1
Walzer, Michael, 52n, 208
war, 25, 159, 280, 292
Weber, Max, 4, 57, 62, 91, 93, 103, 111
Wellmer, Albrecht, 63, 64, 65, 83, 84, 87n26
Welsch, Wolfgang, 246n16
West (Western civilization, Western thought, Western tradition), ix, 2, 15, 17–18, 20–22, 76, 85, 99, 108, 111, 115, 119–20, 129, 141–42, 146, 149–50, 160, 162, 169, 176–77, 189, 206, 208, 210, 213, 231, 235–37, 242, 254, 276–77, 283–84, 287, 301–2, 304, 306, 315, 321, 333, 340. See also Occidental
Western metaphysics, 199, 315
Westernization, 145, 332
White, Geoffrey M., 271n15
White, Hayden, 9, 27n22
White, Stephen, 26n5, 271n7
whites, 299
will, 40, 48
William the Conqueror, 40
Williamson, Chilton, 226n8
Willms, Johannes, 249n46

Wilmer, Franke, ix, 253, 271n8, 271n12, 337
Winch, Peter, 4, 5
Wittfogel, Karl, 233, 245n6
Wittgenstein, Ludwig, 7, 230
Wolf, Susan, 206, 226n6
Wolfenstein, Victor, 344n16
Wolin, Richard, 17, 28n45
Wolin, Sheldon, 8, 56
women, 189–90, 198–99, 217, 232,
    303–4, 340
Woolf, Virginia, 183
words, 38
Wordsworth, William, 159
work ethic, 209
world, 5, 7, 12, 21–22, 61, 88, 97, 131, 152,
    154, 157, 159–60, 168, 255, 279
world civil society, 255
World War II, 281

xenophobia, 144, 207, 213, 220, 329

Yeshuvi, Naama, 202n3
Yiftachel, Oren, 202n4, 202n7,
    203n13
yin-yang, 240
Yizraeli, Dafna, 203n16
Young, Iris Marion, 247n24
Young, Robert J. C., 239

Zarathustra, 1, 2, 26
Zen Buddhism, 115, 235, 241,
    247n19
Zenck, Martin, 57, 85n3
Ziarek, Krzysztof, ix, 114, 330–31
Zizek, Slavoj, 257, 271n5, 334, 336
zoon logon ekhon, 7, 27n16
zoon politikon, 7